W9-BKJ-156

DEGREES
of DISASTER

PRINCE WILLIAM SOUND:
HOW NATURE REELS
AND REBOUNDS

JEFF WHEELWRIGHT

SIMON & SCHUSTER   NEW YORK   •   LONDON   •   TORONTO
SYDNEY   •   TOKYO   •   SINGAPORE

SIMON & SCHUSTER
Rockefeller Center
1230 Avenue of the Americas
New York, New York 10020
Copyright © 1994 by H.J. Wheelwright, Jr.
All rights reserved,
including the right of reproduction
in whole or in part in any form whatsoever.
SIMON & SCHUSTER and colophon are
registered trademarks of Simon & Schuster Inc.
Designed by Edith Fowler
Manufactured in the United States of America

10 9 8 7 6 5 4 3 2 1

Library of Congress Cataloging-in-Publication Data

Wheelwright, Jeff.
   Degrees of disaster : Prince William Sound : how
nature reels and rebounds / Jeff Wheelwright.
      p.   cm.
   Includes index.
   1. Ecology—Alaska—Prince William Sound Re-
gion.   2. Earthquakes—Environmental aspects—
Alaska—Prince William Sound Region.   3. Oil
spills—Environmental aspects—Alaska—Prince
William Sound.
I. Title.
QH105.A4W48   1994
574.5'222'097983—dc20   94-11877   CIP
ISBN: 0-671-70241-6

FOR MIA,
who is always with me

Contents

The method of nature: who could ever analyze it? That rushing stream will not stop to be observed. We can never surprise nature in a corner; never find the end of a thread; never tell where to set the first stone.

—EMERSON

All science is only a makeshift, a means to an end which is never attained. After all, the truest description, and that by which another living man can most readily recognize a flower, is the unmeasured and eloquent one which the sight of it inspires. No scientific description will supply the want of this, though you should count and measure and analyze every atom that seems to compose it.

—THOREAU

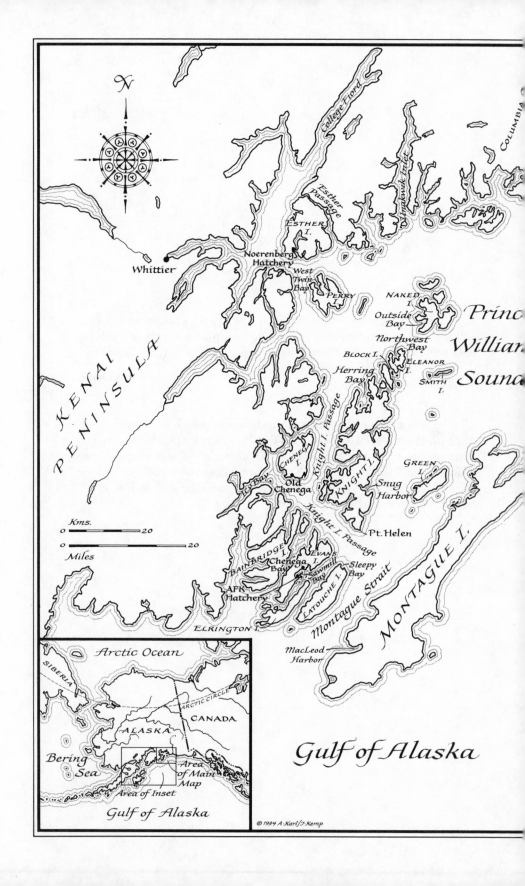

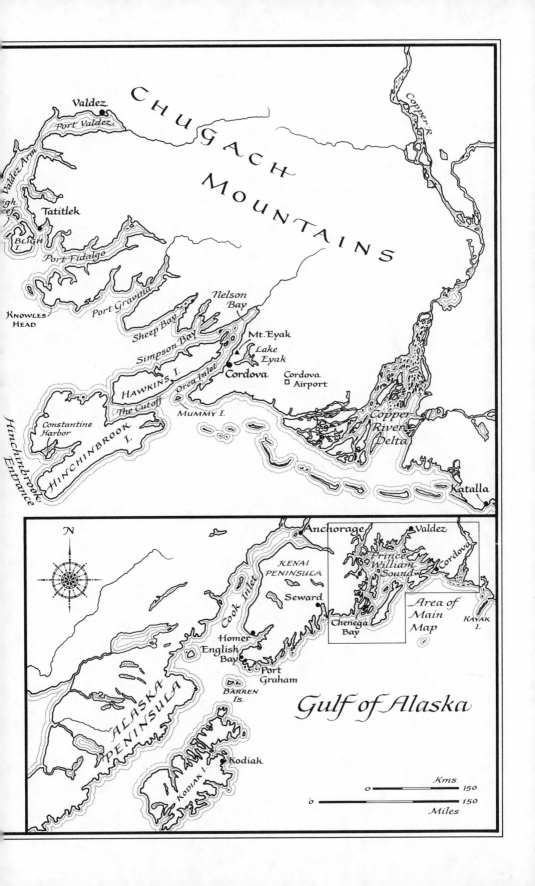

Introduction

EARTH SEEMED to be failing when I began to write this book in 1989. Atop the spread of pollution and deforestation loomed an ozone hole the size of a continent. Species were disappearing, and the global atmosphere was said to be warming. Then came the *Exxon Valdez* oil spill in Alaska, crystallizing the abuse of the environment. The toll of the oil spill on the wildlife of Prince William Sound was terrible and spectacular, on the order of a human catastrophe. People compared the Sound to Chernobyl, Bhopal, even Hiroshima. There was a widespread belief that the ecosystem was ruined, that the pristine Sound would not recover for decades if ever.

I went off to Alaska in May of '89 with a different attitude. I was incongruously optimistic about Prince William Sound. I believed in the life force. I believed that if an organism was assaulted and did not die, it would immediately strive to heal. The recovery would commence with the first clotting of the wound.

It helped that the killing wave had passed by the time I arrived. I surveyed the western Sound aboard a wildlife rescue vessel. Seven weeks after the accident, many beaches were smeared and intertidal life was choked, but there were no more dead birds or sea otters. They had been picked up, or eaten by scavengers, or washed from the Sound. The wildlife off the beaches appeared fit and healthy, their metabolisms fending off the hydrocarbons. Marine bacteria, the platelets hurrying to the cut, blossomed invisibly upon the oil. The Sound struck me as a superorganism, coursing with energy. The sea flushed the straits, the streams fed the sea, the sun seared the stain. Petroleum was of the earth, and the earth was responding to it dynamically.

The disaster had a precedent in the recent past, indeed a

11

coincidence crying out to be examined. The oil spill occurred on Good Friday, 1989. Twenty-five years earlier on Good Friday a monstrous earthquake shook Prince William Sound. Its epicenter was exactly twenty-five miles from Bligh Reef where the tanker grounded. The '64 earthquake literally upheaved the environment. Like the spill it had acute effects, that is, dramatic biological casualties in the short term, and also chronic effects, subtle consequences over time. The quake's record was complete when I began to track the oil spill, and always in the back of my mind was wonder that the earlier disaster appeared never to have happened.

If the acute effects of the spill were severe but short-lived, the question in '89 was: How serious were the chronic effects going to be? What was the long-term hazard of the oil to the ecosystem? Five years have passed, though an eye-blink in environmental history, and I have returned a number of times. Five years is about the soonest juncture possible for making an evaluation. Without question the Sound is different than it would have been had the assault not taken place. But since the system is always changing anyway, as it reacts to environmental disturbances great and small, the Sound has accommodated this latest change as well. The spill altered its ecological spin, but not its ecological integrity, or not for long. The oil has yielded to competing intrusions, although the stain in spots is still there. The lesson gave me hope about the broader threats to the biosphere. Nature would recover if we would ease up a bit.

People are surprised when I say Prince William Sound isn't ruined. What came before, what would come again, is outside their frame of view. To be fair it did not seem possible, not in the searing light of the initial mortalities, that the Sound could bounce back. I found it almost axiomatic that the sharper the distress over the acute effects, the deeper the doubts about environmental recovery.

I had the reassurance of the scientific perspective. Science is a mode of inquiry. It is a way of making sense of the world. Science differs from other modes (spiritual, philosophical, psychological) in demanding that the inquiry be systematic, that the trail to the unknown be blazed with replicative steps. Leaps of faith or of feeling are not permitted. I am most at home with this approach, it beats the others for clarity and content, but all the same the reader should be prepared for leaps.

Although most scientists were not apocalyptic about the Sound, their investigation suffered two handicaps. One was that uncertainty about the oil's effects predominated. Few of the results obtained were black and white. Second, much of the investigation was "litigation-sensitive," meaning that it was conducted under wraps. Even research that was public was subject to political pressures. Thus scientific interpretations were put out according to the biases of the studies' sponsors. The bias did not admit of the uncertainties. So science, as a method of inquiry, performed poorly in the Sound, and other modes gained by default. I will touch on the alternatives, particularly the approach of the Native inhabitants to the disaster.

This book is about the nature of Prince William Sound and the diverse efforts, my own included, to understand how the Sound and its creatures react to stress. The book is not an account of the *Exxon Valdez* incident. To underscore the difference, I will tell a story about the oil tanker.

During my first visit I saw the *Exxon Valdez* in Outside Bay on Naked Island. Emptied of her cargo, she was being cleaned and readied for towing to a shipyard in California. From the helicopter I looked down on her broad red deck, symbol of the worst environmental disaster in U.S. history. Three football fields long, half a football field wide, the tanker looked not as big as that because of the rock faces and conifers rising steeply around the bay.

I could not see inside her gashed hull. The poisonous oil had gone and done its worst to the Sound beyond. Now the Sound was within the tanker, and something strange had happened. Marine life was booming in the cargo holds. The divers made a videotape of it. The sequence inside Hold 3C, at the center of the tanker, illuminates a feeding frenzy. Fish of all sizes twist and snap at darting minnows. A few very large fish swim upside down, possibly because they are oriented to the lights of the divers below. The camera passes through the fish and scans a jumble of protruding plates. Everything in the hold seems to be covered with a thick dust. A gloved hand, as in a housewife's slow-motion nightmare, brushes up white clouds from a surface. The water is clotted with organic matter.

Exxon invited scientists from the National Oceanic and Atmospheric Administration (NOAA) to check out the bizarre phenomenon. The federal researchers happened to be working nearby, taking samples of the seawater, bottom sediments and marine life. Outside Bay was one of their stations for tracking the long-term damage of the oil spill.

The researchers came over readily, for Exxon and the government were still cooperating at the time on matters of science. Screening the tape aboard the tanker, the biologists were awed. The large fish included herring and salmon. William Gronlund, who was in charge of fish-sampling for NOAA, wasn't able to identify the exact species from the monitor, so he and chief scientist

Robert Clark asked if they might collect some. They were taken into Hold 3C.

The atmosphere was Stygian. The pair was lowered in a rubber skiff to the water. Their lanterns illuminated organisms rising and making so many circles on the surface that it looked like it was raining. They observed a floating oily matter, evidently oil loosened from the sides of the tank during cleaning. Paddling into the dark, Gronlund and Clark unfurled a gill net, surely the only fishermen ever to try their luck in the belly of an oil tanker, but they were not able to catch anything.

Clark estimated that the biota were four to ten times richer than in the waters outside. He filled sample jars with jellyfish and the wriggling larvae of crustaceans and mollusks. From the videotape he deduced the presence of zooplankton, marine worms, bacterial mats and algae. Clark had studied oil spills for twenty years and never seen anything like this. But he considered that the tanker was sitting exposed to nutrient-rich water for two months. He theorized that bacteria and other tiny organisms, feeding and multiplying on the oil residues, had attracted bigger predators such as fish. The *Exxon Valdez* had become an aquarium, with a food chain in every tank.

Everyone understands the concept of the food chain, the littlest creatures connected to the largest in a dietary hierarchy. A familiar corollary is that poisons entering the food chain are passed upward, collecting and concentrating in the tissues of ever larger creatures until the compounds reach a destructive level. This scenario was invoked often by those fearing for the health of Prince William Sound. Yet here in the tanker was evidence of the opposite scenario: a cascade of biological enrichment due to the oil.

Which scenario was right? Oil as killer or oil as stimulus? Probably both. Probably the tanker environment was toxic at first (an acute effect of the oil), and subsequently it became productive (a chronic effect). Possibly this is what happened, but not definitely. When you looked below the surface, the Sound was full of uncertainty, full of odd surprises, and the Sound would not stand still.

1

The Earthquake
and the Orangutan

IN THE SUMMER of 1989 I rented an apartment overlooking Eyak Lake in Cordova. Cordova is a fishing town on the eastern border of Prince William Sound. One day from the lake I hitched a ride on a floatplane to Valdez, about fifty miles to the west, over the Chugach Mountains. The plane's pilot commuted to work each morning from Cordova.

The winds bucked the plane on its descent through the clefts. Valdez is situated at a head of a broad, bathtub-shaped fjord, hard against the mountain wall. The setting is like the Tetons in Wyoming if the Tetons were sliced off and put by the sea. The shorter peaks near the town, some shaped like inverted ice cream cones, were white-pointed on top and powder green below. Plunging streams made solid white ribbons on their flanks.

The next day I piggybacked on another plane out to Perry Island in the Sound. It was early August, high summer, the cottonwoods beginning to go ocher. High pressure had swept the morning fog off Port Valdez. On the other side of the fjord, a loaded tanker was leaving the Alyeska pipeline terminal. The alpine fastness was slantingly lit and as sharp and still as in a Maxfield Parrish painting. The day looked to be unstoppably clear. Yet the pilot spoke of bad weather to the south.

Winds in the Sound can be locally unpredictable, because they are bent to diverse quarters by the steep and broken terrain. One of two weather patterns usually prevails. The more common is a rainy southeasterly blow, emanating from a chronic low-pressure center in the Gulf of Alaska. Alternatively, northerly high-pressure winds, also known as drainage winds, flow from fair weather over the Alaskan landmass down through the glacial passes to the coast. The latter pattern prevailed when we took off.

15

Perry Island is located in the northwestern corner of the Sound. At noon I sat on a spit in West Twin Bay on the north shore of the island, facing a 1,200-foot mountain, and watched the two dominant weather patterns clash on high. Clouds like spindrift were rolling up from Perry's hidden flank to the south. As they attempted to crest the mountain, the wind knifing from the mainland gutted and dispersed them. The divide of air must have extended across the width of the Sound. The sea clouds from the Gulf writhed, evanesced and still came on, until, after an hour, the fair breeze failed and the whole Sound filled up with gray.

This was my introduction to the natural forces overarching Prince William Sound. I had begun to see that the environmental tableau was forever in flux. I had begun to realize that the imprint of an event like the oil spill would not long be distinguishable on the swirling backdrop. Most people pictured the Sound as sealed and static, and therefore brittle in the face of disaster. My task would be to liberate the Sound, to set it in motion. I would restore its lifelines in space and time to the broader dynamic.

Hemmed between the mountains and the sea, Prince William Sound is literally a fringe environment, pulled at by opposing forces. On the one hand it is an estuary on the northern arc of the Gulf of Alaska. It is both connected to the open ocean and protected from it. On the other hand the Sound is a submerged mountain range on the south coast of Alaska. White tetrahedrons contain it on all fronts. It is the marine portion of the Chugach National Forest.

Then again, the Sound is a circular complex of fjords. Radiating as if from a hub, the fjords cut deeply into the mainland and the Sound's many islands. The massive glaciers that carved the fjords and mountains retreated before the rising Gulf at the end of the last ice age. But the ice lingers on the shoulders of the heights, and a score of glaciers still finger the water, like landscape architects that can't bear to let go.

The area of the Sound is fifteen times larger than San Francisco Bay, five times larger than Long Island Sound, about twice the size of Chesapeake Bay. Its two main passageways to the Gulf—over the sills of Montague Strait on the west and Hinchinbrook Entrance on the east—measure less than fifteen miles across. The Sound is too enclosed for surf. Stealthily, the tide bears twelve feet of water in and out twice a day. In the long tranquil daylight of summer, I have heard visitors call it a big lake. They are not here in wintertime when high winds from the Gulf generate huge and chaotic waves.

It rains in Prince William Sound more often than it doesn't.

Atmospheric systems fatten on the warm moisture of the Pacific and collide with the cold Chugach Mountains, part of the highest coastal range in the world. The tallest peaks are more than two miles high, straight up from the ocean. Storms are blocked from moving inland and can hold for days. The trapped and laden air rises and dumps rain onto the Sound at an average of ten feet per year. MacLeod Harbor on Montague Island one year had 332 inches of precipitation, the most ever recorded for a site in North America. Cordova, a ward of the sea, is rainy in summer, sleety in winter. Valdez is influenced more by the mountains. Thirty feet of snow is the norm for Valdez winters.

The glaciers work overtime to convert the heavy precipitation to ice and convey it down the slopes. The Sound has no rivers to speak of; the streams feeding it are short and steep, and burst numerously from the forest. Runoff after rains is rapid, with flows in summer up to a hundred times greater than in winter. The salinity of the upper layer of the Sound drops to near zero when the glacial melt and rains are strongest. The glaciers not only loose freshwater but bulldoze fresh sediment to the shores. Landslides topple loose rock into the water, and below the surface unstable formations slump and spread upon the bottom. The erosion won't fill in the Sound anytime soon, as parts of it are a half mile deep.

The Sound sits upon one of the world's most active seismic zones. Over the centuries earthquakes have alternately raised and depressed the coastline, reworking the features of the shore and resetting the interface between mountain and ocean. During the earthquake of '64 Perry Island straddled a geological divide. In fact, the axis of the deformation cut through West Twin Bay where I sat. The land mass southeast of this line lurched up, while the land to the northwest descended.

The physical flux of Prince William Sound carries over into the biological regime. The profusion of its wildlife—the aggregations of seabirds, sea otters, salmon, herring, killer whales, periwinkles, jellyfish, eagles—tends to obscure the variability of the numbers within the species. Individual populations change from season to season and from year to year. Black-legged kittiwakes, for example, the small seagulls I watched scooping fish that day at Perry Island, are among the estuary's most numerous seabirds. There are about 20,000 breeding pairs, but the figure is very approximate. Kittiwake nesting colonies expand or contract by the thousands every year without arousing the concern of biologists.

That population change is normal, healthy, eminently "natural" is an ecological tenet too basic to be debated. Something is always gaining at something else's expense. It is a paradox, difficult for the layman to accept, that a living system like the Sound maintains its stability only by internal flux. Among the factors that cause biological flux are the turmoil of the elements, a change in the availability of food, the incidence of disease, the activity of predators—in a word, disturbances.

The term *disturbance* has a pejorative connotation in ordinary usage, but to ecological scientists a disturbance is simply an event or trend that, brought to bear on a natural system, results in a change. Disturbances may be natural or man-made, and the changes they bring aren't necessarily good or bad. It is scientifically beside the point whether a forest fire is started by lightning or by a careless camper. In either event the forest reverts to an earlier stage of succession, and starts to grow back.

As terrestrial beings we tend to be more familiar with terrestrial disturbances than those to the marine environment. The changes to the land, particularly those from human activity, are glaring and durable. It takes a human lifetime for a forest to grow back, or for soil to be purged of an industrial chemical. The sea, less observably, is more resilient. Resilience is not so much a question of innate hardiness as of time, since marine systems rebound from disturbances sooner or later unless the stress is ongoing. Events overlap, the strong events masking the weaker, and the interactions among them often can't be untangled. But unless a disturbance is unusually pronounced, an overall homeostasis is maintained. Whacked hard, a healthy marine environment like the Sound will tilt like a gyroscope, but like a gyroscope it will continue to spin.

All this related to my visit to Perry Island. I came to observe something called the Prince William Sound Wildlife Volunteer Effort. This was a quasi-scientific program, funded by public donations and attracting volunteers from around the country. According to the prospectus, the objective was to "observe, monitor, and record field data throughout the summer to determine effects of the oil spill and related activities on the Perry Island ecosystem." That is to say, the program would seek to isolate the twin disturbances of the oil and the cleanup—the latter involving hundreds of people and machines on the rocky beaches—from the ongoing natural changes in local wildlife populations.

The same objective, extended Sound-wide, was being pursued by the government. Under the provisions of the Clean Water Act and the Comprehensive Environmental Response, Compensation, and Liability Act, federal and state agencies had launched an extensive program of damage assessment. But the details of this work were being kept secret from the public. Because Exxon was expected to contest the findings, the government did not wish to tip its hand before its case was set.

The spit on West Twin Bay was the location of one of the base camps for the volunteer project. The site was described in the prospectus: "Large diversity of habitat and a good cross section of summer breeding and migrant birds. The area is clean-to-moderately oiled. Based at a beach camp, operations will include counts and observations of birds and mammals from blinds, and offshore & ground transects in mid-treeline subalpine areas."

I made for a tent on the spit and was greeted by Betsy Robbins, of Ithaca, New York. She said she'd been counting wildlife for eight days, mostly in the rain. Two other volunteers, women from New Hampshire, were just beginning their two-week stints. Though the volunteers filled out their logs daily, identifying the birds and animals as best as they could, it was clear that the scientific mission was slipshod. Robbins, who had some biological training, was disappointed by the ignorance of natural history among the volunteers. No transects were being run, at least not by the group here. A transect is a basic survey technique of field biology: A line is laid across a study area, and observations or samples are taken along the line at randomly selected intervals. It makes for a representative and uniform collection of data.

When the summer was over, Pete Mickelson, a Cordova wildlife ecologist and the scientific director of the project, wrote up the results. His report mixed hard numbers with generalization and speculation: "West Twin Bay [of the four base camps] had the greatest abundance [of seabirds] as loons, mergansers, mew gulls, arctic terns, guillemots and murrelets nested near the Bay. . . . Probably 2 pairs of red-throated loons nested in the West Twin Bay area, as probably did a pair of common loons. . . . No young loons were observed suggesting that the adults may have suffered from eating fish contaminated by oil or that oil from the adults' plumage was transferred to eggs resulting in death of the embryos. . . . Sea otters were uncommon except for 2 adult males and a female with a pup in West Twin Bay. . . ."

Mickelson put together a table comparing "expected" and "actual" abundance of birds and animals. It was like a parody of a scientific table. It contained no quantification. Instead there were five ratings, ranging from "abundant" to "rare." A reader of the report was not able to judge "actual" abundance of wildlife, since the volunteers' tallies were not given. To know the abundance of creatures that was "expected" for Perry Island in July and August of 1989, one had to trust Mickelson's experience. Admittedly it was considerable.

"At least 20 species of birds and two species of mammals exhibited a decline from expected population levels," Mickelson concluded. "Although harbor seals were fairly abundant [highest count was 39], possibly twice this number would be expected. Likewise, 9 sea otters seems to be a very low population figure. Sea otters were the most susceptible mammal species to the oil spill." Referring to the noisy cleanup work conducted on parts of the island, he stated that it "severely restricted use by birds and mammals of these areas," but he offered no specifics.

Whether Mickelson was right or wrong about the decline of wildlife (most probably he was right), this was far too soft an approach to control for the flux of the Sound, let alone distinguish the disruption of the cleanup from the harm done by the oil. The report had no value other than its impressions. Though he sprinkled qualifiers like "possibly" and "seems" and "suggesting," he nevertheless advanced interpretations that could have taken on the weight of fact had they been disseminated uncritically—by journalists, for example.

I don't mean to beat up on Pete Mickelson, who lacked the tools to run a proper study and knew it. He, Kelley Weaverling, who administered the project in Cordova, and the scores of volunteers who came to Alaska had no high scientific purpose—they were just trying to do something good for the wounded Prince William Sound. Indeed, their most practical accomplishment was to remove trash left by the cleanup workers.

As for good science, the government had the staff and resources to do it right. At least that's what I assumed in 1989. When I reviewed the official results years later, however, I realized that the government scientists did not master the uncertainties of the Sound either. They fell as short of their assigned goals as Mickelson had on Perry. The difference was that their hypotheses, interpretations and speculations had by then become insinuated as facts.

I SAT on the rounded rocks of the spit and looked up at the clouds. I was an independent investigator, a freewheeler in the Sound. On the one hand, I gathered my facts empirically. I judged what I was seeing by what I had seen before. This was the approach used by the Chugach Eskimos. The Chugach, the original inhabitants of the Sound, had a "sky person" to advise each village on weather and travel conditions. The sky person would lie on his back for hours, studying the speed, direction and shapes of the clouds. Before departure he would take out his kayak and observe the swells. Then he would point the right way to go.

On the other hand, I sought guidance from the theories of

marine scientists. My ecological conception of the Sound had as its seminal grain a 1986 research paper entitled "Estuarine Variability: An Overview." The paper's principal author was Dr. Douglas Wolfe, a scientist with the National Oceanic and Atmospheric Administration in Washington. Crediting Wolfe is more than a little ironic, because, while my ideas about the Sound's resilience were accreting around his thesis, he himself was gathering evidence about the damage of the oil spill for the government's case against Exxon.

The gist of the paper is that estuaries are highly variable because they are subjected to a multiplicity of disturbances. At the same time Wolfe and coauthor Björn Kjerfve argue that estuaries cling to a form of stability; they tend to resist all but the major perturbations. Thus estuaries maintain broad parameters within which conditions fluctuate.

The authors' purpose is to catalog the jumble of disturbances at play. They offer a hierarchy: "Changes occur on a continuum of spatial and temporal scales, in which defined systems at one scalar level are embedded successively within other, larger scales." What they mean by "spatial" scales can be grasped by imagining marine systems as a set of Russian nesting dolls. A particular estuary, the Sound, for instance, is the smallest component in the set. Each system nestles within a bigger version of itself. The systems are dynamically connected, with disturbances transmitted from the larger to the smaller.

The world ocean, commingling all seas, is the primary encompassing system. Theoretically a disturbance at this level can be passed all the way down to the Sound. It is known that deep currents shuttle heat and cold about the planet and influence regional weather. The connections aren't yet understood; storms over Perry Island cannot be predicted on the basis of changes in temperature at the depths of Antarctica, though a relation may well exist.

The connections are clearer at the next level down. The Pacific Ocean is the largest unit in the hierarchy whose energies can be tracked to the waters of the Sound. It takes a very strong disturbance, however: the El Niño phenomenon. The El Niño Southern Oscillation is a periodic climatic disturbance that begins as a warming of surface waters in the equatorial Pacific. When the warming spreads east toward the coast of Ecuador, the atmosphere is engaged and complex meteorological events ensue. Climate can be distorted for a year or more. The effects register in biological communities thousands of miles away—as far, for instance, as the midwestern U.S., where the El Niño that began in 1991 led to severe flooding in 1993.

The major El Niño that began in 1982 has been well analyzed. It brought drought to India and Australia, rains to the west coast of the Americas. The Peruvian anchovy harvest was disrupted. California had severe flooding and lost a number of its prized beaches to erosion. Southcoastal Alaska was wetter than usual, though not drastically so, as low pressure patterns intensified. It has been found that about nine months after the onset of an El Niño, a warming is engendered in the Gulf of Alaska. The change is less than one degree centigrade, which doesn't seem like much. But sea turtles, unheard of this far north, were sighted off the Alaska Peninsula. Tuna and sunfish appeared in Prince William Sound.

Closer to home, in the North Pacific, the principal mechanism of disturbance is the Aleutian Low. Not a storm system per se, it is a path of low pressure, hewn by the jet stream, along which the storms travel from west to east. Where the Low happens to be situated in the North Pacific at any given time is the main determinant of the Sound's weather. In the winter the storm path moves south of the Aleutian Islands. Drawing rain and wind along the island chain, and then tracking northeast across the Gulf, the Low flings storms against the coast every four to seven days. The Low may also move east, by which is meant that the cells of lowest pressure, the most active phases of the storms, occur nearer to the landmass. In summer the Aleutian Low migrates north, to the far arm of the North Pacific in the Bering Sea. In its place comes the gentler (if not much sunnier) weather that some meteorologists lay to a system they call the North Pacific High. Others consider the High to be merely the statistical absence of the dominant Low.

Practically speaking, a scientist investigating the causes of natural variability within Prince William Sound need look no further afield than the Gulf of Alaska, the next-to-smallest doll. Because the Gulf conveys the Aleutian Low, it is known to mariners as the mother of storms. Weather is one of its agents of change, and another is the Alaska Coastal Current, whose impacts are simpler to monitor.

For all the rain and glacial melt within the Sound itself, the bulk of the estuary's fresh water is borne from without. The Alaska Coastal Current is the largest freshwater system in America, with an annual flow 20 percent greater than the Mississippi River's. Collecting the output of rivers and glaciers from as far away as British Columbia, the Current gains volume as it flows northwest. Onshore winds, channeled by the Gulf's coastal mountains, keep it within fifteen miles of the mainland. Mixing occurs, but most of the flow stays above the denser salt water. When the Current reaches Hinchinbrook Entrance at the Sound, it is transporting 50 to 100 million gallons every second. It splits, and a tributary enters the Sound. Circulating counterclockwise, the Current laves the estuary thoroughly and exits by Montague Strait.

The Current is like an intravenous line. It injects not only fresh water but also nutrients, sediments and zooplankton, the minute drifting creatures that support the marine food web. By one estimate, the Current gathers from the Gulf and transports within its narrow band more than 1 million tons of zooplankton each year. The Sound too generates planktonic life, but in springtime samples of copepods, the millimeter-length crustaceans that are the most numerous zooplankters, half the species are found to originate in the Gulf. This means that disturbances occurring unnoticed off British Columbia may reverberate downstream a month later, within Prince William Sound. A dearth of oceanic copepods in the coastal current can cause a serious blow to the food web and affect local populations of birds and fish.

In September at the culmination of the summer melt the amount of fresh water flowing into the Sound is greatest; the Current may attain a speed of three knots, four times the average for March. University of Alaska oceanographer Thomas Royer observed that the flow in March of 1989 was lower than usual. Its rate of one-half knot, in fact, was the lowest in the fifty-nine-year record of measurements. The Current's unprecedented slackness, Royer reported, could have weakened the normal counterclockwise circulation of the surface waters in the Sound—weakened it so much that, near Valdez, the Current could not nudge icebergs, calving from the Columbia Glacier, to the west and out of the shipping lanes as it normally does. Late on the night of March 23 tanker captain Joseph Hazelwood was bothered enough by the icebergs in his path to order a fateful change of bearing, and his ship headed onto Bligh Reef.

I asked Tom Royer to fit the local change—the straying icebergs that diverted the *Exxon Valdez*—into my hierarchy of systems. The linkage is as follows: The Sound's ice movements are affected by the Gulf's current, which is determined by the North Pacific's weather. The weather that winter and spring was very dry and cold, and it caused the input of fresh water from the coast of the Pacific Northwest to be much less than normal. The weather pattern, in turn, resulted because the Aleutian Low, for the first time since 1971, failed to move south out of the Bering Sea in January. And why did that happen? Royer wasn't sure. But he and his associates are beginning to see a connection between atmospheric events around Australia and those in the Arctic. It appears that a southern oscillation, the same atmospheric pressure change that sometimes leads to an El Niño, can cause a rare atmospheric blockage of the Aleutian Low in the Bering Sea.

By connecting the dots, tracking back the disturbances, one could arrive at El Niño as the master culprit of the oil spill. I relate this exercise not just for its amusement. Connections, correlations and coincidences, however intriguing, do not qualify as explanations in science, especially when they exclude other linkages, other potential avenues of explanation. To prove that an effect has a particular cause, or that a change arises from a particular disturbance, the mechanism being hypothesized should be tested. The scenario of cause and effect should be replicated under parallel conditions. This often isn't possible in environmental science, because the whole seething Sound may be the laboratory and disturbances to it can't be reproduced. Environmental scientists therefore make inferences from the evidence available, and then challenge themselves and others to come up with better explanations. Or they ought to.

In making their calculations, good scientists factor in time, both past and future, as much of it as they can grasp. Wolfe and Kjerfve state that disturbances to estuaries operate across embedded scales of time as well as across geographic hierarchies. What impinges on one environmental system as a perturbation may simply be an aspect of a cycle within a larger system. To turn again to the analogy of the Russian dolls, the smallest doll is the present moment in Prince William Sound, time zero, and the larger dolls are the successively longer periods during which exogenous forces may transpire to alter the system.

Thus in the period of a day, there occur two high tides and a transition from darkness to sunlight. In a period of months, the tides of the equinox flood abnormally high. The course of a year brings changes in light levels, temperature and precipitation. The changes become less predictable as the time frame widens, and the less predictable, the easier they are to appreciate as disturbances.

Over the decades the climatic parameters shift. The Sound may experience a phase of warmer temperatures, for example, or fewer storms. A huge hurricane hits, or a monster surge of waves. These episodes seem unprecedented, because one's line of sight, bounded by a human lifetime, perceives the crests but not the troughs or crests behind them. Given enough data and computer power, even the most arbitrary El Niños might be revealed to be the oscillations of some grand climatic mechanism.

The turnover of climate cycles in the North Pacific is shorter than the time that will pass before global warming, a grand-scale atmospheric disturbance, will have an impact on the region. Indeed, as the Russian dolls of time and space expand, the environmental cycles embedded within them collide. To judge by the present trend in the temperature of the Gulf of Alaska, for instance, the globe would appear not to be warming but to be cooling.

The temporal hierarchy does have a limit. The Sound's estuarine entity is only about 5,000 years old, for that is when global sea levels stabilized following the last ice age, or period of glaciation. By the evidence of past glaciations, Earth's present phase of warmth is on the wane. The next oscillation will cause the Sound to disappear under a mile of ice and its myriad creatures to vanish.

The ecosystem reels and rebounds, reels and rebounds, whipsawed by coincidence. The permutations of biological change are endless, because disturbances overlap and affect marine life in ways that are incremental, or offsetting, or inexplicably synergistic.

Take for illustration the plankton regime, the sine qua non of the Sound's estuarine function. The plankton cycle is a springtime phenomenon within the surface layer of the water. The basic sequence is the same, but each spring it plays out differently. First, upwelling nutrients and lengthening daylight stimulate the bloom of phytoplankton, which are single-celled algae. Mushrooming under the lash of photosynthesis, the phytoplankton feed the zooplankton, which are an array of animal life, including minute crustaceans like copepods and the weak-swimming larvae of worms, mollusks, crabs and fish. The zooplankton, as they multiply massively in turn, are forage for the salmon fry tumbling in from the streams, the herring schooling in the bays, the mussels fixed on the rocks and the humpback whales that pass through with their wide-straining mouths.

The plankton cycle would seem to demand clockwork timing in order that everyone be fed. But because the phytoplankton are plants triggered by light (an invariable annual cycle) and the zooplankton are animals triggered by water temperatures (annually variable), mismatches in timing occur. In a cold spring the zooplankton may hatch after the phytoplankton peak has passed, or in a warm spring they may bloom too early. Storms early in the cycle can disperse the plankton. Storms late in the cycle can replace depleted nutrients with fresh upwellings and instigate a second bloom. Plankton populations are subject to so many concurrent disturbances that no one knows how widely the total biomass may vary from year to year. But certainly great fluctuations occur within given species. Copepod numbers have been found to vary by a factor of 20, krill (a larger crustacean) by a factor of 50, certain fish larvae by a factor of 1,000. Something of a balance is being maintained, or else higher organisms would collapse, but the tiny individual components supporting the food web appear to change almost independently.

Higher in the marine food web, among the fish stocks and other adult populations, the swings aren't as dramatic, but since the food web is a cat's cradle of who's-eating-who, the causes of change are just as murky. In their paper Wolfe and Kjerfve looked for long-term patterns in fish. They pointed out that Pacific sardines and Atlantic herring seem to undergo large changes in abundance every fifty to a hundred years. Other researchers have observed cycles in the catches of Atlantic cod, North Sea plaice and Dungeness crab off California. The link appears to be to long-term temperature change. Similarly, the changes in abundance of fish in and near the Sound may be due to oscillations of temperatures in the Gulf of Alaska.

Since 1970 oceanographer Royer and his associates at the University of Alaska have monitored the Gulf at a temperature station just west of Prince William Sound. The instruments are sensitive to the thousandth of a degree and provide readings at depths as great as 900 feet. Why the need to measure so deep? The temperatures at the very surface of the sea are distractingly variable, and would cover up a subtle trend. The Russian dolls as echo chambers, is how I imagined the problem. Tom Royer called the short-term, weather-driven ups and downs "noise that contaminates the Gulf's signal."

The noise/signal metaphor derives from the more discrete disciplines of science, such as physics and chemistry. A physicist or chemist investigating a particular signal is able to screen out the effects he or she is not interested in—the noise. Experiments are controlled. Disturbances are orchestrated. Variables such as temperature are manipulated until their impacts on the signal are understood and then they are dismissed from the equation. Eventually the signal is isolated and defined.

The ecologist, the oceanographer, the meteorologist, building their theories upon observation, are almost never in control of the variables. They do not even know what all the variables are. Exceptional signals, like the splash of the '64 earthquake or the '82–'83 El Niño, stand out in the Sound and ripple for a while, but most others are subject to interference. When environmental scientists do design an experiment to isolate a signal, their models (on computer, usually) are criticized as too-quiet, too-crude substitutes for the real thing. Their inferences are supported by statistics— statistical proofs of a finding's probability being the soft scientists' answer to the hard scientists—but still they are left with inferences.

To get back to Tom Royer. From his temperature history he hypothesized that every fifteen to twenty-five years the Gulf undergoes a two-degree (C.) shift from cold to warm and back again. The cycle seemed connected to the 18.6-year oscillation in the angle of the moon's orbit, which minutely affects the range of the tides, and he posited lesser contributions from the forces of wind and sun. Royer really couldn't explain why the temperature shifts. But when he set his lunar-cum-temperature data next to the annual catch of halibut, he found that the supply of the bottom fish rose and fell in league with his cycle. For king crab, it was inversely so. Royer observed that the king crab harvest was poor in the late 1950s and early 1980s when water temperatures were highest, and best in the 1970s when temperatures were lowest.

Royer's thesis was like a bomb, thrown from the balcony of oceanography onto the stage of fisheries biology. Fisheries managers grabbed onto it eagerly, since if temperature was the driving factor, they might be absolved of past mistakes, but the statisticians and research biologists attacked it and partly defused it.

The halibut connection held up better than the king crab connection. Catch records for Pacific halibut in the region go back to 1927; there was enough data for Royer and two colleagues to detect a recurrent pattern and relate it to the oscillations of the moon. The king crab figures, though, didn't extend that far. The statistical proofs did not confirm the connection. Other disturbances than lunar-driven temperatures, such as the rise of a larval parasite or the toll of overfishing in the '70s, could just as easily account for the disastrous crab harvests of the early '80s. At the very least the noise of one-time factors masked the cyclical signal.

Royer needed more time. His connection would have to hold up through at least one more cycle of warming and cooling, another thirty years' worth of observations, and even then he would have established a correlation, which is something less than an explanation, unless and until he sorted out the Gulf's food web. As the oceanographer was the first to concede, he had two ends of a possible chain—the catch figures for certain commercial species and the temperature data—with few facts about the linked systems in between.

Still, Royer's hypothesis had wide appeal. It was adapted in ways he never conceived. There was an interesting case of this in 1991. When the food web of the Gulf was altered that year by a falloff in copepods, some biologists saw a connection to the mortalities of kittiwakes in Prince William Sound and elsewhere. The copepod decline and the bird mortalities occurred when springtime surface temperatures were abnormally cold. Thus the scenario appearing in Alaskan newspapers: Long-term cooling in the Gulf has brought a cold spring, which dropped surface temperatures, which disrupted the zooplankton production, which caused a glitch in the food chain, which reduced forage fish, which caused seabirds to starve and their reproduction to fall.

It sounded logical. But when I looked into the matter, I found a series of coincidences instead of consequences. The one-degree drop in surface temperatures was too great to have been caused by the Gulf's cycle alone. The zooplankton decline couldn't be shown to be caused by the cold surface waters. (More likely it was due to fewer copepods that year in the Alaska Coastal Current.) The falloff in forage fish may have occurred but was never documented. As for the coup de grace, there was indeed a die-off of kittiwakes, but then kittiwakes also died in 1983 and 1989 when conditions were different. In 1991 around the Gulf, some kittiwake colonies were up, some were down. Other seabirds weren't being affected at all. In sum, overlapping disturbances were making noise, not a signal, which is another way of describing the melange of nature's variables.

Scientists are not so different from the rest of us. Faced with an unfamiliar problem, they think out loud and they look for the simplest solution. It's the conversational equivalent of Occam's razor. Strip away the unfamiliar language, however, and their explanations are often no more than provocative opinions. They understand that—but do we?

If there is a disturbance in the region worth worrying about today, superseding all calculations of cycles and defying explanation, it is the precipitous decline of the sea lion population. The Steller, or northern, sea lion may be on a crash course toward extinction across the heart of its range, which extends from Prince William Sound to the tip of the Aleutians. In the 1970s, when methodical counts began at haulout sites and rookeries, the population was 140,000. It went to 70,000 in 1985, and then the drop accelerated, to just 25,000 animals in 1990.

The problem appears to be the failure of young animals to survive. Breeding and pupping seem to taking place normally, but juvenile sea lions, when they put out to sea from the rookeries, are disappearing from the population. One federal researcher, calling the falloff sickening, said that it was as if an unknown force were extracting sea lions from the ocean before they could get back to land and breed.

A decade ago it was possible to attribute the fall to either a periodic phase or a random spike, but no longer. Biologists are used to seeing steep rates of decline in certain creatures, including birds, mice and fish, but these are equally known for surges of recovery. Short-lived animals mature early and bear multiple young, and consequently they bounce back quickly from drastic setbacks. Large mammals, which certainly include the thousand-pound sea lion, bear single young that develop slowly. Their population trends are gradual. Sea lions can't immediately capitalize on favorable environmental conditions, just as most environmental stresses can be tolerated—literally outlived—without undue loss. But the stress in the Gulf has lasted too long. Even if juvenile survival should miraculously become 100 percent tomorrow, overall numbers would continue to fall for five years. The population stability has been preternaturally shattered.

Scientists agree that the disturbance is probably man-made. There are precedents. Beginning in the 1700s, Russian, European and American seamen hunted the animals for their skins, meat and oil. Severely depleted by the middle of the nineteenth century, the sea lions by unofficial estimates did not start to recover until early in this century. After a high point in the '40s and '50s, they were cropped again, if not as severely, by Alaska authorities seeking to help the fishing industry.

The animal's taste in seafood is identical to our own. Sea lions snatch halibut off longlines, invade purse seines to poach salmon, rip gill nets after taking herring and even puncture the buoys that mark crab pots, this last for no discernible purpose. Not surprisingly, they get shot and killed. Sea lions also drown in trawls, the towed nets of foreign and domestic fishing fleets. But the state's control program ended in the late '60s, and the annual mortalities from human encounters, including a small take by Alaska Natives, cannot come close to accounting for their present plight. The disturbance must be indirect.

The Stellers' slide accelerated as the huge fish-processing ships increased their operations in the Gulf and Bering Sea. Some 2 million tons of pollock are taken annually, plus lesser amounts of flounder and other bottom fish. The growing consensus is that juvenile sea lions aren't getting enough to eat. It may be because there are fewer fish overall, fewer fish of catchable size or maybe fewer concentrations. Though pollock stocks for one are up, the factory fleets may be dispersing the schools so that it's harder for the younger animals to catch up to them. Biologists are just beginning to understand, thanks to radio transmitters, where sea lions feed in the Gulf.

The connections are far from clear. The dynamics are not well known. This is why it was scientifically foolish, in 1989, to try to measure the impact of the oil spill on the sea lions of Prince William Sound and the western Gulf. Although no animals were known to have died during the spill, the government's study plan stated that several thousand could have been exposed to the oil and that delayed effects could lead to mortalities and premature pupping. Surveys and biopsies were duly undertaken. A statistical analysis was supposed to show whether the latest counts of sea lions "were significantly lower than predicted by the historical model." That is, the government argued it could separate the spill from the projection of the ongoing decline.

In 1991 the study was discontinued after an expenditure of a half-million dollars. It was not possible, the government conceded, "to distinguish post- from pre-spill population effects clearly." Like other failures of the damage assessment program, this one was written off to the chances of science. After all, some hypotheses pan out and some don't. However, the real failure was the presumption that the spill was greater than its physical context and that its signal would make itself heard.

The poor researchers. They had a devil of an assignment untangling the threads of the oil spill from the living fabric of Prince William Sound. For their pains they were taken to task by bureaucrats, attorneys, environmentalists, fishermen, Exxon executives, Alaska Natives. The laymen couldn't understand why the answers weren't explicit—why, after millions were budgeted for measuring and analyzing, the explanations of the disturbance did not fall out of the Sound like apples onto Isaac Newton's head. I sat on the spit and watched the clouds writhe.

ON APRIL 29, 1989, Pete Leathard, president of Veco, the Anchorage company handling the cleanup of the oil spill for Exxon, issued a statement to the press. Alaskans and their legislators were out for the scalp of the oil industry, and Leathard sought to calm their rage about the disaster a month earlier.

"Twenty-five years ago Alaska suffered an 'act of God,' the Good Friday earthquake," he observed. "We didn't waste time seeking to punish the cause of that disaster, nor is it productive to spend time placing blame and seeking to punish the perceived cause of this disaster."

Although the Good Friday coincidence of the two events had been widely noted, Leathard's comparing the oil spill to an act of God was rejected as arrogant, blasphemous and self-serving. I never heard anyone from Exxon or Veco ever mention the earthquake again.

But a scientific comparison is not only appropriate, it is vital to understanding how Prince William Sound copes with perturbation. History did not repeat itself in the particulars. The acute effects differed, as the spill struck the ecosystem rather high in the food web, killing many sea otters and birds and injuring intertidal habitat, while the quake hit lower, destroying intertidal and benthic life on a broad scale. What the two had in common was a rapid transition from acute effects to the process of recovery. They made loud disturbances but soon petered out in the ongoing hubbub.

The Alaska earthquake of March 27, 1964, was one of the most destructive geologic events ever measured. Determining the magnitude of the quake was problematic, because no strong-motion seismographs capable of registering it were installed in Alaska at the time. All the seismographs within hundreds of miles of the epicenter in the Sound were driven off their scales. Extrapolating from measurements around the globe, scientists settled on a Richter magnitude of between 8.4 and 8.6. But on the refined scale that exists today, which compensates for the insensitivity of the old instruments by taking into account movement in the earth's crust, the Alaska event has been upgraded to a magnitude 9.2. That makes it the strongest earthquake ever recorded in North America, and the second strongest in the history of the hemisphere.

The quake destroyed the prevailing geologic theory. Prior to 1964 most scientists believed that the continents and oceans were fixed in place and that geological forces operated in a vertical dimension. Mountains formed and the land shook because the earth's crust was contracting and crinkling along vertical fault lines. But in Alaska so much crust was found to have moved so far from the epicenter that a rival theory, based on horizontal thrust, had to be considered. This was the theory of plate tectonics, since widely accepted.

According to the present model of Earth, the crust is fragmented in a dozen moving slabs, or plates, up to twenty-five miles thick. Bearing continents and ocean basins over the earth's molten mantle, the plates grind past each other at some points and at other points collide. Southcoastal Alaska is believed to be the scene of a crunching, continuous collision between the Pacific plate and a western extension of the North American plate.

At a rift beneath the southeastern Pacific, molten basaltic rock is oozing onto the ocean floor. The Pacific plate is born here. The crust, pushing north-northwest as if on a slow-moving conveyor belt, creeps past the American plate at the rate of a few inches a year. The abutting slabs of rock bind, strain and periodically let go in earthquakes. Indeed, the plate's perimeter—from

South America north to Alaska, west to Siberia and south past Japan, Indonesia and Australia—is known as the Ring of Fire because of all the seismic and volcanic activity.

My Perry Island rock emerged some 60 million years ago from a rift west of Puget Sound that no longer exists. The rock was originally in the form of ocean ridges, plateaus and seamounts. Inching toward Alaska on the Pacific plate, the material to make Prince William Sound was overlaid by lava flows and sediments eroding from North America; it was contorted by the chthonic intrusions of granite. About 50 million years ago, the rock arrived much altered at the Aleutian Trench, a fault guarding the Alaskan landmass like a moat.

The trench is located about fifty miles south of the present coast, paralleling the line from Prince William Sound to the end of the Aleutian chain. The fault deflects the force of the colliding Pacific plate by a process called subduction. The ocean plate being heavier, it forces itself beneath the continental plate and descends into the earth. The material of the Sound compressed as it went down. It folded like a rug being pushed through a crack at the base of a wall. While the lower folds melted into the mantle, some of the upper folds were sheared off by the overriding continent and became attached to it, or accreted. This is how the Chugach Mountains originated.

As the conveyor belt still squeezed into the earth, crust was forced back toward the surface, pushing the young peaks higher and uplifting islands from the sea. Mountains were built as far as 200 miles inland, in the Alaska Range northwest of the Chugach, indicating that the Pacific plate is slipping—for the process continues—beneath the North American plate at a rather shallow angle.

Volcanoes, mountains of another kind, spring from the subterranean processing. The Aleutian Islands are entirely volcanic. The melting of plate material many miles below the surface creates pockets of magma and gas. Under pressure, the magma rises through cracks in the folded crust and periodically erupts. From the tip of the Aleutian chain, the line of past and present eruptions curves north along the Alaska Peninsula past Anchorage, and then east into the Wrangell Mountains on the far side of Prince William Sound.

The compression and subduction of crust causes extremely powerful earthquakes. Since 1899 southcoastal Alaska has experienced more than seventy quakes of magnitude 7 or greater, and ten quakes have equaled or exceeded magnitude 8. California, meanwhile, has had but seven that compare, the greatest being the 7.9

event in 1906 in San Francisco. Alaska earthquakes are stronger because the thrust along the Aleutian Trench has a horizontal dimension. When a break occurs, the shock is transmitted both laterally and vertically and affects a greater surface area than along the San Andreas plate boundary in California.

At 5:36 P.M. on March 27, 1964, a break occurred below Prince William Sound. The nearest surface point, the epicenter, was located between Unakwik Inlet and the Columbia Glacier on the Sound's north coastline. The initial break was followed over the next three to four minutes by a series of ruptures, cutting across the direction of the plate thrust, along a 150-mile-long line to the southwest. (The oil spill would take the same path.)

Crustal deformation is the term geologists use when an earthquake moves land vertically and/or horizontally. In this instance 100,000 square miles of southcoastal Alaska were deformed. The Pacific plate had been gradually pushing the North American plate back, compressing and thickening the coastal landmass, until the quake released the strain and the shoreline rebounded. The whole continental margin lurched into the Gulf by as much as sixty feet. The town of Cordova repositioned itself on the globe forty-six feet to the southeast.

In stretching out, the land actually thinned and dropped. The band of subsidence extended for hundreds of miles, from the northwestern margins of the Sound southwest to Kodiak Island. Inland mountains of the Chugach range lost as much as seven feet of altitude. But to the east of Perry Island in the Sound, an equivalent area of the ocean floor went up.

Unlike the horizontal displacement of the landmass, which was determined much later, the up-and-down shifts were dramatically and immediately apparent because of the response of the ocean. The sea fell back from the raised shorelines and rushed in to claim new levels in subsided areas. On the west side of Montague Island, where the upthrusting was freakish, tide pools were left quivering atop thirty-foot cliffs. Cordova's boat harbor was rendered useless when the waterfront rose six feet. Across the Sound, the town of Whittier went down seven feet. And the submerged shoals of Bligh Reef were nudged upward, four feet closer to the bottoms of straying ships.

Probably the person closest to the epicenter was a fisherman named Joe Clark aboard his vessel the *Quest*. Steaming in deep water in Unakwik Inlet, Clark reported he heard "a booming explosion a second or so before the first shock." Immediately the boat began to rock and he saw the shore trembling. About five minutes later, while the earth was still shaking, Clark saw a "big swell moving in." The water sloshed back and forth across the inlet. Waves ran up on shore 100 feet above the tide line and then sharply withdrew, exposing the ocean floor to a depth of twenty-five feet.

The same sloshing and shaking occurred in Port Valdez, east of the epicenter, to devastating effect. The town at the time was located on unstable alluvial ground at the eastern end of the port basin. In the new Valdez, which was rebuilt a few miles to the west, I interviewed a witness named Shirley Scott. Scott said she didn't think much of the tremors at first. When she heard glass breaking in the storefronts, she knew she should get out into the street. She met a hellish scene. A fissure opened beneath a car in front of her. The trees and telephone poles were pitching about. She saw a pile of logs rise up as if they were alive. The ground was reeling so she could hardly keep her balance.

The quake went on for almost five minutes. As the seismic waves rippled through the town, a man saw his son descend to the waist in a trough and in the next instant lift on the crest of a three-foot swell. There was a rumbling sound, a continuous low roar in the air. Like mouths in the earth, cracks gaped and snapped shut, emitting jets of water. Sewerage lines broke and spurted filth. Shirley Scott, trying to get home to her children, fell into an oily crevasse, damaged her knee and was hauled out in shock.

On the waterfront there was chaos. The first waves crashed ashore less than a minute after the quake began. It was fortunate that the salmon cannery was closed for the church holiday. But the freighter *Chena* had just docked with a cargo of supplies and Easter goods, and parents and children had come down to greet her. The 500-foot dock was obliterated; a score of people were swept to their deaths. Repeatedly, the *Chena* was tossed high above the embankment and then dropped hard on the harbor bottom as the sea surged in and out. Somehow the captain started the engines and maneuvered the ship to deeper water, passing over the site where the cannery had vanished. Offshore, buildings swirled in the clutches of a huge whirlpool, while waves raced along the town's main street like speeding cars.

On a beach near the Narrows, at the other end of Port Valdez, a man named Red Ferrier and his son Delbert were amazed to see mountainsides of snow sliding into the water. They jumped into their skiff to get to their boat anchored offshore, but the water ran out and left them stranded. The ocean fell into a rocky channel in the port bottom, sucking their boat down with it. Then the vessel reappeared as the water rose again. Taking advantage of the oscillations, the Ferriers rode the bucking skiff out to the boat the next time that the sea came in. They clambered aboard and got under way. As they headed out the Narrows, a wave pursued them that they estimated to be fifty feet high. It was black with mud, rocks and debris. The wave knocked out the navigation beacon in the center of the Narrows, but before it could overtake the Ferriers, their boat made it to the wider waters of Valdez Arm. The crest leveled out and they were able to ride above it.

The marine effects of the '64 earthquake were more violent and destructive than the consequences on land. It's true that Anchorage, eighty miles from the epicenter, was crippled as streets cracked, sidewalks upheaved and houses slid from their foundations. I remember the pictures in *Life* magazine. But the city had few tall buildings that could topple and kill people. Almost all of the 103 Alaskans who died were drowned. They were caught by waves in the small coastal communities of Kodiak, Seward, Whittier, Chenega and Valdez. Valdez, with thirty-one fatalities, had the highest toll.

The killer waves were tsunamis. Tidal wave is the popular term, but erroneous, since tsunamis have nothing to do with the tides. The most violent tsunamis originated locally as a result of landslides above and below the waterline. Great volumes of rock and snow tumbled from the mountains surrounding Port Valdez. Submarine avalanches occurred when loosely packed sediments, left by the glaciers at the edge of fjords, slid to great depths and displaced massive amounts of water. An undersea slide near the Shoup Glacier generated a wave that toppled trees 100 feet above the beach and left silt and gravel at 200 feet. From above, the basin of the port must have looked like a bathtub going berserk.

A second series of waves originated far offshore and took longer to arrive. This was the tsunami of plate tectonics. In a kind of reverse landslide, hundreds of miles of the continental shelf broke and thrust upward against the weight of the Gulf of Alaska. Waves were dispatched in all directions, with the major crests proceeding about two hours apart. Sharp cones of water appeared on the surface. The sea quaked and slapped the hulls of ships so hard that captains thought they must have run aground.

The tsunami invaded Port Valdez just as the local waves were stilling. The town was already half destroyed; in the night four great surges of water completed its ruin. Boats were lifted into the trees. Fires started. Families fled to high ground. The water reached a tank farm. Fuel oil and asphalt storage tanks were ruptured and hundreds of thousands of gallons emptied into the port. The largest oil spill until the wreck of the *Exxon Valdez*, it left traces that can still be observed high up on the Sound's beaches.

The tsunami was felt throughout the Pacific. Hawaii and Japan were brushed. The west coast of North America took the brunt. Fifteen people were killed that night in Oregon and California. Traversing the southern ocean, the tsunami was still measurable the next morning at the Antarctic Peninsula.

Today any quake in Alaska greater than 6.8 prompts the civil defense to call for evacuations of coastal communities near the epicenter. Residents of the Sound get a tsunami warning once every year or so. Early in the morning of September 4, 1989, a 6.9 event in the Gulf south of Kodiak was recorded. People in Cordova were advised around seven o'clock that the wave would hit an hour later. We were asked to go to the high ground of the elementary school. The police department shifted its communications system to the telephone company building, two streets up. But when I called around, I found few people worried. They told me the authorities were supercautious, and indeed the warning was canceled at 7:30. This particular disturbance, powerful enough at its source to wreck half of San Francisco, rippled through the Gulf and ended in a four-inch wave upon the shore.

THE NATIONAL ACADEMY OF SCIENCES published a multivolume study of the earthquake in 1971. The summary volume had this to say about the biological consequences: "Few earthquakes in history have altered life environments so profoundly and over so large an area."

The tsunami waves, said the report,

> covered sessile organisms and salmon-spawning beds with silt, disturbed and killed salmon fry, leveled forests, and caused saltwater invasion of many coastal freshwater lakes. . . . Walls of water that surged into estuaries scoured out beds of clams and other organisms, or deposited layers of mud and debris that suffocated the life below. . . .
>
> Ocean agitation and underwater mud slides probably caused extensive damage to life in deeper waters, although such changes have been difficult to evaluate. . . . Thousands of large red rockfish and cod were reported dead on the surface near Chenega Island and in Valdez Arm. These fish probably had been forced to return to the surface by violent water turbulence and were unable to return to deep water because their air bladders had expanded. Large numbers of dead flatfish also were seen floating in Knight Island Passage. . . .
>
> The tectonic elevations and depression caused extensive damage to the biota of coastal forests, migratory-bird nesting grounds, salmon spawning waters and gravels, as well as shellfish habitats, and initiated long-term changes in littoral and stream morphology. Clams, barnacles, algae, and many other marine and littoral organ-

isms perished in areas of uplift. Spawning beds, trees and other vegetation were destroyed in areas of depression. . . .

Damage to bivalve [shellfish] resources was extensive, especially in Prince William Sound, where between 11 and 40 per cent of each of the economically important species were destroyed. About 90 per cent of the mussels, probably the most plentiful mollusk in Prince William Sound, were destroyed, and razor clams suffered heavy mortalities in areas of uplift.

The instigator of the National Academy study was George Plafker, a geologist with the Alaska branch of the U.S. Geological Survey. In April of 1964 Plafker had surveyed the earthquake zone by airplane, and when he returned to his office in California he was full of excitement about what he had seen. He set about organizing an expedition to make detailed measurements of the dislocations along the coast. Finding the geologists willing to go was easy, but Plafker had trouble enlisting a biologist. "We needed people who could tell us where the organisms belonged on the beach," Plafker recalled, "what the normal zoning of the algae and barnacles was, so we could measure the changes."

Plafker turned for references to a professor at the California Academy of Sciences, G. Dallas Hanna. Trained as a marine biologist with an expertise in diatoms, the single-celled phytoplankton, Hanna was also an inventor and a student of optics. Once he coated a lens with diatoms and projected them onto a planetarium ceiling to make points of starlight. Hanna was well over seventy, almost twice Plafker's age, and not a candidate, or so the geologist thought, for a rugged summer climbing in and out of boats in Alaska. "When do you want to leave?" Hanna asked.

Hanna, Plafker and others on the research team gathered aboard a USGS vessel in May of '64. Aftershocks from the earthquake were still being felt as they cruised the Sound. "Some people claimed the tremors never stopped all summer," said Plafker. "But we didn't feel them that much on the boat." The eagles and gulls were scavenging the spiny remains of the rockfish with burst flotation bladders. In the far western Sound, downthrust shrubs and trees were withering, their roots steeped in salt water. "It seems odd to a part-time beachcomber," Hanna wrote in his report, "to be able to pick live sea shells from spruce trees."

High on the beaches of the uplifted islands, crabs and starfish were unnaturally congregated in diminishing tide pools. The rims of the oases were littered with desiccated and decomposing invertebrates, and a ripe smell greeted the scientists. Hanna noted that hundreds of square miles of newly exposed littoral areas, once densely populated, had become completely desolate. "The bleached remains of Bryozoa [corallike animals] and calcareous algae were so white that the rocky beaches rivaled the adjacent snow-covered mountains in brightness," he wrote. The organic decay made more food for the birds, he added.

Whether remarking on a barnacle-covered boulder he found tossed eighty feet above the shore, or describing the strange behavior of gulls during aftershocks—they would "attempt to land on the quivering mud of Cordova harbor, touch their feet to the ground, cry and fly up a few feet, then try again and again to land"—Hanna leavened his fact-finding with wonder and style. Hanna was of the old school, before data-crunching became paramount. Plafker remembered him as enthusiastic as a child, rushing about collecting his shells and samples. In truth, everyone on the research vessel was awed and stimulated by the changes the earthquake had wrought. The geologists saw the quake as a grand tectonic experiment, and in recording the results they were being given an unprecedented opportunity to test their theories.

"Geologists look at things from such a long-range point of view," said Plafker, "and not a lot happens over the short term. You tend to learn the most when there are cataclysms, like volcanic eruptions or landslides or earthquakes. But the human and property loss that goes with these events is always something of a damper. It hurts your conscience to be enjoying the science so much when people have suffered."

One of the most intriguing findings, shedding light on both the past and future of the Sound, were tree stumps on the new shorelines of uplifted islands. Apparently the forest once had extended as much as eight feet below the former high tide line. A prior disturbance depressed the islands, killing trees on their margins, after which the ocean covered the stumps with sediment. The '64 uplift allowed wave action to scour away the gravel and reveal the stumps. The coast, it appeared, bounced up and down like a yo-yo, discombobulating its plant and animal communities.

(Plafker now believes that over the last millennium the downs have exceeded the ups—for every foot of uplift there have been two feet of subsidence. The trend has been for the Sound to sink, nudged by seismic disturbances. The earthquakes of the region may even have a cycle, for Plafker has evidence that over the past 6,000 years events on the magnitude of '64 have occurred every 650 to 850 years.)

In their two months of sailing the Sound the researchers stopped at hundreds of points to measure the changes in land level. Eventually the USGS produced a map on which the points of equal change are connected in contour lines. The contours range from minus seven feet to plus thirty, and they parallel the coast, like crinkles in the earth when plates collide. The contour of zero change, the division between up and down, runs from Port Valdez west across Columbia Glacier and Unakwik Inlet, then bends south over Perry Island and climbs into the ice fields above the western Sound.

These sweeping delineations, which helped revolutionize geology, were provided by the lowly barnacle. Plafker and his colleagues seized on the fact that barnacles grow exactly to the limit of high tide. There is a sharp demarcation—the high-tide line—where the white band of barnacles ends. The line is accentuated by the black *Verrucaria* lichen growing immediately above. Barnacles on raised shores were now clear of the water. It was a simple matter, at scheduled high tide, to measure the difference in elevation between the new waterline and the upper boundary of the crustaceans. That gave the amount of uplift at that location.

The same method could be used in determining subsidence. Usually the researchers could see the submerged barnacle line and measure down to it. By the end of the summer, when juvenile barnacles had colonized the new high-tide line, the method became even easier, since one could measure the distance between the spat and the old barnacles without regard for the tide. George Plafker became a champion of barnacles; he would proudly pull them out of his pockets at geological society meetings.

In 1965 Dallas Hanna returned to the Sound at the helm of his own expedition. His aim was to conduct a thorough ecological survey of the altered shore. The research vessel included an invertebrate biologist, to study the mollusks and other small animals, and two botanists, one specializing in intertidal algae and the other in the terrestrial vegetation of the upper beach.

The investigators ran transects at thirty-three sites around the Sound, spending a day or two at each. At uplifted sites they extended a rope from the top of the preearthquake beach down through the new intertidal zone to low water. Then the scientists would creep along the rope, heads bent to the stones, and at random intervals record what they saw living there. Not only beaches were sampled, for in some places the transect was run almost vertically up rock walls.

Ideally, the biologists would take the measure of the disturbance by comparing the same beaches before and after. But they had no prior record of the biological assemblages at their sites: no baseline. This is a common frustration in environmental investigations. So they did the next best thing, which was to establish baseline transects at a site that hadn't been disturbed. West Twin

Bay on Perry Island was selected to serve as a reference because it hadn't gone up or down and because it had been sheltered from the worst of the tsunamis. West Twin Bay, where I ran mental transects twenty-four years later.

Plants and animals group themselves on the Sound's beaches in horizontal zones, according to the tidal elevation. Beach, I should add, is something of a euphemism; there are no honeyed strands up here. Some fine-grained and silty areas can be found, primarily in the east. But in describing the great majority of shore-lines in the Sound it is a question only of the size of the rocks, which range from gravel to boulders. Cobbles, roundish rocks the size of breadboxes, predominate. The biota are richest on cobble beaches that are coarsely mixed and protected from the ocean.

The highest marine zone, the supralittoral or splash zone, is populated by a few limpets and snails and the thin formations of the black *Verrucaria* lichen. Next down, the upper intertidal zone is characterized by barnacle species; by the brown *Fucus* seaweed, also called rockweed, or popweed for its thumbnail-sized flotation bladders; and by beds of blue mussels, these toward the lower half of the zone. The mobile creatures of the upper intertidal include snails and limpets in profusion, some hermit crabs, a few starfish and those small flealike crustaceans, the amphipods and isopods.

The lower intertidal is sometimes called the green zone, because of the green algae coating the rocks. Red and brown algae grow here as well. The animal life becomes more varied, with chitons, urchins, predatory snails, sculpins, sea anemones, crabs, worms and more starfish joining the species listed above. The richest zone for fauna, beginning at low water, is the subtidal, and its principal vegetation is kelp. The spectrum of flora and fauna differs somewhat on the fine-grained beaches of the Sound. Clams live within the soft sediment of the lowest zones, and eelgrass is the dominant subtidal vegetation.

Hanna and his team spent relatively little time studying the downthrust areas. Complete transects were difficult to run because much of the old intertidal zone was submerged. But they found that, though the *Verrucaria* lichen had been killed, the mussels, barnacles and *Fucus* rockweed that had been sent down were thriving in spite of the increased tidal coverage. Fifteen months after the quake, these organisms had seeded the new intertidal with juvenile forms. The snails and limpets had migrated upward to establish their proper zones. In some cases, the herbivores were feeding on the surviving terrestrial mosses. The kelp at the low end and the black lichen at the high end were the only organisms absent from the new intertidal zone.

Life was rapidly reestablishing on the raised shores as well. But the recovery was not as advanced, because the mortalities had been much greater here. With the apparent exception of one limpet species, the snails and the like did not migrate downward. Reacting to the uplift as to a low tide, they died when the water didn't return. The fixed barnacles, mussels and rockweed perished as well. The change in the substrate, the base for life's attachment, was so great that intertidal species on these beaches started over on a clean slate.

Habitats being recolonized after an acute disturbance go through stages of succession. H. William Johansen, the expedition's algae specialist, observed that the order of settlement for vegetation was bacteria, diatoms, filamentous green algae and then the spores of larger algae—each form preparing the way and then yielding ground to more complex species. Fifteen months after the quake, at what was about the midpoint of the recovery, certain organisms were doing better than others in the competition for footholds. Some algae took off. With few herbivores to graze them and little competition from the slower-growing *Fucus* and kelp, the red and green algae had proliferated both above and below their normal zones. Hanna had recorded "dense festoons" of algae even in 1964. "In some places," he wrote, "the general mixture of healthy young plants of many shades of color formed beautiful gardens."

The biologists found that the barnacles were coming back, though slowly because of the algae blocking them. There was a reversal in dominance in the two main species of acorn barnacles. Before the earthquake *Balanus glandula* had been the common barnacle, but now *Balanus balanoides*, a different creature though hard to tell apart, was leading the settlement of the new littoral zone. This was the most curious finding of Hanna's expedition, and the reports remarked on it frequently. Possibly *balanoides* had released its free-swimming larvae before the quake decimated its colonies, while *glandula*, set to spawn later in the spring, was uplifted without issue.

The resilience of the mussels, the mollusk that had suffered the heaviest mortalities, was impressive. The scattered survivors of the uplift seemed to have spawned prolifically, or else larvae were borne from afar. In colonizing their new zone the juvenile mussels were not deterred by the algae on the rocks. Unlike the barnacles, they attached themselves directly to the algal mats. The adaptability of mussels was also observed in a separate report on their return to a barren beach in Port Valdez. In this case the tsunamis had left the beach buried under silt, an unsuitable substrate for mollusks. But at a stream mouth running water had exposed small rocks, on which germlings of *Fucus* could settle. The flotation bladders of the seaweed lifted the rocks, and the tide distributed them along the beachfront. Mussel larvae anchored on the smatterings of habitat. As the mussels grew, their weight caused the rocks to settle in permanent positions. In a few years the mussels had coalesced in beds, in turn offering a foothold to other members of the intertidal community.

What used to be the high intertidal gave over to terrestrial vegetation. The rain leached away the salt, and the decay of the marine organisms fertilized the stones. The scientists found seventy-five species of flowering plants in the new habitat. A few on their list I recognized from my own very limited botanizing, like the ubiquitous salmonberry, cow parsnip and fireweed. The others—monkey flower, black saltwort, Pacific cinquefoil, arctic daisy, Siberian spring beauty, false alumroot—most probably didn't measure up to their exotic names. In any event these plants, some of which were growing beside the uplifted stumps of an earlier subsided forest, were bound to be superseded by trees. In 1965 spruce seedlings already intruded. Today the conifers extend again to the splash zone above the high-tide line.

Hanna and his colleagues called for annual studies to monitor the successional struggles; they speculated that a full recovery of the littoral zone would take a decade. They did not obtain the necessary funding. But when one of the biologists, Stoner Haven, came back for a look in 1968, he found that the old order had been restored. The opportunistic algaes had receded. *Fucus* was once more dominating the upper intertidal, and mussels were affixed to their normal places on rocks. The barnacle *B. glandula* had largely supplanted its upstart cousin, *B. balanoides*. Snails and limpets were abundant, as well as other small animals. Haven noted that a particular starfish was sparse.

Two organisms definitely had not recovered by 1968. One was the black lichen. Although the grazers had cleared the algal film from the new high-tide lines, slow-growing *Verrucaria* was not reestablished on either the raised or depressed shores of the Sound. I know it was ubiquitous again by 1989. It was all around West Twin Bay. I and many others took special notice of the black lichen in 1989. For its blotchy, paper-thin formations resembled nothing so much as weathered crude. Heavily-oiled beaches could be told from a distance, because the stuff glistened evilly, but the lighter coats of oil looked like *Verrucaria*. The cleanup monitors sometimes had to land their planes and scrape the rock with their fingernails before being absolutely sure.

The other organism chronically affected was the butter clam. It has not come back to its former numbers even today. The quake destroyed half the population of the butter clam, the Sound's largest species and the one most sought for eating. On Montague Island it is still possible to see the uplifted beds of gaping shells. If one probes below, in the new subtidal areas where butter clams would have settled, far fewer replacements are found. By contrast, the littleneck clam, another hard-shell species, is common today. A few months after the earthquake the littleneck survivors dispersed millions of planktonic larvae, which took hold in the disturbed subtidal.

The situation of the butter clams cannot be blamed on the earthquake alone. Here is a case of overlapping disturbances. Sea otters, which relish butter clams, were virtually absent from the Sound in 1964. An invasion of sea otters on the heels of the quake hit the clams with a double whammy. Then too, the Sound marks the northern terminus of the mollusk's range along the Pacific coast. Good years for reproduction may occur thirty, forty, even fifty years apart. The butter clam is very long-lived when established, but larval survival during the six-week zooplankton phase is evidently low. Over the years the adult population slowly declines, until one year unknown conditions are just right and the larvae settle explosively in the sediment. There appears to have been no major set since 1964.

The earthquake surely had consequences off the beaches as well, among the fish and marine mammal populations. The swaths of dead rockfish were proof of that. But except for studies by the Alaska Department of Fish and Game of the pink salmon, more about which below, there were no investigations of higher species. Without baseline data none were possible anyway. Probably there were dislocations of animals rather than serious setbacks. I found a report that sea lions using a particular rookery in the Sound dropped by half after the quake, while sea lions at another rookery increased fivefold.

In the Sound today the most durable vestige of the earthquake is the old storm berm. A storm berm is a windrow of loose rock at the top of a cobble beach. It is the ridge just above the high-tide line. On the islands that were uplifted, the 1964 berms are still visible in back of the current formations. Out of reach of the sea, their cobbles covered up with grass and young trees, the old berms look like benches that the land has set down for enjoyment of the waterfront.

Not unlike the intertidal life, the rocks of Prince William Sound were set back to an earlier stage of natural succession. The waves had to rebuild the storm berm, regrade the beach slope and re-sort the sediments. The upended boulders, cobbles, stones and pebbles have competed for space as if they were alive, though the energy driving them is inconstant.

Where beaches are exposed to winter storms, the jostling and pounding have created a stable interlocking of cobbles and boulders, called armor, that guards the contour of the beach. In sheltered areas the sorting has gone more slowly. Boulders lie where the quake left them, cobbles are spread unevenly, and packed grains persist in the crevices. Many beaches in the Sound are said to have juvenile sediments because they literally have not yet sorted themselves out. The waves can't get at them often enough to shape them up.

SYSTEMS IN NATURE evolve toward a kind of stability. Recovering from a disturbance, a seashore, a forest, an estuary will move back toward a state of equilibrium. Stability, equilibrium, recovery: these concepts are similar, but the devil is in the details.

In the summer of 1989 the strict constructionists were maintaining that Prince William Sound must return to its ecological status before the oil spill—the environment clean and the wildlife in the very same condition and numbers as before. Otherwise, the recovery would not be complete. This standard was unrealistic, as I hope I've shown, owing to the climate of perturbation. It seemed to me, though I attributed no teleology to the dynamics of stones and snails, that the Sound was constantly striving for equilibrium and never quite getting there.

The whole notion of equilibrium has been losing favor. In the old concept, equilibrium was seen as the plateau of stability to which ecosystems and animal populations ascended in discrete stages of natural succession. At the climactic stage the predominance of certain species, the balance between predators and prey and the overall inventory of creatures were more or less fixed. A disturbance might disrupt the equilibrium, but time would restore it, again and again, unless the ecosystem had been incorrigibly damaged.

In the newer thinking, nature is so variable that any additional disturbance only changes the course of future variability. This is why biologists being trained today become expert in statistical analysis. They put their data through a series of hoops and rate their chosen explanation of change in terms of its probability. Ecosystems recover from disturbances, to be sure, but since ordinary flux makes it impossible to know what the future might have been, there is no firm standard by which to judge the recovery. The absolutes of the balance-of-nature catechism do not stand up to statistical testing. Chaos theory, which rationalizes the seeming disorder of turbulent systems, has won a place in ecology.

If nature is no longer uniform and orderly, then out too are the sweeping linkages, such as connecting disturbance A with change B and outcome C because the chain makes elegant sense. A famous example in marine science is the thesis that linked lobsters, sea urchins and kelp in the northwest Atlantic. Pondering an explosion of sea urchins off the coast of Nova Scotia in the 1970s, Kenneth Mann and his associates wrote a series of papers relating the phenomenon to an overharvest of lobsters. It was known that lobsters preyed on sea urchins and that urchins foraged kelp. Mann argued that because the lobsters were depleted, the urchins had multiplied and overgrazed the kelp beds, which were necessary for the nurture and protection of the juvenile lobsters. The disturbance altered the environment so as to preclude the recovery of lobsters even after the fishing was halted. This is a bald rendering of Mann's work. The point is that he conceived a simple model of nature in which the lobster was the "keystone species," an animal whose decline could dismantle the entire ecosystem.

The case made it into the textbooks as a classic example of a man-made disturbance. But in the 1980s the hypothesis was attacked by rival biologists, who advanced other explanations for the urchin glut and pointed to interactions and oscillations that Mann had not addressed. The sea urchins, meanwhile, were killed off by an amoeboid parasite. The lobster and kelp returned. Mann in retreat modified his triad with minor chords of increasing complexity, until, in the view of his critics, his music has been lost in the noise. When I talked with him, he allowed that his lobster-urchin-kelp thesis was still not nailed down. He agreed that dynamic theories were more and more persuasive. "The earlier views were too simple, and we have all become cautious about nicely regulated systems," he said.

There is an analogy on the Pacific side. The sea otter, a predator of sea urchins, has been proposed as the keystone species for the kelp beds of the northern Pacific. James Estes, a researcher with the U.S. Fish and Wildlife Service, and his colleagues compared two nearshore ecosystems in the Aleutian Islands. One island had a population of sea otters, one did not. At the former it was found that the otters cropped the urchins, which allowed the kelp to flourish. The kelp forest in turn harbored a host of fish and dependent organisms. The food web reached as far as harbor seals and bald eagles. The island without the otters had many large urchins on the bottom and other invertebrates that the otters favored, but, without any kelp stands, there were few fish and a relatively thin array of marine life. To summarize: Two stable ecological states were said to exist, each resistant to change, and the key was the sea otter.

Too neat, critics countered. A survey of the kelp beds of California revealed that only 10 percent fit Estes's either-or model. There were kelp forests surviving without sea otters, yet hosting varied densities of sea urchins. The range of kelp cover along the California coast was found to be dynamic, not fixed. Estes conceded, "There are regional wrinkles in the model. But I would say, at the risk of being called a cement-head, that my paradigm is not going to go the way of Mann's." He has submitted fresh evidence of urchins being controlled and kelp systems regenerating when sea otters colonized virgin areas in southeast Alaska.

As hard as scientists work to divine an order and make it stick, nature keeps throwing off exceptions. Stability and equilibrium exist only if nature is broadly construed, somewhere between chaos and a Rube Goldberg machine. A compromise is suggested by the idea of nature as "patchy." The Pacific sand lance, to choose an illustration from Prince William Sound, is patchy. A small and common schooling fish, the sand lance holds down a key place in the food web, for it consumes zooplankton and is widely consumed by many larger fish and seabirds. The fish is extremely difficult to measure. Dense schools can show up anywhere. Only the birds, one biologist told me, do a good job of sampling it. The sand lance is a mystery taken for granted, moving unknowably within known parameters, perfectly patchy.

On the beaches of the Sound the patchiness of nature is right out in the open. Why should one section be covered with mussels and the neighboring section, otherwise identical, be covered with rockweed and barnacles? The components of intertidal life are finite, but the combinations seem endless. In theory, the factors that determine the patchiness could be identified and untangled—the history of predation, weather disturbances, tidal height, wave force, sediment composition and stability, etc. In fact a rough start has been made on these questions, since working with intertidal organisms is a lot simpler than chasing schools of sand lance.

Biologists have set cages to exclude the snails and starfish that prey on the mussels. They have scraped off the rockweed and made more space for the barnacles. They have removed adult organisms in favor of the juveniles. By manipulating the system, disturbing its equilibrium, they have been able to watch the biota recover and have sorted out a few of the processes. It appears, for example, that high up on the shore the physical forces, such as weather and tides, shape the biological community, while in the lower intertidal, a richer zone, the physical factors are much less important than the competition among the organisms themselves.

When scientists don't control the experiment, patchiness frustrates their understanding of change. A case from the oil spill is the work done by University of Alaska biologists Glenn Juday and Nora Foster on the Green Island shoreline. Their study was among the few conducted outside the secrecy of the damage assessment process. Juday and Foster, who had made an inventory of intertidal organisms in the summer of 1986, surveyed the same areas on Green Island in the summer of 1989, five months after the spill. Their latest catalog was missing thirty-seven animals and six plants that were observed in 1986. Had the oil eradicated them? Undoubtedly this was true for some. But how to explain that the 1989 survey also found fourteen animals and two algae that *hadn't* been seen in 1986?

Natural variability was broached by the authors. Two disturbances were discussed in addition to the oil. There was—as many other biologists had noted—a potentially lethal cold snap in the winter of '89. Juday and Foster stated that "extreme cold during minus tides has been known to produce damage similar to an oil spill. . . ." Second, two types of predatory seastars were present in '89 but not in '86; the starfish could have cut into the intertidal composition. As for other newfound species in '89, the scientists said natural variability could account for them as well.

Then they suggested another contributor to the discrepancy. Evidently the pair looked harder in 1986 than in 1989. Possibly "a greater taxonomic search effort" resulted in the higher total of plants and animals. This admission undermined everything prior. So when Juday and Foster concluded, "The intertidal environment is dynamic and susceptible to both natural and human-caused disturbances," they should have added a third kind of disturbance, human error and bias. It should be kept in mind that no report in this book is free of the latter, nor is the book itself.

Uncertainties aside, the Green Island surveys are unique in providing before and after views of the same shoreline. From the time of the earthquake to the time of the oil spill, researchers in Prince William Sound have fretted about the lack of baseline references. In 1978, for example, at a scientific conference in Anchorage a NOAA official named Chris Carty called for a comprehensive data bank to be put together, "so that if in the future the Sound does change, we'll have information on the way it was, in order to prove that a change has occurred. It isn't really enough to say we all know there's been a change. We have to have data to back it up, otherwise it's always just attributed to natural variability." Carty spoke with some urgency, because the tankers were already moving oil.

Since the earthquake, the oil industry has paid for most of what we know about the environment of Prince William Sound. Prior to the voluminous spill research, the cost of which the government recovered after the settlement of the charges against Exxon, there was the Outer Continental Shelf Environment Assessment Program. Begun in 1974 and reaching its peak in 1980, the program evaluated the possible impacts of oil drilling off the Alaska coastline. The studies devoted to the northeast Gulf resulted in compendia, for the most part, of coastal resources and wildlife, and were not focused enough to make useful baselines. But their encyclopedic reach was impressive, and the federal sale of drilling leases garnered much more than OCSEAP cost.

Prince William Sound itself was never a candidate for leasing. For one thing, it lay within the three-mile limit of state control. For another, all agreed it was too special a place for drilling. But after the transportation of oil from Valdez began, both OCSEAP and the state commissioned some cursory research of the Sound. These reports included a Coastal Sensitivity Index, which rated the shoreline for its vulnerability to oiling, and a seventy-page companion study, "Description of Prince William Sound Shoreline Habitats Associated with Biological Communities." Moreover, NOAA began to monitor sediments and mussel beds at eight locations along the tanker route through the Sound; the mollusks are especially good indicators of oil pollution because they collect hydrocarbons in their tissues.

The area of most concentrated scrutiny was Port Valdez itself. The focus here was not on potential tanker spills but on actual pollution from the Alyeska terminal. Because the transport system involved a discharge of oily water into the port, permits were required. Alyeska, the oil company consortium that built the pipeline and terminal, funded environmental studies by the Institute of Marine Science of the University of Alaska.

As buoyant as canoes when unladen, supertankers take on ballast on their way to Valdez by filling their cargo tanks with sea water. At the tanker terminal the ballast is exchanged for petroleum from the pipeline. The tainted ballast water, containing about 1 percent residual oil, is run through Alyeska's treatment plant. Newer vessels like the *Exxon Valdez* have segregated ballast tanks that reduce, but do not eliminate, the need for the treatment. The ballast water is processed sequentially—by skimming machines, aerators, chemicals and by oil-metabolizing bacteria in holding ponds—with each step removing another fraction of the oil. Finally, the effluent is piped into the depths of Port Valdez near the terminal facilities. The plant cycles over 15 million gallons every day. The water at the final stage is contaminated only faintly, although the dissolved hydrocarbons that remain are known to be those most toxic to marine life.

The baseline work began eight years before the terminal and treatment plant opened. The environment of the port was quantified. Biological changes were followed through the busy construction period of the early '70s and the commencement of tanker traffic and effluent releases in 1977. Periodically, reports had to be filed in support of the renewal of the discharge permit. It's clear in hindsight that regulators kept a closer eye on Alyeska's handling of ballast water than on its capacity to handle oil spills.

When in the early '80s hydrocarbons were measured in the bottom sediments and in mollusks near the discharge pipe, and subsequently in the bile fluid of certain bottom fish, a debate began about the oil's effects on the fjord's ecosystem. The questions aren't resolved today. Has the abundance of *Macoma balthica*, a tiny clam, been reduced in the mudflats near Alyeska, and if so, is the terminal the reason? The sediments right near the diffuser pipe are contaminated, but the pollution is slight compared with other industrial ports. Are the oil toxins damaging the English sole? One federal researcher assured me, "The fish bile is as clean as we ever find it." Another warned that exposure to the hydrocarbons could lead to cancer in the fish.

The particulars of the debate belong to my upcoming chapters, having to do with hydrocarbons and biochemistry. But the reason the particulars have been hard to resolve has to do with the noise of other disturbances. In 1988 a volume of scientific summaries was published. In the foreword, biologist Donald Hood observed: "At the outset of the studies of Port Valdez it was realized that many types of disturbances, either past or ongoing, occur in this environment with varied intensities and time scales. The most devastating was the Great Alaska Earthquake. Lesser but more frequent disturbance comes from flooding of glacial streams, landslides, storms, and the seasonal alternation between a well-mixed and stratified water column. Other disturbances come from human activities. . . ."

About the ballast water pollution, Hood concluded that "compliance monitoring appears to have contributed little to detecting ecosystem changes since change due to natural disturbance and fluctuations far exceeded perturbations caused by the introduction of the contaminant.

"This does not mean there has not been a change," he cautioned, "but the methods used for its detection were not sufficiently sensitive to separate natural fluctuations, which were overpowering, from those caused by the contaminant."

The competing disturbances were detailed in a chapter by C. Peter McRoy. There were so many at work that McRoy said he could find no stable baseline for evaluating change. When the biological surveys began in 1969, the Port Valdez ecosystem was still pulling itself together from the '64 earthquake. Recovery was slower than in other parts of the Sound, because the scouring tsunamis, the smothering sedimentation and the spilled fuel oil together had stripped the shore and bottom of marine life. McRoy suggested that an investigator of the effects of the ballast effluent plant, if he had no knowledge of the past, might look at the 1969 survey, compare it to the gains observed a decade later and decide that the addition of hydrocarbons, far from being harmful, had stimulated "an unprecedented biological flourishing of the littoral zone." This of course would be a spurious linkage.

Among the latest disturbances, McRoy listed a salmon hatchery and the resurgent sea otters. In his view both were stresses on the food web that might be comparable to the oil pollution. Established in 1983, the hatchery had plans to inject 75 million salmon fry into the fjord on top of the existing consumers of zooplankton. The sea otters—about forty had moved in from the southern Sound—already had eliminated the Dungeness crabs as a harvestable species and were curtailing other shellfish in the port. McRoy asserted that the trophic system of Port Valdez was being changed by these two new sets of mouths to feed, unquestionably but unfathomably. The research to date only scratched the surface.

Ecosystem studies may be feasible when limited to a strip of shoreline, but Alyeska wasn't about to fund an exploration of the entire submarine food web, which in Port Valdez was thirteen miles long, three miles wide and 500 feet deep. So another scientific exercise came up short. Whether we're screening the northern Gulf, or the Sound, or Port Valdez, or a beach on Green Island, the narrowing of focus doesn't seem to make the judgments clearer. Everywhere, patchwork evidence is built upon wobbly baselines. Disturbances overlap and peter out. It takes a clue as glaring as an earthquake to close a case. But the uncertainty that a litigator, say, would find insufferable does not vex the biologist.

As a rule, the marine scientists who came to be involved in the oil spill would have preferred to study its disturbance to the Sound, not its damage. The distinction is not a fine one. Natural Resource Damage Assessment, such as was conducted by state and federal agencies after the oil spill, is a statutory process. It takes snapshots of cause and effect in a deterministic world. NRDA must have links and correlations—it needs for the environment to pare down and hold still. The investigation differs from basic research. Basic research allows the scientific mind to explore nature freely, without interference, wherever nature might point the mind to go. NRDA was applied research, with a legalistic end in mind. In the Sound in the summer of 1989, open-ended and open-minded research went down the tubes.

The scientists at the University of Alaska didn't get it at first. They had a lot of experience in the Sound and they saw the government's NRDA program as an opportunity to enlarge their understanding. Recalled David Shaw, whose specialty is the marine effects of hydrocarbons, "You could study the number of otters killed by direct oiling, versus the effect of the removal of those otters on the Sound's food source." Shaw and his colleagues at the Institute of Marine Science, among them Peter McRoy and Tom Royer, proposed a major study of the ecosystem. Periodically since the '70s, the researchers had made grant applications to the National Science Foundation to do this. Their idea, then as now, was to create a model of the Sound's food web, linking animals, plants and the physical ocean environment.

A model is an approximation of reality. Its goal is not so much to replicate reality but to forecast it. As Shaw explained to the *Anchorage Daily News* in July, "The point of a long-term study would be to understand how the disturbance of the spill propagates through the environment and how long the environment would take to accommodate it." Shaw thought the project would take years of data collection. Raymond Highsmith, another professor, ticked off a shopping list of biological inquiry: "Recruitment [juvenile fish coming of age in a population], growth rates, seasonal variations, reproductive rates, upwelling effects on productivity, the impact of fresh water runoff—if one understands those, then you've really got a leg up on the system, and when there's a disturbance in one area you can have a feel for how other parts of the system are affected." The model was touted for the light it would shed on changes in the Sound's salmon runs.

There was a cart-before-the-horse problem that the university researchers glossed over. The model they had in mind, the long-sought baseline for the Sound, would be valuable during the *next* spill, or other major disturbance. Shaw told me that instead of talking up the applications of the model, they should have stressed how the oil could have affected the plankton and forage fish like the sand lance. They should have harped on the consequences of an injured food web to higher species. Not that he was sure the model could have delivered the answers.

Funding for the project was denied. One state official dismissed it as a "big, semi-esoteric model of ocean currents." Privately, Exxon rejected a similar proposal from the Woods Hole Oceanographic Institution in Massachusetts. The WHOI researchers tried to sell the company on endowing a long-term research effort, a multimillion-dollar trust, that would have involved modeling the Sound.

Nearly all of the government's sixty-three damage assessment studies targeted individual species and probed for specific injuries from the oil spill. Exxon's separate and smaller program had the same focus. Both sides did commission, though, some broader ecologic inquiries. If there was going to be a revelation of the offshore food web of the Sound, it would have to come from a study of marine larvae, Fish/Shellfish Study Number 19, which was assigned by the state Department of Fish and Game to the Institute of Marine Science.

Finfish and shellfish larvae in their early stages belong to the zooplankton. They move at the whim of tides and currents. They are extremely patchy, here one day, or one year, and gone the next. Every week or so following the spill (for it was anticipated in the spring that the study would be approved), the university's research vessels trawled the Sound with fine-meshed nets, scooping larvae from different depths. As the project plan stated: "Larvae of pollock, halibut, Pacific cod, black cod, herring, flathead sole, starry flounder, yellowfin sole, Tanner crab, spot shrimp, pink shrimp, and king crab are vulnerable to oil contamination."

The principal investigators, Brenda Norcross and A. J. Paul, had no hope of measuring direct larval mortalities from the oil, an event as ephemeral as the creatures themselves, nor would the raw numbers of abundance tell much, given the thousandfold variabilities. Rather, Norcross and Paul hoped to learn whether the relative numbers, the composition, of the larval community had been disturbed over time. They planned to take samples for five to ten years, and to compare the proportions of species in the part of the Sound that had been oiled with those in the area that had not. It would demand a considerable labor, beginning with sorting and classifying the multitude of organisms under the microscope.

Six months' collections of larvae were fixed and stored in jars, awaiting analysis. At the NRDA meeting in Anchorage that winter, where the summer results were discussed and the 1990 work plans finalized, the fish larval study was canceled. The NRDA peer reviewers, Outside biologists hired for their advice, raised the kind of objections that in normal scientific debate serve to sharpen a project but that in this forum doomed it. The problem was that even if the results were to indicate that the larvae were different in the oiled part of the Sound, the changes could not be pinned on the spill (on Exxon, that is) for certain. Too many other disturbances could be hypothesized: an unusual lens of freshwater runoff or an unknown current pattern. The fish larvae study was judged not to be worth the cost of continuing.

The investigators were angry. "If fish had been killed, that would be one thing," Norcross told me, "but these long-term effects aren't as provable. The damage assessment approach isn't science, it's counting dead oiled bodies. The lawyers don't want to know what the spill *didn't* hurt. But we should know that, so we don't get all bent out of shape about oil spills. If we can't get something positive out of this, it's not helping the resource. "

Her colleague, A. J. Paul, said, "The studies on otters and birds and sea lions go forward. But the missing data [lower on the food web] is the most critical. Nobody's been funded to get those numbers. We won't have them for the next spill. Twenty years from now, after the oil from the North Slope is gone, we'll need those numbers for the fishermen of Prince William Sound."

And Peter McRoy said, "On the one hand, as Alaskans, sure we're concerned about the environmental damage. But here we have an opportunity to learn something scientifically, regardless of the litigation. We know a lot about how terrestrial systems respond to disturbances, how fire changes the succession of vegetation and animals like moose colonize the burned-over areas. We don't know as much about marine habitats and disturbances. That's why there's an experimental value to the spill. We have a natural disturbance and it's a shame not to study it fully."

"A natural disturbance?" I asked.

"Well, like a natural disturbance," he corrected himself.

Still, applied science had its compensations, and the IMS investigators received ample share. Oceanographer Royer got funding from Exxon to help him analyze the oil's course along the Coastal Current. Peter McRoy contracted to be the scientific adviser to the state Department of Environmental Conservation for damage assessment. Ray Highsmith became the leader of the government's coastal habitat project, an ambitious and costly study of the spill's effects on intertidal organisms. Once he was under way, Highsmith was quoted, "I understand that the people who pay us have to develop their legal positions. But that doesn't mean research will be flawed. My research is going extremely well."

Not long afterward, funding was cut for Highsmith as well. His study tried to clarify the shoreline conditions of the whole western Sound. He was drowning in data, not producing clean answers. The Sound's beaches were coming up too patchy.

THE DAMAGE ASSESSORS smiled upon studies that could show monetary losses from the spill. Under the law a killed eagle or starfish had a dollar value representing the compensation to the public for their losses, but in the absence of a market for eagles or starfish, their worth was problematic. Economists consider the value of wildlife to be a "passive use" by the public. To set a figure on the value of passive use, pollsters ask people in Ohio such questions as, How much is it worth to you just knowing that beaches in Alaska are unspoiled? How much would you personally pay to prevent another oil spill from killing eagles in Prince William Sound? The responses are subjective at best, off the wall at worst, and at any rate highly unscientific, being hypotheses that are never tested. But reckonings of lost value make sense for natural resources that are exploited regularly. Thus, in Prince William Sound there was no better test case of loss than the pink salmon.

Commercial fishing is the largest private employer in Alaska. The oil industry may earn the state more revenue, and government overall employs more people, but fishing for salmon is the prototypical Alaskan livelihood. Many Alaskan communities are dependent on it, including Cordova in the Sound. Thanks to the value of its salmon landings, in excess of $50 million per year, little Cordova (pop. 2,500) was in the top ten of U.S. fishing ports at the time of the spill.

There were no outright salmon kills after the oil spill, no carcasses to total up and value, but several generations of pink salmon were exposed to the oil. The NRDA managers thought that the prospects for tracking the disturbance were good. Salmon reveal themselves more than any other pelagic fish, because they can be counted when they return to their natal streams to spawn. In a small way, the invisible patchiness of the Gulf of Alaska is captured in the veins of the Sound. By foot and aerial surveys, and by automatic sonar counters in the streams, state biologists have recorded the spawning runs of salmon for more than thirty years. With the catch totals recorded too, a reliable idea of the population was in place.

Although all five species of Pacific salmon occur in Prince William Sound—the other four are the red (a.k.a. sockeye), silver (coho), king (chinook) and chum (dog), the terrain greatly favors the pink salmon, or humpback. It is the smallest of the five. Whereas elsewhere in Alaska the larger species make heroic migrations of hundreds and even thousands of miles up broad rivers, the pink salmon uses modest streams near the sea. The Sound has hundreds of such streams, most of them extending a short way from the waterline to impassable mountain falls. The spawning area is so limited that over half the pinks lay their eggs in the intertidal zone, where the freshwater traverses the rockweed and mussels.

From late June until early fall the pinks swarm into the Sound. They are about two feet in length and weigh up to four pounds. Their bright silver coloration darkens to black-olive and their bodies deform as they approach the climax of their lives. The male develops a wickedly hooked jaw and a pronounced hump (hence humpback; pink refers to the flesh color). If they are to be harvested it should be done before they get into the streams, for the fish wear out all at once, like the fabled one-horse shay.

In the gravel of the shallows the female digs a nest with her tail and begins depositing eggs. Hovering close by, the snaggle-toothed male squeezes out milt (sperm) and fertilizes the eggs. Then the female covers the nest and starts on a new one. Eventually she releases about 2,000 eggs. The salmon mill about for another week or two, sluggish prey for eagles and bears, their skins shedding and fins rotting and teeth falling out, until finally they turn white bellies upward.

Over the course of the winter the embryos hatch and turn into alevins, which are larvae nourished by attached yolk sacs. In a bad year, 90 percent of the eggs and alevins perish. They are dislodged by later spawners, gobbled up by trout and sculpins, washed out by storms or heavy rains, desiccated when streams slacken in dry weather, frozen if low flows are accompanied by a cold winter. In the spring the surviving fry wriggle up through the gravel and are swept by the flowing water into the Sound.

The heaviest emergence takes place at night, so that the juveniles have a better chance of eluding predators. The big-eyed silvery fingerlings are about an inch and a half long. The first weeks are the most critical, not only because the fry are most vulnerable then to other fish and seabirds, but also because they need the zooplankton to grow, and the timing of the zooplankton bloom may not match the period of their greatest needs.

Schools of fry linger in the bays and coves of the Sound. In deeper waters as the summer progresses, they acclimatize to the conditions of the ocean. In the fall the six-inch salmon, now called smolts, head out to the Gulf and to the North Pacific. The pink salmon has just a two-year life cycle, the briefest of the five Pacific species. By the following summer they are fully grown and back in their home streams, whence the cycle begins anew.

It is a vicissitudinous life for the humpback. Their survival rate in the marine environment is even lower than the egg survival in the streams, about 2 percent. It works out that two adults return for every 1,000 eggs that are spawned.

Let us relate these vicissitudes to the events of 1989. The intertidal portions of many streams were hit by the oil spill just before the salmon fry emerged. Those juveniles, which were the salmon of the 1988 brood-year (the designation indicates when the fish were hatched), were exposed to oil in the sediments and subsequently in the water offshore. A few months later the adults of the 1987 brood-year came back and spawned in contaminated gravel. Although their abundance could not have been affected by the spill, their breeding may well have been. Their eggs and fry, of the 1989 brood-year, were exposed. I have to defer questions about what hydrocarbon exposure actually entails. The point for now is that if pink salmon populations were going to be disrupted, it would not be in the year of the spill. The effects would show up in the brood-year fish most affected, that is, not until 1990 and 1991.

The biologists taking part in the NRDA studies did not wait for the runs to come in. In the summer of '89, while I idled on the cloud-raked spit at West Twin Bay, Fish and Game personnel were hard at work throughout the western Sound. They counted spawners, dug up eggs and alevins, analyzed tissues and began to correlate their findings with the levels of oiling in the habitat. They found evidence of injury, which they used to make projections about the ensuing returns. Their data was kept secret. Now and then bureaucrats who were privy dropped dark hints, which were meant to counter Exxon's rosy pronouncements—for the company too had biologists probing the Sound—but the statements on either side had little value.

In the end, the salmon runs were not affected, at least not that could be determined. Why not? Too much noise. The returns in fact went up sharply for the two years after 1989. Any signal of the oil spill was swamped. The returns broke all catch records—and then fell just as sharply in '92 and '93.

The pattern should not have been surprising. Fish and Game's graph of the returns since 1960 shows erratic highs and lows, good years zigzagging to bad. The number of pink salmon estimated to have returned to the streams of the Sound has bounced between 1 and 20 million fish. The disturbances responsible for this lack of consistency include the '64 earthquake, the changeable ocean temperatures, the phasing of the zooplankton, the pressure of fishing itself and the extraordinary rise of aquaculture, any one of which, probably, has exceeded the oil spill in impact.

Salmon canneries have operated in Prince William Sound since 1889, but prior to Alaskan statehood in 1959 the record-keeping was poor. The territorial fishery was no doubt overex-ploited. The postwar period is recalled today as the era of Big Fish. Large commercial processors based in the Lower 48 owned the boats, hired the fishermen and took their fill of the salmon. In the Sound any return greater than 5 million pinks was considered a very good year.

The Department of Fish and Game tightened the regulation in the '60s. Creek-robbing, the practice of intercepting spawners in front of the stream mouth, was stopped. Streams were assigned "escapement goals," a set number of fish that would be allowed to escape the nets and lay eggs for the future. In the '70s the number of fishermen was restricted. Permits were granted to the active gill-netters and seiners. Like New York City taxi medallions, the permits could be bought and sold but not increased. Yet in spite of the protective measures, salmon did not gain in the Sound—on the contrary.

The earthquake was the most obvious delimiting factor. The earthquake had attacked the salmon in their spawning beds. In the spring of '64, millions of alevins were crushed in the shock-shifted gravel, or scoured away by the tsunamis, or suffocated under layers of silt. The adults returning a few months later were confronted by a radically different habitat. A number of creeks, blocked by up-lifted sediments, had simply disappeared, the water filtering to the sea underground. Other streams had cut temporary channels, which moved or caved in after the run, leaving salmon eggs high and dry. The downthrust streams maintained their original courses, but trees killed by saltwater obstructed many of them. On both the depressed and raised shores, the prime permeable gravels of the intertidal zone were replaced by silty, unstable sediments that took years to sort out.

Biologists estimated that in 1964 about a quarter of the Sound's pinks nested in intertidal areas where alevins could not survive. Montague Island, where upheavals were greatest, lost the most fish. In September of '64 biologists set stakes in the new spawning sections of a major stream. A year later they could not find the stakes. They discovered that the stream had shifted 100 yards away and was barren of eggs. A run of some 700,000 fish prior to the quake dropped to 20,000 at the end of the decade. It has never come back.

Fish and Game tried to speed the recovery of thirty streams in the Sound, by clearing logjams and regrading channels. The effort was minor, given that 150 prime producing streams had been damaged, and it did not halt the population decline. In eight of the ten years following the earthquake the runs were less than 5 million. The seine fishery was curtailed, and then closed altogether in '72 and '74. The especially dismal returns of those two years were direct echoes of the failed spawn of 1964.

Yet biologists were puzzled that things should be worse ten years after the quake. Now that streambeds had finally stabilized, salmon habitat in the Sound had actually increased. The majority of streams, in being uplifted, gained length on the widened shore. Escapement goals were being met; fry were being produced in sufficient quantity to bolster populations. Scientists were obligated to look beyond the Sound, for runs were down elsewhere in Alaska as well. They talked about poor ocean-survival conditions, which was a tautology (salmon weren't surviving because they weren't surviving) indicating how little they understood the adult phase of the fish's two-year cycle.

In hindsight, two forces appear to have impinged on the pinks in the North Pacific. Foreign fishing fleets began using long drift nets in the '70s, and intercepted an unknown but possibly large number of Alaska salmon. Second was the cycle of the ocean's temperature, as per Tom Royer's model. The cooling trend of the '70s may have caused adverse conditions for finfish such as salmon. Ted Cooney, Royer's colleague at the Institute of Marine Science, has explored a similar idea. He has made links between the spring-time water temperature, the timing of the zooplankton bloom, the emergence of the salmon fry and the strength of the return the following year.

In 1979 the fishery abruptly turned around. The commercial catch tripled and quadrupled, averaging over 15 million salmon through the mid-'80s. Perhaps it was because the high-seas fishery was brought under control, and/or ocean temperatures averaged slightly warmer. Meanwhile something else had changed, easing the urgency of such questions. The wild salmon were being supplemented with fish spawned in hatcheries.

Representing four of the Sound's five hatcheries, the Prince William Sound Aquaculture Corporation is the largest salmon ranching operation in North America. As opposed to salmon farms, which rear fish to maturity in submerged pens, like cattle in feed-lots, salmon ranches let their fry go after hatching. The cofounder of PWSAC (universally referred to as "Pizz-wack") was a courtly German-American named Armin Koernig. I talked with him over lunch one day in Cordova.

Koernig immigrated to Alaska the year before the earthquake. He said he felt desperate, he and his fellow fishermen, as the salmon runs deteriorated. At the nadir in the early '70s, a rival industry loomed, for oil had been discovered at Prudhoe Bay on the North Slope. The fishermen feared a spill and sued to block the pipeline to Valdez, but they were overruled. "In the winters, when we couldn't fish," Koernig recalled, "we sat around wondering what to do. Were we going to sell out and go work for the oil companies?"

Aquaculture in theory would stabilize the supply of fish. Koernig knew nothing of fish culture, but he undertook to learn. He joined with Wally Noerenberg, who had just retired as commissioner of the Department of Fish and Game. Backed by contributions from other Cordovans, the two convinced the state to assist in starting a hatchery in the Sound. "We were just a bunch of orangutan fishermen," Koernig said proudly. Indirectly the oil industry helped too, by providing tax and royalty payments that the state used for new programs. In 1975 the first PWSAC fry were released from what is now the Armin F. Koernig Hatchery on Sawmill Bay in the southwestern Sound.

The facility doesn't look as though anything high-tech is going on. It occupies the site of a salmon cannery that went under due to the poor runs. Isolated at the far end of the bay, its weathered docks, sheds and staff dormitory call to mind a sailing camp that has gone slightly to seed. The gadgetry is out of sight in the main basement. The shiny metal incubation trays are stacked six deep in large rooms, and there are crisscrossing pipes and troughs leading to the outside. On a level below the incubation area, an enclosed stream flows. The freshwater is piped from a lake just above the hatchery. The salmon are bonded to the subtle but individual chemical characteristics of this water.

The progenitors of the first AFK fry were wild fish seized before they could reach streams elsewhere in the Sound. The trick was to imprint their eggs with the new water so that the next generation would lock on and return to it.

The procedures are the same for both start-up fish and the subsequent brood stock. First the eggs are stripped from females and put into buckets. The milt is squeezed out of males directly into the buckets. A freshwater rinse mixes eggs and milt, and fertilization occurs. Next the fertilized eggs are put into the incubator trays, which are boxes with a three-inch substrate of plastic pellets on the bottom. Called saddles because of their shape, the pellets are akin to the gravel of a creek bed. Water flows through the trays, from the top row of stacks to the bottom, at the rate of fifteen gallons a minute.

For four to five months the eggs bathe in the flow on top of the saddles. But when they hatch as alevins in December, they wriggle down into the substrate, insulating themselves from the buffeting of the water. The rooms are kept dark; workers wear headlamps. The reason is that the alevins should expend as little energy as possible, since the yolk sacs are their only sustenance.

Cued by the rising temperature of the water, the fry emerge from the saddles in March. Their progress is pretty much left to them. The fish swim with the flow through the linked trays. They enter chutes laced with salt water, the hatchery equivalent of an intertidal zone, and eventually are channeled into holding pens in the harbor. About one in 1,000 is briefly intercepted for tagging. A minuscule copper wire, coded to indicate the salmon's origin, is injected into its nose. An unneeded fin is clipped from the tagged fish in order to distinguish it in the future.

Seven to 8 million per pen, weighing about a hundredth of an ounce apiece, the fry live on commercial fish food for several weeks. PWSAC biologists determine when the spring zooplankton bloom is peaking, and then they turn loose the fry. The releases are made at night, to try to foil predators. In recent years an average of 120 million fingerlings have fanned out from the hatchery. The juveniles take their chances in the Sound and then in the Gulf with the wild stocks, and the survivors come back as adults.

AFK averages returns of around 5 million fish, the equivalent of the entire run of the Sound before aquaculture. For weeks a crush of pinks fights to attain a small stream tumbling out of the lake. Historically no salmon could breed here because a waterfall makes an impassable barrier. Even if the stream were accessible, there are many too many fish to fit in it. The mating bower is a facade, scented and hung with seine nets.

The actuarial advantages of aquaculture are these: Whereas only 10 percent of the eggs in the streams make it to the fry stage, the PWSAC success rate is over 90 percent. Whereas only 2 percent of wild fry return, the PWSAC success rate has been 5 percent. People dismissed Armin Koernig when he predicted in the mid-'70s that the hatchery system would produce runs of 15 and 20 million fish within a decade, but those numbers came to pass and more.

Pink salmon boomed in the Sound in the '80s. As if responding to the competition, the wild stocks multiplied and stayed ahead of the growing hatchery returns until 1987. In 1988 the ratio changed sharply in favor of aquaculture, and irreversibly, it would now appear. Wild runs plummeted to less than 2 million, the lowest since 1974, while hatchery returns topped 11 million. The decline was attributed in part to severe flooding in the fall of '86, which had dislodged eggs from streams. But with salmon prices high in '88, fishermen were able to exploit the fruits of the hatcheries. They had exciting proof that science could insulate the fishery from the swings of natural variability.

In 1989 the wild pinks numbered 6.6 million, considerably less than forecast. But the hatchery runs topped 17 million, a new record. The fishing that summer was unprecedented in another respect, but this latest disturbance affected the fishermen more than the salmon. Now it was time for me to get off the spit.

A LITTLE FISHING VESSEL steamed into West Twin Bay. The boat was the *Skin Deep*. Kelly and Cece were right on time to pick me up.

In the spring of '89 the *Skin Deep* belonged to the Prince William Sound Wildlife Rescue Fleet, a group of fishermen mobilized in response to the spill. Kelly Carlisle, Cece Crowe and Barbara Logan worked very hard. They saved some animals but mainly collected carcasses. By the time I joined them on the boat in the middle of May, there wasn't anything more to do but to log the sightings of wildlife. I won't tell of the time I had aboard, because it was so askew from the angst prevailing about the disaster. Let me quote nature writer John Burroughs, who wrote in 1899, when *he* first experienced Prince William Sound: "We were afloat in an enchanted circle; we sailed over magic seas under magic skies; we played hide and seek with winter in lucid sunshine over blue and emerald waters—all the conditions, around, above, below us were most fortunate."

Now it was August. I was happy to see my friends again. Kelly Carlisle, the skipper and owner, was in his early forties, with rumpled hair, a straight-as-an-arrow nose and sailor's crinkles around the eyes. Cece Crowe, the first mate, was not long out of college, round-cheeked and blond. Carlisle made his living from shrimp, which he caught in pots in the Sound. On the spit we sautéed some for lunch. The Perry Island wildlife spotters, who were the political descendants of the animal rescue operation, ate with us.

From West Twin Bay the *Skin Deep* headed north toward College Fjord. Carlisle planned to fill his fish hold with ice chunks calved from the glaciers. He had outfitted the boat with a fancy new autopilot, a plum from his Exxon earnings with the rescue fleet. It freed him from the wheel, and he was able to join Crowe and me at the rail, where we watched in awe as the pink salmon flooded into the hatchery at Esther Island.

PWSAC's Wally Noerenberg Hatchery, newer and larger than AFK, is similar in being situated at the base of a captive waterfall.

A lake above guarantees a steady supply of freshwater. How millions of salmon navigate from the northern Pacific back to this particular trickle is not known. Doubtless they pick up the chemical path by which they left, oriented by the currents, perhaps, or by regional magnetic patterns. Scientists have studied the brains of migrating salmon. At the ends of their lives the fish are so bent on olfactory homing that other cerebral functions are nearly shut down.

Nearing Esther, we saw splashes on the green-gray water in front of the entrance to Lake Bay. Two seine boats contracted to PWSAC were harvesting fish inside a line of boom. A large tender stood by to receive them. The nonprofit corporation keeps a percentage of the hatchery production for itself, to recover operating costs and to obtain brood stock. The rest is the common property of fishermen.

When we got closer, we could see silvery glints in the air. The salmon were leaping from the water. Fish were rounding the bend of the island, hugging the shore, coming directly toward us now, thousands of them, streaming in a file no wider than fifty yards, like geese following a trail of corn.

Carlisle cut the engine and we drifted into the line of migration. So many were jumping around the boat that I took a dip net and leaned over the side, certain I could snare us dinner. The salmon threw themselves upward, twisted their backs and loudly smacked down, but a spark of self-preservation must have persisted in their addled brains, because none came within my reach.

Carlisle said he thought that only the female humpies jumped, and that in crashing onto their sides they were trying to loosen the egg sacs in their bellies. (A PWSAC biologist, demurring, said a more likely explanation was that the salmon were trying to shake off a parasite.) We got under way again, angling away from the shore. Behind us the flinging, flying forms were backlit against the sky. For a moment I felt I was at a carnival, looking down a shooting gallery that had fish cutouts for targets—the targets were popping up and down, twenty and thirty at a time, to the beat of a crazy calliope. For every fish heaving itself into view, 500 were unseen below.

The strangest thing about the scene was the absence of fishing boats. Over three days during the week before, the fleet had taken half a million fish here. The PWSAC seiners, behind their protective boom, were still hauling up salmon like gangbusters. Yet the area just outside, where the common property fishery took place, was closed because of oil.

Late on July 28 a sheen about a half mile long had appeared

near the shore of Esther. Nets of several boats were tainted. James Brady, the chief management biologist for Fish and Game in Cordova, invoked what was called the zero-tolerance policy. To maintain the buyers' confidence in the product, the state had decided when the season began that any hint of oil in a particular fishing district would result immediately in its closure.

Stressed-out from four months of dealing with the spill, which had already shut the southwestern districts and denied them their share of the AFK run, the fishermen boiled over in frustration. Several hundred were idled in Cordova, while several hundred others were out working the cleanup—another source of anger, for the men who had hired their boats out to Exxon were making a lot more money than the men who had decided to fish. I sat in on a meeting at the high school gym. James Brady and the state were berated for inconsistent management, PWSAC was berated for taking all the fish and Exxon was berated for everything else.

Stories rippled through town about mystery sheens in the Sound. They were like UFO sightings. Outside the Fish and Game building, Brady stood in a knot of fishermen, parrying heated questions. Someone arrived with a report from Valdez about two chum salmon: Oil had contaminated their flesh. This would be a first. Brady hurriedly dispatched an assistant to check it out. It was hydraulic fluid from a fishing boat.

Hatchery humpies were flowing into the northern Sound at 200,000 a day, milling about uncaught, their flesh going soft. After two weeks of monitoring, the Esther district was declared safe to reopen. Two million pinks were taken in twelve hours on August 14. One net contained 25,000 fish. Cheek to jowl in the salmon, the seiners complained about combat fishing, compared themselves to rats in a cage. Aquaculture's downside is that it reduces the importance of skill. The fisherman used to have to second-guess the salmon, setting his nets where intuition and experience told him the fish would be running.

Undeniably the Alaskan fishermen endured pain and suffering because of the spill in their unspoiled Sound. Many lost income and justly filed claims against the oil company. But within the Sound at least, the spill did not prevent the salmon from being caught. The spill delayed the catch in the Sound, to be sure, and salmon quality was therefore not as good. But because the pinks of '89 were preponderantly hatchery fish, they passed through the restricted zones and were netted in the sanctuaries of the four facilities. The run in the closed southwestern district was poor, as it happened. Because of escapement targets, only about 125,000 pinks made it into the streams that should have been caught.

Fish and Game's zero-tolerance policy seemed to have worked, for the canneries processed the catch and the public accepted the product as untainted. Ironically, it was never proved that the sheen that grounded the fleet in late July originated from the oil spill. Tests by a NOAA lab showed the sheen samples not to be crude oil, but either bilge oil or diesel fuel. A state lab's analysis was inconclusive. As James Brady said, "People started seeing things with a new set of eyes that summer." He said fish processors in Alaska never before had a zero-tolerance for oil.

The next year, 1990, all were grateful that fishing in the Sound was unimpeded. The normal regulations applied, save for a few small areas that were closed off oily beaches. The 1989 fry, having encountered the spill on their way out, now poured in as adults. The numbers were staggering: 31.8 million—yet another record—returned to the hatcheries, plus 14.5 million wild fish to the streams. In August, with the hauls averaging 2 million a day, the processors couldn't handle any more. PWSAC had trouble selling the salmon it needed to cover its costs. Humpies built up again in front of the hatcheries, only this time the sated fleet wasn't interested. Fish and Game had to twist the fishermen's arms to come scoop up the excess production.

Overall it was twice the return of 1989. Exxon exulted, and the NRDA managers bit their tongues. Pressed for an explanation, officials speculated that the run might have been even greater without the oil spill.

Behind the scenes, Fish and Game commissioned a study to estimate the lost fish. Researcher Hal Geiger, extrapolating from the injuries to eggs and fry in 1989, made a case that 2 million additional salmon should have returned to the streams in '90, and an untold number more to the hatcheries. Geiger's report also noted that 1989 was a unique year for the propagation of pink salmon, "a year of excellent environmental conditions that may have strongly counteracted the effects of the oil."

I mentioned Ted Cooney's work relating the strength of a run to the water temperatures and zooplankton of the prior year. Cooney and his colleagues have recorded the springtime bloom and abundance of copepods around the AFK hatchery for more than a decade. He has devised a concept he calls a food-day. Food-days are calculated by multiplying the average daily concentrations of zooplankton in the water by the number of days the bloom lasts. The higher the number, the more the salmon fry have available to eat. Cooney found that food-days fluctuated widely between years, by as much as a factor of 5. His other key variable, surface water temperature, appeared to influence the timing of the emergence of

the fry. Cooney melded the information into a mathematical expression, which he used to predict the size of the following year's
run of the wild stocks.

The model was too simple to be surefire. When Cooney back-
tested it using the existent data of the '80s, the linkage held up only
two years out of three. But his model forecast the returns more
successfully than Fish and Game was able to do. Traditionally the
department has based its projections on the number of alevins
sampled in the stream beds during the winter, and not on the
marine conditions during the spring.

During the spring of 1989 there was concern that the zooplankton may have been damaged. Cooney and his IMS associates
were out measuring plankton stocks during April while the crude
was still on the water. Their findings were kept secret. But I heard
anecdotal reports of a huge bloom, in both the oiled and unoiled
parts of the Sound. One scientist joked that the copepods were so
big he worried they'd eat the fry, not the other way around. Ted
Cooney's private calculation of food-days indicated the second-
strongest zooplankton bloom of the decade. His model predicted
the excellent wild run of 1990. Too bad it wasn't publicized. Some
of the fishermen might have slept easier.

Now we come to 1991. The '89 brood-year fish returned
strongly. The threat facing fishermen in'91 was not environmental
but economic. Falling prices were undermining the success of the
hatcheries. Alaska salmon lost ground to farmed fish from Norway,
Chile, Canada and even Maine. Japan, the world's largest consumer, wasn't paying what it used to for red salmon, the preferred
species. The pink salmon was the least favored and cheapest, bony
and delicate when compared to the others, and thus condemned to
the can in the absence of a better marketing idea.

Before the opening of the '91 season two of Cordova's four
processing facilities went bankrupt. Warehouses were still full of
last year's product. The price processors offered for pinks was
twelve to fifteen cents a pound, down from thirty cents the year
before and seventy-nine cents in '88. For several days the seine
fleet protested the low prices by refusing to leave port. Then the
majority of salmon returned late, guaranteeing an unmanageable
glut in August. Wild runs in the Sound were over 9 million, hatchery returns 31 million. By summer's end it was no longer a matter
of selling salmon so much as getting rid of them.

Sawmill Bay, which fishermen had boomed off and saved from
the oil spill two years before, was tinted brown from an unwanted
writhing mass of fish. It was calamitous. They could not be left
there to rot. The governor had the idea to make a gift of seafood to

the Soviet Union. But who would pay for the canning? Exxon, having committed an environmental molestation that the governor need not mention, was tapped and cheerfully contributed $2 million.

So the Russians, and the poor in Anchorage and Fairbanks, and the sled dogs of the '92 Iditarod race, received over a million PWSAC fish. The less suitable salmon, over 2.5 million in all, were netted from the hatcheries, hauled to the open waters of the Sound and dumped like garbage.

Aquaculture was now perceived as a mixed blessing. Biological questions were raised that hadn't seemed important before. The hatchery fingerlings came out of their chutes bigger and stronger, pegged to the zooplankton, more fit than their wild cousins to elude predators. What was the danger to the carrying capacity of the Sound, with a half billion extra fry to feed? Or to the Gulf, now supporting pinks from hatcheries beyond the Sound? Alaska pink salmon numbered 120 million in 1991, ten times the catch of 1975. What might the hatchery fish be doing to the genetic diversity of the wild stocks? For it was discovered that some of the PWSAC fish, when they came back, were straying into the streams. To critics the cultured fish were becoming a disturbance, not an enhancement.

The prices for salmon did not improve in 1992. And in '92 the returns to the Sound plummeted: the wild pinks to 2.2 million, the hatchery run to below 8 million, the total making the lowest return since aquaculture started. The 1993 returns were even worse— crashing to a total of some 8 million pink salmon, a level not seen since the '70s. The salmon were undersized to boot. Fishing, always a boom-and-bust enterprise, squeezed the weaker fishermen out of business. It was no consolation that Royer's Gulf temperature, inching downward from its '80s highs, might be contributing to the problem, or that Cooney's food-days, calculated for each year prior, had warned of the failures to come.

Cordova believed the oil spill must somehow be at fault. In August of '93 the fleet took out its frustration on the pipeline. Sixty boats of orangutan fishermen blockaded the tanker traffic at Valdez. I remember the men first threatening to do this in the summer of 1989. After a two-day protest, the secretary of the interior persuaded the fishermen to back off. The government committed more money to study the problem with pink salmon in Prince William Sound.

Scientifically, this was a tall order. What exactly was the problem? The fish most exposed to oil had come back strong in '90 and '91. By '92 the oil was purged from the sediments of the Sound except in a few places. The hydrocarbons still in the environment could have had no bearing on the production of hatchery fry, yet hatchery returns fell apace with the native runs.

To be sure, Fish and Game measured injuries to eggs in the oiled streams in '89, '90 and '91. Biologists dug them up after the runs and found a greater number of inviable embryos in the oiled streams than they did in the unoiled streams. The trouble was, the difference in survival never showed up the following spring, when the emergent fry were counted. The government's chief scientist for damage assessment and the peer reviewers for the salmon studies did not believe there was evidence for population damage in pink salmon. Runs had been as poor in the past, and oil not an issue.

What exactly was the problem? On the one hand, we have a creature designed to persist in the face of fearsome losses. From a thousand eggs, a thousand chances in the wild, only one or two successes result, one or two chances to extend life to the next generation of salmon, and yet such long odds seem enough to maintain the species. On the other hand, we have a disturbance, an oil spill, whose effects were probably no greater and probably a good deal less than the winnowings of other disturbances. How many of those 999 fruitless salmon were knocked out by petroleum and therefore not by ice, sun, flood, earthquake, disease, kittiwake, killer whale, etc.?

Nature was like a juggler, a slew of balls in the air. One ball was black. Did it matter which one?

HIGH SUMMER, 1989, and fall coming fast. The first spill-year ebbed. I spent my days in my rooms in Cordova, writing about Valdez. The weather over Lake Eyak got wetter. With the September storms, the greenish water flowing into the lake from behind the mountains was blown toward my shore, a band of green pearl, bled from far glaciers, unmixed with darker depths.

The singer John Denver toured the Sound and afterward gave a free concert in Cordova. The singer was accompanied by the head of a national environmental group who had been making hay with the spill all summer. On breaking into "Take Me Home, Country Roads," Denver said to us, with evident emotion, "Earth is very fragile, and worthy of our greatest attention and love."

Fragile is one thing Earth is not; nor is life on Earth fragile. Life on Earth has weathered meteor bombardments, climate reversals and regular crises of extinction. Individual human beings are fragile, however. We humans project our tenderness onto Earth and then appoint ourselves as stewards of the endangered world. Stephen Jay Gould calls it "the old sin of pride and exaggerated self-importance." He goes on: "We are among millions of species, stewards of nothing. By what argument could we, arising just a geological microsecond ago, become responsible for the affairs of a world 4.5 billion years old, teeming with life that has been evolving and diversifying for at least three-quarters of that immense span? Nature does not exist for us, had no idea we were coming, and doesn't give a damn about us."

But Gould does believe in taking care of the earth, a sort of environmental tough love, which is necessary for the preservation of the human race. Nuclear war, ozone holes and global warming will hurt mankind first and foremost. To me it is the fear of death, never far below the motivations of the human spirit, that elevates the environmental rationale to a moral imperative. A dose of geological history, a short course in ecological disequilibrium, help to steel one for the inevitable. Meanwhile, we should do what we can for nature, within nature.

The anthropocentric instinct to keep our world whole around us, to preserve the delicate and balanced nature that we perceive, impels us, whenever we break the world somehow, to try to put it back together just as it was. I hope to have indicated how problematic the task can be. At a conference in Anchorage on postspill restoration, a marine ecologist named John Teal, of the Woods Hole Oceanographic Institution, spoke in favor of a hands-off approach. "I think there is a great hope for Prince William Sound, particularly if we are not too arrogant about what we can do," Teal said. "I think nature, particularly nature in the oceans, is much more capable of doing restoration than we are."

Teal was in the minority in 1989. The majority of voices cried for an aggressive response. "Everyone's goals are the same," said a government official, "to restore Prince William Sound to its original splendor."

Restoration had not only political and emotional appeal, it was a legal requirement as well. Restoration was more than cleaning up. Under the NRDA statutes, it was to begin when the cleanup of the oil and the assessment of damages were completed. The funds for restoration are those paid by the spiller in compensation for, and in measure of, the damages determined by the government. Eventually Exxon paid $1 billion in a court settlement. And the long and short of it was that people finessed restoration per se. Nature contracted to do the job. The agencies spent the settlement money on acquiring and protecting timber land in the spill zone, and on research and natural resource projects marginally relating to the spill.

While the event was still echoing, however, people were impatient for restoration. There was also this question: How are *we* to be compensated, how are we to be restored, for our spiritual losses? At the Anchorage conference, an attorney for the Natural Resources Defense Council put it, "No matter what we do to Prince William Sound, we all know in our hearts that it will never be quite the same."

About that time in '89, I made my third visit to the Sound. At midmorning in late November, the berms of snow at the Valdez airport were plowed twenty feet high. The sky was flushed pinky-blue. Dark swatches of brush made the only relief on the blank white of the mountain slopes. No more the fun and games of summer, as I was wearing a survival suit sealed tourniquet-tight at the extremities. The little plane had wheels for taking off and floats for landing in the Sound.

I traveled with an oil spotter for the state Department of Environmental Conservation. The young man went up every day if the weather permitted, and marked on his map the beaches that still sheened in spite of a billion dollars' worth of human scrubbing. The tides and pounding storms of winter had taken over the cleanup.

The pilot landed in the east arm of Northwest Bay on Eleanor Island, where DEC's research vessel, *Nautilus II*, was anchored. I had been to Northwest Bay once before, at the end of the summer, and would come several more times. The bay's two arms, east and west, are almost parallel culs-de-sac carved into the flank of the island, north-facing and narrow, with sheltered gravel beaches at one end and at the other a startling view, as if through a keyhole, of the distant Chugach range on the mainland. Bending to the gravel on each visit, to study the minute collusions of oil, substrate and biota, I would straighten up at a prickling sensation from the unseen panorama, and shoot it a backward glance, half expecting the glaciers to have begun their inevitable advance from the heights.

A roomy tour boat under charter, the *Nautilus II* carried about a dozen environmental technicians. They were sampling the intertidal and nearshore zones for oil content and for organisms. It was unclear to the staff (the prinicipal investigators weren't aboard then) whether their mission for DEC fell under the heading of damage assessment, in which case they shouldn't explain to me what they were doing, or spill response, in which case they could. It turned out not to be a problem, for at this stage they were simply gathering raw information.

It was lunchtime when I arrived. The day turned windy and

gray. But soon the beach site—EL-56 by official designation—was busy with people and equipment. Skiffs ran back and forth to the *Nautilus II*. Divers in wet suits collected pinches of the subtidal sediment, emerging onto the beach red-faced from the cold. Researchers laid measuring tapes for transects over the rocks. Two young women, a pair of chemists, dug holes near the tide line. After the water percolated in from below, they scooped samples in a jar. The pore water, as they termed it, would indicate the interstitial hydrocarbon concentrations. Overall the condition of the beach had much improved since summer, so I was told, but sheens nonetheless appeared on the pore-water pits, and the scattered raindrops beaded on rock surfaces that felt too slick, and in the crevices beneath the ice-glazed cobbles, there lay thick chocolaty oil, clotted with hemlock needles.

I looked over the shoulder of a biologist named Patrick Endres, just out of college, who was working a vertical transect from the high intertidal down to the water. To save time, he spoke his general observations into a tape recorder, and photographed the assemblages of beach organisms he had framed along the tape. He set the camera on a tripod above his quadrat, which is like a moveable square window. Pop! went the flash on the dusky beach, and then Endres would paw beneath the surface within the quadrat for other organisms, the infauna, and intone them as well.

Twenty-five years ago, when researchers investigated the disturbance of the earthquake, they may have laid transects on the same beach. Endres didn't know about the earthquake science, nor about the OCSEAP shoreline survey of the early '80s. He was still learning the snails and other critters. "We don't have an established baseline," he said. The principal investigators would probably take note of the earlier studies when they wrote their reports.

On the boat that evening it struck me that I was older than all the DEC staffers. I drifted from their earnest company to a man named Howard Wood, as senior to me as I was to them. Wood wasn't an environmental technician, he ran a skiff and did support work for the expedition. He was an old-time Alaskan with a corncob pipe. He first came up in '63 and "rode out the quake" in Ketchikan in the southeast part of the state. Living Outside at the time of the spill, he returned and caught on with DEC because he wanted to help. It turned out we'd seen each other here in Northwest Bay before. That is, Wood remembered seeing me. "In Alaska you pay more attention to individuals," he explained, "especially in the bush, because of the weather and all. You evaluate people you meet. You might need 'em to stay alive."

We went outside to the upper deck. The boat idled with its

running lights on. Power from the engine's generator was needed below, for the researchers were preparing and labeling the day's samples, the evidence that would help right the wrong. The night was very black. It was lightly snowing in the Sound. In a path of illuminated water a moon jellyfish traveled by the boat, ghostly pulsing, its bowl-shaped body more than a foot in diameter.

Wood talked as one who has seen change come to Alaska, change to the environment that he disliked. But the Lower 48 was worse. "We've screwed it up good," he said. "We've got to live off this earth. You can only rape and pillage so much." Yet he spoke without bitterness. I offered some of my ideas about the spill as a disturbance, and about the limited ability of human beings to fix systems that change. He cocked his head reflectively, sucking on his pipe. My language wasn't his.

"Well," he said, as the jellyfish still flexed beneath the snow-flakes, "let's just say I wanted to help get it squared away—the new Prince William Sound. Maybe I can help guide it to what it's going to be."

2

Oil and Water

NESCIENCE—an excellent word I've never encountered outside of a dictionary—means lack of knowledge or awareness. Nescience is a less pejorative state of affairs than ignorance, which is given as a synonym and implies a certain backwardness. The opposite of nescience, to be strictly literal, is science.

Scientists dispel nescience. If scientists have a social function beyond satisfying their own curiosity about the world, it is to be the intermediaries between nature, the object of their studies, and the nescient public, those of us less inquisitive but nevertheless needing to be in the know.

Crude oil had spilled on water prior to March 24, 1989. Spills as large as the *Exxon Valdez* were rare, but frequent, smaller accidents, together with the results of experiments, had led to a voluminous understanding of the natural processes involved: how an oil slick spreads from its source; how the oil changes form, or weathers, in the sea; and where its components end up—wafting in the air, dispersed finely in the water, stranded on the coastline, filtered to the bottom, absorbed by the biota.

The role of the experimental work was crucial. For unlike the marine ecologists, whose understanding of natural systems was inferential, the analytical chemists could test their ideas about oil in the sea by means of laboratory models. Moreover, they had fair confidence that their models captured the complexity of the processes at work during actual oil spills. These processes they called fates. The physical and chemical fates of oil in the sea set the stage for its biological effects.

Within forty-eight hours of the oil spill there was no lack of expertise assembled in Valdez. The best people in the country were summoned, or they volunteered to come, for the spill offered a rare opportunity to expand their knowledge. Working hard and long, they forecast the behavior of the oil and made recommendations for response. But in Valdez the scientists did not control their own fates. First, their expertise was divided among opposing parties and agencies. Second, the political pressures around them were immense, owing to the public reaction to the disaster. Science doesn't work well when emotions are high. In that cauldron, in that swirling vacuum, facts fell prey to manipulation and ignorance, and nescience in the end emerged pretty much unscathed.

Then too, there were degrees of expertise, adding a further complication. Probably the most influential scientific figure to be heard during the crisis was Dr. Riki Ott, who was not a practicing scientist. Though she had a Ph. D. in sediment toxicology, Ott was primarily an environmental activist and oil-industry critic, and secondarily a Cordova fisherman. She has given up on science, she told me. The technical fraternity looked upon Ott suspiciously, but she had a wide public following because her tireless warnings of a serious tanker accident were borne out. Riki Ott was the sibyl of the Sound. Indeed, just hours before the *Exxon Valdez* left port, she presented a talk to an audience in Valdez (by telephone hookup, since bad weather had stranded her in Cordova) entitled "Spilled Oil and the Alaska Fishing Industry."

Another technical paper by Ott, "Oil and the Marine Environment," summarized oil's fates and effects; it became an important source for journalists after the spill. I sent her text to a number of professionals for comment. Their complaint was that she erred in nuance if not so much in substance. Take for example Ott's statement, "Oil spilled into a subarctic marine environment is very persistent: it tends to remain in the water where it can travel great distances and is partitioned over time into sediment and organisms."

"She should say oil remains *on* the water, not in it," said James Payne, a chemist and a consultant to the government during the spill. Added NOAA's Douglas Wolfe, "You can't measure hydrocarbons within the water column for very long. If oil is to persist in the environment, it's in the sediments or on the beaches."

I pressed Ott on the point, but she wouldn't relinquish "*in* the water." Quibbles such as this are routine in normal scientific discourse, but they become magnified when there is public pressure. "That's why the public gets so confused in these events," Ott allowed. "It's because of differing assumptions of scientists."

In another statement in her paper Ott wrote that "spilled oil does not disappear; instead the mass of oil changes and is transferred into different compartments."

"This is misleading," Wolfe grumbled. "Up to thirty percent evaporates, and essentially it all *does* disappear. There's no clear recognition in her paper that oil is metabolized to carbon dioxide and water, and not in geologic time but usually in a decade or less."

Before delving into the complexities, we should consider that both scientists are right in what they mean by "disappear." Wolfe's view is the narrower. When eventually the oil weathers so much as to become undetectable, it ceases to concern him. Ott, with an eye to showing oil's harmful effects while it changes, maintained that even at the end of the process the oil was not really gone. "I agree that the farther out you go from the source of pollution, the effects get less and less and finally you get carbon and water," she said. "But the ecosystem is absorbing the hydrocarbons for better or for worse."

She seemed to view the earth as a closed system, a sealed test tube. However nature might manage to dilute the spill, transmute it, detoxify it, etc., still the oil adds to the toxic adulteration of the biosphere. The burden was cumulative. To extend the argument fully, the *Exxon Valdez* would always be with us, its cargo measurable in our psyches when no longer a physical residue.

In these times of acid rain, ozone holes, greenhouse gases and fears for fragile earth, I could not dismiss the pessimistic pursuit of the oil in the Sound. But I sided with Doug Wolfe. To be sure, the coauthor of "Estuarine Variability" was a hesitant ally, wrapped up as he was in the government's damage assessment inquiry. With legal action pending, NOAA paid him for his expertise in marine pollution, not for his theories about disturbances rippling through estuaries.

Wolfe explained a lot of chemistry to me, and he readily cited the examples of other oil spills. But when he would fall silent, or I'd hear a sigh over the phone, it was a signal that I was straying too far from basic fates and too close to the effects of the disturbance he was forbidden to discuss. Generally I was impressed by the constancy of the scientific community. The people who were most in the know about the spill were neither subversive nor partisan— perhaps they were too diffident, too willing to follow orders, or perhaps their egos weren't rewarded by confiding in writers. It was just as well that I couldn't get inside information, not from Exxon or from government researchers. I would contend with nescience on my own.

PETROLEUM is of biological origin. It comes from life. Plant and animal forms, buried in seabed sediments millions of years ago, when the earth was largely submerged, decayed to make it. As

Wolfe put it, "Oil is a whole medley of organisms lying down together." Carbon, life's cornerstone, predominates in petroleum, and hydrogen is the next most common element. Squeezed and heated by the ages, the two have combined in thousands of different chemical permutations called hydrocarbons.

Hydrocarbons make up the bulk of crude oil. The nonhydrocarbons—compounds of nitrogen, sulfur and oxygen, and several trace metals—are present in petroleum in lesser amounts.

Here are some familiar hydrocarbons and hydrocarbon products, listed in order of molecular weight, from the lightest compounds to the heaviest: methane, pentane, benzene, gasoline, kerosene, home heating oil, diesel (also known as No. 2 fuel oil), lubricating oil, Bunker C fuel (or No. 6 oil, used by ships), tar and asphalt. The hydrocarbons of commercial value are obtained from crude oil by distillation, a heating and condensing process. Petroleum engineers distinguish between the "light ends," such as the components of gasoline, which are easy to separate from crude because their boiling points are relatively low, and the "heavy ends," like lube oil, which require temperatures of 800 degrees F. to be refined.

The range in volatility among hydrocarbons is extreme. Some of the light ends are gases and some are liquids that evaporate immediately on being released from the ground. If they aren't captured or reinjected into the oil field, these compounds must be "flared off" through controlled burning, lest they build up to poisonous or explosive levels in the air. The hydrocarbons of intermediate weight are much less volatile, and at the far end of the spectrum hydrocarbons are so gunky and inert that practically no amount of heat can drive them apart from each other. About one third of Prudhoe Bay crude (the petroleum that spilled) consists of these nondistillable compounds. I grew used to seeing the term *UCM* in analyses of oil samples from the Sound. It means unresolved complex mixture, a black hole for analytical chemistry. This is the stuff to pave streets with, because it persists unchanged in the out-of-doors for years.

The compounds in oil are also distinguished by structure. The major class of hydrocarbons, the aliphatics, consists of chains or branches of hydrogen and carbon atoms. At low molecular weights the straight-chain aliphatics are gases. For example, ethane, whose formula is C_2H_6, has two linked carbon atoms surrounded by six hydrogen atoms. At medium weights the aliphatics are liquids that evaporate readily, such as octane, C_8H_{18}, a constituent of gasoline. When the number of carbons in the molecular chain reaches twenty and higher, the aliphatic becomes a waxy solid, a paraffin.

The other group of hydrocarbons, the aromatics, is characterized by a ring structure. In benzene, C_6H_6, the lightest and simplest aromatic, a molecule consists of six carbon atoms bonded in a hexagonal ring, with hydrogen atoms on the outside of the structure. More complex compounds—the heavy, or polynuclear, aromatics—have multiple benzene rings linked together like chicken wire. Aromatics are the reason that crude oil has a bad name. Their biological effects can be pernicious.

Hydrocarbons of both types are ubiquitous. They are in the water, air, soil, our food, even our body tissues: most always in trace amounts that pose no threat. Researchers testing a water sample or a fish in Prince William Sound for oil contamination have to allow for this "background" level of hydrocarbons. A certain level of pollution is considered normal in marine systems. I recall a Coast Guard officer announcing that a particular oil sheen, one of many sighted in the summer of '89, was not from the *Exxon Valdez*, but of "natural origin." He sounded relieved. He meant that the sheen was from local boat traffic.

Between 2 and 3 million tons of oil are estimated to enter the world's oceans each year. The contributions from headline-making tanker accidents are slight compared to the multititude of small, routine spills from ships, terminals, offshore drilling operations, and to the more considerable discharges from coastal or riparian municipalities and industries. Some hydrocarbons even reach the water from the air—the wind-borne products of forest fires, power plants and engine exhaust. The seas dilute and degrade these chemicals while dispersing them to remote and virginal corners of the globe.

Not all hydrocarbons are anthropogenic, that is, put into the environment by people. There are also biogenic hydrocarbons, manufactured within the living systems of plants and animals. Certain termites, for instance, squirt noxious hydrocarbons in self-defense. Certain moths communicate by emitting straight-chain hydrocarbons. Lobsters secrete a mating attractant, called a pheromone, which is so similar to kerosene that fishermen sometimes are able to lure lobsters to kerosene-soaked bricks.

The vegetable kingdom—the marine phytoplankton and algae, and on land the trees, shrubs and grasses—produces hydrocarbons for a host of functions. One is as a protective layer on the surfaces of leaves or needles, for the waxy aliphatics are water-resistant. Another is as an energy source; plants store certain aliphatics much the way that animals store fatty acids in their cells. Ethylene, a gaseous hydrocarbon (C_2H_4), is known to be emitted by trees and plants to help ripen fruit and to send various chemical messages. The compound's potency was discovered at the turn of the century, when ethylene escaping from city street lamps induced trees to drop their leaves.

An interesting family of biogenic hydrocarbons is the terpenes, which are a kind of branched aliphatic, more complex in structure than the straight-chain forms. Certain seaweeds secrete terpenes during sexual propagation. Trees make them, it is thought, to attract insect pollinators and at other times to repel insect pests. Terpenes include the scented oils and resins, like camphor and menthol and pine pitch, from which turpentine is derived. The Blue Ridge and Smoky Mountains of the Southeast come by their names because of the terpene haze emitted by the forests. Reacting with gasoline vapors and nitrous oxides from automobiles, terpenes even add to urban smog. (Some may recall Ronald Reagan's campaign comment about "killer trees.")

When vegetation growing in the sea or near the shore dies and decomposes, the detrital matter, including the hydrocarbons, enters the environment and adds to the hydrocarbon background. Background concentrations are by definition faint. NOAA scientists, monitoring the intertidal sediments along the tanker route in the Sound in the late '70s, detected aliphatic and aromatic compounds deriving from plant waxes, plankton and other natural sources. Pristine beaches had levels of hydrocarbons in the range of 100 parts per billion.

Let's explore that gauge of concentration for a minute—parts per billion (ppb), parts per million (ppm), parts per thousand (ppt) and so forth. In the sea, an oil concentration of 1 ppb means that, in a billion units of water, one of those units is oil. The term may denote volume or weight or, commonly, both. When it matters, researchers specify. The oil is considered to be mixed in the water uniformly. One part per billion is a tiny adulteration. To make a 1-ppb concentration using a cup of oil, one would have to blend it with 50 million gallons of water. (What if, hypothetically, the oil spilled from the *Exxon Valdez* had perfused the whole Sound? Eleven million gallons into an estimated volume of 270 trillion gallons: forty parts per billion.)

The NOAA baseline study of hydrocarbons along the tanker route included three beaches within protected anchorages. Here the researchers found that the biogenic compounds were intermingled with chronic contamination from boat activity. The two sources together produced hydrocarbon concentrations in the hundreds of parts per billion. The most elevated readings were from Constantine Harbor near the eastern entrance to the Sound, where the NOAA group reported petroleum hydrocarbons in the parts per million range, an order of magnitude above the rest. Even this was considered background, not a worrisome pollution. But the scientists were in error to attribute the extra hydrocarbons at Constantine Harbor only to fuel spills, ballast water discharges and diesel exhaust.

For there is a third source of hydrocarbons in the marine environment that is neither biogenic nor anthropogenic. The earth itself is a petroleum polluter. A quarter of a million tons of crude oil are estimated to dribble into the world's seas from coastal and submarine seeps. That's equivalent to eight spills the size of the *Valdez* spill every year for untold thousands of years. The seeps tend to occur at plate boundaries along the margins of continents. These areas experience high tectonic activity. Sedimentary rocks containing petroleum are subject to constant folding and cracking, which causes the oil to migrate through faults to the surface.

In southcoastal Alaska there are half a dozen seep sites. A few of the seeps are right on beach faces, where tides lick the oil; the majority are located a short distance inland and the oil enters the ocean by streams or runoff. Probably there are seeps on the near ocean floor as well, but their output is too small to be distinguished from the background. According to a recent paper by two NOAA scientists, historical reports of a number of other seeps on the Gulf of Alaska shore cannot be confirmed today. The seeps seem to have disappeared. Just as seismic activity can induce seeps, it can cut them off. One of the researchers speculated that the '64 earthquake may have scrambled the fault patterns above the oil reservoirs.

Seep sites are obvious places to drill for oil deposits. The two fields working in Alaska today, the big producer on the North Slope and the smaller one in Cook Inlet, each had seeps as clues. The earliest oil production in Alaska took place at Katalla, about fifty miles southeast of Cordova. Active seeps are everywhere in Katalla—at least seventy-five, by one count, in a twenty-five-mile-long band along the Gulf of Alaska coast.

Katalla is an Indian word for oil. There is a story in the local Native folklore about a beach catching fire. In 1894 a white man discovered one of the seeps by falling into it while out hunting. He lit a match to it, "to see what would happen," as he later recounted, and was rewarded by a huge and foully smoking blaze that lasted a week. He and his two partners became known as the Three Greases for their efforts to wheedle financial backing for drilling in Katalla. In 1902 a gusher was struck and a boomtown was born. But the field turned out to be rather insignificant, producing only 150,000 barrels of crude. The wells were shut down and the whole place abandoned after a fire in 1933.

In the 1970s, alarmed by the Arab energy shocks, the United States encouraged oil companies to drill on the outer continental shelf. The Department of the Interior sold tracts off Katalla worth $570 million. Yet the test wells of the most promising geological structures either came up dry or showed deposits too scanty to make pay. One explanation was that sizable oil reservoirs, if they existed at all here, were emptied over time by the tectonic cracking.

After the oil spill, Exxon chemists hunted for PAHs (polynuclear aromatic hydrocarbons) at the bottom of Prince William Sound. In 1993 the company reported that the traces of PAHs they found were not from the tanker but from seep oil, borne into the Sound on the Alaska Coastal Current. Cores of seafloor sediment contained particles of oil that had been settling out of the water for at least 150 years. When the government's chemists looked into it, they could not disagree. Indeed, reanalyzing their data of the late '70s, they found Katalla PAHs preponderant in the beach sediments of Constantine Harbor, which they had cited as the most contaminated station in their study.

How can chemists tell? Since hydrocarbons almost never occur singly, but rather in groups or suites, each sample has its own fingerprint, a telltale complexion of components. Suites produced by the burning of oil, for instance, contain higher concentrations of polynuclear aromatics than those resulting from a crude oil spill. Certain aliphatics, when they dominate a sample, point to a biogenic source. Pristane, for example, the product of a bloom of copepods, can exceed other compounds of the oil background by a factor of 1,000.

Even petroleums of highly similar suites can be distinguished. For example, in 1990 a chemist with the U.S. Geological Survey collected two dozen flecks of tar from upper beaches around the Sound. He identified the signature of *Exxon Valdez* oil, to be sure, but also the widespread signature of a California oil. He speculated that these samples were vestiges of the liquid asphalt spilled from old Valdez during the '64 earthquake.

Analytical tools of extraordinary precision were brought to bear on Prince William Sound, tools that can function virtually at the molecular level. The systems analyzed not only samples of water and sediment for their hydrocarbon content, but also biological tissues and fluids.

I'll give a brief description of the most advanced hardware, the gas chromatography/mass spectrometry (GC/MS) system. It can take up to a week to run one GC/MS analysis. Most of the labor involves extracting and preparing the material for analysis. Once the sample is refined, the final step of quantifying its components in the two machines takes about two hours.

Gas chromatography of petroleum has much in common with distillation. Both processes involve heating the oil so that its fractions boil off and separate. A GC system consists of an oven, an injector and a spiral coil of hollow glass tubing. The sample—a drop of extract, no more—is injected into one end of the coil, through which is flowing a carrier gas. The sample vaporizes in the gas. Then the oven raises the heat in stages, three to four degrees per minute. The sample begins to flow through the coil. It doesn't take much heat at all to move the lighter hydrocarbons—they flow through the column well ahead of the heavy ends. Each time the temperature goes up a notch, a weightier sequence of compounds migrates through the coil. The temperature tops out at 300 degrees C. Finally, as they issue in prescribed order from the end of the coil, the compounds are electrically charged (ionized) by a second device, the mass spectrometer. The intensity of the charge tells their relative concentrations, which in turn give the identity of the sample.

It was by GC/MS that NOOA determined, in the summer of '89, that the sheen appearing outside the salmon hatchery at Esther was not from the *Exxon Valdez*. The diagnostic tools were helpful when the oil was conspicuous, as it was in 1989; but at low concentrations, after months of weathering in the sea, the pedigrees of the hydrocarbons were not simple to determine. This was one reason why the chronic phase of the oil spill was more complex, more contentious than the acute phase.

Our technical ability to track wisps of chemicals in the environment is something of a mixed blessing. It used to be that if we couldn't detect a hazardous substance such as an aromatic hydrocarbon, we didn't have to worry about the possibility of adverse biological effects. Nescience has its comforts. Millions of gallons of oil were dropped like a bomb onto Prince William Sound, and although the explosion no longer echoes in the water or sediments, science won't rest until the last of the compounds disappears into the background.

OIL AND WATER don't mix, at least not readily. Seawater is a poor solvent of petroleum. One part oil per thousand of seawater is considered a high concentration. Oil mostly floats, being less dense than the water. Only a very few petroleums in the world do not float. The specific gravity of fresh-spilled, unweathered Prudhoe Bay crude is 0.89, meaning that it is 89 percent as heavy as water.

When the *Exxon Valdez* ripped open on the rocks of Bligh

Reef, crude oil boiled to the surface at the rate of 2 million gallons per hour. The gush continued for four hours. Then the sea began flowing into the tanks. The remaining oil was floated above the line of punctures and the hemorrhaging slowed. The loss, as close as could be determined, was 10.84 million gallons (258,000 barrels). But four-fifths of the cargo did not escape.

Petroleum spilled on water acts like cream poured onto a linoleum floor. It pools and spreads in all directions. Spreading is the first of its fates in the sea. Gravity forces the oil outward, overcoming the contrary forces of surface tension and viscosity. (Surface tension helps a liquid retain its most compact shape, as when water beads up on a counter, while viscosity, a function of thickness, slows a liquid's flow. Honey is an example of a viscous liquid that flows grudgingly.) If there are no winds or currents, oil will expand like a balloon being blown up in two dimensions. The ocean surface offers almost no resistance, no friction or absorption as there would be on land, although low temperatures slow the expansion process.

Spreading oil forms a slick, from which emanates a sheen. A slick we may define as a dark-colored film thicker than two micrometers. Thinner than two micrometers, a slick becomes a sheen. A micrometer is a thousandth of a millimeter. Two micrometers are 0.00008 inch. An ordinary sheet of paper is seventy times thicker than an oil sheen. The color changes from yellow-brown to rainbow-hued to blue-silver as a sheen decreases in thickness. A single tablespoon of oil can form a sheen covering 625 square feet of water. One can see that 11 million gallons would go a long way.

At first light on Good Friday, 1989, observers flying over the stranded tanker reported a spreading tendril of oil about 1,000 feet wide and four to five miles long. The spill was seven hours old. Skies were gray as normal but the air was unusually still. The crude was in a contiguous pool, moving slowly toward the south. Nothing was being done to halt the slick, which had the raw, somber color of sea and sky.

Usually the winds take over and push a slick—the fate known as advection or drifting—faster than gravity can spread it. The standard formula is that a slick will be transported in the direction of the wind at a rate 3 percent of the wind speed, modified by the rate and direction of the current. But the north wind was blowing at less than ten knots, a breeze more than a wind, and the southwest flow in the Sound was slack this March, as we know from Tom Royer's measurements of the Alaska Coastal Current. The water was quiet, and the spread of the oil was still a greater force than the drift.

Whatever slight chop there was was muffled by the oil. It's true that oil calms the waters; mariners have known it for centuries. Rambling on Cape Cod in 1857, Henry Thoreau met a lighthouse keeper who told him how a ship's crew had poured whale oil over the side during a storm. Their passage smoothed, they made it to the beach in a skiff. Thoreau's landlubber skepticism—he tended to doubt anything he couldn't ascertain for himself—was not misplaced. A layer of oil absorbs energy from a rippling ocean surface, so that gentle waves indeed are stilled. But in a wind greater than ten knots, such as in any storm, the larger waves break up the slick and won't be tranquilized. Yet there is *some* dampening effect, which shows up on radar screens. After the wind increased, Exxon used airborne radar to track the oil along the water.

Initially the weather was perfect for controlling the slick. The most proven technical responses to an oil spill, which are mechanical containment and pickup, are most effective in calm conditions. Boom, a floating barrier, is laid around the slick, and oil-skimming vessels remove the oil from the water. There are many kinds of boom, ranging in depth from one to three feet and in material from stiff plastic curtain to sorbent fabric. As for skimmers, there are at least a dozen types: They use weirs, suction heads, moving adhesive belts, mops, brushes or disks to separate the oil from the surface of the sea. Whatever the array of equipment, it must be backed up with barges or tankers, for the skimmers' own storage capacities are limited.

It wasn't until Friday afternoon, about twelve hours after the accident, that Alyeska got to Bligh Reef with a pair of MARCO Class VII skimmers and a skirt of boom. A pod of killer whales poked their heads up near the stern of the tanker, curious to see what the activity was about. The skimmers nosed into the slick. In its inverted bow the vessel carries a three-foot-wide conveyor belt of adsorbent fabric that oil tends to stick to. (Absorbent material, by contrast, draws oil into the fabric instead of onto it.) The belt takes up and conveys the oil inside, discharging it through a wringer to a hold, after which the clean belt returns to action.

The best the MARCO VII can do is to collect sixty-six gallons, about a barrel and a half, for each minute of operation. By now millions of gallons were spread out over miles—no match for twenty skimmers, let alone two. An Alyeska official figured the boom needed to hold all the oil would have to be twenty-five feet high. No way did Alyeska and the Coast Guard have the necessary gear available in Valdez, nor could Exxon, taking over, have hoped to mobilize the resources in time.

Only about 200 barrels of oil were recovered in the first afternoon. A week later there were eleven skimmers huffing in the Sound and an estimated 7,500 barrels picked up, less than 3 percent of the far-flung slick. According to John Robinson, chief of the NOAA unit advising the Coast Guard in Valdez, the oiling of the shore and the numbers of animals killed probably would have been the same had no skimming or booming been undertaken at all.

Said Robinson's colleague David Kennedy, "If the miles and miles of boom, sea curtain, etc., all the stuff that was ultimately brought here, had been here at the time, perhaps we would have contained up to 40 percent of the spill—I mean that part of it that was on the water. A 100-percent containment isn't possible. You get any kind of current or high wind, or a boom breaks, or something goes wrong, and the product escapes underneath. We've seen it happen over and over in spills. Those little skimmers working on that sea of oil reminded me of ants crawling up an elephant's leg."

The largest oil spill on record, which took place in the Persian Gulf during the 1991 war, was twenty times larger than the *Exxon Valdez* spill. Conditions were excellent for skimming, as the Persian Gulf is gentle and the weather was calm for a month. A converted tanker called the *Al Waasit* picked up 4 million gallons over the course of six weeks, reportedly a record recovery. I flew over the *Al Waasit* while it worked. Its two sweeper arms, like a forward V, extended into the reddish whorls of the slick. The vessel intercepted about 1 percent of the Gulf spill; two other skimmers together recovered somewhat less. Meanwhile the Saudi coast was smeared black for 100 miles in either direction. My point is that megaspills always have hit land if the winds and currents have willed it.

Therefore although Alyeska now keeps a large skimmer in Valdez capable of collecting 2,500 barrels per hour, and although a network of sixteen superskimmers is planned for the Lower 48, there can never be enough boom and skimmers for girding the entire U.S. coastline. Industry and government officials have renewed their interest in two other means to mitigate spills, burning and chemical dispersants.

Burning and dispersants were controversial measures in 1989. Their effects on an oil slick are the very opposite of containment. They change the structure of a spill, transferring hydrocarbons to a vertical dimension above and below the surface of the water. Yet in another regard, burning and dispersants are not so radical, in that they magnify two of petroleum's ongoing and natural transformations. For even as the oil spreads and drifts on the sea, hydrocarbons are vaporizing in the air and, to a lesser extent, dissolving and dispersing in the water column.

Evaporation is the quickest and most cathartic of oil's protean fates. It begins as soon as fresh crude meets the atmosphere. The light ends, both aliphatic and aromatic, disperse as gas or vapor. When gasoline, which is all light ends, spills on pavement, most of it vaporizes before you can get a rag on it. The Coast Guard will respond to a major gasoline or kerosene spill on the water, but won't do much except try to boom it until it naturally goes away. The lighter the grade of the oil, the fewer are the heavy ends left behind in a spill, and thus the easier the cleanup.

It has been estimated that between 2 and 3 million gallons from the *Exxon Valdez* evaporated. As much as a quarter of the spill "disappeared." As Riki Ott surveyed the tanker from above the first morning, the oil was soundlessly, invisibly, massively sublimating around her nose. Ott has long been a critic of air pollution from the pipeline terminal, yet never was she exposed to oil fumes as she was then. "We almost got nauseous," she recalled. "We had to veer off to clear air to get our heads straight." Aboard the tanker itself, the salvage crews wore respirators against the poisonous benzene gas emanating from the holds; at times the gas built to explosive levels. Until the remaining oil was pumped off, the tanker was like a hand grenade pinned on the reef.

The connection between evaporation and burning is simple. While oil's volatility—its vaporousness—is greatest, so is its flammability. It is not difficult to ignite fresh crude while the light ends are evanescing. Canadian and American researchers have experimented with small burns for years. They have ignited test spills with laser beams shot from helicopters. Burning can remove almost all of a small slick, even from Arctic ice. But it is important not to delay. Most of the light ends are gone within two or three days of a spill, and the tarry fractions left behind on the cold water won't ignite as readily.

A unit of the Coast Guard, the Pacific Area Strike Team, has experience in scuttling ships that are leaking oil. Its specialists use explosives and incendiaries when the oil is not volatile. Five days before the wreck of the *Exxon Valdez*, in fact, the Coast Guard ignited a foreign cargo vessel that had run aground in the Aleutians. The fire burned for two weeks, consuming 800,000 gallons of fuel oil along with the ship, at the same time that burning was being debated anxiously in Prince William Sound.

Huge spills involving supertankers have always caused the authorities to hesitate before the specter of an uncontrolled conflagration and its extensive soot and smoke. Belated attempts to burn were not effective on the infamous *Torrey Canyon* spill off Cornwall, England, in 1967, or on the *Arrow* spill off Nova Scotia in 1970. In 1978 French farmers on the Brittany coast squelched talk of igniting the wreck of the *Amoco Cadiz* (which spilled six times more than the *Valdez*), because they feared that soot would ruin their crops. Aromatic fumes blew inland and tainted their farms anyway. In 1990, when the *Mega Borg* tanker caught fire fifty miles off Texas, the public virtually demanded that the smoky blaze be put out, and it was.

In Prince William Sound, evaporation of the oil was slowed by the lack of wind and the low March temperatures. That meant more time was available to burn the slick. Only Exxon championed the use of fire during the first weekend of the crisis, although the company wanted the tanker and cargo spared. Nobody entertained the idea of attacking the ship directly. Proceeding cautiously, the Coast Guard authorized a test burn of the slick by an Anchorage company called Spiltec.

In the darkness of Saturday evening, which was the second day of the spill, two fishing boats, slowly towing a 500-foot-long, flame-resistant boom in a U-shaped configuration, snared a patch of crude. A gelled fuel-igniter was lit and tossed into the boom. When the oil caught fire, flames leaped to 300 feet and continued for more than an hour. After the smoke cleared and the residue was examined, it was estimated that between 15,000 and 30,000 gallons had been eliminated. According to a report written by Spiltec's Alan A. Allen, the effort marked the first time that the high efficiency of test burns had been matched on an unplanned spill. Either 98 or 99 percent of the trapped oil had burned away.

The technical triumph was negated by a psychosocial setback. The residents of Tatitlek, a small Native village that was the nearest community to Bligh Reef, had not been forewarned about the smoke. Dread alone was making the Natives sick—from start to finish they suffered from the spill more than any other group. The morning after the burn some in the village complained of reddened eyes and sore throats. The Coast Guard barred further use of the technology.

Experiments indicate that 10 percent of burning petroleum is converted to soot and smoke. One can imagine the massive volumes that would have billowed if the whole slick were afire in the Sound. Tatitlek would have had to be evacuated, perhaps Valdez too. The plume would have shown up on satellite photos. But a messy fire does not look so bad in light of the biological and financial costs that ensued when the oil escaped across the Sound. Walt Parker, who directed the state's inquiry into the accident, explained, "The feeling now is: Don't horse around. Torch it early. Get the [tanker] crew out of there and make the decision fast. You have to plan to know whether you're going to segregate the spill and burn it away from the tanker, or whether you're going to go for the whole thing."

Ironically, the case for burning has improved since the Kuwaiti oil fires during the Persian Gulf War. Before the war there was much speculation, informed and otherwise, that the holocaust threatened by Saddam Hussein would disrupt the region's weather and perhaps the whole world's. Some scientists drew upon the "nuclear winter" scenarios of the Department of Defense, in which vast layers of smoke blot out the sun. The worries increased when the retreating Iraqis set hundreds of wells alight in late February of '91.

In truth I have never witnessed anything so appalling as Kuwait's Al-Ahmadi oil field in early March. Standing at the center of a wide empty plain, I counted scores of fires. Each well was burning a little differently, one with flames rolling upward like lava, another with straining jagged tongues. The ground rumbled and shook from the pressure of crude oil jetting out at 1,600 pounds per square inch. The oil flowed sluggishly past my feet, the black streams and pools fringed by little meandering flames. Great heat filled my face. Yet surprisingly the air felt fresh, and only straight overhead was it dark and smoky. From all sides clean winds from the desert swept in to feed the suck of the fires.

In Kuwait some 3 million barrels went up in smoke every day, the equivalent of twelve *Exxon Valdez* spills being ignited around the clock. The environmental carnage lasted many months. Although the air pollution was fierce, Kuwaitis were no worse off in health than long-suffering residents of Mexico City or parts of Eastern Europe. Local temperatures dropped, but there were no global changes in meteorology. The overwhelming atmospheric disturbance of '91 turned out to be the eruption of Mount Pinatubo in the Philippines, which, dwarfing the Kuwaiti fires in its effects, cooled the global climate and aggravated the loss of ozone.

Tests have been commissioned as never before—in 1993 some 20,000 gallons were spilled and burned on the ocean off Newfoundland—but whether burning will ever graduate from the experimental stage will depend on the courage of policy-makers. Given the infrequency of large spills, it is the local authorities who are untested rather than the technology. "People worry about all the unknowns, the risks, the air pollution," said James Payne, the leading oil chemist in Valdez. "But look at what happens when you don't burn. Anyway, you're going to burn the oil eventually—a little cleaner, maybe, combusting in the carburetor of your car, but you're still going to put it into the air."

• •

A PRIVATE CONSULTANT from southern California, Jim Payne had been involved with Prudhoe Bay petroleum for a decade. In the early '80s Payne and his associates won a series of contracts from NOAA, under the OSCEAP program, to study the fates of oil in subarctic waters.

Setting up shop at a government laboratory at Kasitsna Bay on Cook Inlet, not far from Anchorage, Payne had several wave tanks built for his experiments. The tanks were about three feet wide, three feet deep, eighteen feet long and open to the air on top. Seawater from the bay was churned into waves by a paddle wheel at one end of each tank. New water was pumped through so that there was a turnover in the tank every three to four hours. To this marine microcosm Payne added fresh Prudhoe Bay crude. (His oil samples were obtained from that particular field. The petroleum that flows down the pipeline is more exactly known as Alaska North Slope crude, because it is a blend from the Prudhoe Bay, Kuparuk and several smaller fields of the Slope.)

The paddle wheels churned steadily from the summer of '82 until late '83. For the first three weeks Payne stayed at the facility and monitored the weathering of his oil samples, and thereafter visited the tanks periodically. By analyzing, through gas chromatography, the evolving suite of compounds, he learned the sequence of the so-called transfer processes that change the makeup of an oil spill. By what remained in the samples, in other words, he was able to trace the movement of hydrocarbons out of the body of the slick.

Payne found that during the first forty-eight hours of a spill the two most important transfer processes were evaporation and dissolution. Like evaporation, dissolution operates on the molecular level. Seawater is a poor solvent of petroleum, but some hydrocarbon molecules do dissolve, that is, mingle among molecules of water. Water molecules are somewhat polar, which means that they have electrically charged poles, positive and negative, and the lightest aromatic compounds are also polar. Electromagnetic attraction overcomes the basic incompatibility between the hydrocarbons and the water.

What is problematic is that the aromatic fractions most able to dissolve are also the most poisonous. Petroleum's toxic gang of four are benzene, ethylbenzene, toluene and xylene, a.k.a. the BETX compounds. In the wave tank Payne determined that BETX concentrations under the minislick peaked at 100 parts per billion within eight to twelve hours and then dropped sharply. The amounts that dissolved were small and ephemeral. The toxic shock does not last because the volatile stuff heads for the sky after a brief phase within the water.

"Evaporation is a hundred to a thousand times faster than dissolution," said Payne. "The fact is that it's difficult to get a significant amount of oil into the water column. For BETX and the naphthalenes [intermediate-weight aromatics]—the only fractions that you really care about biologically—the most you'll get is 200 to 400 parts per billion, and that only right under the slick. In lab studies and wave tanks you can detect the dissolution going on, but in the real world concentrations are so much lower."

Chemists didn't start sampling the Sound until almost a week after the spill. Total hydrocarbons reached one part per million in the water just off the oiled beaches; the levels of the light aromatic compounds averaged two parts per billion. Readings in both categories fell off after April. The heavier aromatics, the PAH compounds, had similarly low concentrations but somewhat longer lifetimes. Overall, the toxic hydrocarbons in the water probably did not exceed 10 ppb, which was the state water-quality standard.

The twin actions of dissolution and evaporation render an oil slick more viscous. After a few days a third transfer process, the dispersion of the oil, begins to exceed the other two in reducing the slick. Dispersing is a cruder process than dissolving. It is driven by wave energy. When the slick is agitated, particles break from the oil mass and scatter into the sweep of the ocean.

The process is made possible by surfactants. A surfactant, a surface-active agent, is any chemical or compound that does its work at the surface of substances. Crude oil contains many nonhydrocarbon surfactants in trace quantities, including metals and compounds of sulfur and oxygen. Also the heavyweight resins and asphaltenes function as surfactants. The surfactants concentrate at the hostile boundary between the oil and water, a chemical foot in both camps, and reduce the surface tension beteen the two. Droplets of oil enter the water. The droplets continually divide and shrink, until they become too minute to float to the surface, and thus "disappear." About ten times more oil disperses than dissolves. The process crests within the first week, for after that the heavy compounds remaining behind require more and more wave energy to be broken from the slick.

Practically speaking, oil spills are a two-dimensional phenomenon, all length and breadth but very little depth. Payne pointed out how thin the killing zone is. Oil sweeps across the ocean and piles in suffocating folds along the shore. To halt it, Payne and others would exploit the third dimension: Send the oil up into the air by burning it, or else down into the water column by accelerating the dispersion.

"If you can put it down in the water only one meter," said Payne, "you decrease a spill's concentration by a factor of a thousand. Ten meters down, you cut it by ten thousand." The way to increase dispersion is to apply extra surfactants to the slick. But chemical dispersants, as such treatments are known in the trade, carry a lot of baggage; their history is more troubled than burning's.

The problem is what happened after the *Torrey Canyon* spill in '67, when some 10,000 barrels of various dispersants were sprayed on the oiled shore of Cornwall. Powerful detergent chemicals, originally developed for cleaning tanker holds and oily bilges, these dispersants cut oil off the surface of the rocks but also devastated the plants and animals of the intertidal zone. One of the agents was subsequently shown to be almost three times as toxic as No. 2 fuel oil.

In the '70s the oil industry adjusted the formulations to make dispersants less harmful. But several biologists who tested oil-dispersant mixtures in the lab reported that the new chemicals were still toxic to fish. However, according to a 1989 report on dispersants by the National Research Council, an arm of the National Academy of Sciences, many of these tests were flawed. The report said that what killed the fish was the *oil* dispersed by the dispersants, not the chemicals per se. Tried separately, the modern dispersants were not found to be very poisonous.

The report recapitulated an important field experiment in the Canadian Arctic in the early '80s, the Baffin Island Oil Spill Project. The BIOS study showed that an oil-dispersant mixture was indeed toxic in the short term, because the dispersants injected aromatic hydrocarbons into the water column, but the test also showed that the chemicals did their job of making oil disappear. Compared to spilled oil alone, the oil-dispersant mixture left fewer hydrocarbons remaining in the subtidal sediments and thus reduced the long-term exposure to marine life.

More vexing to the National Research Council panel of experts was the fact that although the chemicals worked in the lab and in carefully monitored field tests like BIOS, their effectiveness in actual emergencies wasn't good. There was no convincing proof that dispersants worked in large-scale operations, and, further, no consensus on how to go about obtaining that proof. Mervin Fingas, a spill expert for the Canadian government and a leading scientific critic of dispersants, has argued that dispersants tend to push the oil aside—a process known as herding—rather than disperse it below. After the *Exxon Valdez* spill, he estimated that if enough of the chemicals had been sprayed on properly and everything else had gone perfectly, at most 10 to 30 percent of the slick might have been dispersed.

The National Research Council report, concluding that dispersants in themselves caused little harm to the environment, was published just a month before the spill in Prince William Sound, too late to influence environmentalists and environmental regulators, who still considered chemical dispersants a dangerous no-no. As with burning, the unknown risks appeared to outweigh the unknown benefits.

Nothing to do with dispersants went right during the weekend of the spill. Confusion and controversy abounded in Valdez. To summarize: Alyeska and Exxon did not have enough dispersant on hand. In three field trials the aircraft didn't spray the chemicals on the slick correctly. The becalmed Sound provided little energy to make dispersion work, whether natural or man-made. Because state officials argued against dispersants, and because the tests appeared ineffective, the Coast Guard delayed approval of a full-scale dispersant operation. Then conditions changed and further treatment of the slick became moot.

Jim Payne served on the panel of scientists evaluating dispersants. I called him for his opinion on their use in this instance. "I'm kind of neutral about dispersants," he said. "They don't hurt, but they don't always seem to work that well either. But I would have recommended that whatever they had be used immediately anyway, before the slick had a chance to weather." That was also the advice of Harvard chemist James Butler, who chaired the panel.

What about the criticism that dispersants would not work because it was too calm?

"I keep hearing that," Payne said. "A coastie, or someone in Valdez, told me that you have to have wind before you can apply them. I said, 'Where did you get that idea?' He said, 'The National Research Council report.'

"I told him, 'Yes, *ultimately* you need energy. But where does it say in the report that you need wind at the time you put the dispersants on? Spray the stuff and wait for the wind to work.' "

I objected that although I had not absorbed every word in the 300-page report, my inference too was that wind was required at the time.

"We don't say that," Payne countered. "Anyway, this is not a field manual. It's a ponderous volume. We went through three years of rewrites before all the members were satisfied with the handling of the conclusions. You can't just grab it in an emergency and know what to do."

"But this is a major misunderstanding about dispersants," I persisted. It struck me that the decisions made and not made over that weekend, and the fingerpointing of blame afterward, hinged on a faulty knowledge of the technology. In hindsight the panel's report seemed almost irresponsibly unclear.

"So sue me," Payne said, his voice flat and tinny on his speakerphone. I didn't mean to fault him personally. This to me was nescience, an example of it. Nescience was the lag-time between the germination of a scientific truth and its public flowering. Indeed, when the wind in the Sound at last started to pick up, a fourth trial was held, and this time it looked as though the chemicals were starting to work. (One year later, when the *Mega Borg* spill occurred off Texas, Jim Payne came up with hard data, not just visual observations, that an application of dispersants helps to break up a slick.)

Under leaden skies Prudhoe Bay crude drifts southwest of Bligh Reef, like a gray cat languidly stretching, about to make a dash. In two and a half days the slick has spread less than twenty miles. The solution to pollution is dilution. If you can't stop it, then burn it, disperse it—don't just stand there. Owen Myers, a Canadian fisheries expert, has an apt quote: "An hour at the beginning of a spill is worth a month at the end, when beaches are being cleaned up and the damage has been done."

NATIONAL WEATHER SERVICE maps for Saturday, March 25, and Sunday, March 26, 1989, show a low pressure system in the Gulf of Alaska moving north toward Prince William Sound, and a large high pressure system building over the Alaskan interior. On the first map the concentric isobar lines of the two systems are spaced fairly widely, indicating a relaxed pressure gradient and thus not much wind across the systems. In a startling change the next day, the isobars are strongly compressed, as if tectonic plates were colliding above the earth.

Weather systems don't penetrate the upthrust coastal mountains easily. Just as low pressure stalls and brings rain upon the Sound, high pressure, a massing of dense air in the interior, builds like water in a bucket and then spills over the Chugach range through the glacial passes. Late on Easter Sunday, the drainage winds began to flow onto Prince William Sound, stirring a smattering of dispersant into the slick and encouraging authorities to plan a major chemical attack for Monday.

The atmospheric cascade increased overnight. Air flooded in a rush toward the low pressure sump impinging from the Gulf. In the morning near the Valdez Glacier the winds were blowing seventy miles per hour from the northeast. Insulation scattered from the roof of the terminal building at the airport, and volunteers had to hold on to helicopters by their blades lest the machines cartwheel away. Out in the Sound the gusts reached forty knots (46 mph). The bleeding tanker pivoted slightly from the gale, causing hearts to leap into mouths, but it only wedged tighter onto the reef.

March was going out like a lion, chasing the oil in long windrows under sunny, sharp-edged skies. Boats, dispersant planes, animal rescue operations were grounded. Frank Iarossi, the ranking Exxon executive in Valdez, moaned, "The slick is moving like it's on a superhighway. What happened was our worst fears." Scientists went to their drift equations and calculated that the slick was traveling southwest at the rate of twenty miles per day. No one had ever seen oil move that fast. On Monday night the winds rose again to seventy knots.

The oil scudded toward Naked Island, chaotically uncontiguous, a patchwork quilt of gray, brown and black. Between Sunday and Tuesday the area of oiled ocean quintupled, from 100 to 500 square miles. About 80 percent of the petroleum was concentrated at the front end of the slick, bunched there by the wind, and large sheens trailed behind.

According to an analysis by NOAA oceanographers Jerry Galt and Debra Payton, the windstorm had three important physical consequences. First, it broke the pool of oil into diffuse bands and streaks. Second, it accelerated the mixing processes of evaporation, dissolution and dispersion. Third, although the mixing removed about 30 percent of the oil from the slick, the volume of the slick at the same time tripled, due to a process called emulsification.

It's no use contending anymore that oil and water don't mix. When whipped by wind, crude oil incorporates water and swells into mousse. A dessert mousse we know as a spongy blend, or emulsion, of cream, egg and flavoring. Homogenized milk is an emulsion of cream and milk. Basically, an emulsion is a liquid suspended in a liquid. Oil mousse (a bona fide scientific term) is an emulsion of oil and water that looks rather like its chocolate counterpart. Particles of water have been thoroughly dispersed into the oil matrix.

If oil dispersed in the sea is an oil-in-water emulsion, in which the oil "disappears" into the water, the opposite is mousse, a water-in-oil emulsion, in which it is the water that seems to go away. The stuff looks like pure oil, yet under the microscope countless water droplets are sprinkled like beads of light on the brown. Natural surfactants again are the catalysts. The dispersant process works both ways simultaneously, as different sets of surfactants compete with each other. During the storm, oil droplets were dispersing into the Sound, but to a greater extent the Sound was dispersing into the slick, causing its volume to expand. The mousse eventually comprised twice as much water as oil.

In his wave tanks Payne had found that an emulsion of half water and half oil formed after one week and hardly changed during the next thirteen months. Viscous mousse resists breaking down. Aromatic compounds that haven't escaped are bound within. Chemical dispersants tend to wash off of mousse. The water content makes it almost impossible to burn. Exxon tried to torch part of the slick at Eleanor Island on the fifth day of the spill, but it wouldn't ignite.

Mousse also weighs more than fresh petroleum. Payne found that weathering increased the density of his samples to 98 percent of that of water. Skimmer vessels can't lift mousse from the surface as easily as fresh oil. Moreover, in the Sound, the mousse picked up seaweed, feathers and spruce needles, causing weir belts and pumps to clog. Unavoidably the ugly brown clumps came to be known as turds.

The spill scientists in Valdez were dealing now with a transmogrified oil, less acutely toxic, but nastily durable and still moving. Brown-black mousse bowled down the alleys of western Prince William Sound, careening back and forth with shifts of wind, smacking islands and coastline, ducking into bays, flung by the storm into the treetops in some places, and at the end of the lane what oil was left rolled into the Gulf of Alaska.

Oceanographers Galt and Payton have traced two main arteries of oil in the Sound. The larger mass carried on the prevailing current through Montague Strait, hitting Smith, Green and the east coast of Knight Island. This oil exited the Sound at the end of March, having struck Latouche Island head-on and menaced the AFK fish hatchery at Sawmill Bay. A weaker and slower artery followed Knight Island Passage down the west side of that island. A pulse of northwest wind drove parts of this oil deep into Northwest Bay on Eleanor and Herring Bay on Knight.

Other patches of the slick hovered for days in the northwest Sound. Then on April 10 an east wind came up and pushed the last of the free oil onto Perry Island. By this time, of course, the Kenai and Kodiak areas on the Gulf of Alaska coast were getting theirs. Tarballs and patches of mousse bobbed hundreds of miles from Bligh Reef.

NOAA prepared its official map of the oil spill after the fact, by a method called hindcasting. First Galt and Payton compiled all the information bearing on the oil's movements—the daily overflight observations, the radar images of the slick, the weather reports, wind directions and current speeds, the latter radioed to satellites by drift buoys. Then they tested the field information against a computer's version of the trajectory. NOAA's On-Scene Spill Model (OSSM, pronounced "awesome") is a program built upon the trajectories of a number of past spills. The key input in this instance was the pattern of the Alaska Coastal Current through the Sound.

In their report Galt and Payton noted that since neither the computer model nor the fieldwork was totally reliable alone, in combining them the uncertainties and errors could be identified. A sighting of oil upwind and upcurrent of the trajectory must have been a false positive, that is, from a source other than the tanker, and therefore was thrown out by the computer. In another case of a false positive, a sheen was determined to be biogenic hydrocarbons from a large kelp bed. Conversely, if the verified sightings of oil showed the slick moving faster or slower than the computer said it should be, the computer must be wrong. The program was stopped, fine-tuned and run again from the beginning.

Hindcasting is forecasting against a proven outcome, but in fact the rough trajectory Galt and Payton predicted at the time was accurate also. The two researchers told me that everything had indicated a southwestward movement of oil, even when they allowed for winds not yet in force. During the crisis Galt and Payton urged the Coast Guard to direct the containment and cleanup equipment preemptively toward the west and southwest, leaving the southeastern Sound, the town of Cordova and the Copper River Delta exposed. "For the oil to get to Cordova would have required a northwest wind, against the current," Payton said, "and northwest winds are very rare and not long sustained in the Sound at that time of year." But because the town was frightened, some boom was pulled from the west to protect it.

For a week a NOAA plane flew daily over the eastern Sound to check out reputed sightings of oil near Cordova. As late as April 8, with the spill two weeks old and its course irrevocable in the other direction, the town was shaken by a report of "acres of oil sheen" on the flats nearby. Authorities diagnosed a plankton bloom. Another reported sheen was definitely oil, but from a tanker other than the *Exxon Valdez*.

Galt and Payton concluded their trajectory analysis with an unusual commentary on the public reaction: "During the course of the spill, ice, internal waves, kelp beds, natural organics coming from kelp beds, pollen, plankton blooms, cloud shadows, and guano washing off rocks were all reported at one time or another as oil. These, of course, were in addition to the hundreds of reports of real oil, of which there was a good deal to look at. Press, television, and newsmagazine accounts typically treated all reports the same; the most common representation of the spill that was presented to the public was a continuous black blob extending from Prince William Sound to somewhere in the Aleutians. It is easy to see why the several hundred million people who were interested in the spill and had no other sources of information, thought that the spill looked like a six-hundred-mile-long parking lot."

A persistent local rumor about the spill was that oil was sinking and would contaminate the bottom. When I got to the Sound in May, I heard so many reports of this that I believed it for a long time afterward. Kelley Weaverling, the organizer of the animal rescue fleet, told the newspapers he saw oil come up on an anchor. "It doesn't take a scientist to interpret data like that," he said. When the NOAA experts challenged stories about submerged lenses of oil, arguing that Prudhoe Bay crude was not dense enough to sink, the head of the state's Department of Environmental Conservation, Dennis Kelso, insisted, "I believe there's something under the water."

A biologist named John French publicized an experiment in which a piece of mousse, containing "substantial amounts of gravel and other detritus," sank to the bottom of a glass tank. Therein lies the explanation. If hydrocarbons do manage to reach the ocean floor after an oil spill, they are carried there by a heavier material.

Technically, what happens is particulate adsorption. Suspended particulate materials, or SPM, consist of sand, clay, powdered rock, organic detritus—the load of sediment that drifts inertly in the sea. Particulates are usually microscopic, but in high concentrations their effect is to reduce the clarity of the water. Suspended particulates are highest in the turbulent zone where waves strike the beach. In the Sound SPM are also elevated near glacial streams, which discharge plumes of powdered rock, the so-called glacial milk or flour.

Since suspended sediment eventually sinks, any hydrocarbons clinging (adsorbed) to them may be borne to the bottom. The heavier compounds are the ones that tend to stick. If, on the other hand, the near-shore water is clear of particles, adsorption and sinking can't take place. From his experimental data Jim Payne posited a specific level of suspended sediments—one to ten milligrams SPM per liter of seawater, or one to ten parts per million—

below which oil could not be transported to the bottom, at least not in any detectable amounts.

"The water clarity in the Sound is incredibly good," Payne said. Anyone who has boated in this drowned canyon of rock would have to agree. A scuba diver I met likes to watch Pacific octopuses prowling on the bottom; he compares the visibility to the Caribbean's. At the time of the spill in early spring, glacial runoff was limited and likewise the glacial flour. SPM concentrations should have been low off the beaches, and therefore the hydrocarbons measured in the water column and bottom sediments should be very low as well.

Payne had a chance to test his model when the NOAA staff in Valdez enlisted him as a consultant. In early April he was taken aboard a vessel that was gathering samples in the Sound. Suspended particulates proved to be below his 1-10 ppm cutoff nearly everywhere. Oil/SPM interactions were not measurable.

However, it was early in the spill. As part of the damage assessment program, government researchers kept watch on particulate adsorption off the oiled beaches. Whether from the action of the cleanup flushing or from the energy of the waves and tides, the hydrocarbons began to migrate through the intertidal zone and then down along the subtidal slope toward the bottom. Faint fingerprints of the *Exxon Valdez* were identifiable at sixty-foot depths in 1990. At depths greater than that, the oil particles became mixed with other sources of hydrocarbons, possibly from the Katalla seeps.

Jim Payne had a good outing in '89. He demonstrated that the oil never became dense enough to sink on its own. His other projections of oil's fates, including those pertaining to the limited dissolution of aromatics and the high water content of mousse, were upheld. In his formal reports he referred to "an unfortunate but scientifically valuable spill of opportunity," whose field results showed "remarkably good agreement" with prespill studies for NOAA.

"Yes, I was really excited about the findings," he told me. "Every time there's an oil spill, they call me and ask, 'What's it going to do?' And I would tell them, 'Based on the wave tank and other studies, you can expect this and this and this to happen.' Now we have the field data to prove what we were saying."

That phrase of his, spill of opportunity. Payne was not the only scientist in the Sound to employ it. I found it jarring that a disaster in the eyes of most people should be seized by the cognoscenti as a chance to validate their theories. A biologist with the U.S. Fish and Wildlife Service, who was a student of sea otters, cracked, "All these bodies and look at the research I can do," and for months he did not hear the end of it. Some people thought the scientists cold, which was unfair. Rather it was that they had work to do, and something to focus on besides their helpless feelings.

"On the [April] cruise we didn't see many of the mortalities," Payne said. "We weren't working close to shore that much. But yes, we saw oiled birds. Floating in it, you got a heartsick feeling. It was a horrible spill. But was it like Hiroshima? No."

DOUGLAS WOLFE was assigned by NOAA to reconstruct the behavior of the oil spill. He synthesized the field reports and drew inferences from prespill experimental work. The first part of his analysis was a breakdown of the oil's fate during its first month in the environment.

"By the end of April, 1989," Wolfe wrote, "approximately 20% of the spilled oil had evaporated, and approximately 20-25% had been dispersed naturally into the water column. About 25% of the oil had been carried out of Prince William Sound as floating or dispersed oil, and most of the remainder (approximately 40-45%) had beached within the Sound."

I am going to disregard the oil that "disappeared," and also the oil outside of the Sound that didn't. Many tarballs and thick clumps of mousse washed ashore on the Kenai Peninsula, Kodiak Island and the Alaska Peninsula. The oil slick was the farthest-reaching in history, as bits floated to land 500 miles from Bligh Reef. Still, the coastal contamination outside the Sound comprised less than 10 percent of the original volume spilled, according to Wolfe. The western beaches within the Sound took by far the heaviest hit.

What happened to the petroleum after it stranded depended in large part upon the composition and orientation of the shoreline. If the shore happened to be a rock headland, fronting a broad fetch of ocean, the oil stuck uneasily, prone to removal by the next scouring storm. If the shore was a beach of porous cobble, at the head of a crooked bay, the oil penetrated deeply and sheened long after the surface rocks were clean. Heavy mousse deposited high on packed gravel became an asphalt crust; light mousse became a flaking scale. And so forth: The Sound had a dozen types of shore, a dozen dispositions for the oil. The patchiness of the environment was captured perfectly in the diffuse nature of the beached oil.

Science no longer played catch-up, in academic pursuit of its subject, because the oil was no longer in transition in the sea. The oil rested truculently on land, each spot different but each spot the same one day as the next, and something had to be done about it.

Thus a new cadre of experts came forward to advise the authorities on cleanup. These experts were called coastal geomorphologists. Geomorphology deals with the surface features of earth; coastal geomorphology in regard to oil spills is a rare but well-developed subspecialty.

Here is a taste of the calculations made by the specialists. The oil that came ashore was categorized as heavy, moderate, light and very light, depending on the area of coverage. The substrate of the shore, its composition, was categorized as bedrock, mixed sediments, or cobble. The orientation of the shore was categorized as exposed (subject to high-energy wave action), moderate or sheltered (receiving low-energy waves). By these criteria, thirty-six possibilities were created, each deserving a different response by the authorities.

In other words, after the oil was beached, the spill's fate gave way to numbers. Numbers were what the cleanup was all about. People created them and then conquered them, in an attempt to make headway against the patchiness of the Sound. Yet the numbers were never uniform; different sets were put in play. The authorities did not agree on even such basic figures as the miles that were oiled, because of the air of recrimination in Valdez.

For example, in mid-May I interviewed Dr. Al Maki, the biologist who served as Exxon's chief scientist. I had seen Maki the week before on ABC's *Nightline*. The producers had pitted him against the state environmental commissioner, who brought onto the set a bottle of oily gravel and used it to make a point about what the spill could do to a baby seal. In a lead-in piece, an ABC correspondent presented wrenching pictures of the disaster. Holding a three-day-old harbor seal to the camera, the correspondent said, "They talk about this oil spill in terms of water columns, miles of beaches, impact on commercial fisheries. If you want to know what it's all about, really, take a look at this face." Following a break for advertisements, Exxon's Maki was introduced to the screen.

He was still smoldering about it. "When they look at the impact out there," he said, "they're narrowing in, given the extent of the shoreline, so that you have no real concept of what the Sound looks like. You think all of the Sound, all of Alaska, is oiled and dead—there aren't any more animals left, that's the end of the sea otters and the fishery is dead. Well, let's look at the real facts, as I was trying to do on the show. The oil is on less than ten percent of the linear shoreline of Prince William Sound."

The real facts. I was familiar with Maki's 10-percent figure. What it represented was 350 miles of shoreline contamination (light, moderate or heavy), of a total 3,500 miles within Prince

William Sound. The latter figure included both mainland and island perimeters.

Ten percent did not sound like much of an impact. However, if the PWS shoreline measured only 2,000 linear miles, as one government agency maintained, then one could show a greater impact from the slick. If one narrowed the universe further, to the western Sound where the spill had drifted, the proportion would of course climb higher.

Everybody could be correct about the miles. It depended on how closely one applied one's tape measure to the infinite scallops and points of the coastline. Fractal geometry was flexible. By no coincidence, Exxon's 3,500 miles for the whole Sound was the highest estimate in use.

Even the earthquake had a confounding role. The '64 earthquake had thrown the existing charts of the Sound out of whack. The depths of certain channels were uncertain. Maps showed less coast than was actually there, because shoreline mileage had been increased by the uplift (more than was lost to the limited downwarping). In the summer of '89 Exxon had to remap everything.

Some of this I put to Maki. If something so seemingly incontrovertible as the length of a shoreline was open to interpretation, then weren't all of the facts in the Sound up for grabs? The scientist went along with me, cautiously.

It was a consequence of applied science, was it not? Feeling the political heat, science had started to precipitate divergent facts for divergent applications.

"What do you want to talk about?" Maki interjected. "Water quality? What?"

I didn't know. Maki had all the facts. I had feelings, not yet calcified into facts. Maki was prepared to give me figures on hydrocarbons in the water in parts per million. Like other reporters, I was juggling too many numbers, and knew less about the oil spill than before I came to the Sound.

"I can tell you there was tremendous maneuvering in Valdez over the numbers," said NOAA's David Kennedy afterward. "Yet as many different ways as we sliced it and diced it, we didn't get to all the possibilities, such as"—and here Kennedy addressed a key question—"trying to compare how much oil was removed in the first year by the cleanup and how much by natural forces."

We will come back to that question. For although Exxon's $2-billion, three-year project was extraordinary, unprecedented, most of it was unnecessary. The cleanup was mainly an exercise in corporate contrition. It was overkill that fell short, a paradox obscured by an overkill of figures.

My subject is not the political histrionics of the cleanup, but the cast of characters must be given. There were three contesting authorities in the Sound, the federal government, the state government and Exxon. Each employed a coastal geomorphologist.

The ultimate authority lay with the Coast Guard, whose ranking officer was called the federal on-scene coordinator. The junior authority was the Alaska Department of Environmental Conservation, DEC. If dissatisfied at any time with Exxon's voluntary efforts, the Coast Guard could have federalized the cleanup and held the company accountable for the costs. Such a move was threatened but never acted upon. The spill was simply too great for the government to handle. Exxon's authority lay in its purse.

The Coast Guard relied for scientific and technical advice on Hazmat, short for NOAA's Hazardous Materials Response Branch. (It has since been upgraded to Hazardous Materials Response and Assessment Division.) David Kennedy, John Robinson, Jerry Galt and Debra Payton all belonged to Hazmat. Hazmat hired Jim Payne to do chemistry. Doug Wolfe belonged to a different branch of NOAA.

The three shoreline geomorphologists were independent consultants. Hazmat contracted Jacqueline Michel, a longtime NOAA adviser. DEC engaged Erich Gundlach. Exxon's coastal specialist was Edward Owens.

Drs. Michel, Gundlach and Owens knew each other well. "We are the big three of oil spill geomorphology," said Michel. Gundlach said, "I'd say we're the *only* three. Ed and Jacqui and I are the only ones to publish [scientific papers] and stay current. But in this game you don't do spills all the time. Ed says it's as though GM, Ford and Chrysler made one car per year."

In the '70s Owens and later Gundlach earned doctoral degrees at the University of South Carolina under a coastal geomorphologist named Miles Hayes. Michel was not a graduate student of Hayes—but she married him and now they run a consulting business together. Gundlach worked with Hayes and Michel for a while, then went out on his own. Ed Owens left South Carolina earlier; he joined Woodward-Clyde Consultants in Seattle and most of his work has been for industry. It was logical, in the spring of '89, that Owens would sign on with Exxon and Michel with NOAA/Hazmat, leaving Erich Gundlach, who has adroitly served both government and industry, to take the state job.

As Hayes trained them to do, each specialist established fifteen to twenty stations on beaches in the western Sound. They and their assistants collected hydrocarbon samples for analysis, monitored changes in oil cover and penetration and traced the reworking of beach profiles caused by the elements and the cleanup crews. With a budget of several million dollars and a staff of fifty, Owens's project was the most ambitious of the three. "A staggering number of observations were made," Owens said. "But we three saw the same things and basically didn't disagree on anything."

"While not exactly the same," Michel put it, "our results are more or less compatible."

At first I failed to see the big three's collegiality. In individual conversations with me they would casually dismiss one another, sniffing at this or that finding, and their presentations at meetings seemed to have little in common. Each scientist's talk echoed the point of view of his or her sponsoring agency, as did their published papers. But the rivals could have their cake and eat it too. The shoreline and oiling conditions were so variable that it was a matter of emphasizing one set of facts at the expense of examples that did not suit as well. As John Robinson explained, "What happens is not changing data to suit your position. You're always backed with facts. It's the selective omission in what you say." Outside the spotlight the three maintained an accord.

The important thing was the agendas of the authorities applying the science. To begin with NOAA/Hazmat: Based in Seattle and led by Robinson, the unit brought a wealth of experience to the Sound. Since the late '70s Hazmat has provided information on oceanography, meteorology, oil weathering, slick trajectory and shoreline conditions to the Coast Guard during marine oil spills. It also advises the Environmental Protection Agency on hazardous waste incidents. Between October '88 and October '89 Hazmat responded to eighty oil spills and thirty-one chemical spills in the United States. Two of the oil spills involved almost half a million gallons, big by normal standards, but dwarfed that year by the *Exxon Valdez*.

Robinson himself knew the Sound from OSCEAP work he directed in the '70s. Jacqui Michel (with Gundlach and Hayes) had prepared maps for OSCEAP rating the vulnerability of the Sound's shoreline to oiling. Michel and a half dozen Hazmat staffers were in Valdez within twenty-four hours of the spill. The NOAA personnel stabilized at about a dozen, though more than twice that number rotated through their small office. They wore gray jumpsuits, making it easier to get in and out of the orange survival suits they wore on the helicopters. Robinson and Kennedy spelled each other in command in fourteen-day shifts; one of the two was always in Seattle to manage other emergencies.

Ironically, the lesson of Hazmat's experience was that the best course following the stranding of crude oil is to do relatively little.

Its philosophy was to mop up the worst and leave the rest to waves and weathering. "I've said all along that nature does a wonderful job of cleaning up," Kennedy told me. "But anything that's heavy—if you have eighteen inches of oil on the beach, you've got to take that, or else it'll migrate around and hit other beaches."

In intensifying the cleanup process, people could harm the littoral environment more than help it. The blasting of the Cornwall shore with detergents after the *Torrey Canyon* spill was a notorious example; another was the bulldozing that destroyed a marsh in Brittany following the *Amoco Cadiz* spill in 1978. John Robinson recalled that in April, before the cleanup plan was resolved, Hazmat considered recommending to the Coast Guard that nothing be done to the Sound—"whether we should just quarantine the shore and leave."

"Cumulatively on the staff we have seen over 1,000 spills," Robinson continued, "but still we have to draw a lot on intuition to say what might happen. The weight of opinion was to go with a cleanup, knowing we'd incur some damage." He conceded, "There was a [public] steamroller for cleanup, so it would have taken hard evidence, not intuition, to stop it."

The cry for aggressive action was overwhelming. The Coast Guard was not about to buck national and local sentiment, especially as it was given voice by angry state regulators. The Department of Environmental Conservation, though its oversight was spotty before the accident, was relentless in the aftermath. It would never satisfy the DEC or the Fish and Game Department that just the thickest oil be removed, as NOAA would have it. Alaska wished every poisonous drop to be gone from the environment. Its cleanup monitors, clinging to that ideal, became estranged from the Hazmat staff, whose reluctance to belabor the cleanup eventually converged with Exxon's desire to save money. Outgunned by Exxon's superior resources and NOAA's superior knowledge, the state nevertheless had a powerful weapon in passion.

Erich Gundlach recalled, "To some in DEC, NOAA looked like a subsidiary of Exxon. They would say, 'We know it [the oil] is all going to go away. It's not going to be a problem.' They have a callousness toward it. They come in and tell you how it's gonna go and that's it. Instead of a spill in Texas, or Maine or wherever, this one is Alaska."

As for the third authority, Exxon at first had little say or standing in the matter. The company had assumed responsibility for the oil spill and now it had to deliver. Hurrying to get started, Exxon sent workers to Naked Island in April to wipe rocks by hand, bringing upon it ridicule in addition to outrage. The company submitted a formal cleanup plan on May 1, then beefed up its commitment when the plan was criticized as insufficient.

Said Ed Owens, its shoreline adviser, "We in the business agree that oil spills don't do long-term damage and that you can do more damage cleaning them up. What happens is that the scientists make their opinions known, and if the driving forces, socioeconomic or political, are otherwise, then we say, 'Well, seeing as you're having to do this, you might as well do it this way.'

"So the basic method chosen, washing, was better than the alternative, which was to dig up the sediments and take them away. In that sense the rocky nature of the shoreline made it an easy spill. It wasn't oil on a marsh, for example, which is the hardest to deal with."

The company launched a graduated assault. The first washing method that was implemented was to pump seawater onto the beach, whence it flowed down and dislodged oil from the intertidal zone. There was a deluge system, from a manifold, which was a perforated hose laid high up on the beach and parallel to the waterline. At the same time men with fire hoses directed cold water onto spots.

But the Coast Guard and DEC officials became impatient with the system, partly because the mousse became less mobile over time. It was decided to turn up the heat and pressure. A hot-water wash was instituted, with seawater heated initially to eighty degrees F. and eventually up to 140 degrees. The water was applied by hoses and by hand wands, slender spray guns used for spotwashing. The water pressure was increased from fifty to 120 pounds per square inch.

Though the washing techniques were not new, Exxon's engineering was. As the cleanup force swelled, the vessels generating the water evolved into formidable cleaning machines. The first pumps were installed on landing-craft vessels (LCVs), forty to seventy-five feet in length, some borrowed from the military. Then the so-called Maxi-barge was hauled into the field—a barge up to 180 feet long and outfitted with diesel heaters, water cannons and a platform that could lift a man with a hose sixty feet. Finally, Exxon designed the Omni-barge, the pride of the fleet, a self-propelled behemoth that projected 500 gallons a minute through spray heads mounted at the end of a 100-foot-long mechanical arm. The Omni-boom's elbow joint allowed the hot jets to reach angled rock faces and steep beaches that were not accessible to the shoreline workers. Thirteen Omni-barges were deployed, and as many Maxis.

Whatever the washing system, the flushed oil was intercepted at the waterline by sorbent boom, or upon the water by skimmer vessels. Rope-mop skimmers, which circulated a line of sorbent material, and paddle-belt skimmers, which scooped up the oil on a conveyor belt of disks, seemed to work best. Hoses herded the floating crude toward the shallow-draft skimmers, which were stationed close to shore within semicircles of containment boom.

The idea was to prevent free oil from escaping into the Sound, but it didn't always succeed. NOAA took aerial photos of the operation. A barge was attached like a large bug to the beach, with yellow legs of boom and a proboscis fiercely jetting water, and yet off the shore a rogue sheen drifted placidly on the wind. Wolfe, in his estimate of the oil's fates, considered the amount of oil recovered on the water to be insignificant.

Technology was touted, but it was raw human labor that made the cleanup go. Exxon called the men and women on the beaches OSRTs, or oil spill response technicians. A professional put it to me more bluntly: "undertakers of the oil world." Alaskans were enlisted by the hundreds at hiring halls, and dispatched to the field in task forces. Since the job didn't stop on weekends and at times went round the clock, crews were shuttled in and out of the Sound in shifts. The OSRTs did not just aim hoses. Much of it was stoop labor, like farmwork but harder, cutting and bagging oiled rockweed, shoveling and hauling oiled gravel and debris.

Exxon encouraged comparisons to a military campaign, a mighty war against the spill. From the Valdez command center, the company issued a daily operations status report. The filing of 0800 hours on May 14 was a twenty-page document. On this date the cleanup effort, including work in the Gulf of Alaska, deployed 637 vessels, with thirty-eight more enroute to duty; forty-nine oil skimmers; 427,000 feet of containment boom; thirty-six helicopters, seventeen floatplanes and three photo-surveillance planes; and a total of 6,645 personnel, about a third of whom were on the beaches. There was information as well on pinniped haulout status; salmon hatchery protection; vessel cleaning; salvage work on the tanker; current strategy. If such a report had a bottom line, it was the figure of 10,300 yards of shoreline listed as "cleaned" to date.

I carried this document with me when Exxon mounted a press tour to see Task Force 2 at work. The helicopter first passed over Eleanor Island, deeply scalloped, and then circled Block, Ingot and Disk Islands, narrow and knobby. These four were like vertebral extensions of Knight Island, the main mass to the south. Block Island, where we were to land, was the smallest, only about a mile in circumference. Actually, Block was no longer an island. It became attached to Eleanor after the uplift of the shore in the '64 earthquake.

The aircraft came around a bend and abruptly below was a swarm of activity, as if we had sliced off the top of an anthill. There were boats and booms and hoses and dozens of tiny figures in luminous orange slickers moving about on the shiny stones. The pilot banked and descended. We set down on a grassy flat, separated from the beach by a hummock of woods.

The work crews were about to quit for the day, for it was late afternoon, and my colleagues hurried through the trees. I hung back. Here I was at last at ground zero of the oil spill.

Looking in the opposite direction, I was a little startled to see oil behind me. The quiet cove where we'd landed had been hit as well. I walked down to the cobble beach. The oil was pooled along the rough grade to the waterline. I hunkered down to it. It was dark brown with red highlights, the fumes unmistakable. Emboldened, I stuck my finger down into it, brought it to my nose and sniffed closely. When I rubbed my fingertip on a clean rock, not all the oil came off.

After a few minutes I walked back toward the helicopter, where the pilot and a cleanup supervisor, a couple of good old boys, were shooting the breeze in the strong sunshine. They eyed my extended right finger.

"What do you call the oil when it gets brown and sticky like this?" I asked.

"Slime is what we call it. That's what you got there."

"How do I get it off my finger?"

"Wipe it on the ground," said one.

"You lick it off," said the other.

I paused for a second and plunged the finger into my mouth. The two of them yelped.

Slime was a good description for mousse. It tasted like pond scum laced with motor oil. It definitely wasn't appetizing, but I thought it related to a kind of edibility. I spit it out. According to my research, bacteria should have been feasting on the oil, and the worst of its aromatics should have been stripped away after seven weeks in the environment.

Most of them, anyway. Later I queried Doug Wolfe. My experiment was harmless, right? He withheld judgment until he had examined me thoroughly about the condition of the oil. "Sounds like pretty good stuff," he concluded. "It didn't burn your mouth? OK, it was fairly weathered. Pretty good stuff."

I went over the wooded hummock to the beach on the west

side of Block Island. The tide was low and still receding, leaving a long greasy expanse. The smell was stronger than before. An absorbent boom lay like an oily yellow anaconda along the shore. One hundred tidal cycles, and the Sound had not yet licked it off. Now people were attempting it.

Two dozen workers were loading onto a box-nosed landing craft. They were headed back to the troopship. Treading carefully on the slippery cobbles, I went down to see them off.

"They did a good job today," enthused a Veco foreman. Veco was the labor contractor to Exxon. The workers sat quietly on benches on either side of the LCV.

"What did they get done?" Honestly, I couldn't tell.

The Veco guy pointed to a section of the beach where the coating seemed grayer and less shiny. I nodded and looked back at the rows of tired, dirty faces. A Navy seaman in a spotless uniform cranked up the loading platform, sealing the people in. The vessel edged around the point and out of the cove. It was quiet again.

The view to the north was of white tetrahedrons rising from the sea, an endless mountain panorama starting to glow in the low-angled light. It struck me as so beautiful that I had to turn away in a kind of embarrassment. I teetered back toward the head of the beach, where a new green sprout of salmonberry was growing between the dirty stones.

WHEN I RETURNED to the Sound in the summer of '89, the cleanup force was twice as large and the math of the effort had become more complex. Exxon devised a standard called "equivalent yards." Equivalent yards were a measure of the degree of oiling of a length of beach. A heavily contaminated segment had more equivalent yards than a lightly oiled segment of the same length. The productivity of a washing vessel was said to be the number of equivalent yards it could treat in a twelve-hour day. The numbers were crunched, and the result was that the Omni-barge was found to be two to three times more productive than an LCV washer. This was exactly as projected on the drawing board beforehand. It never failed. Whatever the chart or graph, Exxon was constantly shown to be meeting or exceeding its goals.

The Coast Guard, which had to approve the work when completed, got the hang of the math as well. Assisted by NOAA/Hazmat, it came up with a yardstick called "clydes," an acronym for cleanup yield during Exxon spill. As defined in a 1991 Coast Guard report, "The parameters for the calculation of clydes included the type, length, and width of beach, extent of oiling, sediment type, oil permeation depth, and quantity of debris. The calculation showed the relative amount of work in clydes needed to treat each identified segment of beach."

Thus at the beginning of the spill there were some 29,000 clydes to be dealt with. As the weeks passed, the number of clydes went down. There were no clydes left at the end of the summer. But what did this progress have to do with the true state of the Sound, which was still bleeding oil?

For the Coast Guard report continued: "The term 'treatment' was used as opposed to 'cleaning' to indicate that no further work would be required after the initial effort to remove gross contamination." The calculations, elastic to begin with, were stretched to accommodate the difficulty of the task. Even the state DEC came to see that a full cleanup would be impossible in 1989. By agreement the goal was scaled back, and treatment substituted for cleanup.

The problem lay with the oil beneath the cobble surface. According to a technical paper by Exxon: "Where oil had penetrated into coarse sediments, a rising tide would often lift enough oil to the surface to cause previously cleaned rocks to be recoated with a shiny film of oil. This 'tidal pumping' phenomenon was frustrating to the cleanup crews, which ended up cleaning and recleaning some beaches many times." In addition, oil was drifting free and tainting other beaches.

As mightily as it washed, often the best that Exxon could do was to strip off the superficial contamination. Best to scratch off the clydes, count up the miles and move the crews to the next section, before the tide came back and ruined the work. On September 15 it would be moot anyway, for that was the day Exxon would halt operations.

The cleanup created its own language and logic. It created a routine, a rhythm for everyone involved. Once or twice a week, I hitched a ride to Valdez from the lake in Cordova. The pilot and floatplane worked each day for DEC, although Exxon was responsible for the cost of this and other activities of spill response. Dave Beck would take off early. If the weather wasn't too bad, he liked to go straight over the top, between the peaks and the clouds, buzzing mountain goats and unnamed glaciers, rather than follow the shoreline along the Sound and into Valdez Arm. We would land on Robe Lake, the town swimming area serving as a floatplane base. Swans turned in the morning mist. In the hut off the rampway, Exxon had laid out smoked fish and doughnuts, our breakfast. We weren't the only ones eating. The cleanup spending by Exxon had started an economic boom not only in Valdez but across the whole state.

Some began to object to the routine. Fishermen in Cordova turned against the cleanup, as did their scientific adviser, Riki Ott. An Earth First! protester chained her neck to the door of the new Exxon building in Valdez. Earth First! wanted a halt to the project, said a spokesman, because workers were leaving garbage, spilling fuel and generally abusing the wilderness, while the only difference between the beaches that had been cleaned (treated) and those that hadn't was fewer puddles of oil.

A U.S. congressman visited the Sound incognito and wrote an editorial in the *Wall Steet Journal* titled "Turn the Valdez Cleanup over to Mother Nature." The piece was posted in the NOAA/Hazmat office. "What is all that money accomplishing?" the congressman asked. "Not much. Worse, workers may be doing more harm than good to the fragile bays and beaches of Prince William Sound." Behind the scenes, an Exxon-contracted biologist named Jonathan Houghton sent a memo to Al Maki, the chief scientist, urging, "Enough is enough."

NOAA got Exxon to fund a study of the impact of the Omni-barge hot-water cleaning. The site selected for the test, in Herring Bay on Knight Island, had never been treated since being oiled more than three months earlier. Gundlach, Michel and Owens, the three geomorphologists, came to see how much oil would be taken out, and biologist Houghton monitored the effects of the washing on intertidal life.

Enveloped in acrid steam, the Omni-boom pounded two sections of beach, one for almost three hours and the other for an hour and a half. According to Michel's report for NOAA, each round of treatment removed about half of the surface contamination, and much less than that of subsurface oil. Because the longer treatment wasn't any more productive than the shorter one, the duration of the high-pressure, hot-water flushing ought to be shorter. On this her two colleagues were in agreement.

Michel became concerned that oil and sediment were being transported down onto untainted areas in the lower intertidal and subtidal zones where marine life was rich. She considered the treatment to be causing, in effect, a second oil spill. But Exxon's Owens disputed that erosion from the flushing was a serious problem. Gundlach allowed that hydrocarbon concentrations were magnified below, if not sedimentation.

Exxon would not release its biological report on the test, but NOAA officials made no secret of their concerns. "That hot water—what does it do?" said David Kennedy. "It's cooking some of the beach life, and the high pressure is stripping away some of the rest."

Although DEC was constantly nipping at Exxon's heels over violations of cleanup procedures, littering being but one, it wouldn't go so far as to call for a halt. "The state didn't know how long Exxon would play the game," Gundlach recalled. "The thought was, get the oil out while Exxon still has its wallet open. Let the beach life recolonize afterwards. As for NOAA, they couldn't have it both ways. They led the charge for the cleanup."

Exxon bulled ahead. Its managers pressed for approval of a new method, a chemical beach-cleaner called Corexit 9580. Devised for Alaskan conditions, Corexit was a kerosene-based soak, to be sprayed on weathered oil and then flushed with the usual wash. NOAA and DEC were opposed. I covered a meeting held to debate the issue. The company showed a videotape in which a supervisor intoned, "Corexit brings out the natural beauty of the rocks." Exxon's lead engineer was scornful when I questioned computations showing that Corexit increased the number of square feet treated per hour. The Coast Guard never did appprove the chemical.

Another treatment method was granted approval grudgingly. Exxon called it "natural recovery." Natural recovery meant doing nothing. According to a report on its '89 operations, "natural recovery was used frequently at the mouths of anadromous fish streams and other environmentally sensitive areas." It was thought that the salmon should spawn without disruption, even if sediments were oily.

In addition, NOAA/Hazmat conducted a small experimental program of doing nothing, of no cleanup, that is, on select parts of the shoreline. The set-aside program was an attempt to establish what scientists call control or reference sites. The set-asides would be like Jim Payne's wave tanks. How would untreated beaches compare with the others over time? It would give a handle on the efficacy of the cleanup. Ed Owens said he argued for including the whole of Sleepy Bay, a scallop-mouthed embayment on Latouche Island and perhaps the oiliest place in the Sound. Such a large-scale test of long-term weathering was never in the cards. DEC was wary of "sacrifices" and wanted assurances that the set-asides would be cleaned up eventually.

While NOAA wrangled with the state over locations and liability, the cleanup machine nearly made the issue academic. No heavily oiled beaches were spared for the test. "In the end we got only nine sites, nine hundred yards," lamented Robinson, "and one of those might have been already cleaned. The sample isn't large enough." The program appeared to have fizzled, although

Jacqui Michel adopted three of the set-asides among her eighteen monitoring stations in the Sound.

As September arrived, Otto Harrison, Exxon's cleanup manager, was characteristically upbeat. He announced that 2 million man-hours had been expended. The company had a new term to describe the goal of the work: environmental stability, by which it meant that whatever oil remained posed no threat to the environment. "If there's no bad weather," said Harrison, "all the beaches will be treated, cleaned up, environmentally stabilized—whatever."

The September 15 deadline was arbitrary but not spurious. With daylight lessening, working conditions were becoming more dangerous. Rain lashed the windows of my rooms over Lake Eyak. The company publicized records for the Sound showing that after mid-September severe storms blew in every three days. DEC's protest that some form of treatment continue was refused. So I relished the irony, as I boarded the press plane for the company's end-of-cleanup tour, of a stunningly calm and clear day on September 15.

Low fog burned off. Definitely a fall snap was in the air, and a singe to the vegetation of the Sound, tones of gold and rust. With deepening colors a thinness worked down the slopes. The true shapes of the mountains, the bumps and moles on their faces, appeared in relief, the rock emerging to meet the winter.

We flew in a Twin Otter, a roomy floatplane. The Exxon man, Randy Buckley, first showed us boats being scrubbed of oil in a floating dry dock on Naked Island. Then at Eleanor Island's Northwest Bay we inspected EL-52, the pocket beach at the end of the west arm. A DEC vessel happened to be anchored there, and its skiff took a half dozen of us from the plane to shore. The fellow running the skiff was Howard Wood, whom I would meet again in Northwest Bay a few months later. Wood would remind me then, "Yeah, they brought you around at high tide when the oil would show the least, but I guess you had that figured out." What we saw of the beach was quite clean. Pink salmon were scattered in a small stream, played out from the run.

Next was Point Helen on Knight Island. At a press conference the day before, DEC had listed Point Helen among its "dirty dozen" beaches, those most in need of further treatment. Buckley stooped on the shore and pointed out yellow-brown grains of fertilizer, like birdseed on the black-lacquered rocks. This was bioremediation, the newest and most exciting tool in Exxon's treatment box. The idea was to help the resident populations of oil-degrading bacteria. Tests showed that the bugs multiplied in response to nitrogen-phosphorus fertilizer. The boost was applied in fast-acting sprays and slow-acting pellets.

About seventy miles of the Sound had been bioremediated after being washed, including this Point Helen segment just hours earlier. "What I'd like you to keep in mind," Buckley said, "is that the process is not finished. It takes at least a month to work. When we get to Green Island, where we bioremediated six weeks ago, you'll see the end result."

En route to Green we sighted a pair of humpback whales. They lolled on white flippers in the clear water. The plane banked for a closer look, but the animals had disappeared without a ripple. The warm feelings that whales engender seemed to chase away the reporters' skepticism and our guide's stiffness. We all disembarked smiling, and exclaimed at the spotless surface, although bacteria alone could not possibly have cleaned this wave-raked spit, and the oil could be found for the digging.

Six months after oil's fates commenced on Bligh Reef, the crisis was suspended until the following spring. Petroleum still weathered in the Sound. It may have been more dangerous, but the teams of Drs. Michel, Owens and Gundlach continued collecting their separate data on the beaches.

In mid-October of '89 a large storm, coinciding with the highest tides of the year, sent waves breaking over the high-tide berms of the beaches. The upper intertidal, where most of the mousse had lodged and penetrated, was thoroughly agitated, the cobbles tumbling and abrading. Oil was released in dramatic streams. When I called Erich Gundlach, he exulted, "It's what I've been predicting all along."

The experts knew from the histories of other big spills that strong waves purge open shorelines. On the high-energy coast of Brittany, for example, waves stripped off more than half of the Amoco Cadiz oil in four weeks—this was Gundlach's firsthand analysis. If the Sound were as exposed, NOAA might have had a better argument for going slow on the cleanup. But the Sound was an inland sea, many of whose beaches were further sheltered by twists of shoreline. Where the oil lay under gravel it would be triply sheltered. In time the oil would be cleansed, but the question of when gave the experts pause and left the opening for the massive cleanup.

In late November NOAA organized a conference in Anchorage to discuss treatment options for 1990. Michel described the fall storms and the oil's dispersal from high-energy stations. Gundlach was vague about the oil's current status, but showed photos of asphalt crust still conspicuous on a beach in Chile five years after a large spill there, the infamous *Metula* in 1974. He suggested that hard-hit beaches in Alaska might turn out similarly. Owens, when he took the podium, twitted Gundlach about the sheltered morphology of the Chilean shore. Plus the spill there was never subjected to cleanup, let alone to the major work Exxon had undertaken.

By February the impact of the winter storms in the Sound had exceeded just about everyone's expectations. The Exxon managers were ecstatic, pinching themselves when they toured beaches. "Where'd it go?" Owens remembered them asking. After surveys in March and April, a rare scientific consensus was achieved. Over the winter, storms removed between 80 and 90 percent of surface-oil coverage from exposed shorelines; on sheltered shores, storms removed about 50 percent of the surface oil. Subsurface oil, though harder to measure, was believed to have been reduced by about half overall.

One year after the oil spill, there was a sea change in the attitude of the Exxon engineers. Natural forces were hailed as equal partners in shoreline cleanup: "the combination of nature's power and man's perseverance," said a public information video by Exxon. Not only wave action was cited but also tidal pumping, hydrocarbon-degrading microbes and clay-oil flocculation. The latter was a newly identified dispersal process, similar to particulate adsorption.

On the first page of his 1991 report, "Changes in Shoreline Oiling Conditions 1-1/2 Years after the Prince William Sound Spill," Ed Owens stated: "All studies show that the 1989 treatment activities accelerated the natural cleaning, particularly of heavily oiled beaches." In point of fact, there were no studies that showed this, nor that compared the relative contributions of man and nature.

According to DEC's official summary by Gundlach and his associates, the data indicated that "neither surface nor subsurface oiling . . . changed substantially until the winter of 1989/90. . . ." Which implied that the summer's cleanup didn't do much. It is significant that the number of oiled miles in the Sound, about 360 according to Exxon's initial survey, was the same number that DEC found oiled at the end of the summer—a finding the company did not challenge—although the spectrum of contamination had shifted toward the less heavy. The following spring the authorities agreed that 260 miles were oiled to one degree or another, so one can infer that the storms purged 100 miles completely. But no one can show that the level of oiling would have been greater had there been no cleanup at all.

Certainly the cleanup removed some of the oil, but how much? Here is one number never proferred by Exxon. How much oil was salvaged by the skimmers off the beaches? How much was stuck to the tons of oiled gravel, sorbents and debris that was shipped to a landfill in Oregon? According to Ed Owens, the company was more concerned with monitoring trends than with documenting them. Granted a reckoning was very difficult, the more so because the oil was bound up with water.

Estimates by NOAA/Hazmat officials after the first year put the cleanup recovery as high as 20 percent—20 percent, that is, of the original spill volume. The estimate did not distinguish the drifting oil that was picked up during April, prior to its stranding, from the part that was removed from the beaches afterward. At any rate, 20 percent was too hopeful. Doug Wolfe, whose comprehensive analysis covered three years of cleanup, concluded that 8.3 percent of the oil spill was skimmed from the water, almost all of it before the shoreline program started. He found no record of any flushed oil being saved off the beaches, and therefore ignored that aspect of the recovery. He estimated that the shoreline crews got rid of 5.5 percent of the spill as oily solid waste. This measure of efficiency improves somewhat—5.5 percent becomes 14 percent—when related to the amount of the spill that was on the beach, about 40 percent of the original total.

How much, meanwhile, did Exxon's silent partners accomplish? Tenuously, within wide brackets of uncertainty, Wolfe figured that the forces of wave action, bacterial degradation and sediment transport dispersed or eliminated over 80 percent of the stranded oil, equivalent to one third of the amount loosed by the tanker.

All of which confirms that nature had done a better job of shoreline cleanup than Exxon. Yet the idea of a partnership had a certain merit, in that the cleanup helped the environment to absorb the most recalcitrant portion of the spill. By dislodging the heavy mousse, flushing it away where it pooled, the crews spread out the contamination and prevented mats and crust from settling in areas where the waves couldn't reach.

Distilling the ultimate fates from Wolfe's report, one could see that, thanks to natural forces, almost 85 percent of the oil was evaporated, dispersed, degraded and/or weathered to deep-ocean particles no longer recognizable as petroleum hydrocarbons. Essentially, 85 percent of the spill disappeared into the background. As for the remainder, people got it before the elements could. I should say almost all of it. By the end of 1992, according to Wolfe, the amount of oil still present in the intertidal zone was somewhere between .1 and 4 percent of the original volume. I know that for the rest of my life I will be able to go to the Sound and come back with a smudge of the *Exxon Valdez* on my finger. Numbers never tell the whole story.

IN IMPLICIT RECOGNITION of the limits of technology, the 1990 cleanup plan eschewed flotillas, task forces, water cannons and skimmers in favor of small squads of workers with hand tools. The workforce was about a tenth the size previously. The primary target in the second year was subsurface contamination, which was concentrated in about twenty miles' worth of shoreline, and to attack it the crews dug up and then fertilized the beaches. The shoveling exposed hidden oil to the waves, while the bioremediation was meant to augment bacterial degradation. In spots the oil was still very deep. At Sleepy Bay it had penetrated four feet, and the winter storms had cleansed only the uppermost twelve inches.

The secondary target was tar hardening on the higher reaches of protected shores. The workers broke it up and hauled some away in bags. Occasionally, hot-water spot-washing was done with hand wands. The beach-cleaner Corexit was proposed but rejected for the second time. This year there was no attempt at salvage, as the oil that bled from the worked-over sediments was contained by sorbent material placed low on the beach.

The most ambitious work of the summer took place on about two miles of high-energy coastline. The oiliest beaches in the Sound tended to be exposed shores that had been uplifted by the earthquake. Where a veneer of boulders and cobbles lay upon raised bedrock, the oil had seeped into the upper intertidal zone, and particularly into the thick, permeable berm at the top of the beach. The rock armor guarded the subsurface oil and deflected the sporadic probes of high waves.

The solution devised was to excavate the area around the high-tide berm, using backhoes and a bulldozer, and to push the oily rocks down into the mid-tidal zone. There the ocean would not only clean the sediments, but also move them back up, rebuilding the beach profile and storm berm. The technique worked pretty much as planned.

This year a new ideology prevailed. Exxon, the Coast Guard and NOAA/Hazmat had come to see eye to eye on a standard they called "net environmental benefit." Federal and corporate authorities opposed treatment methods whose environmental costs were determined to be greater than the benefits. NOAA resisted intrusive cleanup and Exxon resisted intrusive costs. State officials, however, had gone the other way over the winter. Erich Gundlach and key members of the '89 DEC team were shunted aside; the new managers were more determined than ever to rid the Sound of all the oil. They were regularly outmaneuvered and outvoted.

The conflict culminated in the state's push for a rock-washing machine. Adapted from the hardware of placer mining, the rock washer was in essence a cylindrical drum, like a huge concrete mixer fitted with screens and hot-water sprays, into which beach sediments would be fed for cleaning. Exxon agreed to build a prototype. Parts of the rock washer would have been 120 feet long, which was longer than some of the shoreline segments to be treated. The diesel-powered behemoth would have englutted and extruded entire beaches, roaring and shaking, killing all intertidal life, putting the Omni-barge to shame.

The Coast Guard directed NOAA/Hazmat to prepare a net environmental benefit analysis of the rock washer, drawing on scientific contributions from all three authorities. John Robinson's conclusion was to recommend against the machine. He argued that life was already recolonizing the beaches and that the subsurface oil posed a small and ever declining biological threat. The prototype being built in Seattle was never completed.

As the summer of '90 ended, the state complained that the Coast Guard was signing off too readily on the treated segments. The small squads zipped along with their shovels and fertilizers. Once more the pellets and sprays of nitrogen and phosphorus were the final coating on the Sound. Bacteria as hydrocarbon consumers are overdue for review and will have it in the next chapter. The gist is that bioremediation was underproved and oversold. It wasn't only state officials who saw the fertilizers used as a kind of magic dust, a painless and "natural" substitute for the human labor of tilling and pickup.

The workers' rallying cry was "Demob for Mother Nature." It meant, let's demobilize and let nature do the rest. I heard the expression on the day after Labor Day, from a crew treating a rocky islet in the mouth of Northwest Bay.

About a half dozen hard-hatted men and women came ashore with shovels and absorbent boom. Cigarettes dangling from not-so-tender mouths, they worked for about thirty minutes on a small pocket of gravel nestled in the bedrock. About a half dozen overseers listlessly looked on.

I was with a party of biologists, whose leader, Dennis Lees, called out, "Hey, it's been killed already." Once thick with rockweed, the shore of the islet was now bare as a nubbin.

"Now they're going to remove the sediment," Lees commented, "and there won't be a place for the clams that *were* there to resettle. Oh well, in some other geological era it will recover."

The crew foreman came over and asked what we were doing, crawling about there on the bedrock. I said we were investigating the biological effects of the cleanup program. He uttered a Bronx cheer and stuck down a thumb. "That oughta be interesting," he said.

When they were done tilling, the workers laid a ring of bright yellow boom around the gravel. One sprinkled on the fertilizer with a garden spreader. Another strung up a bright red balloon to deter birds from getting into the chemicals. The OSRTs trooped back onto their vessel. The balloon was painted with a big smile, as if bidding the Sound to have a nice day.

It is time to make the transition from fates to effects, beginning with the consequences of the cleanup. The proposition that the treatment hurt the intertidal ecosystem more than it helped had been debated as early as April 1989, after the first tests of the shoreline wash on Eleanor Island. Clearly, the flushing destroyed invertebrates and algae—destroyed those organisms, that is, that had not already been smothered or poisoned by the oil. For it was fear of the oil's lingering toxicity that swept aside the doubters. By the official logic, the ancillary damage must be a minor and worthwhile trade-off.

In the end, the harm from the cleanup was worse. Such was the formal conclusion of the only in-depth study of the matter. Like most such complex undertakings, it came too late to affect policy. Not surprisingly, NOAA/Hazmat commissioned the study, and Exxon and Alaska have criticized it. The wrinkle is that the scientists who performed it, Jonathan Houghton and Dennis Lees, started out in the hire of the oil company.

Houghton and Lees are marine biologists and longtime friends. They work for environmental consulting firms in Seattle and San Diego, respectively. They were on the phone within twenty-four hours of the spill, trying to arrange positions for themselves in the Sound. They called a number of government agencies and also Exxon. Dennis Lees, the senior partner, had lived in Alaska. For OCSEAP in the early '80s he had coauthored the seventy-page "Description of Prince William Sound Shoreline Habitats Associated with Biological Communities," the only survey since the earthquake report. Jon Houghton had recently studied the intertidal effects of an oil spill on the Olympic Peninsula. The upshot was that Lees and Houghton signed on with Dames & Moore, a consulting firm based in Seattle, which in turn contracted with Exxon. The two got into the field while the oil was still on the loose.

"It was bigger than a 'spill of opportunity,'" said Lees, reacting to my use of the term. "For the consultant the question is always how to further your own specialty and still get work. In this case it was an opportunity to learn and to work, but also to contribute."

By boat and helicopter, the biologists tried to outflank the slick's trajectory. They wanted to establish some kind of a prespill baseline against which to gauge the inevitable mortalities. They went to the east side of Knight Island, before it was hit, and to western Montague, which wasn't, and hurriedly surveyed the intertidal life. They took samples at Outside Bay on Naked before the tanker was hauled there for repairs.

At Northwest Bay, on the west side of Eleanor, they arrived too late. "The snow line was right down to the oil, white on black," Lees recalled. "We were a bit stunned, walking around. You couldn't block your feelings. Hermit crabs trying to crawl out of the mess, chitons going belly-up."

Lees and Houghton and their assistants set up research sites around the Sound in late March and April. When they returned in May, Houghton said, "You could lift up the oily *Fucus* and find barnacles and littorines surviving underneath." Lees added, "You'd look down and see the trails of snails. They were bulldozing it, grazing in and on the oil. We thought the long-term damage would be greater, and each time, coming back here, we waited for the other shoe to drop."

It was becoming apparent that for as many creatures that died as many would not. Houghton and Lees suspected that if the shoreline was already rebounding from the acute effects of the spill, then the cleanup might be counterproductive. When Exxon had them evaluate a test of the hot-water wash and Corexit in early July, they were awed by how the big hoses blew the mussels off the beach. Three-quarters of the littleneck clams below the test site were killed. At one of their favorite research stations, the rocky islet in Northwest Bay, they watched as crews blasted almost all of the *Fucus* off the rocks. This was when Houghton urged Al Maki, "Enough is enough." The pair started to voice their concerns to state and NOAA monitors as well.

A good scientist in a tough position, Maki understood that the trade-offs of the cleanup should be assessed. He believed the set-aside program was necessary and important. He sanctioned the test of the Omni-barge's effects at Herring Bay. "Al was impressed by our warnings," said Houghton. "He was eager for us to get the statistics. But it was too late to stop the juggernaut."

The damage assessment process, picking up steam apace with

the cleanup, fouled the scientific atmosphere. Data on the oil removed from Herring Bay was approved for release, but not the ecological analysis. Gag orders imposed by both sides blocked the scholarly chats between Exxon's researchers and the government's. At a strategy meeting in Texas, when Lees observed that the oil might be slowing the growth of subtidal kelp, one Exxon lawyer looked at another and said, "Are we shooting ourselves in the foot with this study?" The kelp research that Lees had undertaken was discontinued.

Maki distanced himself from Houghton and Lees. There was bad blood with Dames & Moore. Field procedures were burdened increasingly by paperwork. "The bureaucracy hit with all four feet," Lees summed up ruefully. A heart condition took him out of action in September.

A Freedom of Information Act suit by the *Anchorage Daily News* pried out the results of the Omni-barge test. The data confirmed the critics' concerns. Beforehand, in spite of the oily conditions, Houghton had found rockweed and other algae, mussels, snails, limpets, hermit crabs and barnacles living on the beach at Herring Bay, if in fewer numbers than on unoiled areas. But after the Omni-boom treatment the animal and plant life was decimated, particularly the mussels and delicate algae. The shorter washing time proved as damaging as the longer.

Maki put the best face on the results. "You do indeed cause intertidal mortalities," he told me. "You see a reduction in the density of species. But the diversity remains the same. Adult animals are still there to reseed the beaches, and overall you're better off with the mousse out of there." Since a dozen plant and animal species disappeared entirely from the test site, reducing diversity as well as density, Maki was evidently referring to the mature organisms on untreated segments, from which replacements could be spawned.

Houghton and Lees were not rehired by Exxon in 1990. They made a presentation to NOAA/Hazmat to continue their work. The snag was that the intertidal research they had already produced didn't belong to them. The '89 data was proprietary and couldn't be used as the basis for work for NOAA or anyone else. At least the Herring Bay results, and those from another NOAA/Exxon test conducted earlier, were in the public domain. NOAA contracted the two to look at the cleanup's impact on the recovery of the coastline. Exxon agreed to contribute $100,000 worth of logistical support, about one fifth of the study's budget.

"The Omni-barge test indicated that the treatment was worse

than the disease," Houghton said. "We thought we'd save Exxon a couple of billion dollars."

"They gassed it, they blitzed it," Lees put in vehemently, he the less circumspect of the two. "The other shoe that dropped was the cleanup. The spill was horrible, but the cleanup damage, that was probably the hardest to take. It caused decades of damage to the clams. They were surviving fine with heavy oil on them."

The biologists were sitting side by side, their portable computers yoked together, on a boat in Valdez harbor. It was the first of September, 1990, a fine day in Prince William Sound. We were about to set forth on the second leg of their shoreline survey. Data from the first expedition in July was being transferred from one researcher's disk to the other's.

As before there were two vessels, which were chartered fishing boats, and two teams of researchers to divide the work. I was assigned to Lees on the *Carmen Rose*; Houghton boarded the *Sound Investor* with his assistants, and we left port in tandem. We headed for Block Island, the first station on their list and an experimental site for me as well.

Houghton and Lees built their study on sites they had selected during their Exxon work. They created three categories. Category 1, the control or reference group, consisted of beaches that were never oiled. Their intertidal life represented a snapshot of what the oiled beaches might have looked like without the spill. (Eventually they gained access to their '89 data, adding a true baseline to the study after the fact.)

The second category consisted of sites that had been oiled but not treated. Here the '89 set-aside program, slender and maligned, found a purpose. Two set-aside segments were included in Category 2. In an asterisk of methodology, the researchers included as well four sites that were cold-flushed, fertilized and/or tilled by workers with shovels. Their reasoning was that these less-intrusive cleanup techniques had little or no effect on the intertidal community. It was the heat and pressure of the Omni- and Maxi-barges that appeared to have caused the real damage. Thus their third category of sites: shorelines that had been oiled and then treated with high-pressure, hot-water washing.

The scientists conceded they brooked criticism by these qualifications. Had the set-aside program been larger, there would have been a range of untrammeled sites available and no need to stretch the criteria for Category 2. Moreover, it was fairly certain that, on average, the Category 3 segments were more heavily oiled at the outset than the Category 2 stations, raising the possibility of comparing (treated) apples to (untreated) oranges. None of the authorities maintained good work records—exactly what was done to which beach and when. The shortcoming is in keeping with the goal of removing clydes rather than oil.

To approximate the variability of the Sound, Houghton and Lees subdivided their sites according to habitat. Within each category they selected three geomorphological types: protected rocky habitats, characterized by bedrock and boulders; protected mixed-soft habitats, typically gravel with some sand or silt; and exposed (high-energy) habitats of boulders and rounded cobbles. Then they sliced the onion a third way—by tidal elevation. Parallel transects were laid across the upper, mid and lower intertidal zones.

The biologists ended up with twenty-eight study stations around the Sound, each laid with two or three transects. The procedure was to identify and count the organisms living within randomly selected quadrats along the transects. The object was to see whether differences in overall numbers and in community structure, density and diversity were related to treatment history.

In addition to the intertidal census, the researchers collected mussels and snails for growth analysis, sampled eelgrass in subtidal zones off the more sheltered beaches and correlated the levels of hydrocarbons they measured in the sediments with their biological findings.

"And we'll take a break now and then to fish," Lees announced. At this time of year the silver salmon were running strongly in the Sound, so many that people sleeping on their boats in Valdez harbor were kept awake by the slapping of fish against the hulls.

Blue haze, in bands, lay along the shore near the Alyeska complex. It was supertanker exhaust, held down by a high-pressure inversion over the fjord. In the Arm we passed abeam of Bligh Reef, lurking below the rips. As on that night before Good Friday small icebergs cluttered the water, like a spill of broken teeth. The bergs were colored white or blue or in some cases brown because of the glacier-scraped sediment. The boat slowed to thread through.

I climbed to the crow's nest. The air temperature had plunged. For a mile on either side the bergs hissed and popped. The trapped glacial air, releasing, sounded like Rice Krispies meeting milk. Far to the south, perhaps twenty miles ahead, lay a thick discrete cloud bank, which reminded me of the tabular icebergs of Antarctica, whose straight sides would tower above these quirky Arctic shapes.

Block Island, our destination, was the site of my gustatorial beach. I had not seen it in two summers. The change—the absence of oil on the gravel—was startling and gratifying, and not only to me but to Exxon, for photos of Block Island before and after the winter were highlighted in the company's 1990 literature. Block also appeared on the cover of Ed Owens's reports.

Jacqui Michel had established monitoring sites for her weathering study on the east and west shores of Block. It was interesting to review my first impressions through the lens of the geomorphologist. I had been struck by the steepness and stern rockiness of the shore, whereas Michel's report for NOAA described "sheltered pebble beaches with associated tidal flats." Block was now a peninsula. She classified the narrow neck that joined the island to Eleanor after the earthquake as a "washover tombolo terrace." A tombolo is a bridge of low shoreline between a promontory and the mainland.

Our boat anchored off the west side of Block, where I had first observed the cleanup. Houghton's team was already there. While the others set up to work, I headed through the fringe of trees toward the east shore. The spongy terrace above the beach made a good landing spot for helicopters, and in 1990 it had wooden landing platforms and a small fuel depot. Near the high tide line were the red ribbons of a science project. Fuel spills occurred above the ribbons, and, according to Michel, the metal stakes marking her transects were regularly disrupted. Eventually she had to drop the site from her study program.

The late afternoon was quiet. The scene was as beautiful as I remembered, but I was less excited by it now. I still found the view of the Chugach Mountains confusing, implying as they did that one must be looking north toward the mainland, and not southeast as the sun directed, but no: this range was the high picket of Montague, located between the Sound and the Gulf.

Michel's "bayhead beach," where I had sampled mousse sixteen months before, is situated at the end of a channel. It tends to collect flotsam such as logs and loose seaweed. For the same reason it was reached several times by drifting oil after being treated in '89. It looked clean today. My more seasoned eye took in the small rocks and pebbles amid the angular cobbles—the relatively gentle conditions, in spite of large boulders on the bayhead margins, of a sheltered Prince William Sound beach. This "raised seafloor flat" was higher by four feet than in 1964. Though the sharp edges of dislocation had been worn down or filled in, peaty organic material from the old subtidal poked through the gravel.

Michel reported that contamination persisted in the fine sediments below the surface. So it did. I exposed a sand-colored amphipod, a beach hopper, which skittered in faint oil. A sheen glimmered on a little tide pool. Ravens in the distance wheeled and laughed. I went back to join my colleagues.

The west littoral of Block Island, described by Michel as "one of the very few wide tidal flats in PWS," was probably a subtidal eelgrass bed before the quake. It is punctuated by rock outcrops, some of which, mini-islets, one can walk to at low water. The terrain "must have caused the cleanup crews many problems." The big barges bearing the pumps and heaters would have found it hard to approach and maneuver. Ed Owens said he wasn't sure that hot water was ever used here, perhaps only the cold-water deluge such as I saw on my first visit. But NOAA found in its files aerial photos of the cleanup activity. Steam rose from the work, thereby confirming the beach's suitability as a Category 3 site for Houghton and Lees.

In July the pair had established three horizontal transects, each 100 feet long. One transect reached along the high-tide zone of the beach, another along the lower intertidal of the silty flat and a third around the base of a near-shore outcrop. This last represented a mid-tidal elevation but also a different category of habitat, because it was bedrock while the other two sites were mixed-soft. The transects were marked at either end with iron pipes.

Now on the outcrop Houghton and Lees unrolled a measuring tape and set the quadrats upon their prior marks. A quad is a square about a half yard on a side, making a quarter square meter of area. The tool was no more than a simple, gray frame, four tubes snapped together and carried on the shoulder like a plastic popgun, but aimed enough times at the patchy shore it gave a window onto Prince William Sound.

Ten quads were taken per 100-foot transect. On the outcrop the frames were positioned at the 6-foot mark, then at 16, 28, 35, 46, 48.5, 61, 73.5, 80 and finally at 83. These numbers were chosen at random. Scientists can buy a book of random numbers, or generate them on calculators. In a pinch Lees lifts them from a telephone directory, writing down the last two digits from a random column. Random sampling protects scientists from themselves. In removing observer bias, the temptation to lay the quads where they might favor one's point of view, nature's truer view is supposed to be revealed.

My part in the expedition was to help record the information that the biologists read aloud from their quadrats. The person who performs this task is called the scribe. I sat down with my clipboard, rain-proof data sheet and fine-tipped mechanical pencil.

Lees and Houghton worked the outcrop transect together, which was unusual, but it was late and they were the two fastest catalogers.

Lees wore kneepads and half-frame glasses. He peered into the first quad like a dentist into a mouth. Probing with tweezers, he said, "Two *Tectura persona,* two *strigatella.*"

Species were listed alphabetically down the left side of the data sheet. The ten quads were listed horizontally. I put a 2 when I found the box for the one limpet species, and 2 in the box for the other limpet.

Houghton said, "This place had one hundred percent *Fucus* before they cleaned it." He knew this absolutely from his '89 data. Almost as good, a year later, was the evidence of the decayed hold-fasts, the tiny stems that had anchored the missing rockweed to the substrate.

Looking over into his partner's quad, which Houghton had completed and was about to move, Lees said, "Trace of *glandula*— dead."

"He calls me on one stinking barnacle."

Some organisms could be counted individually; others, too small or diffuse, had to be recorded by the percentage of coverage. The "trace" of *glandula* was quantified as 0.5, or one-half of 1 percent coverage within the square.

A thin layer of tarry oil was still evident on the rocks, its coverage ranging from trace to 10 percent. The two discussed how to characterize the oil. "Dry, but not necessarily flaky," declared Houghton. By their code, type 4.

"Live *Fucus* . . . three percent," called Houghton from his next quad. I sat between them on the transect, an ear to either side. Lees said, "I'll go with *Fucus* three percent too, in the interest of reducing natural variability.

"*Fucus* sporelings trace . . . *Enteromorpha* . . . [sigh] . . . *Enteromorpha intestinalis,* put down a trace of that as well." Identifying the rarer algae was taxing. *Enteromorpha intestinalis,* as the name doubly denoted, was like the imagined form of someone's insides: tubular, stringy, greenishly transparent.

Lees's barnacles were identified and entered. There were a trace of *Chthamalus dalli,* a trace of *Balanus glandula* and 8 percent of *Semibalanus balanoides.* "One moth," he added.

About the barnacles: *Chthamalus* is very small, and its white color has a reddish tint. *Balanus glandula* and *balanoides* are larger, and by form or color can't easily be told from one another. The best method is to scrape them off the rock. *Glandula* leaves a calcareous ring, where its base plate has been glued with shell, while *balanoides* does not, anchoring only by a muscular membrane.

I recalled that Stoner Haven, the invertebrate man on the earthquake expedition, found *balanoides* overtaking *glandula* in the wake of the disturbance. The normal mode of dominance between the two was reversed, though only for a time. *Glandula* prevailed when the recovery was complete. A reviewer in the early '80s questioned this finding by Haven, because a photo caption in his report misidentified one of the barnacles. I wanted to get to the bottom of the matter. It happened that Sandra Lindstrom, the algae specialist in our party, had been a student of Haven's. She informed us that Haven had died years ago, quite prematurely, and so there was no way to confirm his finding.

Houghton and Lees thought Haven was correct in spite of the caption error, for in their experience *balanoides* is more opportunistic than *glandula*. It is the barnacle faster to recolonize after a winter's ice or storms have knocked both species off the rocks. After the disturbance of an earthquake, or a spill-cum-cleanup, it would not be surprising that juvenile *balanoides* should be relatively more common. On the other hand, *glandula*'s advantage is a tighter grip. In the face of a hot-water jet the obdurate *glandula* may hold on tighter than *balanoides*. It did look to have come through the spill better, the biologists said, though the data had not been analyzed. Survival had many strategies. I wished Haven were alive.

Many of the Sound's plants and animals have acquired new names since Haven's work in the '60s. The taxonomists of intertidal biology are a restless bunch, scrutinizing for small disparities or congruities that can be used to overthrow some predecessor's designation. The *Fucus distichus* (genus and species) has a new name, *Fucus gardneri* (i.e., Gardner's *Fucus*). The alga's morphological variants from *distichus* were illuminated not by Dr. Gardner but by one of his admirers. It is bad form to name a discovery after oneself. The *Acmaea* limpets that Haven knew are no more, having been split between the *Tectura* and *Collisella* genera. His *Balanus balanoides* now belongs to the new *Semibalanus* association, where barnacles lack base plates. Even the common blue mussel, *Mytilus edulis*, which ranges from the Arctic to Baja California, is under siege in Alaska by splitters calling it *Mytilus trossulus*. At present the splitters are winning.

Lees finished up: "*Mytilus* five percent . . . OK, now the snails . . . *Scutulata*, eighteen times four." To save time surveying the ubiquitous snails, the observers divided the quadrat into quarters. Then he or she would ask the scribe to pick a number, any number, between one and four, and if I said "three," the observer would give me a count of every snail on that particular section of rock, and the whole would be extrapolated by quadrupling. I knew I'd hit upon the densest quarter when they groaned. Maybe just once or twice, at the end of a long stint in the rain, the snails looking like dots in a blur, the spotter would say, "Pick another number." Randomizing protects scientists from themselves, but there is a limit.

The Sound's two algae-eating snails, also known as periwinkles, are *Littorina scutulata* and *Littorina sitkana*. Brown, never bigger than a thumbnail, they look blandly alike, except that the whorl of *sitkana*'s shell is somewhat globular and usually ridged where the other's is conical and smooth. *Scutulata* normally is less abundant, but as with the rival barnacles, it can spurt ahead of *sitkana* after disturbances. *Scutulata*'s advantage is a planktonic larval phase, allowing its young to drift freely, borne by the waves to colonize new shores. *Sitkana* lays eggs, from which its young must crawl, and this method of travel is slower to expand a population than drifting.

Tortoise and hare, the two littorines were competing for space on the denuded outcrop of Block Island. *Scutulata* was winning at the moment. I reflected that without frequent disturbances—no storm, quake, spill or cleanup constantly resetting the competition—there would be room here for only one periwinkle.

The tide fell away and the sea flattened toward sunset. In the channel a silent barge passed, bearing a backhoe from a berm-relocation project.

After the earthquake the most conspicuous change on the shores of Prince William Sound was the blossoming of opportunistic algae, owing to the destruction of the algae-grazing limpets and snails. In the spring of 1990, a number of observers commented on the green slime. Three biologists consulting for Exxon reported that the abundance of filamentous algae in April was "striking" and "sufficient to smother barnacles on some rocks."

Being British, the Exxon consultants were reminded of the *Torrey Canyon*, "the first-ever supertanker spill," after which the green algae exploded on the Cornwall beaches. The next year it was the brown alga, *Fucus*, that was heavy. Bloom masked the disturbance; the impression of health was misleading, like the glow on the face of a consumptive. The abnormal richness of flora was eventually controlled when the limpets and snails recovered. The consultants did not point out that the chemicals used to remove the *Torrey Canyon*'s oil, not the oil itself, had decimated the herbivores and triggered the disturbance. In 1990 the algal bloom in Prince William Sound was both a sign of injury and the first spasm of recovery.

The *Carmen Rose* and *Sound Investor* were tied together at anchor. Back on board we sifted the day's collection of infaunal samples. This aspect of the study counted small invertebrates like clams, cockles, copepods and worms. The animals lived hidden within the soft sediments (hence in-fauna) of the lower reaches of sheltered beaches. They were a separate community from the organisms on the surface, the epibiota, and were more likely to have been suffocated during the wash than to have been overheated or dislodged.

Instead of quadrats, the biologists took six-inch-deep cores along the infaunal transects. A core is a hollow cylinder, like the garden tool used to make holes for planting bulbs. Sifting a core involved dumping the contents onto a screen and dipping the screen into a bucket of seawater. We picked out the gravel and strained the sand through, exposing the critters. It was like washing dishes in ice-cold water.

Dennis Lees noted that one of his cores contained six littleneck clams, which was a lot, all apparently healthy in spite of the redolent oil. "Phew, you should have smelled it," he said.

Seated with his sieve on an overturned bucket, Houghton said, "There are some big mussels there too—eaters almost." Someone asked whether they weren't too contaminated to eat. "Well, maybe the oil will kill you in forty years," he said, "but PSP could kill you tomorrow." Paralytic shellfish poisoning is caused by a naturally occurring toxin that can accumulate in mussels in summer. A man in fact died that year after eating a number in Cook Inlet near Anchorage.

The cores were taken from the lower intertidal flat, between the rocky outcrop and the upper beach. Unlike Block's outcrop and upper beach, which were put into Category 3, the flat was considered to have been oiled but not treated, and thus Category 2. This in spite of Michel's account: "This shoreline segment was intensively washed and there was no way to prevent oiled sediments from being flushed onto the flat."

Houghton and Lees made the distinction that the flat was never directly treated. The 1989 cleanup guidelines stressed that the crews were not to aim hot water at the lower intertidal, partly because the so-called green zone was the richest area biologically and partly because the lower reaches were the least oiled to start. No matter, if the tide was out when the crews were in, the lower zone usually got hosed with the rest, as many witnesses attested.

Evidently the tide was in when the crews got to this segment of Block.

But wasn't the erosion of oily sediments from above a consequence of the hot-water wash that would have biological effect? The researchers maintained that the sediment that was flushed onto Block's low zone was less heavy ("a plume") and less destructive than at other sites. They said the survival of clams showed that siltation had not been heavy. They argued that the high concentrations of hydrocarbons found in the flat were the product mainly of the initial stranding of the oil.

The question matters because subsequently their analysis showed the Block Island infauna to be very rich. It had the densest assemblage of worms, nematodes and copepods of any site that they surveyed. A great number of young littleneck clams were taking hold, in spite of the oily conditions. The data boosted their thesis, since the high numbers pulled up the biological average of the sites grouped in the oiled-but-not-treated Category 2. But if the site had been assigned to Category 3, oiled and treated, the flat's "anomalous abundance," as Houghton called it, would tend to undermine their conclusion that the cleanup hurt more than helped. This is a good example, perhaps, of how assumptions in scientific research are as critical to the outcome as the findings themselves.

There was another possibility, outside the parameters of the study, for the anomalous biological abundance. It may have had nothing to do with whether the lower flat was treated or not, but with the stimulatory effect of hydrocarbons, akin to what occurred in the flooded hold of the *Exxon Valdez*. Houghton allowed that some of the animals may have benefited from the hydrocarbon-degrading bacteria at the base of the food web.

A 200-PAGE REPORT, with weighty appendices, was issued by Houghton, Lees and associates in the spring of 1991. To summarize its main findings:

1. In 1990 the diversity and density of organisms living upon the shoreline was highest at Category 1 sites, unoiled and untreated, followed closely by Category 2 sites, oiled but not hot-washed. The treated Category 3 sites were a distant third in richness of limpets, mussels, snails, hermit crabs, rockweed, etc. The contrast in intertidal life was most marked when comparing the set-asides of Category 2 with the heavily treated rocky sites of Category 3, such as the Block Island outcrop and Northwest Bay islet.

2. The same relationship among categories applied to the infauna of mixed-soft beaches.

3. At oiled, treated sites the concentration of polynuclear aromatic hydrocarbons, the most durable of the harmful compounds,
was greatest in sediments at the lower elevations, just the opposite
finding from the oiled, untreated sites, where concentrations were
greatest at the higher elevations. This suggested that the cleanup
flushed hydrocarbons from the relatively sparse upper intertidal
onto the green zones below.

Houghton and Lees sent a draft report out for peer review. I
retrieved some of the reviewers' comments in order to check my
layman's understanding.

Exxon and the state of Alaska, the two main defenders of the
cleanup, weighed in. At the heart of the complaints was the con-
tention that the natural variability of intertidal assemblies, and the
range of oiling and treatment methods, made conditions in the
Sound so altogether complex that the researchers needed to have
studied many more sites before they could make a firm statement
that was pertinent to the whole Sound.

Having waved my pennant for patchiness, the perpetual, perplexing flux of marine systems, I cannot disagree. No two beaches
were alike. For all the information we collected, as we humped in
the rain from Block to Smith to Naked and back to Northwest Bay
and finally to Herring Bay on Knight, where I left the expedition;
for all the data sheets that were filled out and samples sifted on
what was after all the second time around that summer, much more
indeed could have been done. Greater data would have required
greater funding.

The report was crammed with statistics as it was. Ecology
moves toward ever greater quantitative rigor, and purely empirical
findings, however astute of the observer, are not credited the way
they used to be. The earthquake reports look pretty thin today. By
analyzing large batches of numbers with a computer, a biologist can
establish a pattern (a biological signal) that appears initially as
only a hint, usually one of many, in his field records. This is an
application of descriptive statistics. Analyses of inferential statistics, the next step, are techniques to validate the pattern by comparing it to the products of other data sets. It is in interpreting sets
of statistics, rather than in altering the raw numbers, that the
environmental scientist is tempted to cheat. Therefore, Houghton
and Lees included in their report a long passage of statistical
checks. The tests and proofs were meant to show reviewers that

they weren't seeing only those patterns of numbers in the Sound that they desired to see.

The pair granted that their statistical procedures were looser than the textbooks demanded. This looseness was due to the fact that their twenty-eight study sites were not chosen at random. Houghton and Lees had tried to bring some order to the Sound up front. Their randomizing began only after their stations were picked. The pattern they subsequently discovered was valid, for no critic directly disputed it, but the statisticians wouldn't let them apply their findings as broadly as they would have liked.

Two rival studies of the intertidal zone were being conducted at the same time, both of them under wraps. One was led by Bowdoin College's Edward Gilfillan, consulting for Exxon, and the other by University of Alaska biologist Raymond Highsmith, working for the government. Because Gilfillan and Highsmith must be prepared to defend their findings in court, they had to be statistically unassailable. "Their slavish attention to randomizing," was how Houghton put it, "would have been great for a lab experiment."

Neither investigator tried to separate the initial effect of the oil from the subsequent impact of the cleanup. They sampled the beaches as if they had been subjected to a single disturbance. Thus Gilfillan, for Exxon, hunted for the signal of what he termed the "oiling effect." Looking at randomly selected beaches through tiny quadrats, he showed the oiling effect to be small in relation to the noisy numbers of natural variability.

For Highsmith, proceeding from the opposite expectation, the statistical requirements were a nightmare. He tried to account for all the habitat types and degrees of oiling within the spill zone. A computer generated 150 locations in the Sound and the Gulf, and on each his teams ran four transects. The initial finding, he said, was that "oil was good" for intertidal organisms. What happened was that the computer saddled him with an excess of mainland beaches that were never oiled yet were naturally thin in intertidal life. He had to compare those depauperate sites with beaches on the Sound's islands that were richer in biota even *after* being oiled and cleaned. The results were cockeyed.

Highsmith retooled his study in 1990. His priority now was the most sensitive shoreline type, the sheltered rocky beaches of the Sound's western islands. In this category he was able to show that mussels, barnacles and limpets were reduced by the spill. His costly effort was curtailed thereafter.

Gilfillan and Highsmith were among the critics of Houghton

and Lees. From their statistical high ground, they focused on the study's fudge factors at the expense of its strengths of perception. I kept my eye on the latter. Houghton and Lees documented something indisputable about the consequences of oil spill clean-up—that violent measures to remove oil were more destructive than oil alone. Their analysis has helped to bolster NOAA's go-easy position regarding marine oil spills.

Houghton and Lees have continued their work. Since 1990, the focus of their study has not been so much on the setbacks of the cleanup as on the differing rates of recovery. The recovery of the beach life, by their definition, is "the process observed as the species composing the assemblage oscillate toward the abundance levels and relationships held before the disturbance." Even while I was aboard, the sum of our observations was that the coast of the Sound was recovering from the oil spill. The quadrats framed the fuzz of *Fucus* sporelings, and the set of tiny mussels and barnacles upon the scoured rocks. Likewise Dallas Hanna and crew, setting out in 1965 to establish the destruction of the earthquake, found themselves recording the Sound's rebirth.

Two years after the spill, Houghton and Lees found it difficult to show differences between Categories 1 and 2, the sites that were unoiled and those oiled but not treated. The Category 3 ecosystems still lagged. Where the hot-water jets had been trained, the intertidal community was unlike those elsewhere, featuring a greater abundance of opportunistic snails and barnacles (*scutulata* and *balanoides*) and of young *Fucus* plants, but fewer of other species, such as red algae, hermit crabs, limpets, predatory snails. The worst case among rocky shores was still the Northwest Bay islet, where even *Fucus* sporelings and young *balanoides* were limited on the bedrock. And the scientists estimated that the clams at Category 3 sites were at least ten years from a complete recovery.

The drill snail *Nucella*, a key predator of mussels and barnacles, was not only still lacking on the treated sites but also on the oiled-and-untreated sites. Then in 1992 *Nucella* rebounded very strongly at the Northwest Bay islet, presumably because it had a rich food supply in the new barnacles. The snail remained low that year in Category 2, perhaps depressed by the residual oil or by a lack of food. *Nucella* was up and down, boom and bust, echoing the disturbance.

I kept track of the results from the lower intertidal station at Block Island. The soft sediments of the flat continued to show a higher oil content than elsewhere, yet higher too were the small infaunal creatures, including the littleneck clams. Larval clams continued to settle in the oily sediments. However, when Houghton and Lees transplanted untainted littlenecks to the site, their survival rates weren't as good as the clams they transplanted to clean sites. In other words, the hydrocarbons may have been both stimulatory and toxic, as the effects of the aliphatic compounds and the aromatics worked against each other.

The Exxon researchers saw something similar, at least the first part of it. When the results of Gilfillan's Shoreline Ecology Program were reported in 1993, a principal conclusion was that "infaunal communities found in oiled areas tended to have more individuals, more species, and higher diversity than those found in reference areas. It is very likely that the increased availability of food (resulting from increased biomass of bacteria metabolizing the weathered oil residue) reduced competition for food and allowed more species to coexist. . . ."

In general, the end was in sight. Lines from all three of Houghton's and Lees's original categories were converging on some undulating standard of ecological health, the unknowable patchiness of the future, that would render the categories meaningless. Soon it wouldn't matter whether life was rebounding from the oil or from the cleanup or from something new.

Because of a lack of funding, the earthquake researchers stopped monitoring after 1965, and in '68, excepting the black lichen of the splash zone, Stoner Haven reported a fait accompli. Houghton and Lees have been able to go back every year and track the coastline's recovery. They have had the privilege to look over nature's shoulder.

AND I HAVE BEEN PRIVILEGED. The old feelings stirred as the NOAA helicopter lifted me from Herring Bay in September 1990. The researchers stood small on the beach. Once more the tawny russet slopes of fall, above the ocher shore, and an eroding salmon glinting.

During the winter before, a volcano, Mount Redoubt, had erupted on the west side of Cook Inlet, several hundred miles away. Volcanic ash blew onto the Sound, drifted into Herring Bay and was deposited on the upper beach. Faint white traces were still there. The day I left I saw ash atop the thin tar, and both lay upon Knight Island greenstone, an extrusion of the tectonic forces that also caused the eruption, of the geologic forces that also manufactured the petroleum.

I had the strongest sense of the oil being incorporated by the Sound, even embraced. As I recall this now, two other writings come to me, the way the mind springs across a stream perpendicularly to the current.

The first is Saul Bellow in *Herzog* describing an attractive woman approaching forty: "She was in the time of life when the later action of heredity begins, the blemishes of ancestors appear—a spot, or the deepening of wrinkles, at first increasing a woman's beauty. Death, the artist, very slow, putting in his first touches."

The other is by a friend who lives on the Sound. In the terrible days after the accident this man imagined that a bay on Knight Island, his favorite place, could somehow entrain all of the slick and keep it from spreading and hurting the rest of the environment:

> Oil without a home
> Knight Island opens her arms
> This heart has no bounds

The poet addresses the acute effects, Bellow the chronic. Some thin ice here, as to the sexual element. Robert Clark, one of Exxon's biological consultants from Great Britain, put it in the same terms, but harshly. "The area has lost its virginity," he declared. "You can't lose your virginity twice."

When I got home I called up Mark Kuwada, hard-core foe of the oil. Kuwada was the spill-response coordinator for the Alaska Department of Fish and Game. He and his staff were most concerned with contamination around the mouths of salmon streams. He argued heatedly in 1990 for the big rock-washer machine. He disputed that Exxon's hot-water cleanup should be judged by its shoreline effects exclusively. To him, the universe of the quadrat did not include the possibility that the cleanup of oil was more helpful to the pink salmon fishery, and to other uses of the Sound, than it was harmful to seaweed and barnacles.

I tried to describe to Mark Kuwada the Sound's bittersweet beauty to me, her sadder-but-wiser appeal. "Some people swear by a virgin," he replied.

Then he told me about a friend who kayaked into a wilderness area said to have been spared from the slick. Camped in a beautiful bay, the daylight stealing away, this fellow and his girlfriend made a fire and boiled a pot of seawater. They put in mussels collected from the beach, wild shellfish for a romantic dinner—and watched in horror as the mussels released a sheen of oil.

Hearing that, I did not tell Kuwada about my recent experience on the east side of Block Island. Alone on my bayhead beach, tasting the oil as I had before, this time I swallowed. As the Sound had done.

3

Chemophobia

PETROLEUM IS CAUSTIC and poisonous if you get enough of it on you or in you. But how dangerous is it, really? In the summer of 1990 a Veco worker, shoveling up bits of the spill, accidentally ate a tiny tarball when it popped into his mouth. The man was very concerned, so the Coast Guard reported, and he later complained of a stomachache. But he was told there would be no long-term consequences.

Poison is the dose, pronounced Paracelsus, the sixteenth-century physician. He meant that anything is toxic, even vital oxygen, if absorbed or administered in excess. An Exxon doctor assured me that as much as one cup of crude oil, even if it were fresh with aromatics, would not be fatal to the person ingesting it. There would be a nasty gastric disorder, which would pass. According to other research, the greater danger lies in vomiting and thereby aspirating the oil into the lungs. Petroleum's lethal parameters are well understood, thanks to a smattering of accidents to humans and to years of testing on animal surrogates in the laboratory. Less well understood are its sublethal effects, but a single small dose surely could not lead to problems.

In *Silent Spring*, Rachel Carson's 1962 thriller about pesticide abuse, the story is told of the bold scientist who wanted to assess the risks of a new synthetic insecticide. It was the 1950s and American farmers were beginning to disseminate chemicals like DDT on a broad scale. Toxicology lagged behind. The researcher swallowed what he calculated to be a tolerably minute dose, taking care to have an antidote to the pesticide close at hand. He died reaching for it.

A Cordova fisherman named Tom Copeland evinced the same boldness in April of '89. It was too late to control the spill, spread-

133

ing through the environment like an epidemic, yet Copeland and his crew went out and started picking up oil by hand. Leaning out of rubber skiffs, they corralled clumps of mousse and put it into buckets with flour scoops. The buckets were normally used for carrying herring roe, but the harvest of herring had been canceled for fear that the fish and their spawn might be contaminated. Copeland and crew took the oil to Valdez, collecting a $5 bounty from Exxon for each gallon. They were a splattered mess, and one crew member developed a rash on her face, but they rid the Sound of thousands of gallons before it got too scattered and heavy and then they quit.

An orangutan fisherman if there ever was one, Copeland was scornful of his fellows who stayed in port and wailed. "They were acting as if it was radioactive," he said. "It's just oil."

Just oil? Although the Alaska Division of Public Health declared the risks from being exposed to the oil to be low, a former medical director for an oil company warned that "neurologic changes (brain damage), skin disorders (including cancer), liver and kidney damage, cancer of other organ systems, and other medical complications" would likely result if people working around the spill weren't properly protected. This doctor urged that the shoreline cleanup crews be pulled from the Sound.

Just oil? One worker, whose story came to be known because he filed a lawsuit, was spray-cleaning the insides of a large tank that summer when he swallowed some sludge dislodged from the top of the tank. Moreover, he was said to have aspirated oil; his job exposed his skin to it; he breathed its fumes. Two years later his lawyers claimed that the man's lungs were burned out, that he required an oxygen tank, that he had gained a lot of weight because of a ruined metabolism and that overall he suffered "devastating permanent and totally disabling injuries."

Just oil? The prosperity of America is owed in part to the petrochemicals developed after World War II. Toxicologists were just learning the properties of basic petroleum hydrocarbons when they were presented with a new class of hydrocarbons, highly engineered and resistant to breakdown. We may thank Rachel Carson, who did a great service in exposing the hazards of these compounds. She died of cancer two years after her book was published.

In 1989, a silent spring, her very phrase, was being invoked for Prince William Sound. A spokeswoman for Alaska Friends of the Earth looked beyond the acute effects of the oil to the toxic threat on the horizon. "In addition to the effects on the food chain," she told *Alaska Magazine*, "there are a whole range of what scientists call 'sublethal effects.' Rather than killing outright, these weaken the health of our fish and wildlife. Oil can damage digestive, respiratory or reproductive systems, and increase susceptibility to disease and stress." She added that "all of the life of Prince William Sound should be warned that components of oil cause cancer."

And nearly a year after the spill, a writer for New York's *Village Voice* described a continuing threat: "Otters eating oiled prey will have more hydrocarbons in their fat, sicken in greater numbers and be less likely to produce than those not eating contaminated food. . . . Vets and biologists predict that some amount of liver and lung damage will show up in animals surviving the initial killing wave. Days after the spill, a considerable amount of oil sank, thereby releasing toxic hydrocarbons and poisoning the microorganisms that make up the basic components of the food chain."

The rumor that the oil sank fit neatly with the rumor of its long-term effects. More frightening than the blackened carcasses of 1989 was the specter of a cancer, a literal and figurative sickness, growing upon the marine ecosystem and sapping it for years, just as in years past the eggs of bald eagles had crumbled from the insidious accumulation of DDT in their tissues. The generalizations about hydrocarbons' chronic effects on organisms were true enough, and the concern had the backing of a scientific model, that of the transfer of poisonous compounds within the food chain. But by the time I dared swallow oil on Block Island I knew the model to be false—false in its application to this event and to this place.

Sometimes one arrives at an understanding of a complexity without knowing exactly how one got there. Granted my instincts pointed that way from the beginning. But afterward I plodded back to make sure. I studied a particular idea, this fearful sense about petroleum in the sea, which germinated during the post-Carson age of environmental awareness, took root in America and flowered on a bad night in Prince William Sound.

In 1969 two marine oil spills occurred in the United States. One, off Santa Barbara, California, instigated a national movement, climaxing in the first Earth Day demonstrations in 1970. The other spill, which took place on Cape Cod, was less notorious but colored the thinking of many of the country's marine biologists. Just as significant as the two incidents themselves was the relative lack of incident in the United States over the next two decades. There were oil spills, but none had a major impact, whether ecological or psychological, until the *Exxon Valdez* spill, which invigorated the environmental movement. In the interim, understanding had ossified.

The January 1969 blowout of an offshore drilling rig spewed about a million gallons of crude into the Santa Barbara Channel. Another 2 million gallons were lost over succeeding months. The incident prefigured the *Exxon Valdez* in miniature. There were the same uninformed anxieties about a ruined fishery, the same controversies over the use of chemical dispersants on the slick and of hot-water sprays on the oiled shores, the same heroic attempts to save seabirds, of which at least six thousand died. A major difference was that, although some marine mammals (mainly harbor and elephant seals) were found dead in the aftermath, most biologists did not believe the oil was responsible.

David St. Aubin, a marine mammal expert at the University of Guelph in Ontario, has reviewed the Santa Barbara event and noted the divide between scientific and popular perceptions: "Studies that found minimal effects were dismissed by the public as inadequate, whereas media reports were often overstated and sensational, and found little favor with the scientific community." Another investigator concluded that the intensity of news coverage of an oil spill could be predicted by the proximity of media centers to the scene.

No long-term damage to the ecosystem of the Santa Barbara Channel was measured. In September of '69, while the Channel was recovering, the barge *Florida* spilled about 200,000 gallons of highly aromatic fuel oil off West Falmouth, Massachusetts. The spill killed fish and decimated the crabs, scallops, lobsters, clams and other invertebrates in an embayment of the coastline. A small but violent event was made worse when storm winds pushed the fuel oil into a marsh in Wild Harbor, killing grasses and fiddler crabs.

Three weeks later marine worms invaded the hard-hit benthic zone like Huns. Fueled by the organic matter in the dead organisms and also the carbon in the oil, the worms seized a wasteland devoid of natural enemies. A single species of polychaete, they reproduced unchecked. In each square meter of sediment, from deep water to the salt marsh, wriggled hundreds of thousands of the half-inch-long, threadlike creatures.

In the spring of '70, although other species had begun to recolonize the bottom, the balance of life was still grossly lopsided. When summer came the polychaete worms in the shallow areas crashed and died, glutted by too much of a good thing, and in deeper waters another worm opportunist surged, partly replacing the first. The benthic mix reverberated from the disturbance of the oil for several more years, the populations rising, falling and steadying at last in an orderly recovery. Everything today appears as it should. But if one cares to, one can dig down into the muck of the marsh and whiff the faint sting of oil, and one can measure detoxifying enzymes still at work in the livers of the marsh minnows.

The *Florida* was a worst-case spill. Conspiring conditions outweighed the relatively low volume of oil. For starters No. 2 fuel oil is considerably more toxic than raw crude. While the oil was still fresh, the storm churned the aromatic chemicals into the shallow water and muds below. Winds turned strongly onshore. The coast has a large marsh that absorbed the oil and defied cleanup. The local environment is rarely purged by strong waves, and at first the few storms only stirred up the toxins in the trapped oil.

Finally, and not least, West Falmouth happens to be the backyard of the Woods Hole Oceanographic Institution and its affiliate, the Marine Biological Laboratory. WHOI and MBL make Woods Hole the leading marine research center on the East Coast—some would say the whole country. On the night of the accident, as John Teal, one of WHOI's senior scientists, put it, "We all realized we had a golden opportunity to study the effects of a massive environmental insult, one which we would never duplicate intentionally and hoped would not reoccur by accident."

The researchers made the most of the opportunity. Judging by the number of presentations at meetings and by the publications in the literature, the *Florida*, affecting but a few square miles of harbor and coast, was studied as intensively as any oil spill in history. Though some of the biologists had retired or moved on by 1989, Woods Hole scientists were still tracking the disturbance when reporters called regarding the tanker spill that had just taken place in Alaska.

To me the seminal article is the one that appeared in the April 7 issue of *Science*, the weekly journal for professionals, including the nation's science writers. "Long, Slow Recovery Predicted for Alaska" was the title. The story was properly cautious, but it relied heavily on quotes from three ecologists knowledgeable about the *Florida*.

"The claim will be made that the oil has been partly degraded and evaporated into the air, and that not much will go to the bottom," said Howard Sanders. "But that is not correct." He predicted that "the bulk of the oil will end up in the benthos." Sanders was the one not correct.

"I think we should be very concerned about this spill because it's a cold water spill," said Robert Howarth. "There's good reason to think it's going to put more oil in the water column and keep it there longer, which is exactly what you don't want. . . . I would not be surprised if there is a decade-long effect on fisheries, but I would be hard-pressed to support that with data." He could not know how hard-pressed.

John Teal's remarks, directed toward the short-term mortalities, hold up best. He did not try to fit the square peg of the *Florida* into the round hole of the Sound. When I interviewed him later, he referred to the junior of his two colleagues as an alarmist. He observed, "People don't pay attention to these rare disasters until they happen. Then they overreact. It was true of the Mount Saint Helens explosion, it was true of the forest fires in Yellowstone Park."

For as much as the *Florida* inspired biologists who didn't know better, the few who did were hesitant to make predictions. The category of comparable events, which we may define as big-time tanker spills in cold-water environments affecting at least moderate-energy shorelines, was not large. It included four spills, none in America, that had been studied seriously: the *Torrey Canyon* in '67 (England), the *Arrow* in '70 (Canada), the *Metula* in '74 (Chile), and the *Amoco Cadiz* in '78 (France). In the months and years after these spills scientists identified ecological effects that brought dismay or dismissal, depending on the interpreter. Although the oil never seemed to damage fisheries for more than a year, injuries to other marine wildlife persisted for as long as a decade, especially in sheltered areas and marshes, and one could further make the argument that the oil was weakening organisms beyond the range of human detection. Or one could determine that within a year or two the ecosystems rebounded smartly from the initial loss of life, and that whatever chronic effects remained were so minimal as to be not worth the effort to measure.

Considering the *Exxon Valdez*, the most knowledgeable scientists understood what would happen first—the acute effects—better than they understood what would happen in the future. The question merged with that of marine pollution in general.

Since petroleum-based products were major contributors to pollution, biologists had been studying hydrocarbons for years, both in the laboratory and in the field. They were empowered by the environmental laws and programs created in the 1970s, surely the golden age of environmental regulation. Applicable for our purposes are the National Toxicology Program; the Clean Water Act; the Marine Protection, Research, and Sanctuaries Act; the National Ocean Pollution Planning Act; and OCSEAP, the Outer Continental Shelf Environmental Assessment Program. In 1980 came the Comprehensive Environmental Response, Compensation, and Liability Act (CERCLA), a.k.a. Superfund, which was intended to clean up the nation's toxic waste sites. It was under the

Clean Water Act and CERCLA that government scientists conducted the natural resource damage assessment, the NRDA work, of the *Exxon Valdez* oil spill.

The high-precision analyses applied to the spill, such as gas chromatography and mass spectrometry, had proved themselves in the earlier research. Samples drawn from harbor bottoms or animal tissue or from the air around suspected polluters could be tested for traces of hydrocarbons and other compounds. By the same token, experimenters in the lab could administer the compounds in finely calibrated amounts to rats, mice, fish and other animal subjects. The lab work and fieldwork cross-pollinated each other. The purpose of environmental toxicology is to try to find biological correlations between the doses of a chemical applied in experiments and the amounts of the chemical loose in the water, air or soil.

The lab studies nailed down the lethal ranges of hydrocarbons. They also ascertained harmful, sublethal consequences from petroleum compounds in lesser concentrations. However, in field studies where equivalently low concentrations of oil were detected, the biological changes observed were usually no greater, no more frequent, than the normal setbacks of natural variability. That is, in real-life marine systems the background effects proved noisy. The compounds in oil did not make for a potent blend. With chemicals more durable than hydrocarbons, real injuries to creatures could be distinguished, but noise bedeviled the researchers working out their models about oil pollution.

After the oil spill, scientists in the Exxon camp pointed out the "margin of safety" for fish. No fish were known to have died outright, except a handful of rockfish, and as far as chronic effects were concerned, there was a thousandfold gap between the levels of harmful petroleum compounds measured in the water of the Sound and the concentrations known to be adverse to fish in the lab. That was one margin of safety. Another was the poor correlation between lab and field effects even if the spill's concentrations had been found to be 1,000 times higher. This argument was somewhat less persuasive, having as much to do with the problems of measuring changes as with changes themselves.

The damage assessors for the government circumvented Exxon's margins of safety. They homed in on hot spots in the Sound, areas of the ecosystem where hydrocarbon concentrations were most pronounced and where organisms would suffer the greatest exposure—doses not intense enough to kill them, necessarily, but constant enough to injure them.

For example, although the water in general had low and transient levels of toxic aromatics, the gravel in some of the streams was strongly and persistently contaminated. Much effort was therefore put into measuring the damages to pink salmon eggs. Another targeted fish was the Pacific herring, because some spawned in oily shallows. In addition it was proposed that the fry of salmon and herring acquired hydrocarbons not only through their gills in the nearshore waters, but also by ingesting oil droplets, in which case their exposures might be far higher. Among the mammals and birds, the river otters and the harlequin ducks foraged along oiled shorelines, and so merited long-term investigations. The most critical area was held to be the "bathtub ring" that the spill left upon the Sound, and the fertile nursery grounds just offshore of it.

In other words, the government, bridging the gap between field and lab conditions, measured effects in particular animals and at sensitive stages of development, according to patterns of injury that had been established in experiments.

But there was a third margin of safety—Exxon did not fail to note it—and that is the difference between effects on individuals and effects on populations. The field biologists in Alaska were accustomed to looking at the big picture, such as how disturbances change the abundance and diversity of wildlife populations, but they didn't know much about toxicology, which examines individuals. The investigators of the spill had to do a lot of reading in a hurry, and they lost sight of the forest for the toxicological trees. Not many biologists, let alone fishermen, Natives or others of the worried public, appreciated the distance between the two frames of investigation. Years later, when all was said and done, the spill researchers were able to demonstrate a connection between oil injuries and population damage in only two species, the sea otters and the murres (a seabird). Neither case depended on the oil's bathtub ring, nor on a chronic toxic stress; rather the damage that was reported reflected the high mortality of the first few weeks.

In general, people were made afraid about the long-term ramifications of the oil spill because of the considerable weight of academic references that were cited. These were selections from the record of prior spills and of experiments with hydrocarbons. But I don't wish to imply that people were innocently passive and misled. In fact, we tend to adopt and retain those scientific explications that appeal to preexistent beliefs. "We hear and apprehend only what we already half know," was how Thoreau put it. Here what we half knew about oil was half wrong.

It gets back to the issue of chemicals in the environment. Has the pendulum of concern swung too far? During the 1990 NOAA cleanup study, Jon Houghton said to me, "There are many causes of sublethal abnormalities in marine life. Should the public care if one out of a thousand barnacles has an abnormal chromosome because of the oil? As long as the population of barnacles isn't affected?"

The *Sound Investor* was anchored in Herring Bay on Knight Island beneath a high haze. While we talked in the stern, Houghton tended a line baited for rockfish, that spiny but delectable denizen of nearshore ledges. We were aware that the rockfish were being tested for toxic injury. "Marine life has such a tremendous spawn," he continued. "It's life and death and so many don't make it. In our society we try to protect individuals from exposure to pollutants and their possible long-term effects. I'm not sure we've decided to do that for marine plants and animals."

An otter lolled a few yards from the boat, as if on perpetual vacation. "Sea monkey," observed Houghton, using the sailors' moniker for it. We watched it play. An abnormal chromosome there, in a creature much closer to a human being than to a barnacle . . . now that would be a different story. We had feelings for sea otters that pushed explications to the side.

IN EARLY JULY of '89, when the spill was still new and the attorneys had not yet put the fear of God into scientists, I went to NOAA headquarters in Washington, D.C., for a briefing on oil. Dr. Douglas Wolfe took me through the biochemical basics. "We have a long evolutionary tolerance for oil," Wolfe began. "It has been in the environment for a long time, and we—I mean living organisms in general—have learned to deal with it in limited exposures." While recommending no hydrocarbon for ingestion, Wolfe observed that humans and most other creatures have developed enzymes that can break oil down.

The aliphatic hydrocarbons that make up the bulk of crude oil are similar in structure, he said, to the fatty acid compounds in animals. When our systems encounter aliphatics, we metabolize a portion of them as if they were fatty acids. In fact, the first step, biochemically, is to convert the aliphatics to fatty acids by adding oxygen to the molecular chain of hydrogen and carbon. Eventually, energy is derived from the oil as it would be from fat, and the by-products of the process are carbon dioxide and water.

"So one could say," I suggested, "that fat equals aliphatic oil plus oxygen?"

"No comment," Wolfe said with a smile.

He stressed that mammals, birds and fish would rather get rid of hydrocarbons—excrete them as quickly as possible—than use them as a source of energy. The stable aliphatics go rather quietly.

The aromatic hydrocarbons, on the other hand, those of the benzene-ring structure, react readily with living cells, challenging the animal's capacity to disarm and expel them. The lighter aromatics, in relatively small amounts, kill organisms. I've mentioned the BETX compounds, petroleum's gang of four, led by the simplest and most toxic, the single-ringed benzene. Then there are the double-ringed naphthalenes and the heavier, multiringed aromatics, which we may group as PAH compounds. The polynuclear aromatic hydrocarbons, a.k.a. the polyaromatics, are less lethal as a rule than BETX, but, as the number of rings increases, the more the PAHs resist breaking down, and the longer they are retained in organisms.

If an animal is exposed to aromatic compounds in less than fatal doses, enzyme systems come into play to process them, but it's tough going, a defensive response to a poisonous hot potato. "When the aliphatics are metabolized, there's no pain involved to the organism," said Wolfe. "But the aromatics have to be sent to the liver for detoxification, and there can be pain along the way." By pain he meant histologic, chromosomal, reproductive and/or behavioral damage.

Wolfe had recently returned from the Sound, where he assisted on the first leg of a NOAA investigation of bottom fish. The analysis of the hundreds of fish collected wasn't complete, although Wolfe would not have been permitted to reveal the results even if he had them. "The fish are metabolizing that oil," he could safely say. "As a result of that exposure, there are potential effects."

So went my first lesson. In time I understood that exposure to hydrocarbons, a body of chemicals that once belonged to living creatures, can lead to contradictory developments, from oil as poisonous carcinogen to oil as organic stimulus. It depends not only upon the composition, concentration and duration of the exposure, but also on the route of uptake, be it ingestion, respiration or superficial contact. However the chemicals are acquired, if life doesn't die straightaway—if exposures aren't too great—the general biological response is one of grudging accommodation.

Let's consider human exposure first, the exposure from the cleanup. Just three weeks before the accident, oil spills were brought under Occupational Safety and Health Administration (OSHA) regulations governing hazardous waste operations. Although Alaska health officials advised that the threat was low, the oil on the beaches was considered to be a hazardous waste product. Cleanup workers had to decontaminate themselves at the end of the day. They left their protective rubber suits and gloves outside the showers on the shower barge. After washing, they exited the showers by a different route, so as not to come in contact again with their splotched clothing, and their gear was cleaned each night. In practice if not proclamation, Prince William Sound was a hazardous waste site.

OSHA was guided by crude oil's "material safety data sheet," a summary of health effects, warnings and first-aid procedures. The agency requires industries to post safety information on chemicals that are handled in the workplace. Accordingly, everyone working on the beaches was required to take a safety course that included a presentation of Exxon's facts about crude oil. I took a short form of the course and received the sheet prior to joining the Houghton-Lees expedition.

At the top of the six-page document, crude oil was described as "a dark liquid," with a "strong hydrocarbon solvent odor."

Page 3: "This product may contain benzene . . . as a natural constituent. Benzene can cause anemia and other blood diseases, including leukemia (cancer of the blood-forming system), after prolonged or repeated exposures at high concentrations (e.g., 50–500 ppm). It has also caused fetal defects in tests on laboratory animals."

Further: "Crude oil has been shown to cause skin cancer in animal tests. In such lifetime skin painting tests the substance was applied to the shaved backs of mice at regular intervals without cleanup between applications. In view of these findings, there may be a potential risk of skin cancer in humans from prolonged and repeated skin contact with this product in the absence of good personal hygiene."

The second reference was to the PAHs. OSHA did not regulate petroleum per se. Benzene and the PAHs, although minor in proportion to other compounds in crude oil, were the chemicals that prompted the safety procedures. I looked into the toxicological history of each.

The link between polyaromatic hydrocarbons, poor hygiene and cancer is long-standing. As early as 1775 a surgeon in London, Percival Pott, made the connection, though he wasn't able to identify the particular compounds, only that something in coal soot seemed to be causing scrotal tumors in chimney sweeps. Had there been a safety sheet on coal soot, the chimney sweeps would have been warned to wash thoroughly at the end of each day. When modern scientists induced tumors on the skin of mice, they identified PAHs as the cause. The skin cancers have been brought about by extracts of oil-contaminated barnacles as well as by direct applications of crude oil.

The National Cancer Institute lists more than a dozen PAHs as suspected carcinogens in humans. Which is to say, many cancers have been induced in animals, but in the workplace or elsewhere where people have been exposed to high doses of heavy aromatics, a connection to cancer is strongly suspected but not absolutely proved. Americans ingest PAHs in smoked meats and roasted nuts and seem none the worse for it. The threat to human health from the heavy aromatics in the spill appeared to be slight if basic precautions were followed.

A number of shoreline workers contracted dermatitis, a heavy rash, on their hands and forearms, and by no coincidence these people declined gloves or failed to tape their gloves to their sleeves. An analysis by the Coast Guard stated that the risk of skin cancer caused by sunburn was statistically much greater than cancer from the workers' contact with PAHs. As for the consumption of oiled seafood, another possible route of PAH exposure, people simply stayed away. The Alaska Natives, as we'll see, would not believe that their shellfish and salmon were safe, in spite of vigorous arguments by the authorities that the contamination was too minor to matter.

Benzene is the only aromatic hydrocarbon listed as a "known" human carcinogen, that is, shown to the satisfaction of science. The rap sheet on C_6H_6 is as long as my arm. OSHA regulations characterize it as a clear, colorless, noncorrosive, highly flammable liquid with a strong, rather pleasant odor. Extracted from petroleum, it has value as a solvent and a motor fuel. It has been widely used in industry since the turn of the century. Pigment readily dissolves in benzene to make "oil-based" paint; benzene likewise makes an excellent paint-thinner. But no one handles it so casually today. Vaporizing, benzene may enter the body by inhalation or through the pores of the skin. The chemical has been linked to blood and bone marrow disorders and irreversible anemia among workers in shoe factories, rubber plants and oil refineries. As early as 1928 researchers called attention to the association between benzene exposure and leukemia.

Benzene does not cause anemia and leukemia overnight; the rubber workers, like the chimney sweeps, got sick only after many years of exposure, just as the lab animals got skin cancer near the end of their (short) lives. But when exposed to high concentrations of benzene, humans may suffer grave effects at once. "In the old days," said Dr. James Huff of the National Toxicology Program, "it wasn't only leukemia—people handling benzene would just keel over and die." Unlike the PAHs, benzene is both acutely and chronically poisonous.

OSHA has ruled that over an eight-hour day workers may be

exposed to a benzene level in the air of no more than one part per million. If readings should reach even half that level, 0.5 ppm, the industry must initiate a medical monitoring program and other precautionary measures. The regulations apply to enclosed workplaces, like factory interiors, where vapors can accumulate. Conducting an experiment underneath a wharf with one side blocked off, Coast Guard researchers spilled fresh crude and measured benzene up to 7 ppm, which they called a short-term, worst-case occurrence. OSHA specifically exempts oil fields, drilling operations and other open-air sites from the benzene standards, because exposures there have consistently been shown to be less than 0.5 ppm.

Oil spills were another matter. Safety inspectors toured the beaches of the Sound in the summer of '89. Their air sampling program found that both benzene and oil-mist concentrations were below the level of regulatory concern. According to the official report, weathering had dispersed most of the harmful vapors by the time the spill hit the shoreline. Diesel and gasoline fumes from the cleanup operation, and even tobacco smoke from workers, were thought to have interfered with the chemical signals from the oil.

At the end of 1989, some 1,800 workmen's compensation claims were filed in connection with the cleanup. The majority were for "slip/trip/fall–type" accidents, no surprise there. Fifteen percent were categorized as "weather-related," including a common respiratory infection. (This nasty flu left a smell on a victim that was instantly recognizable in Valdez; usually the person had a jaundiced face to go with it.) The "potentially chemically related" category, including forty-four cases of dermatitis and nineteen "nervous system" complaints, counted for less than 5 percent of the total. Finally, about 7 percent of the claims were grouped as "symptoms ill defined."

The vaguer ailments interested me, because people tended to attribute them to hydrocarbons. I talked to a physician who cared for the crews in the Sound. He described workers complaining of dizziness and nausea, particularly female workers on warm days.

"We didn't run any blood chemistry on these people," he said, "nothing fancy other than a physical exam, which didn't show anything, so we can't be sure why they felt sick. They always got better after resting. Most weren't malingering—they really wanted to get back to work. They'd been on the job for weeks in most cases when this happened to them. It was puzzling to me, definitely."

In the dozen or so lawsuits that were brought afterward, the poor health of the plaintiff was laid to his or her general exposure to crude oil and cleanup agents. These lawsuits were long shots. There are ample records of people blacking out (this didn't happen in the Sound) after breathing intense concentrations of hydrocarbon fumes, and in the worst cases victims have fallen unconscious and died. But those who recovered did so fairly quickly and had no chronic illness. I myself am evidence in point, since my capacious inhalations of fumes in the wrecked al-Ahmadi oilfield in Kuwait. Those fumes, fresh from the ground, immobilized me within fifteen minutes, and I had to be pulled clear of the field.

The lower but steadier doses were harder to figure. The cleanup worker whose job kept him in an enclosed tank in '89 had a stronger basis for litigation than others. A doctor who examined him in support of his suit told me that the initial injuries to the man's lungs probably never healed. The doctor, who runs an environmental health clinic in Texas, asserted that the damage was aggravated by the victim's subsequent exposures, far from the oil spill, to household solvents, dry-cleaning fluid vapors and the like. It seems there is no escaping the toxicants of modern life.

Of course the poisoning of animals in the Sound was proof as well that people should be concerned for their health. Although it wasn't explored at the time, there was a possible link between the plight of the oiled harbor seals and the hazards of oil fumes to humans.

The spill tainted an estimated three out of four seals living in the western Sound. Several hundred remained blackened for months, clambering on and off the oiled beaches, some even bearing pups in the oil, as they clung to their regular haulout sites. Yet few dead were found, in part because seal carcasses sink, and the calculation of mortalities by the damage assessors was complicated by an ongoing, prespill decline in population. (The problem with harbor seals in the Sound is similar to the fading of sea lions across the Gulf of Alaska, and no more explicable. If the acute toxicity of the slick killed about two hundred in 1989, as was estimated, the chronic decline took an additional one hundred.)

The splotched survivors were acting strangely. Biologists and cleanup workers reported that many seals seemed lethargic, or tame, and wouldn't be spooked by the approach of a person or the noise of a helicopter. Reluctantly they moved off the beaches into the water. Two years later, when a summary of the spill toll was released, seals were said to have been brain-damaged. A veterinary pathologist hired by the government concluded that identical neurological injuries had occurred in industrial workers stricken by the vapors of gasoline and hydrocarbon solvents.

The scientific evidence for this connection was slender, resting on the brain tissue of one seal, with corroborating signs in the tissue of five others. Twenty-seven animals were examined in all. "We had only one good seal," said the pathologist, Terry Spraker of Colorado State University, "which was the first one collected, thirty-six days after the spill. It was sick and wasn't going to survive. The others were collected in late June and their brain lesions [injuries] were milder. These seals were still coated with mousse, but probably they were recovering. These lesions *are* reversible."

Specifically, Spraker's microscope revealed "axonal degeneration," which he compared to stripping the insulation off the brain's electrical wires, and "intramyelenic edema," a swelling within the sheaths around the nerve fiber. Such conditions are reported in the medical literature on humans and hydrocarbon solvents. Besides head pain, the brain injuries would have caused the one seal such confusion, Spraker believed, that the animal was doomed to drown. She was a pregnant female, heavily oiled in Herring Bay. Her sense of direction was addled; she wouldn't have registered the water pressure or temperature when diving for food.

Other seals must have been as gravely hurt by their acute exposures to the oil. To find out, the pathologist should have been sampling earlier. But by the time the permits to shoot two dozen animals were obtained, most of the volatile compounds had fled the oil and the harbor seals were shaking off the effects, like the workers who recovered after being felled by fumes. The critical difference was that workers could go home and rest, while the pinnipeds still had to forage for themselves in the subarctic waters.

To return to the wooziness and vague symptoms of some cleanup workers, the interesting question is why those relative few were affected and not the rest. An OSHA scientist suggested an explanation to me. In occupational medicine there is a syndrome known as the healthy-worker effect. Within large labor pools a certain minority will be allergic to a substance in the work environment. Those affected weed themselves out. They leave and take work where they're not bothered. The laborers who remain are stronger and healthier overall.

Employment on the oil spill was different. Here was an opportunity for fishermen, clerks, bank tellers, what have you (I met a man whose business was selling ballet and theater costumes), to cash in on a boom. Alaskans jumped at jobs paying $17 an hour. Historically the economy has been driven by bursts of temporary employment, a midsummer night's dream of riches, and be it the Klondike gold rush or the Trans-Alaska Pipeline construction there is no telling when a boom will come again. Veco, the labor contractor, wasn't picky about hiring. People with pacemakers in their chests dragged hoses over the slippery stones. The healthy-worker effect didn't stand a chance. The sufferers of allergies wobbled all the way to the bank. From there some proceeded to lawyers' offices.

THE OCCUPATIONAL health inspectors said they saw no reason to recommend long-term monitoring of the cleanup workers. But an epidemiological show of force might have quashed the rumors in Alaska about cancer. For cancer was at the bottom of the concern about petroleum hydrocarbons. Benzene was known to cause cancer in humans; benzene and its sister aromatics were constituents of oil. The fact that cancer was not alleged in the lawsuits or compensation claims of the cleanup workers did not mean the disease would not strike in the future.

Since the biochemical squence of carcinogenesis has not been clarified, scientists cannot show precisely how benzene (or how cigarettes, for that matter) trigger the disease. The proof must be inferred. The National Cancer Institute declares a substance to be a known human carcinogen on the strength of double-barreled evidence—first, an epidemiological finding, such as an elevated rate of disease following exposure, and second, toxicological corroboration in the laboratory. Mere correlation, remember, is not an explanation of causality.

In the late '70s, as the epidemiological evidence of a connection between benzene workers and leukemia grew stronger, OSHA moved to lower the exposure limit from the 10 ppm ceiling then prevailing. Industry fought the new regulation, and was upheld in court because the government had not established sufficient proof of the hazard. Possibly the excessive leukemias had a source other than benzene, or a combination of sources in which benzene was not the lead agent.

Toxicologists redoubled their work with rodent surrogates and benzene. In feeding and inhalation experiments it was relatively simple to induce blood diseases such as anemia, but not cancer. Then, in the early '80s, a number of laboratories, among them James Huff's group at the National Toxicology Program, an arm of the National Institute of Environmental Health Sciences, confirmed that benzene was a powerful animal carcinogen. The rats and mice developed an array of tumors. Still, the rodents did not provide the extrapolation to humans that was sought, because the cases of leukemia induced were very few. It was on the evidence of the other rodent cancers that OSHA went forward. In 1987, with industry acquiescing, the agency tightened its standard for airborne benzene to 1 ppm.

Benzene is regulated even more strictly in drinking water, where the route of uptake, ingestion, is more direct. EPA and the Food and Drug Administration permit a concentration no higher than 5 parts per billion. In a 50-million-gallon reservoir, in other words, EPA would allow no more than five cups of dissolved benzene. At concentrations any lower, instruments can't reliably detect it.

In 1990 (before the FDA standard, adopted from EPA, formally went into effect) there was a benzene scare in the United States. Tests performed on bottles of Perrier mineral water in North Carolina and Georgia revealed benzene contaminations ranging between 10 and 20 parts per billion. In the brouhaha that ensued, all 72 million bottles of Perrier for sale in the United States had to be recalled. The company's sales in this country have never recovered.

An FDA spokesman was largely ignored when he said that, at such a minor level of contamination, "if you consumed about sixteen fluid ounces [of Perrier] a day, your lifetime risk of cancer might increase by one in a million." The agency, in fact, did not order the recall. The government felt unable to justify a recall given the paucity of the risk—but to save its reputation the Perrier Group of America had no choice.

Also discounting the hazard was Bruce Ames, a noted biochemist at the University of California at Berkeley. He is the originator of the Ames test for mutagenicity, a standard means of using bacterial cultures to assess whether a chemical might be a carcinogen. "We have to stop getting hysterical about all these hypothetical risks," Ames told the *New York Times*.

Was there a practical way to understand the risk of cancer from drinking Perrier? I went back to Huff's experiments with rodents, which helped to justify the 5 ppb limit for human exposure.

Huff's group fed benzene to rats and mice for up to two years. The top dosage for the mice was 100 milligrams of chemical for each kilogram of the subject's weight. (Another way of expressing this dose is 100 ppm—that is, for every million units of mouse-weight, 100 units of benzene were administered.) Every animal received the same relative amount, which was of course minuscule since mice don't weigh much. The benzene was delivered by stomach tubes, five times a week. The animals receiving the maximum dose developed the highest numbers of lymphomas, carcinomas, and adenomas.

I did some extrapolating and the FDA confirmed that the equivalent dose for a 150-pound person would be a bit more than a tenth of an ounce of benzene per day. By the logic of toxicology, one would be assured of contracting some form of cancer if one stomached such a regimen for a lifetime. But drinking contaminated Perrier would be a ludicrously inefficient means of administering the carcinogen: A person would have to consume 2.5 million of the bad bottles each week to approximate the intake that had sickened the rodents. If the Perrier were officially clean—say, no more than 5 ppb benzene—one would have to drink at least 10 million bottles (160 million fluid ounces) per week to match Huff's top doses.

In setting their standard for benzene in drinking water, government regulators have stated that if they err it should be on the side of safety. The 5-ppb ceiling not only guards against any possible short-term injury to human health, but also, it would seem, any conceivable long-term threat. This is the same kind of divide, Exxon's "margin of safety," between the BETX concentrations found in the Sound after the spill and the dosages required to produce harmful effects in fish.

I do not fault the regulators' conservatism. Where I have difficulties, and I'm not alone, is with the calculations of risk assessment that accompany the stringent limits on potential carcinogens. When an incident of contamination occurs and an exposure ceiling is breached, a risk assessment formula is invoked showing an increase in the likelihood of someone contracting cancer.

Risk assessment produces hard numbers on the incidence of infrequent and unfortunate occurrences. It is a social science, the utility of which isn't known until after the fact. Thus in 1986 Alyeska figured that a major tanker spill would take place in Prince William Sound once every 241 years. That was not a good risk assessment. There is less guesswork involved when a wealth of data exists. Life insurers, for instance, use risk assessment in pricing their policies. A company gathers the statistics on prior mortalities, considers the present contingencies and then computes the probabilities of a person's dying in the future.

Imagine a company issuing a policy to a mouse that is based on its studies of human morbidity. That is more or less how cancer risks are assessed. Following long-standing procedures, scientists analyze the induced effects of a chemical on rodents, and then, with an eye to the epidemiological histories, derive a cancer potency factor that is extrapolated to humans. What emerges is a one in a thousand (or ten or a hundred thousand) chance of becoming ill with cancer from a particular exposure. Delving into the number, one finds assumptions, weighted variables and hypothetical models of a chemical's distribution, uptake and metabolism in the test species and in humans, all of which may represent the best judgments of experienced toxicologists, yet the figure nevertheless issues from the same kind of rubbery algebra Exxon used to show the efficacy of its cleanup machines. Something gets lost in the leap from animal testing to human risk, and from human risk to regulatory policy. In exchange for being protected from chemicals, the public is made more anxious about them.

If the tainted Perrier water made for an unlikely promoter of cancer, what about the risk from an unavoidable, long-term exposure to a carcinogen? Americans worry most about the invisible chemicals they don't even know they're absorbing. For example, daily life in Valdez, Alaska, exposes one to benzene in the atmosphere. Petroleum vapors released during tanker-loading operations at Alyeska, a few miles from town, inject an estimated 450 tons of benzene into the air of the port each year.

Though the epidemiologists haven't found anything, the Alyeska emissions have been a concern for years. EPA and DEC have studied the problem; regulations have been proposed and debated. Alyeska accepts that controls of some sort are inevitable. Not only benzene emanates from the terminal, but also lesser amounts of ethylbenzene, toluene and xylene, of the BETX fraternity, and hexane, an aliphatic hydrocarbon having deleterious effects when inhaled. The ballast water treatment facility vents aromatics as well.

Federal legislation passed in the wake of the spill required the oil industry in Alaska to fund citizens' groups that would serve as industry watchdogs. The Prince William Sound Regional Citizens' Advisory Council (RCAC) pressed the inquiry into Alyeska's air pollution. In 1992 it released a study of the airborne hydrocarbons, the most thorough examination to date. The report found benzene to be the chemical of most concern. The risk assessment: A lifetime resident of the Valdez area stood a one in 20,000 chance of contracting cancer from benzene vapors. The report made an alarming story in Alaska newspapers. Valdez's benzene hazard was said to be comparable to Los Angeles's.

The pollution specialist who conducted the RCAC study was Dr. Yoram Cohen of the Unversity of California. His central piece of data was the estimate that, over the course of a lifetime, the average person in Valdez would absorb two thousandths of a milligram of benzene per kilogram of body weight per day (0.0021 mg/kg/day). Admittedly this exposure was no more than an informed guess, built upon the consultant's contamination model. It was not a lot of benzene, considering that the mice in the National Toxicology Program experiments got up to 35,000 times as much.

Cohen multiplied a person's exposure by the cancer potency factor of benzene (the latter derived by EPA in the mid-'80s), and came up with a 1-in-16,420 probability of cancer, which he rounded off to one chance in 20,000.

Cohen referred to this risk as an approximate and conservative one, in keeping with EPA safety margins. Indeed, the RCAC number was in the ballpark of the EPA's own assessment, issued two years before, of a cancer hazard of one in 10,000. EPA considers such a risk, and any other that is higher than one in a million, to be unacceptable. It triggers the regulatory machinery. Although an individual's odds are remote at one in 20,000, another way to see it is that among 20,000 people there will be one extra case of cancer. Valdez doesn't have that many residents, but still the regulators are bound to protect the one vulnerable person (the one-fifth person, actually) from benzene.

Alyeska, predictably, did not endorse the RCAC findings. The company released its own study, three years in the making, which showed the risk from the terminal to be substantially less, about two in a million. According to its monitoring data, 90 percent of the benzene in town was produced by engine exhaust, wood smoke and the like. Still, the overall odds of cancer were found to be in the range of the EPA and RCAC figures. The company's argument was that even if Valdez had a million people, the terminal's small contribution to disease would not be detectable amid the environmental noise—noise that did not include, by the way, the benzene that was generated and copiously consumed by cigarette smokers.

Whom, in this fraught world, to believe? Benzene-wise, one day of breathing in Valdez is decidedly more dangerous than drinking a sixteen-ounce bottle of tainted Perrier. Alyeska, EPA, the state DEC and the citizens' council are still arguing about the hazard, and commissioning further studies, but no one challenges the first-order assumptions of cancer risk.

The fearsome power of risk assessment depends on a "linear," or "no threshold" view of carcinogenesis. By this it is meant that there is no amount of a cancer-causing chemical so small as to eliminate a hazard entirely. When a substance is shown to cause cancer in test animals, and the equivalent dose is derived for humans, reducing that dose, even drastically, never ends the threat, but only lengthens the odds. According to this way of thinking, if Alyeska cut benzene emissions in half, then half as many residents would be predicted to get cancer in the future. But for the individual as for the group there would never be a statistical escape.

However, biomedical critics point out that the body does not passively tolerate the invasion of hazardous chemicals. The liver and immune system actively work to detoxify them, and there must be a level below which human defenses are strong enough to prevail without paying the price of cancer. A threshold must exist, that is, below which all bets of risk assessment are off, even if regulators do not acknowledge one. If forced to halve its benzene emissions, Alyeska might possibly move everybody below their exposure thresholds.

A second criticism of linear thinking is that, as exposures are reduced and the chances of *not* getting cancer expand, the signal of the chemical merges with the background rate of disease. As Alyeska argued, a certain percentage of people will get leukemia "naturally," from unknowable causes. To demonize benzene just because we can detect it in the environment is to admit how little we understand the development of cancer.

Biochemist Bruce Ames has taken the lead in a movement to challenge the conservative standards set by the government for chemical contaminants, particularly for pesticide residues in food. The tests on which the standards are based were flawed, argues Ames, because they have extrapolated the results of feeding huge, lifetime doses of chemicals to rodents—doses calibrated to fall just short of killing the animals outright. The mice who got cancer, usually late in their normal life spans, may have responded to the unrelenting load of the chemical and not to its inherent carcinogenicity. The high doses may cause cells to divide more rapidly, increasing the likelihood of harmful mutations.

Siding with Ames, the respected journal *Science* editorialized in 1990, "The standard carcinogen tests that use rodents are an obsolescent relic of the ignorance of past decades . . . [when] . . . extreme caution made sense." The journal said the public's "chemophobia" was diverting money and attention from more pressing hazards to human health.

The editorial did not name her, but in her grave Rachel Carson surely turned over. The writer of *Silent Spring* prepared the ground for the testing of chemicals on animals and for the extrapolation of cancer risks to humans. In the early '70s, when his bacterial mutagen test was introduced, Bruce Ames had promoted Carson's dire prophecies. Now he thinks she went too far.

"Everyone ignores the natural background," he told me. He was referring to the chemicals occurring naturally in foods, compounds that outnumber the contaminant substances 100 to one. According to his recent research, fully half of the natural chemicals that have been tested in rodents at high doses have been shown to cause cancer.

James Huff, the benzene toxicologist, has rallied to defend the traditional methods. Unmoved by Ames's arguments, he has urged that the use of rodent surrogates be extended. For example, tissue from fish in polluted harbors could be fed to rats and mice, and if the rodents got cancer, people could be warned of threats to their health from the fish. Huff told me, "It's too bad Rachel Carson isn't here to defend herself. Remember, if it weren't for her, you wouldn't be seeing any bald eagles flying around."

THE AMERICAN BALD EAGLE—if the sea otter was the animal that pulled most at the heartstrings during the oil spill, the situation of the stricken eagles was the most infuriating. The environmental crime, the blackening of our country's symbol was all the worse because of the bird's struggle to recover from pesticide poisoning a generation earlier, when its population in the Lower 48 dipped toward extinction.

The chemical responsible then, DDT, is a kind of hydrocarbon, one that has been altered by the addition of chlorine; it belongs to the malignant family of chlorinated hydrocarbons. DDT was introduced as an insecticide in the '40s, just at the time, ironically, that eagles were starting to recover under the Bald Eagle Protection Act of 1940. States used to pay bounties for eagles, which were known to take fish and thought to prey on livestock, and over the years Americans shot many thousands of their national bird. DDT worked more subtly in the large, long-lived raptors. It took until the 1960s for biologists to realize that DDT was just as dangerous as its spin-off poisons, such as dieldrin and heptachlor and chlordane, which could and did kill songbirds and small animals outright.

Sprayed onto fields and forests, the chlorinated pesticides ran off into streams and collected in rivers and lakes. Bacteria in the bottom sediments metabolized them. DDT, the most widespread of the chemicals, converted to metabolites DDE and DDD. Fish took up the compounds and processed them further. The bald eagle's body burden of organochlorines grew with each consumption of the tainted fish. When the concentrations in the birds reached the hundreds of parts per million, the female produced eggs that were either inviable or had shells so thin as to break under the brooder's weight.

The bald eagle's reproductive rate fell to near zero. The species was saved only by the banning of DDT in 1972. But since the chemical still lay in the environment, resisting degradation, and since eagles are not sexually mature until five or six years old, the recovery must be slow. The eagle population in the Midwest took fourteen years to double. Several states in the eastern United

States, where numbers were even lower, have stocked their refuges with eaglets imported from southcoastal Alaska.

Bald eagles are a spectacular example (wolves are another) of a species that is threatened and rare in the Lower 48 but is as common as crows in Alaska. Bounties were paid for carcasses from 1917 until 1953; the territory was exempted from the Bald Eagle Protection Act. More than 100,000 were shot and cashed in because fishermen held that the birds took too many salmon. As many more were shot and not redeemed. It wasn't illegal to kill eagles until Alaska joined the union in '59. Today the statewide population is put at about 40,000, five times the number living in the other states combined.

Ideal habitat for bald eagles consists of tall trees next to sheltered waters with plentiful fish: an apt description of Prince William Sound. The Sound's eagle population is estimated to be 4,000. Marjorie Gibson, a raptor specialist who assessed the birds' health after the spill, called the area a "high-rent district," meaning that the eagles that keep nesting territories here are the best of the breed, the top of the competition. Weaker and younger birds, she believes, are banished to less favorable ranges on river drainages and lakes inland. The rich proceed to get richer. It is not unusual for eagles in the Sound, as in the other prime breeding areas along the Gulf of Alaska coastline, to lay clutches of two and three eggs, whereas one egg tends to be the rule in the Lower 48.

On first coming to the Sound a visitor is likely to stop open-mouthed—I know I did—at each sighting—magnificent—of a bald eagle. One feels a bit foolish gaping because residents take them for granted. In Cordova in the spring of '89, far from the spill, a pair courted directly over the town, turning together in stiff-winged gyres. I watched a crow drive off one of the eagles, after which indignity it flapped to a nearby spruce. The bird teetered on the slender treetop and leered down at me like a gargoyle.

Benjamin Franklin accused the eagle of cowardice and low morals. In 1782 Franklin backed a rival candidate, the wild turkey, for national emblem. After observing an animal for a while, inevitably one makes anthropomorphic judgments, and so I could appreciate Franklin's animadversions. Eagles scavenge carrion, forage garbage in dumps and rob other birds of their catches. From my window over Lake Eyak that summer I witnessed a powerful enactment of its bullying ways.

The local eagle made a pass at a seagull, trying to get it to drop a fish. The eagle managed to knock down the gull instead. The eagle repeatedly dived onto the bird on the surface of the lake, aiming to slam its head with its talons. The gull was stained pink with blood, but it resisted by diving or by splashing up water with its wings each time the raptor swooped.

The eagle was methodical (Franklin would say lazy). It rested for long minutes on a tree, like a boxer between rounds of its own choosing, and then rose again to the attack. The gull kept splashing and wouldn't give up. Eventually the eagle refused to come out, and the other gulls settled about their comrade on the water, fluttering in a kind of victory if seagulls could proclaim victory.

Tough love for nature spares one from undue pain, and anyway, the bad taste is cut through by the next keening cry and soaring view, the lordly head blazed white against the deep green banks of the Sound.

At the time of my arrival in mid-May, dozens of eagle carcasses had been picked up and turned in to the freezer morgues of the U.S. Fish and Wildlife Service, a collection for which Exxon would pay a latter-day bounty. The majority were never recovered because they were believed to have fallen in the forest, back from the coastline. But the wave of mortalities, lasting about a month, was not seen to be as damaging to the eagle population as the poisoning of the survivors and of their reproductive potential.

Eagles were feeding on oily carrion, mainly waterfowl that had washed ashore. One bird reputedly made a stack of carcasses on the beach. The handful of live eagles that were brought in by fishermen were not in good shape. A raptor expert from Minnesota, Dr. Pat Redig, flew over the spill zone in April and called the situation "exceedingly grim." He reported eagles with oil-smudged tails, some in labored flight.

The FWS announced a major rescue program, to be funded by Exxon and run under FWS guidelines. The regional director of the Service said that the sickened raptors would probably die if they were not brought into captivity for treatment and cleaning. Alaska veterinarians lobbied for a role in the rescue. The logistics of trapping and tending who knew how many oiled eagles—birds with slashing beaks and seven-foot wingspans—presented an unknown challenge, but as with other exigencies of the spill, the public will and corporate resources were there to make it happen. The seabird and sea otter rescue programs were by then operating at full speed. Initially reluctant, Exxon committed $100,000 to construct a rehabilitation center in Anchorage strictly for eagles. It was expected that the sickest birds would have to be held for a year or more.

The program, however, was scaled back before it began. By evidence that became plain in the Sound there simply wasn't a need for extreme measures to save eagles in the spring of '89. Why the need was perceived in the first place makes for an interesting scientific story. People were caught up in the sweep of the emergency, but it went deeper than that. Several threads of knowledge converged in the bald eagle—the bird was positioned, if you will, at the top of an epistemological food chain, that having to do with toxic compounds and wildlife.

One concern was the concentration of chemicals in birds of prey. In the past, not only bald eagles but also many hawks and falcons had been brought down by ingesting chlorinated hydrocarbons. There was much talk in '89 of bioaccumulation and biomagnification in eagles, terms that tended to be used interchangeably. It is important to understand the difference. Bioaccumulation indicates only that a substance is retained. Biomagnification is a broader idea. It indicates that tissue burdens of the substance (or its metabolites) increase with each step up in the food web, because the organisms accumulating it cannot eliminate it, or if so not enough, and therefore they pass it on.

Both effects can occur in humans as well. An infamous case of biomagnification, told hauntingly in photographs for *Life* magazine by Eugene Smith, occurred at Minamata, Japan, during the '50s and '60s. Mercury in industrial waste ran off into Minamata's bay, where it was taken up by small invertebrates and then by fish. Humans who subsisted on the fish accumulated greater and greater amounts of a metabolite of mercury. This sinuous augmentation led to birth defects, blindness, paralysis, coma and death, yet the path of the poisoning eluded scientists for a long time, rather like DDT's role in the decline of raptors.

Many biologists were not aware that oil acts differently. Animals such as birds store petroleum hydrocarbons in their tissues much less readily than they retain organochlorines or metals. Moreover, birds as a group metabolize and excrete crude oil components better than marine organisms do, better, for example, than the cold-blooded fish, although not better than the mammals. This is not to say that hydrocarbons do not register in birds. After experimental feeding of oil, the heavier compounds are detectable, particularly in the fat reserves and in the lipid-rich material of eggs. The levels exceed the background concentrations in untreated subjects, which is proof of bioaccumulation.

Petroleum hydrocarbons can be transferred among animals in the food web, but biomagnification stops at the taxonomic transition between invertebrates (such as marine worms and shellfish) and vertebrates (fish, birds and mammals). Among vertebrates, the accumulations may be linked, but not exponentially so. NOAA's Douglas Wolfe told me, "Even in the literature as late as the mid-'80s there are erroneous references to food-chain magnification of hydrocarbons. All of us were claiming that fifteen years ago, because we didn't know, but it's a dead issue today." Rather it should be, he added, having seen a reference in the '90s. Here again was science lagging behind nescience.

Because higher animals get rid of them so fast, tissue analysis for petroleum hydrocarbons is not often performed on wild birds. Biochemists have discovered more sensitive indicators of exposure to oil, arising from the activation of certain liver enzymes. These markers of accumulation can be measured even when a bird's muscle and fat come up clean.

If the idea of magnification, a long-term threat, was misplaced, not so the belief that crude oil was acutely hazardous to seabirds. Eagles were seabirds as well as raptors, and the lesson of past spills was that marine birds got hit with a lot of oil at once, with profound and shocking results. The lesson was repeated on an unprecedented scale in Alaska, as many hundreds each of loons, grebes, ducks, puffins, guillemots, gulls, cormorants and murrelets, plus tens of thousands of the murres, were killed or wounded by the slick. Between the Sound and the Alaska Peninsula, some 36,000 carcasses were eventually recovered, which was only 10 percent, or perhaps less, of the total. By the final reckoning, several hundred of the Sound's bald eagles also died. Therefore it made sense, on those grounds alone, to protect eagles from coming into contact with the slick.

There are three main pathways by which oil attacks birds: by the fouling of feathers, by poisoning after heavy ingestion and by the contamination of eggs.

The first is most important. The majority of seabirds expire of the cold, because the oil disrupts their insulation and prevents them from flying and feeding. The birds' outer feathers interlock, keeping cold water out and body heat in. In that regard the toxicity of oil is secondary, for rafts of seabirds have perished after being gooped in spills of vegetable oil. Most of the labor at the bird rescue centers in Valdez and elsewhere went toward cleaning and restoring the water-repellency of plumage. The staffers were somewhat surprised that eagle feathers absorbed rather than repelled water; the eagles took a long time to dry after being washed.

The problem of contaminated plumage leads directly to the other two afflictions. Birds are forever preening in the normal order of business, but when fouled they tend to their feathers almost frantically, trying to clean themselves with their bills, and they can't help swallowing a portion of the oil. In one of the first experiments of avian toxicology involving petroleum, conducted in the early '60s, it was found that ducks ingested about half of the oil that they were painted with.

Caught in a slick when it is new, seabirds take up the spectrum of aromatic hydrocarbons, from the evanescing BETX, inhaled as well as swallowed, to the durable PAHs. The average marine bird weighs just a pound or two. A half cup of oil, which a 150-pound human might ingest and shrug off, wreaks catastrophic effects. The bird's intestines, bone marrow, liver, kidney and immune system are attacked all at once. The aromatic compounds also interfere with the function of its adrenal and thyroid glands, with its system of converting saltwater to fresh (resulting in dehydration), with its capacity to break down food (resulting in malnutrition).

Hemolytic anemia results from the destruction of red blood cells. It is probably the most common symptom of hydrocarbon poisoning in seabirds. The condition has been straightforwardly induced in experiments with naphthalene, an intermediate-weight aromatic. Blood is drawn, and the red blood cells are separated in a centrifuge. A healthy seabird generally has a packed cell volume, as it's called, of around 50 percent of whole blood. If the packed cell volume is reduced to 40 percent, the bird is anemic. At 25 percent, the bird is desperately ill and will live only if kept warm and carefully tended. It needs force-feeding, usually with supplements of iron.

Less than 30 percent of the birds at the Valdez rescue center were kept alive. The acute effects of the oil cascaded. An anemic bird instinctively boosted its metabolic rate, which aggravated its need for warmth and nourishment, which further strained its thermoregulatory capacity, already compromised by oil-clogged feathers, and its digestive system, already inflamed by hydrocarbons raking its gut. Oiling creates so many severe and overlapping stresses that postmortem exams are pointless.

A bald eagle, swooping onto a loon struggling in the slick, would have been subject to the same cascade of oiled plumage and unwitting ingestion of aromatic hydrocarbons. Wet, sick, hypothermic, it might then break a wing in wobbly flight, or be drawn again to the oil, desperate now for easy pickings, but the more it ate the more it would weaken, and thus expire quite blackened, to be scavenged by eagles in turn. So the tattered carcasses came in. A few eagles died before the spill, from the stresses of winter, and became marked with the evidence after the fact.

The eagles that concerned the authorities were the lesser oiled, those holding on, it was feared, with their red blood cells declining, until they would succumb to the elements. At the same time, egg-laying was starting. Even if it wasn't sick, only slightly spotted, a brooding bird could transfer oil from its breast feathers to the eggs.

An impressive body of literature exists on the impact of oil on seabird eggs. As far back as the 1940s, the Fish and Wildlife Service reduced herring gull colonies on the coast of New England by spraying nests and eggs with oil. More recent knowledge was gained thanks to government grants under OSCEAP, the Alaska environmental program. Here is one area of toxicology where field experiments can be scientifically controlled. Seabird colonies are easy to get at. The brooding birds temporarily fly off at the approach of the scientists bearing their pots of crude oil. Eggs can be brushed with a range of applications, and nests can be monitored throughout the incubation period. For confirmation of results, similar tests may be run on eggs in incubators back home.

Oil in the most minute amounts disrupts or halts the development of avian embryos. Mere thousandths of a gram can have the gravest effects. "A quarter of a drop of oil on the shell is lethal to 50 to 80 percent of embryos," said Michael Fry, an avian specialist at the University of California at Davis. Toxic PAHs invade the shell pores, and the embryo within is very sensitive. Unlike the mammalian embryo, it is cut off from the defense mechanisms of the parent. In many cases, Fry noted, the fatal wisp of hydrocarbons isn't even detectable in its tissues.

When research biologists trapped laughing gulls on the nest, dabbed their breasts with fuel oil and then let them return to brooding, 40 percent of the eggs failed to hatch, compared to a mortality of only 2 percent in nests of birds treated only with water. Using the same small amount (two milliliters) of weathered crude oil on feathers, Michael Fry and colleagues were able to bring about a total hatching failure in a group of Hawaiian wedge-tailed shearwaters, a colonial nester. In this instance Fry believed that ingestion of the oil during preening caused the effects.

As a general rule, birds are most vulnerable to chemicals early in incubation, and rapidly less so as they develop and hatch and mature. In one test on chicken eggs, embryos eight days old were killed by faint appplications of Prudhoe Bay crude to the shells. But at eleven days of age the embryos survived. The extra days allowed their livers to develop enough to neutralize the hydrocarbons. This was deduced through measurements of the liver enzymes I mentioned, the telltale indicators that the chicks had not only been exposed to the oil but were mobilized against it.

Biologists in the Sound had these and many other citations, all pointing to the extreme sensitivity of seabird embryos and hatch-lings to petroleum. The research provided one more reason to try to rescue and clean the mating eagles. If there was an extrapolation to make to a different avian species, one never subjected before to experiments with oil or to a major oil spill, the general assessment of risk was valid.

Symbolism iced the scientific cake. Exxon wouldn't have ded-icated a rehab center to the common murre, the bird that took the biggest hit. The bald eagle stood for our dwindling wilderness, for all that was still unspoiled about America. Thus the company later made the bird a symbol of the Sound's recovery, as in its 1991 brochure, "The Abundant Bald Eagles of Prince William Sound, Alaska." On the other side, the head of the Alaska Department of Environmental Conservation once stalked into a meeting with Exxon and the Coast Guard carrying a dead eagle in a bag. He said he had just picked it up on an oily beach in the Sound. He used it to press the state's case for more cleanup.

In May of '89, at least, the cooperation was good among Exxon, the Fish and Wildlife Service and a private group, the Interna-tional Bird Rescue Research Center of Berkeley, California. Once the company agreed that the bald eagle operation should go for-ward, expense was put aside. Exxon hired veterinarians and biol-ogists to supplement the government personnel, and installed blood centrifuges on the chartered rescue vessels.

The capture teams scouted the spill zone by airplane. Six weeks after the accident, the biologists observed that most eagles were not oiled, and that they were behaving as if there were noth-ing wrong with their health. Recalled Marjorie Gibson, the eagle expert brought in by IBRRC to run the capture program, "Not in our wildest dreams would we have expected them to be breeding or defending their territories the way they were, especially where cleanup activity was going on."

The group leaders had to rethink, for if the eagles were not that ill, then captivity—in itself quite stressful to wild birds, caus-ing adrenal, blood and liver changes akin to that from poisoning—would best be avoided. If nesting was going forward, might not it be better to keep pairs together and let the eagles lay? The pro-tocols of the program were revised: There would be a veterinary exam in situ. If the captured birds were not seriously oiled, and if they passed a blood test and seemed strong enough to rear young, then they would be released on the spot.

For three months several teams trapped eagles in Prince William Sound and also around Kodiak Island in the Gulf of Alaska. Since from a distance it was hard to tell whether an eagle was tainted, the capture teams went after most any bird in the vicinity of an oiled shoreline. They took advantage of its opportunism. High on its perch, the raptor would notice a dead fish being dropped from a skiff into the water. As the skiff motored slowly away, the bird would descend and make off with the bait, but when it arose, its talons would become ensnared by loops of transparent fishing line. The fish was attached to a floating log, whose weight would bring the bird down to the water, and the boat would speed back. Restraining its wings, the capture specialists would slip a hood over its head and then take the bird to the main vessel.

Anesthetized by the darkness, the eagles did not resist their half-hour checkups. Besides a thorough physical inspection, and the spot-cleaning of oil if necessary, about ten cubic centimeters of blood were drawn from each bird. A small portion of the blood was separated in the microcentrifuge and analyzed. The flash tests measured the packed cell volumes (PCV) of the red cells and the various protein components of the plasma. The rest of the sample was saved for shipment to Dr. Pat Redig at the Raptor Center at the University of Minnesota, who performed a detailed analysis.

At a scientific symposium in 1990, Marjorie Gibson and Dr. Jan White of IBRRC summarized the findings on the 113 birds that were examined. (Gibson told me that the blood chemistry and other technical data were based largely on the eagles of the Sound, where her own rescue team worked.) Ninety-eight eagles were healthy enough to be released at once. Only one-third of the 113 had any oil on them; only two birds were more than lightly oiled.

"On the whole, blood work performed on these birds was within normal ranges," Gibson and White reported. Redig put it more bluntly: "Nothing could be detected. I had blood from a hundred-plus birds. I concluded, they looked good. What you're looking for in these tests are abnormal levels of enzymes from the liver and kidneys that are signs of organ malfunction. You don't really expect to find these indicators unless seventy-five percent of the liver has been destroyed."

I asked him about the worst case he saw. "There was one immature bird that was sent to me," he said, "that had been heavily oiled and had a broken wing. There were indicators, but even she wasn't internally damaged."

Of the fifteen eagles deemed to require care and conveyed to the rescue centers, most got well and were freed within two weeks. Perhaps the best indication of their health was their behavior on release. Rescue workers made the mistake of letting some eagles go along with a batch of seabirds. Smiles froze as the raptors snatched and ate some of the rehabilitated fowl.

In addition to the eagles captured by the specialists, the public rescued twenty-four. These were in worse shape than Gibson's fifteen, more anemic, five with fractured limbs, and some too far gone to save, but only half showed signs of oil. It was determined that most of the injury and illness in this group antedated the spill—these birds were casualties of nature, like trees that should have fallen in the forest and not made a sound, except that volunteers heard them and gathered them up. Generally, they needed a longer rehabilitation too. Gibson herself took home a bird that was found oiled and crippled in Herring Bay. It would never again be able to survive in the Sound. But whether or not the *Exxon Valdez* was at fault, "it's as healthy as a horse today," she said.

In a separate report, veterinarian White calculated that Exxon spent over $10,000 per eagle in 1989. She divided the overall program costs of $1.4 million by the 137 birds that were handled. Was it worth it? Almost all the bald eagles that died from the spill perished before people were organized to help them. The rest survived with little or no assistance. The other rescue work was more effective: Half of the 1,630 oiled seabirds taken into the four rescue centers were made fit for release, and half died.

Granted the eagles were less injured than other birds to start with. Still I was curious about the split in survival among eagles. I knew that large, warm-blooded vertebrates detoxify hydrocarbons. Why if so many shook off the contamination did several hundred others succumb?

"There is, of course, significant doubt about whether most eagles even ingested oil," wrote Gibson and White. Eagles have a crop, an enlargement of the gullet where food initially lodges after being swallowed. The authors speculated that the oil on carrion might have been expelled from the crop along with bones, feathers and other indigestible material.

Redig believed that eagles ingested hydrocarbons, but he said that if the causes of death were to be rated, drowning and exposure to the cold and wet, as a consequence of superficial oiling, would rank well ahead of poisoning. Hemolytic anemia was not demonstrated in the necropsies. Michael Fry, whom the government hired as an adviser, or peer reviewer, of its bird studies, said, "Most eagles were waterlogged and starved, probably because of external fouling." If acute toxicity was a factor, it would have been greatest in the first week of weathering of the slick.

Perhaps a bird's character—I should say behavior—played a part too. The discriminating eagles may have avoided the tainted carrion. The capture teams didn't observe eagles hunting in oiled areas, and found that birds would not take their fish if the traps were dropped within thirty yards of an oily beach. The stranding of oil wasn't uniform, noted Gibson and White, so there were clean sections for eagles to feed in.

"The less proficient hunters might not make it," Gibson suggested when I questioned her. "The ones that would settle for oily carrion would be at most risk. But we learned that the best territorial defenders would not take carrion. I remember an eagle that lived near Sleepy Bay, it was absolutely clean, head and tail. That summer it fished 100 yards off the shore of one of the dirtiest beaches in the Sound."

"You almost seem to be saying that the oil spill acted like a force of natural selection," I remarked, "weeding out the eagles that were less fit." Of course this was pushing it. I was thinking of the spill as a disturbance, a bearer (in man-made form) of stress to the Sound's community of raptors.

"I projected it would be Armageddon," she said. "I felt strongly when I went in that the oil would have a toxic effect. I also believed, we can do a lot for them. But then we saw they were making it better than we thought. It was a relief, but also humbling, looking back on what nature can do. It also helped that the area had almost no immature eagles—that the strongest birds were there. I guess I'd say that the forces of nature and luck were with them equally."

THE SHORT-TERM EFFECTS did not tell the whole story. A large and still expanding body of information about bald eagles and the spill was in the hands of the U.S. Fish and Wildlife Service. It was kept secret for three years, under the restrictions of the natural resource damage assessment (NRDA) program. Before I had an opportunity to review it, I talked with Philip Schempf, the lead biologist on the government project. Schempf has worked with eagles in southcoastal Alaska since 1980, and he collaborated with IBRRC and Exxon in 1989 even as he launched the damage-assessment study.

"I disagree that everything's rosy," was the only comment he would make about the report by Gibson and White. His superiors did not allow Schempf to show his own hand. Gibson too was most eager to know whether there might be chronic sublethal damage in individual birds or in the eagle population, but she was not privy to the inquiry.

From the beginning, or at least after the first month, one could see the extended effects of the oil spill as a glass either half empty or half full. The legal polarization pushed scientists toward one view or the other. I learned to distrust the pronouncements of both sides, as well as the infrequent summaries of research findings. Without the full studies, it wasn't possible to check the basis of the pronouncements. In that sense the Gibson and White report, though appearing eighteen months after the event, was exceptional. By the time a comprehensive picture of the eagles was made available in 1992, with details and shadings, most questions were academic and the public was preoccupied with other things. The state of understanding rested circa 1989. When I told a newsmagazine editor that my book would contain some surprises, he assumed I had uncovered evidence of "three-legged ducks," or other mutant offspring of the biological catastrophe.

The first rundown on the damages to species was issued by the Trustee Council (made up of representatives of three state and three federal agencies) in April of '91. It was meant to justify a settlement of criminal and civil charges against Exxon. The press accounts of this summary said the overall damages were worse than believed, although it was not clear whose belief the damages were worse than, no figures beyond a morgue inventory having been released before.

According to the status report on bald eagles, "Productivity surveys in 1989 indicate a failure rate of approximately 85 percent for nests on moderately or heavily oiled beaches compared to 55 percent on unoiled or lightly oiled beaches. Bald eagles have a delayed sexual maturity and have a relatively long lifespan under normal circumstances. Consequently, although reproduction apparently rebounded to more normal levels in 1990, population impacts as a result of poor productivity of nestlings and the death of hundreds of adult eagles in 1989 may not be readily apparent for several years."

In focusing on long-term population impacts, the government was invoking scenarios about hydrocarbons and birds that looked beyond the toxicity of ingested oil, that is, to the twin specters of the lethal contamination of eggs and the wounded reproductive health of adults.

When damage assessment commenced in the spring of '89, aerial surveys immediately found trouble in the eagle nests of the Sound. After the peak hatching period in mid-June, the FWS reported that far fewer chicks were seen than normal. The investigators climbed trees and collected twenty eggs that didn't hatch. It was not possible to obtain a representative sample of dead embryos, because the seagulls would make short work of abandoned eggs. Researchers also collected eggshell fragments and the remains of food in the nests, lest the birds be absorbing aromatic hydrocarbons that could impair their reproductive organs.

I've gone back through my news clippings of the time. The early stories talk about "nest abandonment," but after '89 one didn't hear about eagles having forsaken their nests, only about that year's nesting "failure." The FWS even listed the missing eaglets—"at least 133 chicks" that should be living in Prince William Sound but for the oil spill—as if such exactitude counted for anything in the contingent world of wind and water.

Bald eagle nesting suffered in the Sound not just because birds had died or didn't lay or because their eggs were poisoned. These upshots of oil were found to have impact. But the most important factor was that eagles were driven from their nests by the furious interference of the shoreline cleanup.

Alarmed and agitated, as anyone covering the cleanup could tell, the birds circled their craggy treetop structures. Eleanor and Smith Islands, where crews worked full-bore during spring, produced no eaglets whatsoever. Knight Island had 118 nests occupied by adult pairs, yet only eleven young were observed in June. The FWS biologists couldn't do anything about it. Glumly, they would tell a cleanup supervisor not to worry about disturbing a particular segment—the eagles there had just abandoned their nest.

Gary Sonnevil, the biologist in charge of the Valdez office, told the *Anchorage Daily News* in July, "There's a massive quantity of people—a small army supported by a navy supported by an air force. These birds haven't seen levels of activity like this ever in Prince William Sound. . . . The real intensive cleanup area is where we're seeing abandoned nests at high rates."

Perhaps because he was not involved in damage assessment, Sonnevil put forward the most obvious explanation for the nest abandonment. So did Jill Parker, another FWS biologist, whose assignment that summer was eagles and seabirds. Phil Schempf on the other hand was more cautious (a correlation is not an explanation), and told reporters that what was happening must await proper scientific study. It may not be just the cleanup, he said. Birds may have left because oil contamination made eggs inviable, or because the spill reduced the fish and the dearth of food affected reproduction.

Legally speaking, the explanation didn't matter. Exxon was as liable for wildlife hurt by its cleanup as by the spill itself. Or so the government was prepared to argue in court. The company would have maintained that the poor nesting was a trade-off approved by the Coast Guard in ordering the cleanup, just as the damage to rockweed and mussels was a necessary consequence of the hot-water, high-pressure technology. There was some merit in the corporation's complaint of double jeopardy. The question was never put to a test.

In its public statements the government emphasized the continuing threat to the ecosystem from the oil, not the disturbance from the cleanup nor the other pressures on wildlife due to the extraordinary human presence in western Prince William Sound. Why multiply the uncertainties, when one explanation for the chronic damage, the toxic oil, could explain it? Many scientists, to maintain the funding for their research, went along. Thus, at the conclusion of his preliminary NRDA report on eagles, Phil Schempf wrote: "We believe the close relationship between nest fate and the linear extent and intensity of oiling lends support to the hypothesis that the observed response in the eagle population was due to the oil itself and only secondarily to the disturbance created by oil cleanup activities."

This was the only reference in his lengthy paper to the alternative explanation for the nesting failure. Schempf was claiming that the cleanup did not matter as much as the degree of contamination, which had been determined by official surveys and delineated on shoreline maps.

The reasoning was subtle. In a majority of the nests sampled in the western Sound, a chemical analysis showed that eggs had been tainted with hydrocarbons. The shells of birds' eggs retain the compounds, whether or not chicks have hatched successfully. Schempf's tree-climbers took inviable eggs from some nests and shell fragments from others. By this the investigator demonstrated exposure to the spill, a key first step. (Later Exxon would claim that many of the government's samples bore the signature of diesel fuel, a background condition in the Sound.)

Schempf reasoned that the highest number of nest failures would be expected to occur where the likelihood of exposure was greatest. That would be in areas where, according to the maps, oil lay heaviest on the shoreline. These assumptions were borne out by his reading of the data. The fewest failures, by the same token, correlated with the lightest extents of oiling. As for the disturbance from the boat traffic, aircraft and overall human interference, these pressures did not correspond to the degree of oiling or to the outcome of nesting. Therefore the cleanup factor was not as strong a determinant of nest fate as the oil itself was.

When he was free to elaborate, Schempf maintained that the records of the '89 cleanup were too sketchy for him to make the necessary correlations. "I can make a tie [from nesting failure] to the oil," he said. "I can't make it to the disturbance. There was no good way to measure it." Hence it was excluded from the analysis.

Such were the calisthenics of logic that researchers employed to whip their theses into shape. I knew that I could summon figures showing that the cleanup presence was earliest, loudest and longest on the oiliest shores, and thus correlated very nicely with the failure of resident eagles to produce young. Conversely I knew that the rating of shoreline contamination—the data most fundamental to Schempf's construct—had been a rather subjective exercise.

Schempf conceded that the cleanup "probably" was most intense where the oil was greatest. We left it that the two factors were too intertwined, really, to be scientifically untangled.

NRDA aside, in 1990 the FWS saw to it that the cleanup crews respected the broods of the eagles. A buffer zone was established around each nest, within which no activity was allowed while the nest was occupied. Aircraft and boats must stay clear by a quarter mile. Eagle monitors posted with cleanup squads consulted frequently with the Coast Guard supervisors, so that work was stopped if the birds seemed upset. It helped of course that the shoreline project was much smaller than in '89. The eagles may also have gained a certain tolerance for people.

To its credit, the FWS did not hold back the sanguine results of the 1990 summer surveys. Exxon was gratified that nest production rebounded. Al Maki, the company's chief environmental scientist, reported in a scientific journal, "61 of 75 previously active nests (81%) in PWS cleanup sites produced an average of 1.4 eaglets per nest, thus matching historical productivity statistics for this area." Exxon's three biological consultants from the UK, pressing the argument for the species's recovery, said that the breeders killed in '89 would have been replaced quickly. There existed a pool of birds cooling their heels at sites inland, the ones that had lost the competition for the prime coastal territories. But the FWS disagreed, pointing out that nest occupancy was still down, and the agency warned of further trouble within the population.

Later when Schempf's study came out, one understood how the glass in 1990 could be half full (a healthier production of eaglets than in '89) and also half empty (adult pairs occupying nests were fewer than normal). What happened was that the eagles in the western Sound redoubled their efforts. Fewer birds made more young, as there was an abnormally high incidence of multichick broods. Over half the nests that succeeded produced two chicks. In two nests, both barren the summer before, three eaglets were raised. Nature was compensating for last year's losses.

The vigor of the rebound wasn't enthused upon in Schempf's paper, nor in our discussion did he go in for sweeping statements about nature's resilience. "Maybe it is a big rebound," he said. "Eighty-nine was aberrant, because of the spill, but who's to say that '90 wasn't aberrant the other way for some other reason? What's normal for Prince William Sound? There's no way to know, because we haven't been following the nest production in the years since."

Unquestionably, the eagles whose territories were hardest hit in '89, whether from the oil or from the cleanup, would have found the environment on both fronts much improved in '90. Although these birds still had to deal with residual oil and harassment, nevertheless they outdid the eagles nesting in the eastern Sound and other parts where it was clean and relatively quiet.

Michael Fry, who reviewed Schempf's data, suggested that there was more going on in the western Sound than a rebound. Was he saying to me that the oil spill somehow enhanced the eagles' ability to procreate? Not exactly. But the breeding environment may have improved in 1990 in a third respect. The spill thinned the population in what was a high-density, high-rent habitat for eagles. "Saturated" was Fry's term for it, though the maximum carrying capacity of the system wasn't known.

Fry's theory was that the Sound provided food enough for all comers but not space. Acquiring and defending a breeding territory is stressful. The energy that eagles expend in Darwinian duels they also need for bearing and rearing young. In the spring of 1990 the competition was temporarily eased. As a result, birds bore fruit in greater numbers than ever, oblivious to the lingering spill, and with this surge the population zigzagged back toward its elusive equilibrium.

Principal investigator Schempf was not impressed by such speculations. He had further concerns. He wished to know whether eagles from the western Sound were perishing in greater numbers than in unoiled eastern sections. Protracted mortalities of adults that had been exposed to aromatic hydrocarbons could drain the population just as surely as nest failures.

In the summer and fall of 1989 the FWS researchers trapped dozens of birds from the two areas, both adults and fledglings. After drawing blood, they harnessed the eagles with lightweight radio transmitters, battery-driven devices about the size of a roll of breath mints. Picking up the individualized signals in their survey aircraft, the biologists tracked their subjects through the winter. If an eagle didn't move for six hours, the transmitter was programmed to double its rate of beeps, a signal that the subject must have died. Where possible, the observers retrieved carcasses and did necropsies in the lab. In 1990 additional birds were radio-tagged, bringing the number of eagles in the monitoring study to 134.

Results after two years were negative. Birds in both groups died over time—from emaciation or trauma, the wild eagle's winnowers—but Schempf and his colleagues did not find more deaths associated with the oiled habitat.

The one finding distinguishing the two groups had to do with uric acid in the blood of eagles trapped in the western Sound. To Schempf the elevated levels of uric acid indicated possible kidney damage from the oil spill. But Pat Redig, who conducted the blood work for the project, believed that the difference in the levels was not significant. Uric acid rises and falls depending on when the animal last ate, and Redig said that in the absence of more compelling indicators of oil, this factor ought to be disregarded. Fry, the peer reviewer, told me that the birds with the highest levels had food in their crops. Though it had been his idea to look at uric acid, he concluded that the findings were "an artifact" and unrelated to hydrocarbon exposure.

Schempf went along, deferring to their greater experience. He did not relinquish his suspicions. The FWS team drew more blood from the Sound's eagles in the winter of '91–'92. This time, the uric acid levels were higher in the birds from the unoiled east. Uric acid was a dead end.

Exxon of course was not party to the forensic debates. But from the sideline the company questioned whether the FWS would be able to show a population trend of any kind, good or bad, now or in the future, that could be hung upon the oil spill. It was the old problem of a lack of benchmark. In the Sound the most recent aerial census, prespill, had been taken in 1982. Who knew how the eagles may have varied in number in the years since? On what basis could a change be demonstrated?

The government's answer to this objection was illuminating. Federal biologists argued that the eagle population could only have gone up since 1982, as the birds continued their recovery from the Alaska bounty program and as the production of hatchery salmon swelled their food supply. If the population were found to be reduced, the government said, only the oil spill could be held responsible.

When the population charts were subsequently made public by the government's chief scientist, the 1982 numbers were indeed the lowest. In 1989, notwithstanding the mortalities from the spill, the Sound's eagle population had grown since '82. The census in 1990 showed a small dip, which was said to be within the range of error of the sampling technique—call it no change from '89. The 1991 population was the highest, if by the same insignificant margin, of the four years being compared. Chief scientist Robert Spies said that, if one put 1982 against the three latter years, the data indicated an upward trend.

But now Schempf's position was as Exxon's had been: that the census samples and statistics were too vague to prove a change in the Sound. The signal of the oil might yet be heard. He still worried about a long-term population decline, which he feared he would never be able to pinpoint because of the termination of his damage-assessment funding in 1992.

"The response to the spill will be muted by the nature of the bird," he said. "Eagles may live twenty years in the wild. If you go in and knock out sexually mature adults, what are you doing to the population dynamics down the line?

"Maybe it's true," he went on, "that we could spend zillions of dollars and not come out with a better understanding. I just think that we've read half of the novel and then put the book back on the shelf. Maybe we would never finish it."

"Maybe it's *War and Peace*," I suggested. Schempf was not consoled.

On a limited basis with private funds, the biologists continued to follow the radio-tagged eagles. The government, meanwhile, threw in the towel. In its 1992 update on the damages, the state and federal Trustees said that the population figures "suggest that the spill has not measurably affected the bald eagle population in Prince William Sound."

End of story, though "measurably" was a caveat, the refuge of the unyielding scientist. What can't be measured can't be known. Bishop Berkeley, who wondered whether a tree falling unseen in the forest made a sound, would have approved. Berkeley must have seen the eagle's soar. The philosopher made a sojourn in colonial America, when the virgin population, Alaska excluded, is estimated to have been as high as 75,000 birds.

IN THEORY, a wild creature whose system was weakened by petroleum hydrocarbons was more likely to sicken, more likely to die, when buffeted by additional stress. Lab tests on fish, birds and rodents had plainly shown this. But in the field it would be no easy demonstration, as the NRDA managers started to realize, because of the quicksilver nature of hydrocarbons in animals. And the oil would not remain in the Sound forever, not measurably.

Four hefty catalogs of natural resource damage assessment plans, separate from the summaries of NRDA results, were issued in the years following the spill. The cover illustrations on the paperbound volumes seemed to reflect the government's mounting disquiet. The 1989 plan showed a tanker leaking in a fjord, a bald eagle flying overhead. In '90 and '91 the eagle on the cover was gone, and the oil spill, not encircled by boom as pictured in '89, was blacker, larger and had spread to either shore. For '92 a new concept: a map of the Sound and western Gulf and the spill as a continuous band along the coastline. The oil's magnification was just the opposite of its fate over the period, and at odds too with the message inside, because, each year, species of concern dropped out of the catalogs.

Research on crabs, sea urchins, sea lions, storm petrels and seagulls ended after one field season. So did the fish larvae study, to the chagrin of its designers at the Institute of Marine Science. Work was shelved for want of useful results, or merged with other studies, and sometimes new studies were launched when biologists saw possible pathways of injury they had overlooked. Long-term funding was not necessarily a sign of the gravest damage. With almost nothing to show for themselves, brown bears got three years of research funds and nearly consumed a fourth, thanks to tenacious lobbying by state Fish and Game officials. Finally the chief scientist managed to kill the bears off.

Terrestrial Mammal Study Number 6 was originally intended to last two years. It was titled "Influence of Oil Hydrocarbons on Reproduction of Mink." The idea was to give oil-laced food to captive mink during breeding. It was one of the few attempts to approximate in the lab what might be happening in the Sound, specifically to the intertidal mammals. Biologists suspected that not only mink, but also river otters, bears and deer were being exposed to hydrocarbons in their diet. If the oil disrupted the production of the captives' offspring, a case might be made for population losses in the wild.

Mink were to be the "model species" for the carnivores, wrote investigators at the University of Alaska in their '89 prospectus. "Detrimental effects on the reproductive cycle of mammals are well documented for a toxic chemical group of hydrocarbons, the PCBs." The animals were to be obtained from commercial sources that raise mink for their fur.

The study drew fire from animal welfare groups, almost causing it to be aborted. One of the investigators, veterinarian John Blake, told me he has kept files of hate mail in his closet. "The popular press dragged us through the mud," he said. "We were said to be creating a second oil spill in captivity. I even had professionals tell me, 'You shouldn't do this. We know already what the oil will do to those animals.' "

Blake and his colleagues were fighting the images of sea otters and birds acutely poisoned by ingested oil. In fact they were going to administer weathered crude, in much smaller amounts, no more than might be needed to induce a reproductive response. Blake knew the difference firsthand, having analyzed the severe organ damage in dead otters following the spill. If there was a cruelty in the test, it would be because his subjects must be killed at the end in order to be examined.

The challenge to the experiment was beaten back, thanks in part to national environmental groups suing Exxon over the spill, for they favored as broad an inquiry as possible. No one challenged the study from the opposite perspective: that the metabolic defenses of mink would rebuff the petroleum hydrocarbons and the work would lead nowhere.

Tests had been done on ranched mink using PCBs and chlorinated pesticides and trace metals, which accumulated and resulted in such reproductive damage as smaller litters and increased mortalities of kits. But as for experiments with oil, the literature offered little on reproductive effects in mammals of any kind. It had been demonstrated that pregnant rats had more fetal deaths when the rats were orally dosed in the early stage of pregnancy with Prudhoe Bay crude.

Mammals purge hydrocarbons from their systems even faster and more thoroughly than do birds. This capacity has tended to discourage long-term experiments involving mammals and oil, not because injuries cannot be shown, but because scientists understood that in order to bring them about, they had to boost the doses beyond the exposures that animals would receive in the wild, say, from eating tainted shellfish all summer after an oil spill. Also, it was not a simple matter to work experiments upon large animals in captivity. Canadian scientists have subjected seals and even polar bears to brief regimens of oil in the diet—the animals' systems were duly stressed—but the chronic effects were unknown.

Still, the duty of scientists is to test their hypotheses where possible, and the hypothesis that petroleum in the diet of mink might interfere with their reproduction is a perfectly good idea to explore. Blake, however, was warned by his managers at Fish and Game not to use the term "science." When referring to the tests he should say "damage assessment." Science—basic research—was for the sake of general knowledge, and the costs of conducting it could not be reimbursed under the NRDA. This exercise was to be, at best, applied science.

Blake was disgusted by the semantics—and by the whole affair. He felt besieged on multiple fronts. What's more it was not for me to doubt his hypothesis because it lacked guiding precedents. Negative results, strictly speaking, are just as worthwhile to science if not to the law.

The study didn't begin until early 1990, since it took the researchers nine months to establish the breeding colony of about 100 mink. Whereas Blake had envisioned a two-year trial that would monitor the animals through more than one breeding cycle, the study upon review was cut back. The damage assessors, with an eye to costs, banked on the first litters to tell them what they needed to know. Field studies would presumably reveal the rest.

The mink females were put into two groups, the larger group subjected to a short-term ingestion, seven days in duration, with the doses administered at different phases of the breeding cycle. The smaller group was fed oil for 120 days, a course encompassing all phases of the cycle, from before insemination through the weaning of the kits. Presumably, if the wild mink mating on the coast of the Sound were exposed, the oil that they would absorb would be weathered. Therefore, samples of Prudhoe Bay crude were heated gently and stirred in order to expel the volatile compounds. The oil was mixed into a commercial mink ration of ground meat. The researchers decided against force-feeding, because wild animals aren't force-fed.

Blake's team felt its way toward the proper dose. Too much oil in the food and the mink would reject it, too little and the hydrocarbons would have no consequence. As a pretrial test they offered some of the animals food that was tainted at 1,000 parts per million, the oil representing about a tenth of a percent of the ration. They considered this a high concentration.

"We didn't think the mink would eat it," Blake recalled, "but they did—and even when they were offered a choice between the oiled and an unoiled diet, they showed no preference."

Since the animals would stomach contaminated meat, the scientists were free to pick a lower dose in line with the conditions in the Sound. They settled on 100 ppm, a diet consisting of one ten-thousandth oil. To placate their critics, the scientists pointed out that in a cup of mink food this represented less than a drop of oil, from an eyedropper no less. One hundred parts per million was about the maximum contamination in the shellfish found on the worst-oiled beaches, so possibly some wild mammals were being exposed to that degree.

The dose of 100 ppm also happened to be the lowest that would produce a response in the bile fluid of the subjects. For in detoxifying and excreting the components of oil, animals produce hydrocarbon metabolites that emanate in liver bile. When the bile fluid is extracted from the animal, these chemicals can be measured. I'll explain the procedures later. Liver bile became very important material in Prince William Sound. It was where the spill would most likely be revealed when a creature was healthy on the surface, the equivalent of digging for oil beneath the cleaned beaches.

To get to the outcome of the study: There was no difference in reproduction between the mink that consumed the oil and the animals in the control samples that did not. Subjects remained healthy, and kits were born normally on both oiled and unoiled regimens. The only effect tied to the short- and long-term ingestions was that the oiled diet caused the mink to pass the food from their digestive tracts faster. This made sense, given that their systems would have been mobilized to eliminate the unwanted chemicals.

Blake cautioned that the mink in his pens were permitted to eat as much as they liked. Thus there was never a risk of malnutrition from digesting too rapidly or incompletely. Out in the Sound, where animals had to work to eat, such a problem, if it were occurring, could be debilitating. The scenario depended of course on intertidal carnivores having no alternative but to consume the most contaminated seafood they could find, and sticking to it for months.

In the beginning it was planned that a companion study, tracking wild mink and also river otters in the Sound, would indicate whether deaths or declines in population were actually taking place. The scientific case against the oil, like the one indicting benzene as a human carcinogen, would be made stronger within the pincers of observation and experiment. But coordination between lab and field was short-lived. After the field sites had been scouted in '89, and study procedures costed out and submitted, it was decided to drop the wild mink from the research plan. The 1990 workbook put the focus on river otters alone.

The reasoning for the change was not given until the government's first presentation of damages in April 1991: "Mink and other small mammals that are known to feed and spend part or all of their time in the intertidal zone are difficult to study. They are known to crawl off into burrows or the brush if sick or injured and carcasses are unlikely to be found. Also, information on pre-spill populations of these animals is minimal."

By contrast the river otter, sometimes called the land otter, demarcated its movements by the droppings of scat at "latrine sites" within a home range. In addition, otters were larger than mink. The animal is usually associated with freshwater environments, but in this part of Alaska the seacoast provided the richer habitat and very abundant otter populations. The government's implication was that the river otters were easier to keep tabs on than the mink. Moreover, a few carcasses of otters had been recovered over the summer of '89 by cleanup crews. Bile samples showed exposure to hydrocarbons.

The truth behind the scenes was somewhat different. According to Terry Bowyer, a University of Alaska ecologist who designed Terrestrial Mammal Study Number 3, the mink and otter field study, the river otters were no less elusive than the mink, and no less prone to dying in dens. There was no population baseline to work with. Otters proved harder to trap than mink, and, having once been caught, were too wary to be trapped again. "The mink," he said, "were a lot more numerous, and easy to follow. We had them walking into our camp that summer. We had bought all the radio transmitters for mink, and then they were carved out of the study."

From what Bowyer and others related, it appears that the management team figured that the river otters would bring more bang for the buck. The logistics may have favored mink, not to mention the scientific tie to Blake's study, but the compensation from Exxon promised to be greater if a case could be made for river otters. Their pelts were not only worth more than minks', which was a basis of calculating the value of their losses, but they also occupied a higher place in the hearts of the public.

Who has not warmed to scenes of river otters in wildlife documentaries, the furry family sliding in the snow, or sleekly diving for fish, and generally romping before the camera? I remember otters as regulars on TV's *Wild Kingdom* a generation ago. Mink were not like that. Mink were unsociable and skulked by night and savaged farmers' chickens. It was a fact that such differences in public esteem would be reflected in dollars under the economic contingency valuations of the NRDA process. At a minimum, so went the thinking, river otters would repay their assessment costs.

During the discussions on how to proceed, Bowyer like Blake had to be reminded that "research" was not the goal. He accepted the terms and went to work. The (modified) objectives were to see whether there were differences in population, movements and food habits between two groups of river otters, one inhabiting an oiled area and one a clean area of Prince William Sound. This was the approach of all the field studies. Since the biologists did not have their subjects in hand before the disturbance, they could not follow any changes directly; they could only infer, by comparing two sets of animals.

The first otters were trapped in December of '89, and others in the springs of 1990 and 1991. Their blood was drawn. Radio transmitters were surgically implanted in the abdomens of the animals, and also tablets of mildly radioactive compounds that would register in their scats. Then the subjects were released and tracked.

The biologists came up with no difference in mortalities between the two groups. Nor was any change in otter populations reported, though if anything the scats showed, contrary to expectations, that otters declined at Esther Passage, the uncontaminated study area. In their preliminary report, the investigators said the study samples were too small to permit generalizations about survival. Absent otters may not have died but rather moved out of the study area. Bowyer and colleagues might have put it that the Sound's river otters were patchy, too patchy for the bounds of their two snapshots.

Other findings, however, suggested that animals were being stressed. In 1990 male otters at Herring Bay, the oiled site, weighed less when they were trapped and subsequently ranged farther afield to obtain food. The government highlighted the erratic movements in the damage summaries, projecting them onto river otters at large, but the sample size here was even smaller than in the population study.

It turned out that the weight comparisons were based on just four specimens from the oiled site and seven from the unoiled area. The comparisons of home-range movements involved a total of twenty-two radio-tagged subjects, which was better, except that the distances were hugely variable. Some animals hardly budged, some traveled many miles along the coast. In spite of the assertions of statistical significance, the distillation of a single figure to represent a small and disparate sample was suspect. I didn't question that differences were found between the otter groups. But if Jack Sprat weighed 100 pounds and his wife twice as much, would it be meaningful to report that their average weight was 150 pounds? And thence to compare the Sprat avoirdupois to another couple's? What was more troubling than the dearth of otters being compared was the dearth of sites being compared. A Sound-wide projection of the variance was not valid.

I talked with Jim Faro, the Alaska Fish and Game biologist who led the fieldwork on the project. "It could be argued," Faro said, "that the otters at Herring Bay had a larger home range to start with. And yes we are looking at small sample sizes. But I'm convinced that the otters in the oiled areas were moving so often, and moving at night too, because they were frantically searching for food."

What about human disturbance as an explanation for their behavior? I myself had been one of the many intruders at Herring Bay in 1990. The report didn't go into that factor. Faro said, "If disturbance was part of the effect, it was still oil-related, so to me it's pretty much the same."

The field exams showed no trace of hydrocarbons on river otters. However, of the several sublethal markers that were ascribed to the oil, the researchers made much of one: blood haptoglobins. A component of the mammalian immune system, haptoglobins are proteins generated by the liver, and their function is to clean up damaged red blood cells. They show up in reaction to an acute stress.

The stress that induces them needn't be exposure to hydrocarbons. Rather, haptoglobins are associated with a raft of illnesses and injuries in mammals, humans included. Trauma, inflammation, infection and poisoning may generate the proteins. Experimenters have found elevated haptoglobins in captive rabbits after injecting the animals with turpentine. It had been previously demonstrated, in other words, that blood haptoglobins could be spurred by the toxicity of certain hydrocarbons. These markers offered a possible connection to the oil in the river otters' environment.

Bowyer, a field man, had not set out to look for haptoglobins. His study supervisors at Alaska Fish and Game expressly told him to stay away from the intricacies of blood chemistry. Nevertheless, he turned to a biochemist at the university, Lawrence Duffy, who thought that the test might be revealing. The government was quick to reimburse the costs on receiving the results: In both 1990 and 1991, otters from the oiled site at Herring Bay had higher levels of haptoglobins than did the group at Esther Passage.

"We are sitting on killer data sets," said Bowyer in 1992. "We know—I mean, we strongly suspect—that otters are still being exposed to oil. If otters are messing around with mussels, they're definitely being exposed, because other studies have shown that oil's still in the mussels. Plus some of the beaches are still sheening, we saw that in '91, so that another exposure route could be when the otters groom their fur."

In the 1993 draft of their study, the authors stated: "We believe that significantly elevated Hp [haptoglobin] levels, and a significant reduction in body mass, are the first evidence of chronic, oil-related effects in river otters in Prince William Sound. Likewise, we noted significantly elevated Hp and IL-6ir [a protein that promotes the formation of haptoglobins] levels for otters living in oiled areas in 1991."

The river otter championed the argument for long-term damages in terrestrial mammals. Originally, nineteen species were said to be at risk because of the oil on the beaches, from the burly bears to the tiny voles. Of these, fourteen animals were studied in 1989, three in 1990, two in '91, and only the river otter drew NRDA funding in '92, to wrap up the analysis of the prior years' data. Yet fieldwork on otters continued under a different heading. Payments in hand from the settlement in late '91, the government studied how to "restore" those species that its research had shown to be damaged.

I learned later that Bowyer and Faro had a major doubter, more informed than I, in chief scientist Bob Spies. Although the interim reports were embraced by project managers, Spies would not give his final approval to the river otter study, on the grounds that the conclusions were overstated. Meanwhile, the results from the 1992 field season came in. In '92 the Fish and Game team had worked new sites in the Sound, oiled and unoiled, because the animals at Herring Bay and Esther had become too savvy for trapping. The differences in blood proteins between the two new sets of otters did not match the earlier findings, which meant, depending on one's point of view, that river otters had recovered from their hydrocarbon exposures or that haptoglobins had been extraneous from the start.

"I'd qualify our haptoglobin results this way," said biochemist Duffy. "It could be the oil, but you need a whole battery of tests. Maybe the otters [at Herring Bay] had more viruses, or higher rates of infection to start with, which could have influenced their immune response. The variation in the blood parameters of wild animals is a lot greater than in a batch of captive mink.

"Let me make an editorial comment," Duffy added. "People are loath to put money into baseline studies that look at the overall health of animals. Then there's a stress, like the oil spill, and we find we don't have the proper markers in place. I've been up here twenty years, and we've been talking about the need for a baseline all along."

Over $1 million was spent on the river otter project over four years. That sounds like a lot, but to run persuasive science on the rain-wracked edge of Alaska takes money beyond that. If Bowyer and Faro had been funded to work more than two sites, they might have strengthened their statistics. If they could have incorporated mink, they might have strengthened their model of contamination. They might have a case today.

After all, being biased doesn't necessarily make one wrong, only unreasonably determined to be right.

•   •

AS THEY WENT FORWARD, the government's studies of the Sound's wildlife were monitored by project peer reviewers as well as by the chief scientist. I described Michael Fry's overview of Phil Schempf's work on eagles. In the normal give-and-take of science, the function of peer reviewers is to offer judgments on research papers submitted to the professional journals. If a journal's panel of consultants should find errors or shortcomings in the work, and if their objections aren't satisfied, the paper will be rejected—not published. Since the experts are drawn from the same competitive field, their critiques often raise hot yelps from the scientist under scrutiny. The system is far from perfect, yet scientists accept it as the best check on what they do.

The NRDA peer reviewers provided quality control and advice to the researchers in the field. But they also served the management team and the attorneys. More was at stake than publication in a journal, for periodically the experts made recommendations as to which studies might pay off and which might be cut. The reviewers walked a fine line. They encouraged the studies that showed a link between oil and injuries, and at the same time tried to restrain the researchers from unwarranted leaps.

"The researchers tended to accentuate the negative, in order to get funds," observed chief scientist Spies. "The attitude of the PIs [principal investigators] was that oil was a drastic poison. In the peer review process, we tried to correct that."

A specialist in marine pollution who started out with a piece of the NRDA work, Spies became the government's top consultant late in 1990. He was the only scientist I interviewed who excused the behavior of the lawyers and NRDA bureaucrats. Rather, he blamed the coercion and manipulation on the federal statutes themselves, principally CERCLA. He strived to soften the hard edges of the inquiry and to build in the proper caveats and complexities. "Science is a process, not a product," he liked to say. He admitted that his correctives never went far enough. Spies did not stop overdrawn interpretations from being disseminated. That wasn't his job.

The mass of information alone made for headaches. (My initial boxful of NRDA reports, though incomplete, weighed twenty-five pounds.) In a major presentation to the Trustee Council in Anchorage in early 1992, Spies organized the material by degree of damage. By his ranking, the most serious but least common effect on a species was a population decline, resulting from its lethal and sublethal exposures to oil. A half-dozen other effects, acute and chronic, figured in his hierarchy of injuries. Exposure to hydrocarbons was not in itself proof of injury, but the case for the latter was stronger for the former.

For example, the lot of the bald eagle fell near the high end of the injury spectrum—there were exposures to oil, considerable mortalities of adults, reproductive losses for a year, no discernible dip in population, recovery well under way. The river otter, not manifestly damaged but possibly stressed, fell in the middle of the spectrum.

At the low end, to select another mammal, was the Sitka black-tailed deer. The dead deer were controversial during my first trip to the Sound in '89. The carcasses picked up after the spill were winterkills, not casualties of oil. But because healthy deer may have eaten oiled kelp, forty-four were shot that spring and summer for analysis. Most were clean as a whistle. In a small minority, liver and muscle tissue showed evidence of exposure to aromatic hydrocarbons. The concentrations, in the low parts per billion, may have been from background sources. No pathologies that might be due to oil were found. Many deer were infested with lungworm parasites, which in some cases could lead to pneumonia, but this was a condition of the wild.

Of the individual species studied, the murre and the sea otter were found to be the two worst injured. The sea otter, emblem of the Sound, we will look at in the next chapter. The murre got a double whammy from the spill, both acute and chronic impacts, the one damage cascading into the other.

Together the two species of murre, the common and the thick-billed, are the most numerous pelagic birds of Alaska. Murres are large alcids, of the penguinlike family of divers and underwater swimmers. Other alcids are puffins, guillemots, auklets and murrelets. A bit smaller than crows, and sleeker, with white breasts and sooty dark heads and backs, the murres band together in huge colonies during breeding season. Side by side on steep rock faces, the females lay single eggs, while the juveniles and courting pairs flap about on the water below in gregarious commotion. Tens of thousands of murres in one place are not unusual.

Nearly everything about alcid behavior makes these birds vulnerable to floating oil. It need not take a major spill. Prior to the *Exxon Valdez*, the region's most deadly event to seabirds was the Kodiak Oil Pollution Incident of March 1970. The source of this oil was never pinpointed. It was believed to have come from several inbound tankers, which flushed their ballast tanks in the western Gulf of Alaska on their way into Cook Inlet. Globs of weathered oil came ashore for a thousand miles, from Prince William Sound to the Alaska Peninsula, and with the oil came smeared carcasses of birds, most of them alcids. The minimum estimate was 10,000 seabirds killed; the maximum, by the Fish and Wildlife Service, was 100,000.

Not surprisingly, when seabirds began dying six weeks later, this time further west and on the north side of the Alaska Peninsula, the authorities again suspected oil pollution. There were initial reports of a large slick and also dead sea otters. Several hundred miles of coastline were surveyed in late April 1970. No oil was found, but the density of murre carcasses dotting the beaches was several hundred per mile, and in some stretches was several thousand. The birds were emaciated. Other explanations failing, biologists attributed the die-off to a fierce Aleutian storm that blew through days before. The toll of the natural disturbance was estimated to have been 100,000 common murres.

Prince William Sound lacks large murre colonies, as the birds prefer more open and isolated sites, but murres were killed within the Sound by the southwest-tracking spill. About 500 carcasses were turned in to the Valdez morgue. The major mortalities were reserved for several colonies in the western Gulf. No observer was at the remote Barren Islands, south of Cook Inlet, when the clots of mousse swept onto the rafting birds about to breed there. The dead murres drifted to the mainland and to the shores of Kodiak Island. More than 20,000 were eventually recovered, representing about three-fourths of the oil's documented kill of seabirds. Since the carcasses were subject to sinking and scavenging, the projection of the acute toll was an order of magnitude higher.

Poisoning did not cause the chronic damage to murres that was measured subsequently. According to the analysis by the Fish and Wildlife Service team, so many adult birds died all at once that the springtime mating synchrony, the critical mass of breeding behavior, was disrupted for several years. Younger birds were disoriented, not knowing how to mate successfully. Some adults laid eggs, but late, and not all together as was usual, that is, without having safety in numbers. It was hypothesized that the eggs produced were targeted in succession by the seagulls and ravens. In the colonies that the slick hit hardest, the production of chicks plummeted to zero or near it in both 1989 and 1990. Censuses indicated that reproduction began to improve in 1991.

Loyal to their natal rookeries, murres don't readily migrate to niches that may be open on distant cliffs. Therefore for these colonies biologists predicted that the recovery to former numbers would not happen for decades. If so, it would be a classic example of a disturbance echoing over time, above the buzz of annual variability. Fortunately, other large congregations in the Gulf of Alaska were spared the oil. The two species are millions strong in this part of the world and not in danger of extinction.

About the natural variability. The FWS investigators noted that populations of murres, like other colonial nesters, fluctuated up and down in the grip of environmental perturbations. The El Niño of the early '80s disrupted murre colonies on the Pacific coast outside of Alaska, apparently by changing the food supply. There were no good baseline numbers for how the Gulf's colonies may have shifted prior to the spill. But the researchers had confidence in their spill effect, because the breeding failures they saw applied to the oil-struck colonies and not to the population on a regional scale, as would be expected if the change was related, say, to Tom Royer's deep-ocean temperature cycle. Spies and the peer reviewers endorsed the findings too.

In my accounts of the NRDA work I have tried to stay away from the Exxon response. I'm not referring to the public relations static that played down the damages. The company engaged scientific consultants, biologists of good reputation, who without fanfare looked into many of the same species the government was examining. It was like a chess game being played on two boards. Exxon lined up studies to counter the major moves it expected from the other side. The company didn't bother with terrestrial mammals like river otters, and ignored birds and fish where the acute damages were marginal. Salmon, herring, eagles and certain seabirds were the species of concern for Exxon.

Neither side was in a hurry to reveal its results, even after the settlement. The state and federal Trustees, having released summaries of damage in 1991 and '92, held a public symposium in Anchorage in early 1993. The NRDA reports still were not finalized, but the principal investigators gave detailed presentations. The Exxon scientists were invited but did not attend. A few months later they made their own presentations at a forum in Atlanta. Their reports described injuries nowhere near as extensive as reported in Anchorage. Furthermore, going second allowed these scientists to include rebuttals to their government counterparts.

This late in the game, I did not pay much attention. But if there was a common theme to the Exxon studies, it was that the uncertainties and variabilities at play in the Sound were no match for the strict requirements of statistics. The Sound was patchy, the data were extremely noisy, the baselines very crude. What was a poor biologist to do? You really couldn't say much of anything about the ongoing effects of the oil spill on the ecosystem. Even regarding the murres in the Gulf, the government's best case.

After studying the Barren Islands population and offering findings of her own, Dee Boersma, a University of Washington professor, concluded that "there is no justification for claims of either a dramatic reduction in colony attendance, or of substantial failure of the remaining birds to settle and reproduce in the years following the *Exxon Valdez* oil spill."

The polarization was never necessary. The statutes allowed the spiller of the oil and the public agencies to cooperate on damage assessment. The company offered to collaborate on science in 1989, but was shut out. The government did not trust Exxon, probably with good cause, and in the climate of outrage the government decided to go for all the marbles.

Chief scientist Spies's presentation at the Anchorage symposium was entitled "So Why Can't Science Tell Us More About the Effects of the *Exxon Valdez* Oil Spill?" His subtext was the limits of certainty. He sketched questions that his peer reviewers had raised behind the scenes since the beginning. His speech was an admission, or so it seemed to me, that the scientific management of the NRDA work was flaccid. The government had already picked up the marbles.

I'm harder on the government side. The work was piecemeal and erratic, and bereft, for all of its millions, in intelligence of purpose. For years the NRDA researchers were not permitted to consult one another, let alone talk of their findings to anyone who cared about Prince William Sound. Sealed inside their reductionistic spheres, they never really grasped how their work was portrayed, how their hypotheses and interpretations were stamped as facts and conveyed to journalists and thence to the public. To be sure, the researchers hated the adversarial process. They were well aware that their findings were half-formed. But they provided what was asked of them because in the end they meant to see their work published in a proper journal and their proper credit paid.

BEFORE LEAVING the warm-blooded realm we should consider one other animal, the marine mammal *Orcinus orca*, or killer whale, and its place on the injury hierarchy. The killer whales garnered much attention and concern; they fared well in the competition for NRDA funds. It was not just for the losses they sustained, nor the appeal of their slashing presence and high intelligence. Nor was hydrocarbon exposure ever established, whether acute or chronic, so by rights the orcas do not belong on the injury chart at all. Killer whales had one great advantage over the other species in the Sound, which was a baseline, a strong estimate of the prespill population. The postspill count in one pod of whales, called AB pod, was alarmingly down.

Owing to their large size (twenty to thirty feet long), their conspicuous group behavior (orca pods, ganging up on seals and salmon, are the wolf packs of the sea), their individually patterned dorsal fins, protruding sharklike into the air, and not least because of their acquiescence to human approach, it has been possible to identify hundreds of different killer whales in the Pacific Northwest. The cataloging in the Sound began in the late '70s under OCSEAP and intensified in 1984 when Sea World, the private aquarium near San Diego, sought to capture whales for its exhibits. Sea World and the National Marine Mammal Laboratory, a division of NOAA, mounted surveys to assess the impact of removing animals from the population. In the end Sea World was denied. Yet the killer whale catalog has been steadily augmented, with fresh impetus from the oil spill.

From the start nearly all fieldwork has been contracted to an Alaskan team led by Craig Matkin. He, Graeme Ellis and their associates use a photo ID technique developed by cetacean researchers in British Columbia. A newly observed animal is photographed and named by number and pod. AB 8, for example, refers to whale 8 of the B pod of Prince William Sound. "Her identifying signs were a little sickle-shaped fin," Matkin recalled, "and a small black circle in the white saddle patch behind the fin." For uniformity's sake the photos in the database are left profiles only.

AB 8 was entered in 1984, an adolescent female. She was nicknamed Bubbles because of her fondness for playing in the prop wash of Matkin's skiff. More than likely Bubbles would be alive if Sea World had been allowed to take whales, for she was very accessible, and the right age to adapt to captivity. In '88 she appeared with a calf (only then was her gender confirmed), which was named AB 41. "She became more serious as a mother," Matkin said, "and wasn't as drawn to the boats as before."

As the friendliest pod, AB was easy to keep track of. Some whales of other groups have been photographed only once in the Sound, though probably they've been seen more often. Usually, the more effort that biologists put into wildlife surveys the more animals they find, and population figures are revised upward. For killer whales the sightings abounded, giving a false idea of numbers. Even professional spotters were deceived. Matkin's photo IDs showed the same animals to be ranging widely, or else shifting places each time they surfaced, "so that thirty whales spread out looked like a hundred." As the picture sharpened, the numbers turned out to be less than believed.

The total population, according to 1991 estimates by the Marine Mammal Lab, was 297. Each of these animals has been photographed at least once. Thomas Loughlin, the Lab's senior scientist for Alaskan species, said the figure was accurate "plus or minus six"—that is, he was confident that the population was no higher than 303 and no lower than 291. Other biologists in the Sound would love to have such statistical certitude. Quadrats, extrapolations, oiled groups vs. controls, etc., most of the machinations of scientific approximation can go out the window when the universe is known.

Matkin preferred to stand behind a narrower population figure for the Sound: 126. It comprised the current members of the six resident pods that he has made his study groups. The Sound is traversed by eleven "resident" and eight "transient" pods. The latter are whales that don't remain on a year-round basis. But not all residents are constant. The true way to distinguish them, said Matkin, is by feeding habit, the resident pods taking only fish, mainly salmon, and the transients selecting marine mammals like porpoises, sea lions and seals. No killer whale seems to care for sea otters.

If the Sound's orcas represented the antithesis of patchiness, the trouble for NRDA was that one couldn't examine them. One couldn't make any measurements other than by a camera. However, a whale's fidelity to the pod is so strong that an individual that is absent is presumed to be dead. As Loughlin and Marilyn Dahlheim, project leaders for damage assessment, noted in their report: "No animal consistently missing from a resident group has ever returned to its pod or appeared in another pod in 24 years of research in the United States and Canada." This was the basis for the allegations of injury from the oil spill.

AB pod was reconnoitered six months prior to the spill, in September 1988. It numbered thirty-six individuals. When next sighted, on March 31, 1989, seven days after the spill—Loughlin, in the air, dizzy from the fumes and the frantic search, in radio contact with Matkin on the boat—AB pod appeared to have lost seven members. There were sheens around the whales sighted.

The missing animals did not turn up that year. Worse, an additional six dropped out in 1990, they too never to return, making for an ongoing mortality rate of 20 percent if one accepted the presumption, and even if one did not hold they must be dead, such severe reductions in a pod were unprecedented. Two missing females left behind juveniles, which also was unprecedented. Bubbles, AB 8, disappeared in the second year. Her calf, AB 41, was adopted by a female relative, an aunt or cousin to AB 8, for pods are organized along matrilineal lines.

AT pod, a transient group, was also believed to be missing

whales. Members of AT were observed at Bligh Reef near the tanker on the third day of the spill, when a photographer from the *Los Angeles Times* snapped their picture. The government conceded later that the AT animals, which behave differently from residents and were much less familiar to the researchers, might have left the group yet still be alive.

The case for mortalities would be built on the abrupt disappearances from AB pod. Abrupt, because for the initial losses it was assumed that nothing untoward had happened to the pod in the six months between the two sightings. The seven deaths must have taken place in the first seven days of the spill. In private, the investigators and their managers wrestled with scenarios for fatal injury. Were the matter of the killer whales actually to come to trial, the scientists must not only argue that the missing cetaceans were dead, they must also explain why and how the deaths occurred—the equivalent, in a murder prosecution, of presenting the oil's motive and method. Scientists often conduct detective work, but not often under such pressure.

Precedents were lacking. There was almost nothing in the literature about killer whales and hydrocarbons. Experiments have been run on captive dolphins but never orcas. Necropsies have not pointed to hydrocarbons. For that matter, killer whale carcasses are rarely recovered in the wild, and thus how and why orcas die at large is little understood. (In 1990 a carcass was beached and discovered, thanks to the eyes peeled, but the tissues were degraded past any analysis.)

In a 1988 report for the U.S. government on the threats of offshore oil development, Canadian pathologist Joseph Geraci wrote that "there is no gripping evidence that oil contamination has been reponsible for the death of a cetacean." Reviewing the records of cetaceans and spills, Geraci observed, "The drama of certain mortality no longer seems reasonable. Instead, we find whales and dolphins in the vicinity, and some in the midst of the spill, behaving quite normally." Geraci initially served as one of the NRDA peer reviewers, but bowed out when he saw where things were headed.

Still, could not killer whales have been blinded by the caustic aromatics (some sea otters had been) and doomed to starve? There was discussion too of cataracts possibly caused by the oil.

Or were hydrocarbons possibly ingested in killing amounts? For a huge mammal, that would take some doing. If the model of the lab mouse were any guide, a large killer whale could stomach twenty gallons of raw crude and swim away.

How about the respiratory pathway? An orca's blowhole, its

only avenue to the air, is located at the top of its head. The blow-hole would be in proximity to the oil-water interface when the animals surfaced to breathe. Toxic fumes sucked into the lungs could cause panic . . . disorienting brain damage . . . death. Or the pathway could be aspiration, the direct uptake of oil into the lungs. Whichever, the most dangerous exposures would have been near-est to Bligh Reef. It would help to be able to place the AB whales there.

The respiratory scenario looked good until Bob Spies pointed out that for inhalation to be lethal, the concentrations of volatiles in the air would have to be very high—in the hundreds of parts per million at least. Intense concentrations surely occurred close to the surface in the first hours of weathering, but not days after the slick had been churned and broken. As for aspirating oil, the orca's blowhole has a flap over it, and the animal exhales with a blast that would probably clear anything from its breathing passage.

In their report, Loughlin and Dahlheim did not speculate on the pathways of death. The case was built upon Matkin's faithful surveys of AB. At the time the AB whales were spotted, they were off Point Helen at the far end of the Sound. But citing the record of the pod's movements in years past, Loughlin and Dahlheim wrote, "It is very possible that AB pod was in the Naked Island area [only twenty-five miles from Bligh Reef] when fresh oil was blown down into that area on 27 March 1989." Such whereabouts were plausible because AB was in the habit of hanging out west of that area to steal black cod from fishermen.

Many years ago the whales learned the trick. Black cod, a common name for sablefish, are caught in the spring on a longline, a several-mile-long line of baited hooks. Fishermen put weights on the line, suspend it at depth for half a day, then winch the catch in. Alerted by the sound of the winching, or sometimes just waiting in the vicinity of the line's marker buoys, the AB animals would rip off fish as the line was reeled to the surface. Only heads were left on hooks. A quarter, even half of a catch would be lost. Fishermen tried various measures to fool or frighten them, but the poachers wouldn't desist. Fortunately, only the one pod seemed to be in-volved.

When Matkin and crew had looked into the problem in the mid-'80s, their photos of AB pod revealed evidence of bullet wounds. Between 1985 and 1987 seven whales, including some observed to have been wounded, dropped out of the pod. They were presumed dead. The group's mortality rate was unusually high, though only half what occurred in '89 and '90. In the inter-vening two years, as Loughlin and Dahlheim pointed out in their report, the dropouts were few. The rate of missing was normal. They and Matkin believed that the pod had stabilized before the spill, that interactions with angry fishermen were no longer an issue and that therefore the latest losses must be from the spill.

The case was highly circumstantial. In truth, the scientists did not spend their time honing and reconciling their presentations for court. It may have come out that the two PIs were of somewhat different minds as to the fate of the missing cetaceans. Dahlheim was convinced that the AB thirteen were dead, Loughlin less so. Loughlin said that a survey in the Gulf, if the whales didn't show up there, would persuade him. As of '93 the missing had not been spotted in the Gulf either.

Craig Matkin was convinced from the start that they died, and while he couldn't say exactly how, he thought it might have to do with the pod's inquisitive and trusting temperament. "They got involved with the black cod because they were less afraid of boats," he suggested, "and for Sea World, AB had great candidates for capture. Among ourselves we sometimes say these whales were marked from the beginning. Maybe that's what comes from being too friendly with people."

The good news about AB is that the situation stabilized in 1991. Another whale disappeared; a calf was born to the pod. In 1992 two more calves appeared, and in '93 yet another, making for a current total of twenty-six animals. But the coincidence of the oil spill remained glaring and maddening. The two years' drop in numbers, the disrupted dynamics within AB—something bad had happened and it seemed too extreme to be laid to adjustments of nature.

The argument for an oil effect might have been stronger if the methods had included tissue and blood sampling. Such tests may have indicated exposure or even possibly an accumulation of hydrocarbons in the animals. It was rejected not so much because it couldn't be done—nooses and tranquilizer guns would be needed—but because the approach was invasive and controversial. "Everyone's afraid of doing biopsies," said Matkin, "because killer whales have become something like sacred cows."

Or liver bile might have been taken, a more drastic and penetrating assay. In vertebrate animals, the liver is the primary organ to detoxify foreign chemicals. The liver converts them to metabolites, which are somewhat different compounds, in preparing them for excretion. Aromatic hydrocarbons become aromatic hydrocarbon metabolites.

From the liver the metabolites are carried in the bile fluid to the gall bladder. When the animal eats, bile is released from the gall bladder into the digestive tract to aid digestion. Finally the bile passes out in the urine along with whatever contaminants.

Bile metabolites reveal a chemical much more tellingly than do changes in blood chemistry. Blood tests in veterinary science aren't specific for hydrocarbons. The uric acid workups didn't connect the oil to bald eagles, and the haptoglobins in river otter blood were a reach. When John Blake ran basic blood parameters on his captive, oil-fed mink, he found no consistent signal, but tests of their bile were uniformly positive for hydrocarbons.

Terry Bowyer could have had bile from the river otters trapped at Herring Bay in 1990. He could also have had the liver tissues themselves analyzed for hydrocarbons or for signs of toxic injury. However, like the orca researchers, to do so he would have had to kill his specimens.

"We had a heck of a time catching them, and I wasn't willing to kill them off for bile values," Bowyer said. "You have to behave ethically, and not do more damage than what's been done."

Ethical standards varied by species. No one would dream of shooting a bald eagle or a killer whale to look for aromatic metabolites, but seabirds, shorebirds, ducks and deer were routinely taken in the Sound, and of course thousands of the faceless fish. Also some sea lions and harbor seals, whose populations were more endangered than river otters'.

The investigators had little success with what one called "opportunistic necropsies." When an animal is found dead and the cause is suspected to be hydrocarbon exposure, the bile and liver samples must be taken at once, before decay starts to skew the chemistry. All of Schempf's eagles, for example, were past testing by the time carcasses were brought in.

Everett Robinson-Wilson, the chief of environmental contaminants for the Fish and Wildlife Service in Alaska, managed the chemistry on the birds and mammals killed or hurt by the spill. "I told them, I want liver, I want bile, but I didn't always get it," he said. His colleagues were not familiar with toxicological procedures, and in the first months of the emergency not enough care was taken in drawing and preserving samples.

"On river otters," recalled Robinson-Wilson, "we had six bile samples turned in. We looked at the bile hoping they weren't dead too long. Otherwise you get anomalous peaks in the metabolites. Only two specimens were any good. I was certain of exposure to oil in one animal. And that one, I think, was still alive when it was brought in to the rescue center." (The single finding led to the official statement, two years later: "Analysis of river otter bile indicated that petroleum hydrocarbons are being accumulated by this species.")

When it came to the harbor seals, Fish and Game collected a score of live animals to work with in 1989. Their hides in most cases were obviously spotted with oil. The seals produced better hydrocarbon data than any bird or mammal studied. Two bile samples were flagrantly high for metabolites, the rest low or moderate. There were durable PAHs detected in the blubber of some of the subjects, indicating an accumulation of potentially harmful compounds. There were scattered traces of aromatics in liver, brain and mammary tissue, and also in milk.

The seal meat was clean, however, and pathologist Terry Spraker found nothing in the seals' blood that could be tied to the oil. "I made fifteen or twenty different diagnoses," he said. "There was a lot wrong with those animals, parasites, infections, et cetera, but the only damage that fit exposure to oil were the brain lesions I described." The findings of brain lesions did not line up nicely with the exposures, because the bile and blubber metabolites were not the ones that caused the damage. The seal necropsies were late too, having captured the processing of well-weathered oil.

"The body wasn't dealing with it anymore," Spraker suggested. He believed that the seals had managed to detoxify the oil by the time they were sampled. "Just because an animal had oil on it, it didn't mean the animal was going to be hurt," he said. "But you couldn't say that in Valdez in 1989."

DESCENDING THROUGH the animal kingdom, and setting aside plaints and politics, we come to fish.

Fish are vertebrates, like mammals and birds. When they absorb petroleum hydrocarbons, fish activate the same basic system of metabolism, in which the liver is central, but the process of ridding the compounds is slowed by their cold-bloodedness. Hydrocarbons have a somewhat longer life in fish than in other vertebrates. As a result, the biological connections between oil and its cryptic effects are easier to trace.

Fish take up hydrocarbons in three possible ways. Most often it is through the gills. In effect, fish breathe the concentrations they encounter in the water. Sometimes fish are superficially tainted with oil, if they happen to run into a patch. Finally, bottom dwellers like sole and flounder may consume oiled prey. New research after the spill suggests that salmon fry may ingest oil droplets—not deliberately, it is assumed, but in mistaking the oil for zooplankton, or perhaps in consuming plankton that themselves have swallowed the droplets.

For all of that, fish readily sense petroleum in water and as a rule try to avoid it. The story went around Valdez in '89 about the researcher who put some salmon into a tank of water and added oil—the fish leaped out onto the floor. Kills in the open ocean, where there is room to dodge a spill, are extremely rare, though mortalities to drifting larvae have been documented. In a field experiment managed by OCSEAP in Puget Sound, homing salmon were presented with a choice of two fish ladders to climb. More fish mounted the watercourse not spiked with oil. The avoidance increased as the aromatic concentrations in the water were increased.

Another researcher, Roy Nakatani of the University of Washington, concluded after a literature review that salmon are not deterred by hydrocarbons in their migration path if the aromatic concentrations are under five parts per million. To learn whether these exposures could throw off their homing sense, Nakatani caught some fish returning to a hatchery stream, exposed them in a laboratory tank and then put them out to sea again. The treated salmon, he reported, found their way back with no less success than the untreated controls.

Fish have made attractive subjects for environmental toxicology. Many experimenters who cut their teeth on rodents have shifted to the aquatic models. Fish may not be as easy as caged mice, since bulky aquariums are required, and "flow-through" systems to administer the test chemicals to the water, but otherwise, their care is simpler than for the larger mammals or birds. Fish are not picky about taking tainted food. Just as important, critics of science don't object as much to experiments on fish. I think the bioassays are more acceptable because fish are not regarded as individuals. Their identity lies in schools, spawns, stocks: One's as good as another.

At first, fifteen to twenty years ago, the emphasis was on establishing acute toxicities for various chemical pollutants, including hydrocarbons. Scientists calibrated how much of a substance was necessary to cause lethal effects in the captive fish. The results are expressed either as LD_{50} or LC_{50} values. The LD (lethal dose) is the precise amount of a chemical that if ingested or injected causes 50 percent of the subjects in the sample to die within a set period, say ninety-six hours. The lethal concentration (LC) is the amount of chemical maintained in the water of the aquarium that kills half the subjects.

As an example, toluene, the light aromatic sibling of benzene, is said to have a 96-h LC_{50} value for striped bass of 7 ppm. Translation: Half of the striped bass in a tank infused with toluene at seven parts per million would be expected to die within four days. The light aromatic hydrocarbons have been tried on a breadth of marine species, since after a spill those are the compounds known to dissolve. Called WSF (water-soluble fractions), they are dangerous because they become "bioavailable" to fish in the water column. The chemicals don't dissolve easily and don't stay long—ninety-six hours is therefore an unrealistic exposure for a mobile creature—but a brief encounter with one part per thousand may be bioavailability enough to be fatal.

In tests directed by NOAA's Stanley Rice, Alaskan species were found to be more vulnerable to fresh oil than fish and invertebrates from temperate seas. Why? Because in the colder conditions they received greater exposures, the aromatics evanescing less rapidly into the air, the toxins remaining longer in the water.

Lab and field cross-pollinate. After fuel oil spilled from the *Florida* in 1969 and disrupted marine life in West Falmouth, bioassays delineated the particulars: how the compounds in the mix did what they did. Similarly, the crude oil spilled by the *Amoco Cadiz* in '78 was put through its poisonous paces again under controlled conditions, so as to try to understand what happened, and what might still be happening, along the Brittany coast.

The earlier models were not very sophisticated. In its seminal 1985 report, *Oil in the Sea*, the National Research Council, an arm of the National Academy of Sciences, criticized scientists for not doing a better job of recreating authentic field conditions. Biologists were experimenting with dosages that were implausibly high for most situations of oil pollution. In other words, tests ignoring what Exxon would later call the "margin of safety" led to flawed or pointless extrapolations. "This inability to transfer information obtained from laboratory studies has been an intractable problem throughout this report," warned the Research Council.

With more money it was possible to construct tests at the level of parts per billion. The modeling of the subtle effects of chemicals on aquatic organisms is a new-fashioned field. Toxicologists stress fish today without killing them. They start by figuring out the maximum dose the animal can absorb and still stay alive. With that as the ceiling, a range of lower dosages is administered. Care and patience are vital. The experimenter must have the craft of a Borgia to keep the fish nourished and free of infection and extraneous ills for months or even years, all the while afflicting them with an unwanted chemical. If cancer is the object of the study, for instance, it won't do to have the subject expire of organ failure. The tests might sound as cold-blooded as their subjects, but as yet no painless substitutes are available for deriving this knowledge.

Although cancerous tumors have been found on the livers of fish living in polluted harbors, nobody has succeeded in bringing about the identical conditions in the lab. Compared to the rodent model, cancer's gestation in fish is long-drawn. One productive attempt did manage to induce liver lesions that are believed to be precancerous in a species of Pacific flatfish, the English sole.

The work was done in the mid-'80s by the Environmental Conservation Division of NOAA's Northwest and Alaska Fisheries Center in Seattle. Tumors in wild sole in parts of Puget Sound, after they were discovered in 1975, became a troubling public issue, in part because the fish was consumed by humans. The incidence of cancer and other liver disease in the fish correlated with the amount of heavy hydrocarbons, the PAHs, in the soft bottom sediments. In the places where pollution was heaviest— the two worst for PAHs were Eagle Harbor on Bainbridge Island and the Duwamish Waterway in Seattle—the livers of the sole were especially diseased. In addition, reproductive organs were impaired. Lest I seem to be picking on Puget Sound, let me add that the same ills have plagued fish in Boston Harbor, the Southern California Bight, the Hudson River near New York City, the Great Lakes region and elsewhere.

The heavy aromatic compounds, along with toxic metals, chlorinated pesticides and PCBs, reached the bottom of Puget Sound from long-standing runoff from Everett, Tacoma and Seattle. Eagle Harbor was exceptional, a different story. It is a pretty little port removed from the urban centers. The quaint metal buildings of an old creosote plant perch at the mouth of the harbor. Creosote, a wood preservative loaded with PAHs from coal tar, seeped into the water for seventy-five years before the operation was shut down.

Beneath its tacking yachts and bright marinas, Eagle Harbor is officially a U.S. hazardous waste site. The Environmental Protection Agency discovered hot spots in the harbor sediment where aromatic particles reached into the parts-per-hundred. One spot measured 540,000 ppm, meaning that the bottom there was half PAHs. A 1985 health notice from the county warned people against eating any of the clams, crabs or fish such as English sole, advice that most residents had practiced for decades. Territorial and sedentary, the sole in Eagle Harbor became diseased by their proximity to the bottom sediment and by feeding on benthic worms and crustaceans that were also contaminated. That was the hypothesis anyway. The NOAA scientists devised experiments to verify it.

So as to have unexposed specimens for their tests, the biologists netted several hundred young sole from the clean sections of Puget Sound. Six to eight inches long at the start, the fish lived twenty to a tank, through which flowed sterilized seawater. They were watched for infections and fed daily. Once a month a group of the fish was injected with extracts of sediment taken from the bottom of Eagle Harbor. While this exposed them to a range of PAHs, another group of sole received shots of just one compound, benzo(a)pyrene. So far as is known from other animal studies, benzo(a)pyrene is the most carcinogenic of all the PAHs. A third group of sole got clean sediment extract, or nearly so, containing just background concentrations of the aromatics. Finally, the controls, the fish that received no injections.

In a related experiment, a batch of English sole took up PAHs another way, via their food pellets, which were laced with the Eagle Harbor extract.

"The one-year exposure phase was followed by a six-month holding period," wrote the scientists in their 1987 report, "after which the fish were sacrificed." Pathologists cut them open and examined their livers.

The feeding experiment had unclear results, as all the fish grew and turned out much the same. Pathological changes relating to the contaminated diet were not statistically significant. But the injection tests produced real differences. In the fish that got either the PAH extract from Eagle Harbor or the straight benzo(a)pyrene, liver tissue was strongly discolored and showed cell death and precancerous lesions. In the fish that got clean extract or none, the color of the liver was the normal white or creamy, and otherwise the tissue appeared to be healthy.

The method that produced the injuries was a radical one, not the way that fish are exposed to pollutants in the wild. Feeding the chemicals to the sole was not as effective as injecting them, whether because the doses in the pellets were too low, or because the sole were able to enlist their digestive systems before the contaminants reached their livers.

Still, the toxic injections did not achieve the advanced pathologies found in wild sole from Eagle Harbor. That PAHs cause cancer of the liver in this species was still hypothetical, not proved, and the scientists were careful to say so in their report. The clues were stronger, tying lab to field. Cancer may not be an unusual development in organisms, but to give healthy organisms cancer is unusually difficult.

The NOAA group obtained part of the funding for the test from the National Cancer Institute. For the liver tumors in the fish of Puget Sound raised questions about impacts on consumers. Addressing the issue, the researchers reported very low PAHs in the flesh of the English sole. They also found "a general lack of muta-genicity (Ames test) . . . associated with muscle tissue extracts."

Even before they had the results, several of the scientists took home sole from Eagle Harbor to eat, disregarding the health advisories to the citizenry. Here was an experiment after my own heart. But why would they do it?

"They caught some big ones and they really like fish," one member of the team said. "I didn't care to. The sediment just stank when we pulled it up. But they knew that the edible flesh of the fish was clean."

A final point: This same laboratory of NOAA researchers studied the effects of the oil spill on the fish of Prince William Sound. They didn't look at every species, because some were in the purview of Alaska Fish and Game biologists. The reader will guess which group was conservative about the long-term threats to the health of fish, including the risk of cancer, and which group was up in arms.

LET'S LOOK CLOSER into the liver's metabolism of harmful hydro-carbons. Liver enzymes convert the compounds to metabolites. The molecular modifications make the metabolites more suitable for excretion. The addition of oxygen, for one, makes the compounds more soluble, and thus more easily passed out in the bile and in the urine.

The liver bile is the key pathway of elimination. There are other processes of petroleum by fish, other avenues and transformations, such as the conversion of some of the hydrocarbons to carbon dioxide and water; the elimination of some of the aliphatic fractions unaltered; the transient storage of metabolites in muscle, fat and the fat-rich tissue of eggs and brains; and even some venting of compounds through the gills. I wish to keep the focus on the bile and the liver, for it was understood at the time of the oil spill that the liver, leading the charge against hydrocarbons, would be the most prominent target of chronic injury, and that the bile would be the first messenger of exposure.

Whatever their routes and stopping points, the elimination of hydrocarbons by fish takes but a few weeks after uptake. (A mammal might accomplish it in a few days.) Unless fish are constantly being exposed, there is soon no sign of contamination. This is called depuration. Depuration undoes the evidence of bioaccumu-lation.

As NOAA's Doug Wolfe explained, "The whole process indicates why PAH levels are not measured often in fish tissue, and when they are, the levels are always low. They are not as easy to identify as PCBs or other substances that accumulate."

In polluted harbors, where polyaromatic hydrocarbons were plentiful in sediments, researchers had learned that the liver and other tissues of fish might not show any PAH metabolites. It was more likely that the PAH metabolites would show up in the bile fluid. Accordingly, the procedure of NOAA investigators in the Sound was to screen the bile fluid first, and only if the levels were high were more painstaking evaluations of organs and flesh undertaken.

Scientists collect the bile from its reservoir in the gall bladder. In humans this organ is a pear-shaped sac about four inches long. In fish the gall bladder is pea-sized; when removed from its membrane its looks like a blueberry. A tiny drop, pin-pricked from the organ, suffices.

A word now about the hardware. Whether hydrocarbons are in the bile is determined indirectly, by a method using fluorescent light. First a filtration system, called high-performance liquid chromatography, separates the various metabolites in the fluid and passes them in sequence through a column or coil. The sample is subjected to fluorescent light, the light tuned to one or two wavelengths indicative of PAHs. The strength of the signal emitted as the compounds progress do not tell the precise molecules present nor their precise amounts. Rather the readings, in units called FACs (fluorescent aromatic compounds), gave the general level of bile exposure.

A result positive for FACs sends the detective back to the liver. The metabolites of the aromatics may not be in evidence. But other tests are able to uncover signs of a biochemical struggle. Enzymes have been activated, certain reactions have taken place. They are called MFO (mixed-function oxidase) reactions.

MFO is a generic term, the name for a complex of biochemical steps. Many of the individual processes have been explored since the term was first applied. New enzymes have been identified, the most important being of the cytochrome P450 family. The P450 enzymes are catalysts of MFO activity. I offer these details in order to dispense with all but MFO, which shall stand (as it did for most scientists on the spill) for the mobilization of the organism's basic response to aromatic hydrocarbons.

Simply put, components of oil induce MFO in vertebrate animals. Bile metabolites are the products of MFO activity in the liver. And here is another, more cautious generalization: In experiments on rodents and fish, MFO induction appears to be associated with cancer of the liver.

How the two are connected is not clear. It seems that when disarming and dispatching aromatic chemicals, the MFO enzymes render some of them briefly more dangerous. Cancer arises from mishaps of DNA, the genetic material within cells. It has been demonstrated that certain PAH metabolites bind to DNA. The metabolites also bind to receptors in the cell that may in turn interfere with the DNA.

What transpires is not well understood. At one intermediate stage of transformation, some of the metabolites become what are known as free radicals. And as free radicals, they become keys to the locked door of carcinogenesis. Since the DNA almost always repairs the damage caused by free radicals, keys besides these must be activated before a cancer is unlocked.

The sequence linking aromatic hydrocarbons, MFO and cancer is neither straightforward nor inevitable. MFO is an evolutionary adaptation to the general problem of toxins in nature. Naturally occurring toxins may induce MFO on the route to cancer, just as man-made chemicals may be inducers but not necessarily carcinogens. The process is complicated by the fact that, in fish at least, MFO is influenced by the season, by temperature and by the stage of the animal's reproductive cycle. Therefore, toxicologists prefer to use MFO to look backward to the degree of contamination rather than forward to a potential tumor or injury.

Since MFO activity in itself is not proof of hydrocarbons at work, other tests must be employed to confirm the presence of oil. That achieved, MFO becomes an excellent "bioindicator" of exposure to oil. The enzymatic assays have proved to be more sensitive, if no less indirect, than fluorescent screening for bile metabolites. The MFO tests can track the enzymes down to zero—no induction taking place, thus no exposure, thus no oil.

For investigators of marine pollution, it would be preferable of course to catch the oil red-handed, the PAHs tainting the tissues in unmistakable concentrations and the fingerprint of the compounds pointing to their source. Gas chromatography and mass spectrometry (GC/MS) provide exact concentrations of contaminants, but those tests, as I've described, are costly and time-consuming and often come up with nothing. Bile screens may be inconclusive too, because the fluorescence is subject to noise from innocuous compounds. Hence the interest in sensitive MFO. The tests for it offer a litmus of environmental quality. With MFO it might be possible to detect pollution before it even qualifies as pollution.

Lest they jump to conclusions, however, the investigators ought to proceed along the same path that the aromatic hydrocarbons take in the fish. Is there elevated MFO? If so, look at the bile.

Elevated FACs? If yes, look for hydrocarbon metabolites accumulated in the tissue. Elevated metabolites? Now factor in the lesions, pathologies and other clues of chemical harm, and make your case for injuries from oil.

Alaska Fish and Game investigators often went by the opposite sequence. Tissue samples were screened en masse, a host of lesions identified, and the most statistically significant of these were highlighted if they could possibly be related to hydrocarbon exposure. The ascertainment of the exposure was secondary.

The rockfish made an interesting case in point. In the spring of 1989 Fish and Game biologists examined twenty dead rockfish that had been brought in from around the Sound. Decomposition of specimens was a major problem. It was determined that five had probably been killed by oil. (This was the only record of mortalities to adult fish, of any species, in Prince William Sound.) That summer, bile metabolites were measured in eleven of thirty rockfish collected off oiled shores, suggesting the possibility of damage.

In 1990 and 1991, a hunt for chronic injuries commenced. The department contracted with histopathologists (specialists who identify microscopic tissue changes caused by disease or injury) at the University of California, Davis. Reading hundreds of slides of sectioned rockfish tissue, the histopathologists noted a score of different lesions. There were tissue changes not only of the liver but also of the kidney and spleen. Four of these conditions were analyzed, because they might be expected to arise from exposure to a toxin. Two liver conditions passed the statistical hurdles. It was duly reported that the rockfish from the oiled sites had a greater incidence of liver lipidosis (excess fatty tissue) and sinusoidal fibrosis (vascular scarring) than did the rockfish from unoiled sites. These changes were attributed to chronic damage from the oil spill.

However, the biologists did not conduct experiments on rockfish that might tie the two conditions to petroleum hydrocarbons specifically. More importantly, when the levels of bile metabolites and MFO in the fish were measured, neither indicator showed any difference between the rockfish collected off oiled beaches and those from clean sites. One of the California histopathologists told me that, given the range of the lesions he saw on the slides, he might well argue that a toxic agent afflicted all of the specimens. Alternatively, the manifold conditions may have characterized rockfish from both sites before the oil ever got into the water.

Again, it wasn't that Fish and Game was wrong about the oil's effect on rockfish, it was simply that its study had not shown the presumed effect to be right. "Fish and Game," said Bob Spies in the department's defense, "was not established as a pollution-control agency." In general, there was a tendency among the damage assessors to call MFO an injury, to call bile metabolites accumulation, to categorize any cellular change or PAH value as an adverse consequence of toxic exposure to hydrocarbons. Sometimes the confusion was deliberate.

John Stegeman, a biochemist at Woods Hole Oceanographic Institution, straightened all of this out for me. I went to see him because Stegeman's test for MFO was used extensively during the spill. (His assay hinges on cloned antibodies to particular MFO enzymes.) I first heard of Stegeman's work in 1990, when the Alaska Department of Environmental Conservation hired him to analyze several fish, principally pricklebacks, to see whether they were taking up hydrocarbons from the shoreline. Pricklebacks are small creatures of the tidal zone. One sees them hovering in rocky pools on the Sound's beaches when the water has withdrawn.

In 1990 DEC was contesting the notion that the cleanup was doing more harm than good. Because the agency operated on the "response" side of the spill, it was barred from the secret NRDA studies of intertidal marine life. DEC realized it needed a biochemical basis for its recommendations to the Coast Guard. That's where Stegeman came in.

In late June Stegeman was given several dozen pricklebacks collected at both oiled and unoiled shores. He also examined fish that had been maintained for a time in cages off oiled beaches. In August he passed on to his sponsors the preliminary results: His assay found MFO induction higher in the oiled samples than in the unoiled controls. "The significance of this induction to these animals is not fully understood," he advised.

The next year, after securing more funding, running more experiments on pricklebacks and weighing all results, Stegeman was able to report to DEC that induction of MFO closely correlated with the degree of oil contamination remaining on the shoreline. He was pleased to note that his test provided "an exquisitely sensitive marker" for charting the persistence of hydrocarbons in Prince William Sound.

DEC no longer cared. The agency had taken Stegeman's preliminary work and run with it in press releases. The gist of the announcements was that harmful concentrations of oil were still being measured in intertidal areas in 1990. The specter of cancer in fish was raised. The agency's admitted motive was to keep the heat on Exxon, NOAA and the Coast Guard to continue removing the oil. Back at Woods Hole, John Stegeman did not want to say he'd been burned. "Let's just say I was more trusting than I should have been," he allowed.

Stegeman went on to do other work for the state, including the MFO testing of rockfish. In 1992 he was not bothered that his prickleback report was gathering dust in Juneau, because his private purpose had been to obtain data on the workings of MFO in an unfamiliar fish. Having analyzed fish from polluted sites around coastal Massachusetts—having tested species from around the world—he had learned a context for the enzyme activity. The gross effects sometimes associated with MFO, such as liver tumors, were limited to the most contaminated rivers and harbors. MFO in flatfish from Boston Harbor was ten times greater than anything Stegeman found off the oiled beaches of Alaska. Yes, some flounder in Boston Harbor had liver tumors. The Sound's pricklebacks were a long way from that.

As part of my tutorial, Stegeman sketched the shadings of histopathology:

"What is a change and what is a lesion? Necrosis [cell death] is a change. A neoplasm [a growth serving no function] is a change. So is a difference in the membrane. A tissue change may be a consequence, or a compensatory response, to a chemical insult. But is that a lesion? It's hard to get two histopathologists to agree on any one slide. One of my colleagues describes it as a social science."

At least liver cancer, an extreme development, should be considered a lesion, should it not?

"Yes," he said, "but then, an injury that threatens an organ— does it threaten the organism too? You can live with only 10 percent of your liver functioning, as long as the injury or tumor is contained there."

Still rhetorically, Stegeman summed up the situation in the Sound:

"Is the oil in the environment? Yes.

"Is it getting into organisms? Yes.

"Are there changes as a result? Yes.

"Are those changes signs that doom is upon us? No.

"That is not to say there won't be deleterious effects on individuals in the future."

By doom he meant changes across populations, in particular to fish stocks of commercial value. He doubted that the arousal of MFO enzymes, the production of hydrocarbon metabolites or even the appearance of liver lesions would affect overall health and numbers. At any rate, to document such a change would take a wider net than either scientists or fishermen had available.

A saying among fisheries scientists is that contamination becomes pollution only when it hurts populations. Jerry F. Payne, a

Canadian fisheries expert and MFO researcher, sent me a batch of papers, one of which analyzed the potential effect on the catch if a large spill were to occur on the Grand Banks off Newfoundland. Payne and others projected a loss of less than a ton of plaice (a commercial flatfish). In a side-note Payne scrawled that the value of the loss was "equivalent to a portion of the bar bill at one of literally hundreds of oil-pollution conferences, workshops, etc., that have been going on for the last fifteen years."

CLASPED BY MOUNTAINS, Snug Harbor corkscrews into the southeast flank of Knight Island. It is one of the most protected anchorages in western Prince William Sound. Yet it was whacked by the slick when winds pushing the oil past Knight shifted to the east.

In May of 1989 I came into Snug Harbor on the *Skin Deep*, a wildlife rescue vessel. Alpine snowfields reached a half mile into the sky. There was a shadowy wall of green forest in the middle scene, and a rocky shoreline stained with oil at the base. Terns filigreed the picture, the only things moving. Then a bald eagle flew into the late-day light and harassed the terns. A silvery fish fell to the water, the eagle hard after it.

Several research vessels were at anchor in Snug. The largest was the *Fairweather*, 230 feet long, belonging to NOAA. A voice hailed us, "Want some fish for dinner?" I took the skiff over, and, climbing aboard, confronted a mess of scientific samples.

Scores of fish were splayed in the trawl. The ship was collecting bottom fish and bottom sediments for damage assessment. I picked out a twenty-five-pound Pacific halibut. For all its heft it seemed to be missing a third dimension. Halibut are extremely flat. As the fish grows from its larval stage, one eye migrates from the whitish underside to join the other eye on the dark flip side. To its prey on the bottom the halibut looks like the sky, and to its predators above, it looks like the bottom.

I hesitated. "Is there oil in the tissue?"

"We've been eating 'em," said the researcher, smiling broadly.

I had no inkling then that I would have to wait three years to examine the *Fairweather*'s results. Subtidal Study Number 7, as the project came to be called, reached well beyond the bounds of Snug Harbor. In 1989 alone, the vessel trawled from the spill zone 3,269 fish for analysis. (Make that 3,270.) The species sampled included halibut, flounder and three kinds of sole, which are bottom fish, and also pollock and Pacific cod, which range somewhat higher in the water column and swim in and out of the Sound in large schools. In another category, Dolly Varden char were taken by gill net. This sport fish is an anadromous, nearshore resident, migrating from lakes to the littoral and back.

Subtidal 7 towered over all the NRDA fish work except for salmon. Thousands of bile and liver specimens were extracted. MFO and histopathology screens were run. Tests of sex hormones illumed the fecundity of female sole and Dolly Varden. Researchers thought there might be reproductive dysfunction from the oil, such as PAHs had brought about in the contaminated sole of Puget Sound. Fish were also checked for parasites and fin rot. Past tests showed that hydrocarbon uptake could make fish more susceptible to infection and general ills.

The study's hottest finding, about pollock, became known in the spring of 1990. The news broke not through a breach of litigation security, but from an unrelated NOAA survey of fishery stocks in the Gulf of Alaska over the winter. The pollock had been disregarded by the damage assessors; no one thought them particularly at risk from the oil spill. But when analyzed, the fish showed metabolites of oil in their bile. Moreover, the range of exposure matched the track of the spill. Concentrations were highest in the pollock caught within the Sound and fell off along the Kenai coastline in the Gulf.

The principal investigator of Subtidal 7 was Usha Varanasi, chief of the NOAA's Environmental Conservation Division in Seattle. "What is interesting," she said about the pollock, "is that since depuration is only a matter of weeks, the exposures must be recent and ongoing." This was a year after the spill.

I asked Varanasi to compare the pollock findings with the metabolite levels in the sole of Eagle Harbor.

"The types of PAHs in creosote are not the same as in crude oil," she advised. A comparison of the two situations was difficult. "But overall I would say the *Exxon Valdez* fish are less exposed."

I telephoned Varanasi often, always dancing around the specific facts I wished for. But at this juncture of my education, a lightbulb went on in an adjoining mental room. I said, "I think I understand it—what these markers tell. What's exciting is to see that the animals are doing just what they should do when a chemical is put into their environment. We know that oil is still in the Sound. Something would be wrong with biology if you put oil into their environment and it *didn't* show up in their systems."

"Yes," she lightly agreed. "Results are quite enigmatic, but slightly predictive."

Meaning . . .?

"Enigmatic because we cannot see whether fish might be dying or whether diseases might be resulting. We do not know for how long the level of exposure would have to continue before there would be seen effects. But the fish are processing the compounds the way we have predicted."

In the 1991 trawls, the same geographic spread applied to the bile of pollock. The Sound still showed the greatest exposures. But now all the levels had dropped considerably, lessening concern about long-term damage. Indeed, when the study was concluded, the examinations of pollock had failed to find anything other than exposure—no lesions or reproductive impairment. PAHs were not detectable in the pollock meat or the females' eggs.

The question still remained how a restless, oceangoing fish acquired hydrocarbons from the depths of the environment. Although the basin of the Sound was far less contaminated than Eagle Harbor, heavy aromatics reached the benthos in 1990. Abraded from oiled shores, traces of oiled particles were drifting into sediment traps placed upon the nearshore slope. But the chemical concentrations in the sediment were very faint, and anyway, pollock didn't live their lives at the bottom like sole or halibut.

The best guess was that the pollock were exposed via their prey, consisting of a smorgasbord of smaller fish and crustaceans. These might have ranged closer to the tainted shoreline and taken up oil. Unfortunately, a collection of stomach contents removed from the pollock in 1990 was not preserved properly. The dietary pathway could not be explored.

As for Subtidal 7's other findings: Bile metabolites in the Dolly Varden char were the highest of all sampled in 1989. When the metabolites fell sharply in '90, almost to background levels—NOAA credited the winter storms for having purged the shoreline—the Dollies were dropped from study. But Fish and Game continued to monitor the fish and claimed that the Dolly Varden, and also the cutthroat trout, were suffering mortalities and reduced growth from the oil.

Exposures in the three species of sole persisted for a year longer, not fading until 1991. No sublethal changes, no liver lesions marred any fish, nor was there any reproductive damage. The study did turn up one change that may well have been due to the spill. In 1990 the rock sole caught at the oiled sites had a greater incidence of cell abnormalities in their gills than rock sole at unoiled sites. Though supported by the statistics, the NOAA scientists expressed caution about this finding because they felt it was not surefire for oil. Parasites could cause the same condition.

And my Snug Harbor, whose deep twisting bottom mirrored the alpine spine of Knight Island, had the dubious distinction, of all stations sampled, as "the site at which fish had highest concentrations of metabolites in bile." The yellowfin, flathead and rock sole living in Snug displayed the highest enzyme activity too. Bile and MFO levels for '89-'91 were given in the NOAA report. The internal markers held true to what was happening in the submarine environment, for each year the exposures of fish diminished in concert with the weathering of hydrocarbons from the fjord.

If the commercial groundfish stocks were unaffected, at least in ways that could be measured, there remained a deep concern about the pink salmon and the herring, the money fish, one and two, of Prince William Sound. Fishermen cared most about the salmon and herring because they spawned here. A successful catch depended on a successful spawn. The salmon and herring that were at an early life stage when the spill was fresh suffered explicit harm, not just exposure.

Alex Wertheimer of NOAA's fisheries lab at Auke Bay, Alaska, focused on the pink salmon fry. In the spring of '89, pink fry from both streams and hatcheries entered the Sound hard on the heels of the oil. Wertheimer found salmon fingerlings with little globs of oil in their stomachs, indicating that hydrocarbons could get into fish by means other than respiration from the water.

Wertheimer added oil to the food pellets of pink fry held in tanks. He didn't model the ingestion of droplets per se—technically it was too difficult to replicate. But he was able to show that fish on the oiled diet grew slower, which paralleled the results obtained from the field in April of '89. Both Fish and Game and NOAA had found that juvenile pink salmon, when netted near oiled shores, were slower growing and smaller than the fry caught off uncontaminated shores. The pink fry research challenged the "margin of safety," Exxon's argument that exposures to fish within the Sound were minimal and harmless that spring.

Sam Sharr of Fish and Game studied the eggs of wild pink salmon in the streams. Following the runs of 1989, '90 and '91 more eggs were found dead in oiled streams than in unoiled streams. In the idiom of the investigators, that was a good hit. But the trends were perplexing. The worst year for mortalities was not the fall of 1989, when the oil in the streambeds was heaviest, but the fall of 1991, following two and a half years of constant flushing. It didn't make sense when exposures to eggs were declining.

The difference in egg survival persisted in '92 and '93, even though oil in the gravel was no longer a factor. The peer reviewers of the salmon studies wondered whether the baseline conditions of the two sets of streams had been different to start with. It might be that a stream's orientation to weather and waves had a greater influence on egg survival than the degree of contamination.

"Apparent functional sterility," said Fish and Game biologists, proposing an interesting new hypothesis for the oiling effect. There may have been genetic damage to the hatchlings that survived their exposure to aromatic hydrocarbons. The scenario was that the '89 brood-year salmon, though plentiful when they came back to the streams in '91, laid an unnaturally high proportion of inviable eggs. The same may have happened to those of the '90 brood year.

The idea needed testing. The NOAA lab at Auke Bay set up an experiment. Salmon embryos were to be stressed with oil, raised to maturity and then bred. Would their sexual productivity be less than that of a control group? The results won't be known for several years.

Another confounding fact, as discussed earlier, was that investigator Sharr never saw the damage to eggs reflected in the number of viable fry. In the spring there were no differences between the two groups of streams in terms of the juveniles emerging from the gravel. Natural losses over the winter had evened the score. So where beds had been contaminated, the disturbance at one stage (eggs) was distinct, but its echo had vanished at the next stage (hatchlings)—vanished at least from the hearing of statistics. Hence a discrepancy in terms of the numbers of returning adults would be impossible to measure.

The record-breaking pink salmon returns of '90 and '91 flew in the face of worries about poisoned eggs or slower-growing fry. But when the runs were poor in '92 and worse in '93, fishermen had as much proof as they needed that pink salmon in the Sound were inherently damaged. They blockaded the pipeline terminal in '93. I called Sam Sharr, who told me, "Though we do have evidence of a chronic problem [to eggs in certain streams], there's no quick-and-dirty way to relate the poor runs to the oil spill."

NOW FOR THE HERRING. In the years following the oil spill the Pacific herring also spawned in numbers that broke records. At the same time the proposition of genetic damage was explored, and of adverse changes in fry. Again, as if in corroboration, an unusually bad herring run occurred in 1993.

Herring are silvery schooling fish about nine inches long. They live for up to a dozen years, and breed annually after the age of three or four. Each April when they arrive the Sound is white-ringed with their fecundity. Milt spewed from the males fertilizes the eggs laid down by the females. Eggs are deposited from the intertidal zone to a depth of sixty feet, with survival greatest for those that adhere to the subtidal fronds of kelp. Birds and other fish feast on the surfeit; sea lions move in upon the feeding frenzy.

Overhead, spotter planes flash sightings of dark-massed herring schools to the assembly of fishing boats.

The market is driven by Japan's taste for the roe. Herring are captured before they spawn and exported whole, leaving the buyers to remove the egg sacs, or, in a separate and smaller fishery, the eggs are gathered upon the kelp, the two served together in Japanese restaurants. Lest the resource be overtaxed, Fish and Game permits the seine boats to fish only in half-hour bursts. A season's success depends as much on the scheduling and management of the openers as on the size of the run.

One billion fish, on average, breed in the Sound. The spawning population consists of herring of different ages. In 1989 they ranged from the herring that were larvae in '86, just three years prior, to the oldsters spawned in 1979 and now producing their last eggs. Herring are told apart by the year of their birth. The term *year-class* is used, which is the same thing as brood-year.

The size of each year-class varies widely. In Prince William Sound at the time of the spill, the year-class contributing most to the fishery was the robust group of 1984, its members just entering their prime. Had there been a harvest that spring, four out of five herring caught would have been from '84. Waiting in the wings was another large cohort, the 1988 year-class, consisting of juveniles not sexually mature.

The 1989 season was shut before it could open. James Brady, who made the call for Fish and Game, said he was being conservative. The tanker was still on the reef, the slick still adrift. Fortunately, the heaviest spawn occurred along shorelines in the northern Sound that were not affected. Each spring the schools leave a somewhat different pattern of egg deposition. For example, Green Island was hit, yet the herring did not go to Green that year. Exxon argued that 95 percent of the spawning shoreline that fish used in '89 was untouched by the spill. This figure disguised the degree of deposition. Definitely, eggs were thick around Naked Island and eggs around Naked Island were oiled.

Although many of the spawners encountered hydrocarbons on their swarm to and from the beaches, no fish were known to have died. There were some findings of short-term injuries, namely inflamed vents and gall bladders, and some evidence of sublethal tissue changes. These damages were measured to individuals. The thrust of the NRDA investigation was directed at the year-class of '89, representing the eggs, embryos and larvae struck by the spill when the oil was freshest. It was known from the literature that hydrocarbon exposure led to increased rates of larval abnormalities.

The biologists knew that the herring fishery would continue to be dominated by the '84 year-class. Those fish would be running hot and heavy no matter what. Any injuries to the early life stages of the '89 class would certainly not matter at first. Only 1 percent of herring eggs, and less than half the larvae, make it to maturity in the best of circumstances. The issue really had to do with the inherent size of the class, a complex happenstance that is regulated by unknown factors. All that was certain was that big classes didn't come along back to back. If the '89 class should turn out to be large and a linchpin of future harvests, then developmental damage to the larvae might well have an impact on the fishery. If the year-class should be small, any losses making it smaller would be a drop in the bucket.

With managers confident and openers extended, the herring tonnage pulled from the Sound was great in 1990, and even greater in 1991, thanks to the seniors from '84. The '84s had begun to decline, yet in 1991 they still made about half of the catch. Another 38 percent of the catch were freshmen recruits from '88. The next largest group was '85, with under 7 percent. Other year-classes contributed negligibly. Such lopsidedness was not unusual.

In Cordova, Fish and Game's Brady pointed out clouds within the silver lining. "The biomass of herring increased in part because there was no harvest in 1989," he said. "Maybe the harvests would be even better but for the spill.

"Anyway," Brady said, "there are things you can't argue about—the ocular tumors, the defects, et cetera, that occurred at the larval level."

Our conversation took place in 1991, before the work on developmental defects was known to be flawed. For instance, the eye tumors Brady spoke of. In 1989 herring eggs were collected and incubated in the lab. After hatching, the embryos and larvae were analyzed. The next year it was reported that herring were deformed if their progenitors had spawned near oil. Big headlines: no cigar. Histopathologists at the University of California subsequently told Fish and Game that the eye tumors, for one, were artifacts. They were protuberances resulting from tissue decay in defunct samples, not from the "mutagenic petroleum hydrocarbons" cited in the preliminary report. Another pathologist, after analyzing embryos and larvae for three years, made a better case that the oil exposure of the first year increased the incidence of deformities. The question of a population impact was still open.

I asked Brady, "Say you're a lawyer, and a twenty-five-year-old man wants to sue because he was abused for a time as a child. Yet he has turned out normal. What kind of a case do you have?"

"I don't know. But if you had a disturbed man, a criminal, you could point to the childhood abuse as the explanation."

"How would you show that it was the abuse that made him a criminal? Unless the entire year-class of twenty-five-year-olds was deformed—half of them psychotic? Will that be the case with the '89 herring?"

He conceded that background factors would probably mask the oil's effect. He said that didn't mean scientists shouldn't go after it. Brady was not a damage assessor, and glad of it. He remarked how much worse it would have been for the herring, had the winds of that fast-fading Easter blown differently.

The 1992 herring harvest set another new record. Stubbornly, the investigators pursued the spill into the very nuclei of cells. They commissioned tests to see how aromatic hydrocarbons injured the chromosomes of herring. They started looking for reproductive impairment in the '88 year-class, whose members may have lingered as juveniles close to the oiled beaches. This was the cohort to worry about, because it was going to be the successor to the '84 class in carrying the fishery. The '88s represented over half the catch in 1992.

Making roe for the first time that spring, the year-class of the *Exxon Valdez* showed itself to be weak. It was too soon to know how weak. Not all of the fish were yet breeding.

In 1993 their paucity was pronounced. By number and by weight, the '89s contributed less than 3 percent of the herring biomass. A picture was emerging of their scant place in the population. The '88s, now five years old, again provided over half the estimated spawning biomass. I say biomass instead of harvest, because there was no seine harvest at all in 1993. After testing the waters, neither Fish and Game nor the herring buyers thought the fishery was strong enough to open. The return was small. The '88s, feeding poorly that spring, were not gravid enough to make pay. In a commercial sense, the run had totally failed.

So here was another disaster, which many people laid in whole or in part to the oil spill. You couldn't say it wasn't so. You couldn't say it was, either.

Into the uncertainty new funding was injected. The state and federal Trustees agreed to study the problem with the pink salmon and herring stocks. The project that commenced in 1994 was an ecosystem model, an attempt to map out the food-web dynamics affecting the major fish species of Prince William Sound. The model was to include life histories, predator/prey relationships and the role of climatic and oceanographic disturbances. Things had come full circle. This type of project, sought by Alaskan marine biologists in the years before the oil spill, was rejected by the government in the summer of 1989 on the grounds that it was basic science.

DESCENDING, still descending, to the level of marine invertebrates. By the look of them, the invertebrates have nothing in common except for the lack of a backbone. Not having a backbone frees an animal to assume divergent and multifarious shapes. Mussels, starfish, shrimp, worms, amphipods, barnacles, crabs, anemones, jellyfish—soft or hard, big or little, faceless or faintly recognizable as our animal kin, the invertebrates tend to grow from their outside covering in, and not, as we do, from an expanding skeletal substructure topped by a brain in a case.

Invertebrates' insides are different too. The management of alien chemicals, such as aromatic hydrocarbons, is primitive. Very often there is no management. When mussels take up hydrocarbons, filtering them from the water along with their food particles, they store the PAHs in fatty tissue (shellfish are fatty throughout), and only when the contamination eases do they purge the compounds, very slowly, not speeding them through at all. In invertebrates the bioaccumulation of hydrocarbons is pronounced, a telling difference from fish and higher animals.

MFO activity in most invertebrates is very low. There is no bile fluid, no liver/gall bladder system for detoxication. The organ nearest in function is the digestive gland, which, disseminating the compounds, may show the adverse effects of toxic stress. So may the gonads, the sex organs of the animal. Mollusks in polluted harbors develop neoplastic conditions, which are not cancerous tumors, but rather the proliferation of useless cells. Pollutants alone don't appear to induce the growths; at least the conditions haven't been induced in experiments. Biologists think that a virus must be present as a coconspirator.

Though not metabolizing them well, most invertebrates are able to screen off harmful hydrocarbons from their vital functions. They are more resistant to oil contamination than fish, mammals and birds. Intertidal organisms seem the most tolerant, more so than the benthic fauna, perhaps because the intertidal zone is more stressful in general than the cold and constant bottom.

Two exceptions are worth mentioning. Oil readily kills certain kinds of amphipods. The absence from the sediment of these tiny crustaceans is looked for after spills. Because of their sensitivity, amphipods have also been used in the lab to calibrate the acute toxicities of different crudes and aromatic compounds. In the years after 1989, NOAA gauged the declining toxicity of the sediments by exposing amphipods to samples from the beaches.

At the other extreme, certain marine worms, called poly-chaetes, thrive after spills, turning over quickly so that each ex-panding generation of larvae is more adapted to the hydrocarbons than the previous one. This happened after the *Florida* spill in West Falmouth. In the Sound one often heard biologists talk about "*Exxon Valdez* worms."

Like the biomarkers in the bile and livers of fish, the bio-accumulation of chemicals in tolerant invertebrates makes them useful indicators of pollution. For decades the United States has looked to mussels and oysters as sentinels of coastal environmental quality. Monitoring has not been continuous, but the current ef-fort, NOAA's National Status and Trends Program, also known as Mussel Watch, dates from 1985. It samples mussel and sediment from 100 bays and harbors around the country. Contrary, perhaps, to public perception, the samples tell a story of improving condi-tions, as concentrations of PCBs, DDTs, metals and PAHs have declined from their peaks in the '70s.

Mytilus, the common blue mussel of the Sound, was mobi-lized after the spill to abet the damage assessment. Bioaccumula-tion might prove where the oil was, or had been. In one program, mussels were suspended in cages around the Sound, from which posts they combed the water for compounds on the move. In an-other, NOAA scientists scrambled out to check historical monitor-ing sites on the coastline. Four were located in Port Valdez, where the mollusks were keeping tabs on the tanker terminal, but two sites were in the central Sound within the spill trajectory. The slick bypassed both. The researchers staked out a number of new sta-tions to the southwest, ahead of the oil. Three of these sites were hit heavily, the mussels there absorbing PAHs in the hundreds of parts per million. By contrast, unaffected mussels had concentra-tions in the low parts per billion, which was the background level.

Periodically over ensuing field seasons, the NOAA scientists compared a total of ten intertidal sites, taking sediment as well as mussel tissue for analysis. Houghton and Lees would classify these sites as "mixed-soft"; by another designation, they were low- or moderate-energy. The smaller, sandier grains on the more pro-tected beaches retained oil and made for more consistent readings of hydrocarbons than did chunky gravel or cobble. Still, the levels declined each year.

In 1991, something startling emerged from the mussel watch. Beneath several large beds of mussels—found at new sites, but still within sheltered areas—investigators turned up unweathered oil. There was quite a lot of it. Evidently the oil sank in and the layer of mussels screened it from the winter waves. In the worst cases mollusks were contaminated at 10 parts per million, a high reading for this late in the spill, and the PAH levels in the supporting sediment were ten times higher. The phenomenon had not been recorded because large mussel beds on gravel are uncommon in the rocky Sound, and also because the mollusks by all appearances were healthy.

The government stated in its 1992 damage summary, "These beds were not cleaned or removed after the spill and are potential sources of fresh oil for harlequin ducks, black oystercatchers, river otters and juvenile sea otters—all of which feed on mussels and show signs of continuing biological injury."

The hot mussels prompted feverish postulation. Actually, it was the other way around. The mussel beds were discovered in the course of a wider search for pathways of hydrocarbon exposure. For the damage assessors had a problem: If animals were still being hurt as claimed, two and three years after the spill, how were they acquiring their sublethal doses of oil? Routes were easy to outline for fish, less so for mammals and birds. Most probably the oil would be in what they ate. Yet no firm evidence existed that otters or birds were consuming tainted food.

We must ascend for a moment to the level of the harlequin duck. The ducks got it started, this last act in the fading melodrama of the oil, and the first act in the story of the Sound's "restoration."

According to Fish and Game's *Widlife Notebook Series*, a guide prepared just prior to the spill, "The male harlequin (*Histrionicus histrionicus*) is a flashy, bull-necked, muscular looking little duck, with a wheezy squeak like that of a child's plastic squeeze-toy. . . . The common name harlequin, as well as the Latin name . . . come from the male plumage, said to resemble the gaily colored tights of pantomime buffoons."

Dark-headed, ring-necked and splashed with white, the harlequin is fairly common in the northern Rockies, the Pacific Northwest, Alaska and Siberia. The duck maintains a separate range in the northwest Atlantic as far east as Iceland; but in the northeastern United States the species has become rare, and it is considered endangered today in eastern Canada. Harlequins nest only beside freshwater torrents. Their habitat needs are unique, and they are sensitive to changes in the environment.

In southcoastal Alaska the harlequin breeds upstream from the shoreline. Until the spill nobody had ever located one of their nests in Prince William Sound, hidden as they were beneath the brush on steep banks at 1,000-foot elevations. "Flightless young have been observed playing in rapids and even waterfalls, which are felt to be used as escape habitat," says the *Wildlife Notebook* entry. "Predation probably contributes less to juvenile mortality than does joy-riding!" At the end of the summer hens and broods move down to the sea, and the ducklings begin to fly.

I first heard about the harlequins when out with Houghton and Lees in 1990. The skipper of one of the vessels passed along a rumor that damage assessors had "shot out twenty-five percent of the population" in order to have tissue samples for study. This was an exaggeration. Some harlequins were fully residential and some only wintered, so the population was not a fixed one. Sam Patten, the principal investigator for Fish and Game, and his associates collected less than one hundred harlequins in the Sound, when up to 10,000 may frequent the area throughout the course of a year.

But in another sense, the take of harlequins in the southwestern Sound was less than wise, because the biologists had no idea of how sparse the breeders had become there. The one harlequin family noticed near the oiled shoreline in the summer of '89 was shot for analysis.

When no broods were observed at the end of the summer in 1990, the magnitude of the problem started to sink in. The breeding of harlequins appeared to have completely collapsed in the southwestern Sound. The scientists decided to survey the ducks the following spring, when pairs should be courting at the stream mouths. They were dismayed to find a remnant population of only 220 birds in the oil-spill area. None were seen courting.

The investigators set up mist nets across the mouths of the more turbulent streams. To ducks flying downstream at dawn, the fine strands of the nets were invisible. This method of trapping was practiced by the Chugach Eskimos. Each stream was staked out for only a day, yet nowhere were harlequins ensnared, suggesting that none were nesting on the upper reaches. At the end of the summer of '91, no more than two broods were observed in the nearshore regions of the spill zone. By contrast, surveys of the northern and eastern Sound turned up many harlequins breeding successfully.

Why? What could account for the reproductive failure? From his postspill liver and bile samples Patten had indications of exposure to hydrocarbons. What if the harlequins, diving in the shallows for limpets, chitons, small clams and small mussels, were consuming invertebrates that were still tainted? Four percent of the birds collected had food in their gullets that tested positive for hydrocarbons. From the literature he learned that it did not take much oil to interfere with the hatching of seabirds.

Patten's energetic questions led others to discover the tainted mussels in the Sound. Post hoc ergo propter hoc, the government said, "Oil-contaminated mussel beds may be the source of this apparent continuing problem."

The situation was a little more complicated than that. In his ongoing status reports, and in subsequent conversation, Patten ruminated on the causes of the reproductive halt. The initial mortalities obviously had cut into the resident population. Some two hundred harlequin carcasses were recovered in the spring of '89, no doubt a minority of the total losses. Patten believed that birds had been, as he put it, "blasted" from the spill zone. His phrase called to mind the hot jets of the Omni-boom blowing mussels off the rocks. Harlequins are loyal to their home streams, so the niches opened up in the southwestern Sound would not soon be filled by pairs prospecting for new territory. Patten said the ducks he saw there "just sit on the outer rocks and don't do anything."

Beyond the acute effects, the scenario bifurcated. In searching for chronic injury, Patten favored the pathway of the food chain. The newly discovered mussels were a possible link. The PI and his team chased harlequins all around the western Sound, binoculars poised, but they never caught ducks in the act of eating oiled mussels.

He believed he had evidence of toxic stress, as some of the ducks from oiled areas were in poorer condition (lower fat reserves) when they were collected than those from unoiled areas. This finding was thrown out by the peer reviewers, because he took samples over the course of a year without allowing (controlling) for the influence of the seasons on the ducks' weight and fitness.

What the food-chain scenario lacked were lesions, or cellular changes, or any sublethal symptom that might result in reproductive damage. As for bioaccumulation, Patten couldn't show that compounds were retained in the harlequins' muscle tissue or fat, because these analyses were never performed. Nor had he conducted experiments with breeding ducks that might shed light on the question. And now, further collecting in the field was out. The agencies, stung by public reaction to their research methods, wouldn't allow any birds to be shot in 1991 and 1992.

Of course, there was another scenario for the breeding problem—human interference. Patten did not think it was as likely, but he did not stint on documenting it. His study detailed voraciously the human presence in the Sound between 1989 and 1991. As he summarized: "Massive amounts of human disturbance to stream mouths and other Harlequin habitats included thousands of man-days of manual cleaning, mechanical tilling, hot-water treatment, Inipol [the fertilizer for oil-eating bacteria], weir construction, agency and contractor visits, ship and boat traffic in bays and lagoons, and low-level overflights by fixed-wing aircraft and helicopters. Since Harlequin ducks are sensitive to disturbance, and high levels of disturbance can be correlated with poor reproductive performance, this is the alternative hypothesis of the cessation of Harlequin reproduction in the oil spill area of western Prince William Sound."

Reproduction remained extremely low in '92 and again in '93. Since the cleanup was no longer a factor, Patten's reports turned away from the human-disturbance hypothesis. "To be precise, we have reduced three hypotheses to two," he said, "because we can't tease apart the effect of the initial mortalities from the oiling effect." The missing harlequins were not being replaced, whether by breeding or immigration; the resident birds weren't pairing, as if in a state of shock, the spill still sounding in their ears. In '93 forty ducks were collected, from the west and from the east (and at the same time of year), to learn under the microscope whether differences existed between the two populations.

The government pressed its claim that the ducks' failure to reproduce was tied to the oil in mussels. But how many contaminated mussel beds were still left in the Sound? These were defined as densely packed colonies, twenty yards square at minimum, that still shielded oil on moderate- or low-energy beaches. Official estimates in '92 put the number at about twenty-five. Chief scientist Spies went to see the extent of the problem. He wasn't impressed: "We made a full-speed survey in the boat and still the beds were twenty minutes apart from each other." In '93, however, NOAA and Fish and Game hunted for additional beds and raised the total to fifty.

This research, like all other new projects since 1992, was conducted not so much to study damage to species but to lay the groundwork for their "restoration." Let me now strike the quotation marks. I've been gingerly about restoration because the term is a poor fit for the actions undertaken in its name.

Under the provisions of CERCLA and the Clean Water Act, restoration has three meanings. The first is the conventional one. The funds gained from Exxon were to be used to rehabilitate the natural resources found injured by the spill. A resource need not be a physical or biological entity. The category included such lost or damaged services as fishing, kayaking and enjoying the outdoors.

The law provides two fallbacks if restoration is judged not to be feasible. The government may use the money to replace the injured resource with something "similar," or to acquire a resource deemed to be "equivalent." The language in the settlement with Exxon also allowed for the "enhancement" of natural resources. In brief, the door to restoration was open to pretty much anything that might come through.

While the spill was still new, many notions were put forward on ways to restore the Sound in the literal sense. One could build extra fish hatcheries, for instance, or transplant seabirds, otters or even strips of rockweed to replace the life that was lost. By the time the money began to flow—$1 billion over ten years, the largest settlement of an environmental damage claim in history—such hands-on techniques, which were dubious and expensive, did not appear to be called for. "Natural recovery is a very potent tool," Spies advised the Trustees. "Nature's doing most of the job, and we would be working around the edges."

That was all right by the Trustees, a six-person council representing three state and three federal agencies, because the settlement funds were already spoken for, several times over. The Trustee agencies reimbursed themselves for their considerable costs to date. Spun off from the damage assessment, the research projects of the agencies went forward while the public was consulted and the formal plan devised. For a species to qualify for interim restoration monitoring, the oil spill should have injured its population, not just individuals or early life stages. This criterion was waived for species of commercial importance such as salmon.

The restoration plan took a long time forming. In response to public demands, the Trustees earmarked a major portion of the money to purchase or protect wildlife habitat. The ocean and coastline already being in public ownership, the nearest unprotected resources to the spill were terrestrial—upland, as it were, from the scene of the damage. There was pressure to bring the coastal forests of the Sound and Gulf under the restoration umbrella in order to save them from logging.

The logic fashioned was that the injured wildlife required extra territory to recover. Here is where the harlequin duck, having passed NRDA's tests, repaid its research funding, and to a lesser extent the river otter, and another species too, the marbled murrelet. The marbled murrelet is a secretive little seabird that nests in the pinnacles of mature conifers. Its breeding behavior was even less understood than the harlequin's. After the spring of 1989, when several hundred dead murrelets were retrieved from the Sound, the oil had not caused the bird any harm that could be determined, but the population was believed to be declining.

No matter that the linkage was fuzzy. The murrelet, the river otter, the harlequin duck were like the spotted owl of the Pacific Northwest, only there was little opposition to protecting the woods they inhabited. The lands at risk were owned by the Natives, for the most part, and the non-Native opposition to the cutting had preceded the oil spill. But afterward, the justification was always there in the fine print, what the Alaska attorney general, who was a Trustee, called the "legal-slash-vertical factual link" from the dearth of harlequin broods in the Sound to the purchase of timber rights elsewhere.

The tainted mussels must also play their part, being at the toxicological crossroads of the Sound. Over two field seasons the government spent some $1.5 million to study the mussels and their possible connection to river otters, juvenile sea otters, harlequin ducks and oystercatchers, the latter bird an intertidal feeder and nester. Coordination among the study components was poor. The PIs were supposed to test for hydrocarbons in feces, but only the oystercatcher researcher did so, with equivocal results. Scats couldn't be obtained for the others. The river otter biologists pursued blood proteins, the harlequin team liver enzymes. The mussel researchers tested ways to rid the mussels of their oil. The solution was to remove them, replace the gravel of the bed and put the mollusks back down like sod.

For all the talk about bioavailability, little was learned about it. The investigators did not establish ongoing exposures to the four species. Nor did they experiment with oiled mussels in the diets of their subjects. Invasive research, difficult to set up in the best of circumstances, had no appeal. Besides, the captive mink had eaten food that was contaminated at the hydrocarbon level of the worst-case mussels, and nothing had happened to the mink.

The Trustees ended the funding for the investigation in 1994. The mussels clung to their parts per billion, having served their purposes for restoration. Whether their own health was affected was still not known.

A FRENCH BIOLOGIST named J. C. Dauvin, an expert on the *Amoco Cadiz*, has summarized the impact of oil spills on invertebrate assemblies. He lists three chronological stages: 1) a brief period of mortality, especially for amphipods, following exposure to fresh oil; 2) a medium-term change in which some populations continue at normal levels, while a few populations of opportunistic worm species proliferate greatly; and 3) an eventual return to the original community state. An extreme example of the sequence is the explosion of opportunistic worms in West Falmouth, after poisonous aromatics destroyed the balance of invertebrates.

It should be clear that oil can kill, but how does oil enrich? Where does the toxicity leave off and the opportunity begin?

The enrichment phenomenon is not unusual. Marine life is known to congregate at sewage outfalls in urban harbors. A city's waste products, including organic matter and hydrocarbons from street and industrial runoff, support thriving animal communities. The *Exxon Valdez* itself sustained a miniature food web, from fungus to fish, within its ruptured tanks. In these instances the aromatic hydrocarbon concentrations are rather low, the harmful pollution diluted, so perhaps it's not surprising that toxic effects are absent.

Let's revisit Eagle Harbor, PAH paradise of Puget Sound, EPA hazardous waste site. Officially the waste site consists of three units, a section on shore where the defunct creosote plant is located and two sections of the harbor bottom. The East Harbor unit, the bottom nearest the plant, is where the PAH contamination is heaviest.

The liver tumors plaguing the fish of Eagle Harbor seemed to justify the need to fix the bottom. In lab tests the sediment proved toxic to amphipods; it had caused precancerous lesions in captive sole. Creosote seeping from the plant to the waterline had reduced the number of clams. But how was the invertebrate community of the bottom responding? Ellen Hale, EPA's assistant site manager for the harbor units, sounded a bit glum on this score. In spite of the obvious pollution, she said, the benthic community was impacted less than one would expect.

"There's not a pure correlation, the way there should be, between the levels we're finding and the biological effects," she said. "Probably the most distinct effect is a shift in the community toward more tolerant species."

Hale sent me a copy of the agency's formal investigation. Biologists compared the Eagle Harbor ecosystem with unpolluted sites in Puget Sound, termed background areas: "Abundances . . . of benthic animals were not significantly lower in Eagle Harbor than in background areas." Just the opposite: "Most striking was the increase in total macrofauna abundance within Eagle Harbor compared to the background stations. . . . This increase was largely due to the increase in abundance . . . of polychaete worms."

However abundant, the Eagle Harbor benthic life was considered unhealthy. The EPA dumped a layer of fill three feet thick onto the fifty-acre eastern section, capping its PAHs.

For one further example, consider the Santa Barbara Channel, site of the infamous 1969 blowout. There is oil pollution in the channel of natural origin, emanating from a potent group of subtidal seeps. Near a place called Coal Oil Point, as many as 1,000 barrels of petroleum are being released subtidally every day. By another estimate, the aromatic components in the seepage total thirty tons a year. Slicks on the surface sometimes stretch for ten miles.

After its black eye from the well blowout, the oil industry decided to examine the environment more closely. In the early '70s the American Petroleum Institute, an industry group, funded a study of Coal Oil Point by a marine biologist at UCLA named Dale Straughan.

The hypotheses underlying Straughan's 1976 report were typical of the state of knowledge at that time. She set out to look for malformations, reproductive damage, scanty populations, or any other harm that might be resulting to marine organisms from chronic exposure to petroleum from the seeps. She and her assistants sampled more than sixty species, from the high-tide mark down to the channel bottom at 180 feet.

Her 120 pages of findings can be distilled in a word—zilch. None of her measurements showed any differences between the animals at Coal Oil Point and those at clean sites in the channel. It didn't seem to matter to the barnacles, snails, abalone, urchins, lobsters or worms whether oil was present or not. Certain larvae from the seep region seemed to have developed a tolerance for the crude. Everything was "patchy," Straughan observed, describing both the density of organisms and the oil within the sediments.

Straughan did not attempt to analyze the community structure at Coal Oil Point, the ecosystem approach. That more comprehensive work was done in the early '80s by marine biologists from Lawrence Livermore Laboratory in central California. They chose the largest individual seep in the channel, known as Isla Vista, and compared its benthic community to a section of ocean bottom where there was no seepage.

The benthic organisms around the Isla Vista seep are crustaceans, worms, mollusks and other invertebrates, unremarkable creatures several inches long at most. The Livermore team sampled them in cores driven into their hiding places in the soft sediment. Isla Vista turned out to have a richer ecosystem than the unoiled site. The number of species, or diversity, was about the same, but the seep had the greater density—higher populations within species. The oil was again acting as a stimulus.

The principal investigator of the study was Robert Spies, later to be head of damage assessment in Prince William Sound. The irony of his insights was of some comfort to me during the period while I labored in the forced dark. I asked Spies to explain how oil could be both bane and boon.

Spies thinks the key to the phenomenon is the concentration of aromatic chemicals at the boundary between seawater and sediment. The level determines whether benthic organisms suffer toxic effects or make gains. He postulates a threshold of, roughly speaking, one part aromatics per million. Above this concentration, the immediate environment is too hot for most invertebrates. Just at the threshold, harmful compounds can be neutralized or biologically tolerated. At dilutions just below, marine life is able to enrich itself on the stores of organic carbon being offered in the oil proper.

Different organisms take part in this process. At the Isla Vista seep, Spies explained, the process starts with the activity of the single-celled microbes. Like shock troops, bacteria meet the oil deposits below the ocean floor and start to consume what to them are the choice components, the lighter aliphatics. As a result the petroleum issuing into the ocean is relatively high in sulfur, aromatic compounds, heavy aliphatics and tars.

The zone immediately around the point of emission is too toxic for other benthic life, but the bacteria, some of which are so thick as to be visible in strands and mats, are fat and happy and multiplying. Biologists who dove in Eagle Harbor noticed the same thing. Alluding in their EPA report to the model of the petroleum seeps, they described bacterial increases and what appeared to be mats of organisms upon the harbor bottom.

Some of the microbes at Isla Vista are able to metabolize the sulfur compounds in the seepage, and other bugs go for the aromatic hydrocarbons—they adjust their enzyme systems to break the benzene ring structure, a capacity lacking in higher organisms. The bacteria are detoxifying the oil even as they feed on it. Most importantly, they themselves are a food source for the creatures on the next link in the chain.

As one moves away from the seep's ground zero, the enrichment becomes apparent. At Spies's threshold of toxicity, there is a transition zone populated by numerous worms. The worms consume the abundant bacteria, or forage on microscopic crustaceans nourished by the microbes, or simply prey on each other.

Further out still, the level of aromatics declines enough for a full range of benthic invertebrates to capitalize on the carbon. Anemones, abalone, clams, large crustaceans and starfish join the ubiquitous worms. The decay of organisms at the end of their life cycles adds to the nutrients in the system. Animal populations remain denser than normal until one passes beyond the reach of the oil.

Those are the community effects. Analyzing thousands of individual specimens, other researchers reported no visible harm from the oil—no tumors or deformities in the sedentary seep creatures. When Spies's team sampled fish, they found MFO arousal in one species, a two-inch-long flatfish called a sanddab, indicating that livers were taking up PAHs. But he and his colleagues weren't able to make a good survey of abundance, so they didn't know whether fish were benefiting from the enhanced food web. It was not impossible that the fish could be more numerous and more stressed at the same time.

The oil did reduce some organisms. The amphipod population at the Isla Vista seep was found to be only half that at the comparison station. A certain copepod was less numerous. Spies also found that seep starfish had reduced sexual function and a shorter breeding season than starfish elsewhere.

Spies told me that when he published his statistical picture of enrichment, he was accused of being a patsy for the oil industry. In 1990, when we first talked, he was beginning to investigate the oil spill in Alaska on behalf of the opposite point of view. He was struck by the millions the government was prepared to lay out. "I've got fish born every day in San Francisco Bay with anomalies," he said. "We don't seem to pay attention to the right kind of problems."

AT THE ENDPOINT of our descent, the bacterium: a single life within a single cell.

In April of '89 Don Button, a microbiologist at the Institute of Marine Science of the University of Alaska, observed that the oil spill might not be such a bad thing for one organism in the Sound, but that "nobody ever takes anything from the bacteria's point of view." He calculated that if no weathering or cleanup took place, metabolism by microorganisms would make the spill disappear in 10,000 days, or about twenty-seven years. He was aware that this was too long for people to tolerate.

Years before, Button had studied the marine bacteria living within Port Valdez. His was one of the environmental projects monitoring the tanker terminal. He found hydrocarbon degraders to be abundant in the rainy fjord, but he was puzzled because he could not tie the bacteria to oil pollution by Alyeska.

Raising his eyes to the spruce and hemlock above the water, Button theorized that terpenes bleeding from the forest canopy were providing a food source for the bacteria. Terpenes are a kind of biogenic hydrocarbon, produced by trees.

He devised a test. He took flasks of seawater containing the microbes and laced the samples with a terpene mixture. Other flasks he laced with toluene, an aromatic petroleum hydrocarbon.

The bugs that were fed the terpenes metabolized it at dramatically faster rates than the others metabolized the toluene.

The experiment indicated that the bacteria of Port Valdez had been primed. Although they were able to break down either hydrocarbon, they had a greater affinity for the terpenes than for the toluene. The results suggested to Button that, on the one hand, Alyeska wasn't overloading the port with toluene, and, on the other, terpenes must be present in the water in significant concentrations.

Button subsequently found that the principal source of the terpenes was not the runoff from the local slopes, but rather the Alaska Coastal Current sweeping up from British Columbia. The Gulf of Alaska is bordered by a conifer forest of some five million acres, a huge purveyor of terpenes to the coast-hugging flow. Terpene concentrations were higher off the Gulf coast than within the Sound. Button was even able to correlate the fluctuation of local terpene levels with the rainfall patterns in southeast Alaska, hundreds of miles away.

Other microbiologists agree that the bacteria are prevalent in the region; but they maintain that priming by terpenes is beside the point. Bacteria with the capacity to degrade hydrocarbons are ubiquitous in the sea. Normally they represent about 1 percent of the total microbial community. They feed on ambient carbon sources, but when they sense an infusion of hydrocarbons, whether from living vegetation or a dying oil tanker, the bacteria can respond to it within hours and multiply greatly. The bugs keep it up for as long as the supply lasts. The composition of bacterial communities is extremely malleable. Where the hydrocarbon supply is constant, as at the petroleum seeps of the Santa Barbara Channel or the creosote seeps of Eagle Harbor, the microbial mix is permanently altered, with the hydrocarbon degraders predominant.

Creatures neither animal nor vegetable, the bacteria are nearly as old as the earth itself, having arisen four billion years ago. They are 100 times older than *Homo sapiens*, and may boast as many different species as we have individuals. More than a billion microbes inhabit a gram of soil; there are a million in a milliliter of seawater. Marine bacteria and their protozoan and fungal cousins represent 50 percent of the mass of life in the ocean.

Bacteria are far simpler than vertebrates or invertebrates, but to think of them as primitive is not correct, given their complex biochemistry and impressive adaptive mechanisms. The ultimate opportunists, bacteria have populated all manner of environments, from the frigid stratosphere, to the airless hot depths below the earth's surface, to the acid channels of mammalian stomachs. Bacteria were the first ashore when the '64 earthquake created a new intertidal habitat in Prince William Sound; they laid the basis for subsequent colonists.

The bacterial cell is structured differently from those of higher organisms. Bacteria are called procaryotes; plants and animals are eucaryotes. The difference is that our DNA—the genetic material of eucaryotes—is enclosed within a nucleus inside our cells, while inside the bacterial cell there is DNA but no distinct nucleus. Procaryotic organisms propagate not by sex but by cell division, as individuals. A bacterium grows until reaching a certain size, then splits into two identical daughter cells.

Aerobic bacteria, such as live in the sea, require oxygen. They respire. If oxygen is in short supply, the cells' reproduction is curtailed. The ocean contains much dissolved oxygen, so that's not a problem. In the suffocating muck of a salt marsh, aerobic bacteria don't do well, which partly explains why oil stranded there is slow to degrade.

The bacteria also require nutrients, mainly nitrogen and phosphorus in addition to basic carbon. These elements are also present in seawater. In order for bacterial growth to be accelerated, nutrients must be provided in amounts equal to or exceeding the microbes' needs. A bacterial culture, pampered in a lab dish, multiplies exponentially. Cells double every twenty minutes or so when nourished properly. The growth rate is not a straight-line progression. Initially there is something called the lag phase, during which little appears to be going on in the dish. The bugs are making internal adjustments to the blend of nutrients being provided. If oil is offered, the microcrobes that favor hydrocarbons mobilize the requisite enzymes, converting themselves internally, and then begin to metabolize the compounds and reproduce.

In bacteria, fates and effects merge. Scientists who study the weathering of slicks include bacterial degradation as a companion to evaporation, dissolution, dispersion, etc. Bacterial degradation is in fact the ultimate fate of the oil, the last metamorphosis, after which the components disappear into the chemical background.

Scientists have never tracked the response of the microbial community in the open ocean after an oil spill. From lab tests and wave-tank experiments it can be surmised that the bugs are set back at first. The more soluble compounds in high concentrations are toxic to most bacteria, as they are to other organisms. The light fractions in the oil can cause cell walls to burst.

By rights the acute effects on bacteria should have been considered among the natural resource damages. But biologists did not bother with the bacteria. Their concerns began at the level of the phytoplankton, which are single-celled algae, and the multicelled zooplankton. These organisms represented the vital next steps, after bacteria, in the food web of the Sound. Nothing amiss was detected in the limited sampling of the plankton. Basically, the hydrocarbons moved through the rich-laden waters like a cannon-ball shooting through a cloud. Some damage to ambient organisms must have occurred, but the hole quickly closed, as replacements swirled in on the currents.

The bugs start to break down crude oil once evaporation has removed the most poisonous light ends. Dissolution and dispersion make the oil more available to the bacteria, and to the marine fungi and yeasts that play a role in the process. The microbes position themselves at the oil-water interface. Here they have access to both the nutrients in the water and the less-than-soluble hydro-carbons. Bacteria produce their own surfactants, the chemicals that reduce the tension between oil and water. The surfactants promote emulsification of the slick—help disperse it in droplets. The drop-lets in turn provide them a greater surface area of oil to get at, and so the process spirals.

The proof of bacterial activity is shown indirectly, by record-ing the changes in the constituents of the oil. The microorganisms favor the intermediate-weight, straight-chain aliphatics and attack those compounds first. The branched aliphatics, the heavier waxes, tars and PAHs are considerably more resistant to breakdown. Fewer bacteria are at work when the choice components have been eliminated. The rule of thumb is that populations peak in the water column one week after a spill and fall off after a month. Twelve days after the oil spill, Don Button collected a water sample off Knight Island. He found that the bacteria were primed—their potential greater than that of bugs in Port Valdez—to break down toluene.

At one stage in digesting the aromatics compounds, the bac-teria add oxygen, making metabolites that dissolve. Some scien-tists, among them Button, worry about these metabolites, because they are similar to the free radicals, the intermediate hydrocarbon products of the vertebrate metabolism. The question is: Does the bacterial degradation of oil create compounds that endanger other marine species? Injuries to sea urchin embryos have been demon-strated in the lab. In the open environment, the metabolites react quickly with other chemicals and disappear, like quarks of marine toxicology. Doug Wolfe tried to measure their potency in intertidal sediments oiled by the *Exxon Valdez*, and though he thinks he heard a toxic signal, it was quite dominated by the overall decline in the potency of the original aromatic fractions.

The bottom line is that bacteria use hydrocarbons to make

energy and especially to make more bacteria. At the end of the process, as a kind of waste product, they leave behind carbon dioxide, water and the mineral constituents of the oil.

"The rate of petroleum biodegradation," notes Ronald Atlas, a leading microbiologist in this field, "is the single most important parameter in the self-purification of the marine environment." The oceans would be awash in oil were it not for microbial cleanup. Atlas's statement extends as well to the past. Most of Earth's petroleum was lost eons ago, not long after being formed. Oil seeped up through cracks and was broken down in the watery biosphere. Chemist Jim Payne told me, "If organic deposits had not been sealed from aerobic bacteria, we wouldn't have any oil fields today." Saudi Arabia happens to be situated above cap-rock formations that have held the petroleum in place.

Studies to harness the bugs for oil cleanup began in the late '60s, after the wreck of the *Torrey Canyon* off Cornwall. In Alaska, Ron Atlas sampled the indigenous bacteria of Prince William Sound and Cook Inlet. He discovered that microbes were being stimulated by the ship traffic in and out of Anchorage. On the North Slope oil fields, he found that bacteria worked slower in the cold, yet never stopped unless the water froze.

Atlas and a number of other researchers had a simple idea for helping the microbes. Where carbon (a.k.a. oil pollution) was in ample supply, they tried to improve the conditions by adding extra nutrients, namely nitrogen and phosphorus. Make more bugs and they would remove more oil. Small-scale tests indicated that the nutrients helped increase the rate of degradation. Bioremediation, as the technique was called, was by then showing good results on contaminated soils. The marine environment, being less stable, was a greater challenge, both to achieve results and to measure them.

In 1986 Alyeska upgraded its ballast-water treatment plant by adding a stage for bacterial cleanup. The facility separates the vestigial oil from the aqueous ballast carried by tankers to Port Valdez. At the end of the process the oil is fed into ponds of seawater. To stimulate the microbes, Alyeska aerates the water and adds nitrogen and phosphorus fertilizers. According to its reports, this last step reduces the aromatics in the effluent before the effluent is discharged into the port.

The *Exxon Valdez* provided an opportunity to learn whether the bacteria already at work within the pores of the shoreline could be boosted further. When EPA proposed the idea in May, the mechanical washing was already under way. EPA joined forces with Exxon on the project. A liquid fertilizer was on the market,

Inipol. Developed in France following the *Amoco Cadiz*, Inipol was designed to stick to oil, but it had never been employed in a large-scale emergency. All available supplies were rushed to the Sound, and also Customblen, a granular blend for agriculture that released the same nutrients but slowly.

In June the first trial of bioremediation produced exciting results. Inipol was sprayed onto a cobble beach in Snug Harbor. After about two weeks of bathing by the tides, a large white rectangle appeared where the liquid had been sprayed onto the black stones. The surface of the rocks was clean, though oil remained below.

In July an EPA press release enthused about the preliminary findings. On the test beaches there were "between 30 and 100 times greater levels of oil-degrading microorganisms than in control plots."

Exxon moved toward a full-scale application of the fertilizers. There were some questions raised about Inipol's toxicity, but publicity for bioremediation continued to build. EPA chief William Reilly visited the Sound in early August and plugged the bugs. At the same time, the NOAA-approved, hot-water wash was developing detractors. "Bioremediation is very promising," Reilly said, "and if we could only get enough of the stuff [Inipol], they'd do more."

Summer ran out with seventy-five miles of shoreline treated. Bioremediation seemed like a benign and low-tech alternative to the high-power hoses. I wrote an editorial in a Valdez newspaper in praise of the bugs. Meanwhile, Exxon and EPA scientists looked at their data with greater scrutiny. In September the agency announced it had been in error about the boosted microbial populations. Upon analysis, all oiled beaches, sprayed or no, saw a hundredfold increase in numbers of hydrocarbon degraders. "Natural bioremediation is a hard act to follow," said Hap Pritchard, the PI for EPA on the project.

More troublesome to the scientists was their inability to measure oil being removed. The startling white rectangle was one thing; and other beaches looked superficially cleaner. But the oil within the sediment appeared undiminished. Analysis of the constituents showed that certain compounds were indeed dropping out, which was evidence of degradation, but the fertilized bugs didn't seem to be working any faster than the others. Hydrocarbon consumers quickly reached a plateau of about 10 percent of the microbial community, and wouldn't be nudged higher.

EPA and Exxon microbiologists worked all winter. In December I attended a meeting in Washington, D.C., that was chaired by

Hap Pritchard. He brought his peers together to critique his promising if preliminary results from Prince William Sound. With each test plot having generated different results, his statistics were all over the place, but he had the white rectangle in Snug Harbor. There were collegial joking references to "visual science." What looked to be true, in other words, was not yet true according to analytic chemistry or gravimetric tests or statistical controls. On the second day of the meeting, "visual science" began to lose its amusement for Pritchard, but he never ducked.

Afterward Pritchard said, "What's been exciting to me, in Prince William Sound, is to find what a hell of a good job the bacteria are doing in the first place, and secondly, that it's been possible to manipulate them."

"Who are these bugs?" I wanted to know, for I thought they would be more appreciated if the scientists would put out the names of the species. In the summer, a junior EPA researcher had deflected my question about the species, saying, "The physical characteristics of the slime are what matters, not the name."

"The bacterial kingdom is so diverse," Pritchard said. "It's hard to sort out the otters from the polar bears. Basically you've got two organisms, the *Pseudomonas* and *Flavobacteria* genera—in cultures they're the two most common anyway. Within those genera who knows how many species there are."

Pseudomonas bacteria are rod-shaped cells, about a micrometer (0.00004 inch) in length. They are fringed with hairlike structures called flagella that whip about and propel the organisms through the water. Alyeska had a picture of *Pseudomonas* in its literature about the ballast-water treatment plant. The micrograph was fuzzy but the body and flagella were clear. "Alyeska's Microscopic Clean-up Crew." I liked that.

In the summer, on the sill of my window overlooking Lake Eyak, I had conducted my own experiment. One of the scientists gave me a cough-syrup-sized bottle labeled "Microcosm—Augustine Expt. MAO4-454." Inside was a pinch of oiled gravel collected from a fertilized beach on Knight Island. Looking closely, I could see that the black pebbles and the bottle's interior were lightly coated with a pale slime.

To keep things going, I was advised to add a few drops of oil (whatever was in the garage), a dollop of seawater, some plant food such as fish emulsion, and air.

I put in a little oil, some gravel from outside the door, tap water, salt and a piece of banana. Mostly I kept the top on, the way the bottle was given to me. Off, there was a faint scummy odor. This was a large error. The sealed system evidently went anaerobic.

The bottle really started to smell and look awful. I confess I threw it away. Anaerobic (un-air-breathing) bacteria are another class. Some degrade oil, according to Ronald Atlas, but they are not very good at it. I had overseen the death of bioremediation and the triumph of a foreign culture. This is why marsh muck smells when it's dug up.

To this day EPA and Exxon have not succeeded in convincing critics that their own bioremediation truly worked. There were some positive signs in tests held in 1990. Microbial activity, and perhaps microbial numbers, were shown to have been enhanced by the fertilizers. Some hydrocarbons were definitely lost. But was the rate of degradation demonstrably higher than elsewhere in the western Sound? Yes, said Exxon's reports, backed by consultant Atlas, rates were up to five times higher. PAH concentrations dropped faster because of the treatment.

For its part, the EPA review board kept demanding revisions in the analysis by the Pritchard team. Many interim versions of the report were put out, but as of late 1993 the final stamp of approval had not yet been granted. I talked with a project statistician. "The beaches are variable, the oiling of them was very variable," he said. "The more variation you have, the greater the effect must be in order for you to show that it's real." He was trying new statistical approaches that he hoped would bring forward the reality.

Bioremediation worked best of all in the test tubes and microcosms. The frustration was the same as in the damage assessment program, where proofs of toxicity, illumined in the lab, could not be mirrored in the field. The white window at Snug Harbor was never satisfactorily explained. It may simply have been a physical effect of the Inipol, abetted by tidal pumping. A more hopeful hunch is that biosurfactants, the chemical degreasers produced by the boosted bacteria, were responsible. *Something* in the experiment helped to speed the removal of oil from those particular rocks in that particular plot of Prince William Sound during that one fortnight in June. The white patch is not there today.

4

The Native and the Otter

A man was out looking for chiton [a mollusk] when he was surprised by the tide. Before he drowned he cried, "I wish I might turn into a sea otter!"

—CHUGACH LEGEND OF THE ORIGIN OF THE SEA OTTER

FROM THE VERY BEGINNING I intended to save the sea otters until last. They were a special case requiring special elucidation. The sea otters were an inconvenience, actually. Something about the otters challenged my view that disturbances in the Sound were transitory and that scientists who set out to explain them usually failed. The sea otters emitted a keening sound, a signal of distress, that cut through the white noise of environmental instability.

More money, by far, was spent on the sea otters after the oil spill than on any other species. Biologists went to great lengths to rescue and rehabilitate the otters from the oil, and to study the disaster's acute and chronic effects on the animals. My unease wasn't due to their injuries, which were serious but, insofar as the population was concerned, remediable. The cry I heard was a rejection of the scientific approach altogether. Biology and statistics were not sufficient to describe what had happened to sea otters in Prince William Sound. Their situation evoked emotions, unquantifiable emotions in people, which, ironically, was why the rescue and research efforts were so urgent and extensive.

The reverberations from the sea otters were both ecological and historical. At the time of the oil spill, the population was stronger in the eastern Sound than in the west, a pattern reflecting a prior disturbance. The sea otter was still recovering from the hunt for its fur that ended in 1911. The hunt, which left the species close to extinction, began in the Sound in the 1780s, some forty years after the discovery of Alaska by Vitus Bering. It took that long for Russian adventurers from Siberia to sweep up the chain of

Aleutian Islands. Since the Russians could not get the otters without the aid of Native hunters in kayaks, they used the one to kill the other. They enslaved the Aleuts of the chain and the Koniags of Kodiak Island and chased the sea otters all the way to Chugach Sound.

The Sound's inhabitants, the Chugach Eskimos, were too tough and too few to be conquered. But they were induced to join the hunt. The Chugach killed otters in the Sound for the Russians, for English traders (whose name for the Sound prevailed) and finally for the Americans. Even after its sale in 1867 Alaska was valued mainly for its sea otter fur. The toll of the hunt was harder on the Natives than the otters. Although the animals proved almost miraculously resilient, retaking the last of their haunts in the Sound by the 1980s, the Natives' recovery from disease and despair was not assured. Certainly the Natives would never be the same as before. So it was their cry too I heard, distantly from the past, reaching to my rooms above the misty lake.

History helped explain—as neither science nor journalism could do—why the Native and the sea otter were the two denizens of the Sound that suffered the most from the events of 1989. Indeed I mean to put them on the same level of indigenousness. The studies made of the Natives after the spill were as extensive as those of sea otters. The Native and the sea otter were the most sensitive to disaster because they were entwined by disaster through the past.

In the account that follows, I have tried to synthesize the two investigations, and I have used a broader brush than previously. Four characters are involved: the otters, the Natives, the scientists and the public. For just as the sea otters stirred public passions that were beyond science to assuage, so the Natives, in their deeply private view of the Sound, were passionate, and mistrustful of the explanations of scientists. The Natives were guided by a knowledge of nature that might be called nescient. At the same time, they harbored quite different feelings from the public about sea otters.

Let me start with the otter's fur, because it is the link between the historical crisis and the latest one. The pelage of the sea otter is a wonderful material. Its color ranges from a lustrous gold to a deep chocolaty brown. The Russians called the animal "sea beaver," but in the opinion of Georg Steller, the naturalist with Bering and the first Westerner to describe the animal, its coat "so far surpasses in length, beauty, blackness and gloss of the hair of all river beavers that the latter cannot be compared with it."

The hairs of the fur are of two types. The superficial layer is the guard hairs, which are about an inch long, and beneath them is the underfur, which is shorter and downier. The underfur is the densest of any mammal known; it consists of more than half a million hairs per square inch. The hair shafts are kinked and interlocking, trapping air in myriad spaces, and making for a great warmth and water-repellency. This insulation helps the sea otter to survive in subarctic temperatures alongside the blubber-laden pinnipeds and whales, which are much bulkier animals. Not that, at eighty to ninety pounds for the males and forty-five to fifty-five pounds for the females, the sea otter is small. But as the smallest mammal to inhabit the ocean, the sea otter was something of a physiological curiosity to modern biologists.

When they tested properties of insulation, researchers determined that the fur of the sea otter is actually a better insulator than seal blubber. Yet the seal should be warmer overall, because, having a greater volume-to-surface ratio, its body should generate relatively more heat. The otter's fur, in other words, could not conserve enough heat to make up for the animal's lack of bulk. For this animal to survive in the ocean, the difference must be made up by its metabolism: by an extraordinary output of heat.

Metabolism, in the broad sense used here, means converting food to energy with the input of oxygen. (The metabolism of oil, a topic of the last chapter, is an unusual subprocess.) All mammals metabolize their food in about the same way, using about the same amounts of oxygen to make units of heat-energy from given amounts of nourishment. Therefore the pace of an animal's metabolism—its metabolic rate—can be measured by the amount of oxygen it consumes while it's fed under laboratory conditions. When scientists monitored sea otters in sealed test chambers, they measured their metabolic rates to be twice as high as those of other mammals of the same size. The otters were burning twice as many calories.

Sea otters sustain their high metabolisms through ravenous eating. For their size they eat much more than other creatures do, as can be illustrated by showing daily food intake as a percentage of body weight. Thus a 205-pound writer consumes about five pounds of food and drink per day, less than 3 percent of his body weight, and finds that proportion more than adequate. A sea lion, operating in a more demanding milieu, eats fish equivalent to 6 percent of its body weight daily. But the sea otter has been found to eat 25 percent of its weight every day, four times as much as the sea lion and eight times as much as the human.

They forage for hours at a stretch. After studying them at Amchitka Island in the Aleutians, where the pods are among the thickest in Alaska, Fish and Wildlife Service biologist James Estes estimated that, for each square mile of habitat, about 100 sea otters were consuming some 350,000 pounds of shellfish per year. But if they are gluttons, they are gluttons on a razor's edge. Burning calories instead of storing them, the animal maintains a fat mass, or energy reserve, of only 3 percent. In stormy weather, buffeted and unable to dive, an individual might lose as much as ten pounds in a day, and starve to death in three. They actually get ulcers from not eating enough.

Part of the energy derived from its diet the sea otter plows back into grooming. The animal spends a considerable portion of its time pulling, rubbing, fluffing, whisking itself. For unlike blubber, the fur must be actively kept up or it won't insulate. The forepaws, which have stubby digits and retractable claws, do most of the work, while the hind feet, which are webbed and floppy, knead the lower body. Looped about with kelp, its head raised with a quizzical look, the sea otter seems disconnected from itself, like a ventriloquist trying keep a straight face at a dummy's antics. When an otter somersaults over and over, it is not doing it for fun, it is blowing air bubbles into its underfur. A quick, final spin leaves a silvery film of water that seals in the air layer.

Since the water conducts away the animal's heat more rapidly than the air does, the sea otter likes to keep as much of itself as dry as possible. When the water is particularly icy, the animal will ride very high, like an empty tanker. It adjusts its buoyancy by means of its outsized lungs. If needing to cool off, the animal deflates and rides lower in the water. It has the ability to augment or constrict the blood flow to its peripheral tissues, yet another means of managing its temperature.

Thermoregulation, scientists came to realize, was the key to the sea otter's survival. A breach in the system, such as from a smear of oil it couldn't get rid of, might cause a fatal breakdown. An animal with oiled fur, fighting off the cold, might boost its metabolic rate beyond its capacity to fuel itself. Hypothermia and death would ensue.

The prehistoric Natives well appreciated how the fur staved off the cold and wet. Eskimo chiefs wore robes covering their bodies from neck to ankle. People used otter fur for trim on sealskins, for armbands, penis sheaths and soft bedding. The Chugach showed off the fur to Captain Cook in 1778, when the English explorer discovered the Sound. But overall, the sea otter was not so useful to the Natives as the seal or sea lion. This was because its flesh was not good to eat. Some said it tasted like mud, others said it was like cormorant, and by the time you finished cooking and eating it you were hungry all over again.

If the otter held a special place in the world, it was for reminding the Chugach of themselves. The sea otters were social animals that behaved individually. They maintained a parallel community on their side of the waterline, bobbing in a kind of mirror of Native life. Plucking a clam from the bottom, an otter cracked it open just as a person would do, against a rock brought up for that purpose. They used their chests as dinner tables. They groomed and fidgeted, they rolled from side to side on the surface like synchronized swimmers, eyes shut and paws together as if in prayer. They were expressive and fickle, comical and nasty. A male would sometimes seize a pup and swim about with it, until the desperate mother ransomed her young with a crab. The Natives, who knew all about hostage-taking, would be entertained as if at a movie.

The otter they believed was sprung from humans. They had a literal basis for their anthropomorphism. The creature's skeleton looked like a little person's. Its leg had a tibula and fibula just like their own, and the internal organs were similar. The Aleuts (neighbors, but ethnically different from the Pacific Eskimos) were able to perform small surgeries, and they rehearsed their procedures on the sea otter.

In Chugach Sound, the sedentary otter was the one animal that could be hunted year-round. The compact between the hunter and prey was that the animal would agree to be taken only if the hunter paid the proper respects. It was absolutely taboo to laugh at an otter in its death throes. For an animal, not just the sea otter, was doubly alive. It had an immortal soul, which took the form of the creature itself, and also a spirit-owner, a powerful overseer, which looked something like a human only brighter.

The great spirit-owner of the sea creatures was Imam-shua, a goddess who lived at the bottom of Chugach Sound. Whenever one of her sea otters died, its soul was transferred to another. Therefore the hunter, if he initiated the death, must follow through properly; otherwise there would be no more sea otters. He must not drink any water until he purified the carcass on the beach. He must pour fresh water into the otter's snout, because its life in the salty ocean would have left it very thirsty. The bones must be buried in the ground, befitting a creature that had once been a person who drowned.

When the Russians and, subsequently, the Americans took over, they perverted the bond betweem the Native and the otter.

They turned the Natives into killing machines. Fleets of kayaks were dispatched along the coastline. The men would surround an otter in their kayaks, outflank its desperate dives and slay it with harpoons or arrows. The overseers did not object to the hunting and purification rituals the Natives performed, because they got the pelts afterward and the hunters were able to maintain their obligation to the renewable form of the animal—except that eventually the animal did not come back. At that juncture, around the turn of the twentieth century, the Native and the otter were severed. Each population was left alone to recover if possible from the onslaught.

Working backward from their recent expansions, biologists have figured that small colonies of sea otters held on in a dozen places. Perhaps a thousand or two lived in wave-beaten refuges, hundreds of miles apart, from the far Aleutians to southcoastal Alaska. Prince William Sound was their easternmost refuge, maybe fifty animals hiding in coves on the outer skirts of Montague Island.

The descendants of the Chugach maintained four villages, which over the years contracted into two. They shared the Sound with miners, fishermen and fox farmers. They knew of the sea otter from stories but not from experience. In the early 1960s, when the otters started to come back strongly, an odd, sad thing happened. The sense of feeling for it, of identifying with its humanlike qualities, no longer belonged to the Native exclusively. To hunt the animal was forbidden by the state. The spirit-owner of the sea otter was now the conservationist at large.

ON THE AFTERNOON of March 27, 1964, an Aleut named Paul Kompkoff Sr. was out by himself in the eastern Sound, not far from Cordova. It was Good Friday for most other Christians, but he was Russian Orthodox and his time to be in church was a few weeks hence.

Kompkoff, in his early forties, and his wife, Minnie, were living in Cordova in 1964 because they had children attending the high school there. Normally they resided in the Native village of Chenega, which was located in the far western Sound.

As he recounted it to me, he took his skiff down Orca Inlet and into the Cutoff, the shallow channel separating Hawkins and Hinchinbrook Islands. In the Cutoff he saw two animals acting strangely on the beach. A bald eagle and a sea otter were fighting over something, tugging at something. He drew closer. The animals had hold of a fish, a red Irish lord, a kind of large sculpin. The strange scene made him feel dizzy.

Kompkoff didn't remark on it, but it was strange enough to see an otter in the Sound, let alone see one contesting with an eagle.

He had grown up without sea otters. And though he called himself an Aleut, Kompkoff actually wasn't. The Russians applied their initial designation to all the indigenous groups that they met on their sweep up the coastline to the Sound. Thus any man in a kayak was an Aleut, and useful for the hunt. Kompkoff's name, his faith and some of his blood were Russian, but primarily his stock was Chugach. To avoid confusion, anthropologists now group the Natives of the Sound and the Pacific Eskimo people to the west under a new heading, the Alutiiqs.

Kompkoff continued his tale, matter-of-factly. The otter and the eagle were pulling on the fish. He cut the engine. Then he noticed, above where the otter and the eagle were, that the trees were swishing back and forth. He felt really dizzy then. He thought he was going to be sick.

He didn't know what was going on. He was rocking. He smelled the acrid smell of fresh mud, and looked and saw the shallow water boiling. He yanked the cord on the kicker and turned back out. There were strong swells. He saw harbor seals leaving the water, clambering onto the bars because they knew. Then he knew, too, what it was, that they were experiencing an earthquake.

Kompkoff ran his boat back to town. Cordova had come through not too badly—some damage to the docks, and the harbor bottom uplifted. He learned that Valdez was hard-hit and many there killed, and that Tatitlek, a Native village near Valdez, was rattled but unscathed. There was no word from his village of Chenega until later in the night. Then a party of seal hunters who had been clear of the village radioed the news that Chenega was totally obliterated. One-third of the seventy-six residents were missing and presumed dead.

Here is what happened: The ground began to shake a little after 5:30 P.M. People ran out of their houses. Many elders went for the church, their instinctive sanctuary, and others headed up the hill toward the elementary school. During the four or five minutes of endless shaking, a small wave of water came up on the beach. It broke gently, withdrew and, to the dismay of those who were watching, kept withdrawing. The water dropped back 100, 200, 500 yards, exposing the bottom of Chenega Cove. Some realized it was gathering to return.

Simultaneously the whole of Chenega Island, though impossible to perceive, was lifting up and lunging to the south on a buckling plate of earth. Thirty miles away, an even more violent upthrust was taking place along the axis of Montague Island. The fatal tsunami originated here, it is believed. From the shock at Montague the water reeled to the northwest, a straight shot through Knight Island Passage, and rolled into the horseshoe-shaped cove. The little wooden houses were built close along the curling shore. The exposed site of Chenega, occupied by the Chugach for at least 1,000 years, was chosen to give the widest possible view of approaching enemies.

People were running up the hill, some clutching religious icons. It was fortunate that the snow crust was hard so they didn't break through. The tidal wave was thirty-five feet high when it hit the shore. It crashed down upon the houses and flooded swiftly up the hill. It caught a man with his three young daughters. His three-year-old was snatched from his grip; the nine-year-old disappeared from his side; he managed to keep hold of the four-year-old and these two survived. Tumbling in the froth, a woman was stripped of all her clothes except one ankle sock, but she too survived.

Several who looked back saw the church crack, bow and break apart under the force of the first wave. One recalled saying, on seeing the church swept away, "I guess that's the end. We'll all go now." The people praying inside were never seen again. Two more waves followed. Splintered spars and boards and rooftops floated offshore in a mass. One woman called from the wreckage, but the others had no boats to go get her. She was rescued hours later by the returning hunters.

Sea spray had wet the base of the school, at an elevation of ninety feet. That and a single house were the only buildings left standing in Chenega. The schoolhouse was roomy and heated, but, frightened by an aftershock, the survivors decided to move to higher ground for the night. They made a campfire in the snow, and counted themselves and cried.

The destruction of an entire community along with a third of its residents represented the worst human toll of the '64 earthquake. Only Valdez, with a population of 1,200, had more deaths, thirty-two. What was worse, just six bodies from Chenega were recovered. Several drowned children were found in the treetops. The few adults found were naked, which was dreadful and ominous. All the other people were sucked into the Sound.

Paul Kompkoff Sr. set out from Cordova a few days after the disaster. "We searched for bodies all along the way," he said, "because so many had been reported missing. It really sank in when I saw the miles of dead rockfish along Knight Island, and red Irish lords, big ones too. I lost my dad and mother and my youngest brother. Never found any trace. We looked for a couple weeks trying to find them." Minnie Kompkoff lost both her parents as well.

Kompkoff never said that he was the lucky one or that he was glad to have been away. "When your time comes, it comes, you go," he said.

So Chenega was abandoned. The survivors dispersed to Tatit-lek, Cordova, Anchorage and beyond, but they never stopped missing their home in the western Sound. For years it seemed beyond their hopes, but they would get a chance to return, because of oil. The discovery of oil on the North Slope led directly to the Alaska Native Claims Settlement Act in 1971. Native groups, including the displaced Chenegans, were awarded money and land to clear up the claims blocking the pipeline construction.

The impact of the earthquake on the sea otter population was a question that couldn't be quantified. But there was an indication that the expansion of the otters in the Sound was interrupted. A young Alaskan biologist named Calvin Lensink, flying census surveys in southern Prince William Sound in the late '50s, had estimated the otter population to be roughly 1,000 as of 1959. Lensink reported a count of 545, which he rounded up to allow for the animals he missed from the plane. Six months after the quake another biologist counted 392, a number that for all practical purposes was the same as Lensink's. Considering the animals' rate of increase, however, the census taken five years later should have come up with more otters, unless a disturbance of some kind had intervened.

Under ideal conditions, that is, when presented with virgin habitat and unlimited food, sea otters multiply by as much as 20 percent per year. The pattern is one of an expanding front. A high-density wave of males is at the lead, and the female animals come behind. Otters segregate themselves in pods by sex except during the time of breeding.

After a new area is colonized, the females settle the choicest zones, where they raise their pups. The males among them are few, but they are the established breeders, patrolling their territories and rubbing their chests furiously at the approach of rivals. With seniority they develop large white heads. Young male otters, their mating prospects nil, swim five, ten or fifty miles to join with other young males. They settle the outskirts and the most weather-beaten shores; their survival rates are not high. They are the ones to probe the frontiers for new and better range.

Prince William Sound is not classic sea otter habitat. Across their historical range—which extends from the northern islands of Japan through the Aleutians and down the coast of North America to California—the animals are densest when living among canopies of kelp and feeding largely on sea urchins. Kelp in turn is densest, the so-called kelp forests, when growing off rocky, exposed and somewhat shallow coastlines, such as characterize the Aleutian Islands. In the Sound, its waters deep and ice-fringed, its bottom loose with glacial sediments, the kelp and sea urchins are only minor elements of the ecosystem. Consequently it came as something of a surprise, recalled Cal Lensink, when the otters invading the Sound in the '60s and '70s took crabs, mussels and clams. "We didn't put it together that butter clams, which have better nutrition than sea urchins, would become their favorite food," he said.

Researchers have since learned that sea otters select food in a new habitat in a most rational manner. They start with the invertebrates that offer the greatest amount of calories for the least amount of work. In the Sound, that would have been the Dungeness crabs in shallow water, followed by clams, which take a bit of digging. Butter clams, growing to four inches in diameter, live within soft sediments and range from the lower intertidal zone to depths of 100 feet. As the easy prey is reduced, the stronger otters dive deeper offshore, investing greater energy in clams, and the juveniles turn toward intertidal mussels, which though not as nutritious are within their reach. When the earthquake uplifted the beaches and shallows, it damaged the most accessible shellfish. Thus weaker animals would have found it harder to forage and mortality may have increased.

The setback to the sea otters, if there was one, was short-lived. From the islands bordering the Gulf, the otter front moved north, to no great notice at first. As the riddle has it, lily pads doubling on a pond each day don't become a problem until one day before the end. Fish and Game surveyed about 2,000 in the mid-'70s, and calculated the population at twice that. The extra traffic of oil tankers didn't deter the sea otters from moving into Port Valdez. From one individual sighted there in 1974, before the pipeline opened, counts rose to seven in '79, forty-five in July of '85, 116 in February of '86.

Meanwhile the Chenegans moved back to the western Sound. They would not return to the old village site, because the memories of the missing dead were too painful. As part of their 75,000-acre entitlement under the claims act, they chose Crab Bay on Evans Island. Fifteen miles south of Chenega Island, Crab Bay and abutting Sawmill Bay were well known to the people. Three salmon canneries and a herring saltery once operated there, providing seasonal employment. Except for the AFK salmon hatchery at the far end of Sawmill Bay, the area was quiet, and distant from the tanker traffic. Then as now the only access was by boat or float-plane.

The move back would not have been achieved but for the efforts of a younger couple, Larry and Gail Evanoff. Larry Evanoff had been away at a Native high school in southeast Alaska when the earthquake took his parents and his home. His situation struck a chord with Gail Sherman, an Inupiat Eskimo student from the northwest part of the state. Her own village of Candle had burned to the ground and was abandoned. After their marriage, they lived in Cordova and Anchorage, where Larry worked as an air traffic controller and Gail attended college.

Gail wangled state and federal building grants. Larry supervised the construction. On a promontory above the old saltery, above the reach of the '64 tsunamis, the workers put in a diesel generator, a community building, a gravel road flanked by faux-Victorian streetlamps, and twenty-one prefabricated houses, each having a picture window that looked east onto the snowpeaks of Latouche. The families were in by the summer of 1984: the Kompkoffs, Vlasoffs, Selanoffs, Totemoffs, Vigils, Eleshanskys, Evanoffs, etc., some seventy-five people in all. They named it Chenega Bay. They built the blue church themselves.

What joy to be with wildlife again, to partake of it. To cut up a forty-pound halibut on the clean-smelling planks of a new dock—to call out, Come! Everyone come down and get a piece of fish! To roast a fat seal for a party, to explore the island for deer trails and berry bushes, all shiny with raindrops, to catch a hiding pink octopus at the month's lowest tide.

Many old skills they dusted off, even the taking of sea otters. The Marine Mammal Protection Act had been passed in 1972. While safeguarding the animals from everyone else, the new law restored the Natives' traditional rights. An exemption allowed them to hunt sea otters and to make and sell "authentic" handicrafts of the fur, as long as the species was not endangered by the activity. As the statewide otter population topped 100,000, a tentative harvest commenced in the coastal villages.

In the vicinity of Chenega Bay the otters were as unpracticed at the hunt as the people. "They were extremely abundant," Gail Evanoff remembered. "My son went out for them in his kayak [of fiberglass now, bought from a store in Anchorage]. He went right up and knocked the sea otters over the head, there were so many. I salted down the skins and sent them away to be tanned. When they came back I did the sewing, though I'm not the best. The fur makes really great hats."

But there was no commerce to speak of, and no villager tried to make a living at it. "The majority of people in Chenega weren't interested in otters," said Pat Selanoff, a fisherman who served as the village tagger. (The government began to keep records of the pelts in 1988.) Selanoff added, contrary to what Evanoff recalled, "There weren't too many around here anyway." According to a survey by Fish and Game, five households harvested a total of fifteen otters over the winter of '85–'86, winter being the season when the pelts were thought to be at their prime.

The overall Native harvest in the Sound, maybe fifty otters per year, did not dent the burgeoning population. Retaking first the west, and then the north, the sea otters spread lastly to the southeast, along a series of fallow inlets toward the fishing town of Cordova. They came into Port Gravina, then Sheep Bay, then Simpson Bay, finally Nelson Bay. Nelson Bay is the northern extension of Orca Inlet, on which Cordova is situated. You could run up to Nelson Bay in 1979 and see there was going to be trouble. Scores of otters, each one gobbling a dozen crabs per day, and the crab pots floating nearby.

People forgot, if they ever did know, that the elimination of the otters at the turn of the century had allowed invertebrates of all kinds to flourish. Shellfish became bigger and more abundant. Then came two majors disturbances, the earthquake and the sea otters, superimposed on the natural cycles of supply. The causes of change were difficult to apportion, but the sea otters were a conspicuous factor. Thus when Chenega was resettled, and the Natives had trouble finding clams, most in the village faulted the otters, according to the household survey by Fish and Game. But elders such as Paul Kompkoff Sr. knew that clams had been scarce since the earthquake.

In Cordova, Dungeness crabs were a big business in the late '70s, employing about one hundred people in fishing and processing. The Dungies slipped after the quake, but then numbers seemed to stabilize. In hindsight, Fish and Game biologists think they let the harvest periods run too long. Crab populations are tricky to manage because of natural fluctuations. The resource might have been under strain even before the otters appeared.

Strictly speaking, it was not proved that sea otters moving into Orca Inlet ruined the Dungeness fishery, because the effect of the one on the other was not scientifically measured. It surely looked to be the case. David and Judith Garshelis, two researchers from the University of Minnesota, plotted the harvest totals against the otter numbers. In 1977 the Dungeness crab take was 115,000, while the otters sighted were "a few." In '78 the harvest was 311,000 crabs, the otters still "a few." The harvest dropped to 62,000 in '79, when eighty-five otters were counted (eighty-five the average of censuses throughout the year). And in 1980, in the presence of 371 foraging otters, commercial crabbing was canceled in the district because crabs were undersized and scarce. About this time sea otters started getting shot around Cordova.

The razor clams went next. Cordova in the '20s and '30s called itself the razor clam capital of the world. The area is dominated by the mighty Copper River, which, debouching into the Gulf of Alaska just east of the Sound, created an extensive delta and mud-flats. The miles of shallows between the river and the town were rife with clams. As late as 1960, when the taste for them was no longer fashionable, the commercial harvest was half a million pounds. The earthquake damaged the clams twofold, first by ex-posing beds to the air, and next by choking them with silt from the upraised Copper River Delta. During the 1970s harvests fell. Then the arrival of the sea otters drove them lower, until there was no point. Fish and Game closed the Cordova district to commercial clamming in 1981.

The otters spilled out of the Sound. In '86 the U.S. Fish and Wildlife Service counted about 1,200 in Orca Inlet and the nearby flats. Pods were hauling out on the bars and packing into the sloughs of the Copper River Delta. Here another conflict occurred, the most violent to date. In the springtime the fishermen lay their gill nets to snare migrating salmon, the world-famous Copper River reds. Sea otters tangled in the nets, especially the young and in-experienced ones. "The tide would run out through the channels," recalled Chuck Monnett, a sea otter biologist in Cordova, "and otters would literally be filtered into the gill nets."

On the flats the otters got caught in a long-running war be-tween fishermen and pinnipeds. Sea lions and seals were known to "work the gear"—to chew salmon right out of the mesh. The fish-ermen were entitled to use guns to defend their equipment. The smaller sea otters did not work the gear nor damage the netting when they got tangled up, yet they were pests that not everyone cared to let go alive.

Conducting a population survey in 1986, FWS biologist Terri Simon-Jackson took a boat along the sandbars during a red salmon opener. Within a two-mile stretch she found four otters washed up dead and one wounded. The dead ones had either been clubbed, indicating they had initially been caught in nets, or else shot in the head at close range. The other animal Simon-Jackson saw being shooed away by a fisherman in a skiff. The otter was swimming in unnatural circles, she reported. Captured and put down, it had a fractured skull.

Salmon in 1988 brought high prices. Hundreds of boats came to the flats for the early runs of reds and kings, and for the later runs of cohos. Surveying once a week during the four-month season, University of Alaska researcher Kate Wynne reported a total of 100 marine mammal carcasses beached on the delta. Forty-one were sea lions, twenty-seven were sea otters, nineteen were harbor seals. No doubt some had died of natural causes. Gunshot wounds and skull fractures were noticeable on carcasses that were not decomposed or scavenged. Other fatalities doubtless escaped her detection.

Probably just a few bad apples were wantonly destroying marine mammals. Wildlife managers tried by various means to enlighten the fishermen. Sea lions were of greatest concern, because they were in decline throughout the Gulf of Alaska, while the otters were increasing. Yet the conflict with the otters was feared to get worse as the wave spread eastward. Fortunately, the pink salmon fishermen inside the Sound were not having a problem, because the gear used there, the heavy purse-seine net, the otters could ride right over.

In the years since the earthquake the otter population within the Sound had grown to approximately 10,000, close to the ecosystem's limit. Overall its numbers in Alaska were said to be as high as 150,000 in 1989, and the otters still had empty habitat available. Biologically, psychologically, the situation was complex. Within the state Natives and non-Natives alike were not enamored of the hungry animal, but people Outside were, as had already been shown in California.

The sea otter had many fans in California. A remnant population, long isolated in the Big Sur region, expanded to the south in the 1970s. The otters got into trouble with fishermen for taking the abalone and Pismo clams. When tankers began moving Alaskan oil down the coast, the population, numbering only about 1,500, was seen to be vulnerable to oil spills. The Fish and Wildlife Service listed the southern sea otter as a threatened species.

The animal's supporters were led by a group called Friends of the Sea Otter. The Friends became concerned about its status in Alaska too. When in 1988 the FWS proposed a new regulation that would bar Alaska Natives from selling handicrafts sewn of otter fur, the Friends and other conservation groups applauded. The fear seemed to be that Natives would kill otters wholesale, then sell parkas and fur trinkets to tourists and retailers. Items of this nature had been confiscated from a Kodiak gift shop, and from a hunter in Sitka, prompting Native skin-sewers to sue the government.

The Friends wrote to its members: "For Alaska's Natives are now seeking to reopen a tragic chapter in the otters' history, pressing the federal government hard to open up a new sea otter fur trade. . . ." History was stood on its head, with the Natives cast as the despoilers, and the Friends attacked by a Native group in return for "tearing at the very fabric of the life of indigenous peoples."

The Alaska sea otter population was not endangered by the small Native take of some 500 per year, nor by the sporadic hostility of fishermen. At least that was the scientists' opinion. But scientists preferred to sit these arguments out. They knew that when emotions ran strongly about a wildlife issue, the merits as they saw them tended to get squashed.

"Thirty years ago," said biologist Cal Lensink, "we managed sea otters in Alaska for their populations. Now, because of TV, which brings you so close to animals, people love them as individuals, but they don't have an understanding of populations or ecology. So there's more protectionism today. We can't do as much."

Indeed, I had a part in the process he was talking about. I wrote a narration script for a television documentary on sea otters. The show was filmed in California in the '70s. The animals were endearing and seemed made for the camera. They jackknifed and somersaulted under the water, now speeding down to the darkness through tunnels of kelp, now pressing their amusing bewhiskered faces into the lens.

Although much had been learned about *Enhydra lutris* since Steller's initial description, the creature was still an irresistible subject for anthropomorphism. For example, Steller wrote: "The male caresses the female by stroking her, using the forefeet as hands, and places himself over her; she, however, often pushes him away from her for fun and in simulated coyness. . . ." On the contrary, during mating the male bites the female on the nose to hold her still. "It's no honeymoon for the female," I wrote. "Her nose may bleed and she has to struggle to breathe. . . . This otter is probably shading her eyes, but she looks like she's holding her head—small wonder, after what she's been through." I added that the gestation period was similar to a human's, almost nine months.

Lensink affably conceded that it was impossible not to identify with them. Yet he like other biologists did not approve of anthropomorphism. It encouraged sentiments that interfered with their work. It ranked animals according to their appeal to humans, whereas nature played no favorites (I anthropomorphize). The sea otter was the perfect specimen of the "charismatic megaverte-brates," one biologist's term for the large fuzzy mammals that people sent donations to protect, at the expense of cold-blooded, odd-shaped others.

The professionals did share the general concern about sea

otters and oil spills. They understood, much better than the public, the critical connection between the animal's fur and metabolism. They knew this because, ten years before the *Exxon Valdez*, scientists had tried oil on the otters of Prince William Sound.

The late '70s was the period of offshore oil exploration and its scientific offshoot OSCEAP, which assessed the environmental impact of drilling. The program funded Daniel Costa and Gerald Kooyman, of the Scripps Institution of Oceanography in California, to experiment with sea otters. In lab tests on five captives, the two researchers demonstrated the supercharged nature of the animals' metabolism. On average the metabolic rate, as shown by oxygen consumption, increased by 40 percent when 25 percent of the subject's coat was covered with oil.

Oil clearly taxed their capacity to stay warm. However, after the otters were shampooed, their metabolic rates rose even higher, to twice the normal level. The clean animals shivered uncontrollably in the cold water of the holding tanks. Costa and Kooyman realized that scrubbing the otters had made their thermoregulatory stress worse. The wash destroyed the insulation of air within the interlocking hairs, allowing water to reach the skin all over. The shampoo stripped away the sebaceous oils that made the fur healthy. Two of the three animals in this test fell sick with pneumonia, and one died. Obviously there was a lesson for rescue workers who would clean oiled otters.

In 1979 the researchers went to Prince William Sound to try a similar experiment under field conditions. They set up camp in Constantine Harbor, a few miles from where the tankers passed through Hinchinbrook Entrance.

However playful they seem in appearance, sea otters are violently toothy at close quarters. The usual capture method is to deploy a long drift net, one end anchored to the bottom, the other end drifting free. An otter swims into it and becomes entangled. Then the biologist hauls it into the skiff, and, with a pad of some sort, holds it down while a colleague delivers the anesthesia. (In a training film the FWS likens the animal to a chainsaw buzzing in a burlap bag. The film advises, "If an otter escapes, remain calm. It is not necessary to leave the boat.")

The tangle nets have to be checked often, lest the captives drown. In Constantine Harbor, tending a pair of 150-foot nets, Costa, Kooyman and assistants were vigilant but still lost, they reported, three of the thirty-one otters they caught. Two were rival males that got snarled up together.

The researchers anesthetized the otters with gas, administered through a bucket slipped over the head. They put radio collars on all the otters, oil on some of them, and let the animals go. Measuring metabolic rates wasn't possible in the field. The object was to compare the responses of those that were oiled with those that weren't. Presumably the oiled subjects, like their counterparts in the lab, would need to generate more heat than the control animals, and would spend more time at what the scientists called "high-level activities," such as "vigorous grooming or foraging." Each radio transmitted a twenty-four-hour pattern of activity. Where possible, the biologists checked their understanding of the signal patterns by watching the otters through binoculars.

Owing to problems both behavioral (otters swam out of range) and technical (collars detached; one oiled animal died of an infection), the final comparisons involved fewer than ten subjects, which, as in the earlier work, did not permit statistical generalizations. Still, no differences were observed between the two groups. The oiled otters were no more active than the others. Costa and Kooyman suspected they hadn't applied enough oil. They had decided at the outset to be conservative, and to cover no more than 10 percent of any otter's coat. Most were treated with less.

"I was convinced from our lab work that sea otters were fragile," said Costa, "and that any amount of oil could kill them. It was puzzling, in the field, that they did relatively better. We hadn't considered that captivity was so stressful. The point that we later realized was that for all the stress of the wild environment they were adapted to it, and they weren't adapted to the lab."

The pair completed their report for OCSEAP in 1980. Their conclusions would be upheld to the letter in the terrible unplanned experiment nine years hence. They wrote: "Contamination of large areas of the animal's fur (greater than 30 per cent) will most likely result in death. Sea otters *may* [their emphasis] be resilient to chronic *low-level* oil contamination, where the probability of large surface oil contamination of the fur is low. . . . Rehabilitation of oil-fouled sea otters would be very costly requiring holding facilities to keep the animals for at least two weeks. Even if adequate facilities were available, the success rate of rehabilitating oil-fouled sea otters is likely to be rather low."

The findings by Costa and Kooyman were buttressed by a second team of researchers, led by Donald Siniff of the University of Minnesota. The Siniff group conducted tests on sea otters in the eastern Sound. They reported that four animals, having been lightly oiled, groomed themselves hard for several weeks and appeared to stay healthy. But a heavily oiled animal died quickly. One other heavily oiled subject, which they scrubbed clean, looked to be expiring when they lost radio contact with it.

Together the two experiments suggested a threshold of oil contamination, below which sea otters would probably survive on their own, and above which they would probably die in spite of human intervention. Dan Costa recalled that at scientific meetings in the '80s he spoke up that sea otters might be better off if they weren't rescued after a spill. "But in Valdez," said Costa, "a lot of what was known was ignored—what we and others had shown before."

There was an opposing view, however. Randall Davis and Terrie Williams were biologists from the research unit of Sea World in San Diego. In 1985 they obtained a dozen sea otters from the large population in eastern Prince William Sound. In their lab in San Diego, they and two colleagues tainted six of the otters with oil. Like their predecessors, they recorded the dangerous acceleration of the animals' metabolisms. The goal of Davis and Williams, however, was to develop a system to clean the fur so that metabolisms and activity patterns might come back to normal.

The oiled otters were sedated and scrubbed with Dawn detergent. Released once more into their holding pool, the animals groomed and shivered abnormally, as they strived to restore their fur, but within two weeks all but one had regained their health, or at least their conditions prior to the experiment. Davis and Williams concluded in their report that "sea otters that have had 20% of their surface area oiled can be successfully cleaned and rehabilitated using techniques developed in this study."

Both in approach and in results they differed from the other researchers. Whereas Costa and Kooyman and Siniff returned lightly oiled otters to the wild, and watched them survive with no treatment, Davis and Williams used captive otters, more oil (20 percent body coverage versus 10 percent or less), and after careful treatment they too saw their subjects survive. Whereas one side found cleaning to be counterproductive, Davis and Williams put together a manual on rehabilitation techniques.

Don Siniff told me that the two were a small minority, that "all of us who worked with sea otters thought that rehabilitation was a waste of time." This hindsight is too sweeping. It was still an academic issue, as no one had tried to save otters in a real emergency. Davis and Williams were willing to bet on the scientific merits of rehabilitation, and more importantly, their position aligned with the instinct of the public. For there was an overwhelming urge to do something for the animals after the disaster, the man-made disaster. Davis and Williams got the call to come to Valdez.

Of all the things that we have lost since non-Natives came to our land, we have never lost our connection with the water. The water is our source of life. So long as the water is alive, the Chugach Natives are alive.

It was early in the springtime. No fish yet. No snails yet. But the signs were with us. The green was starting. Some birds were flying and singing. The excitement of the season had just begun. And then we heard the news. Oil in the water. Lots of oil. Killing lots of water. It is too shocking to understand. Never in the millennium of our tradition have we thought it possible for the water to die. But it is true.

—WALTER MEGANACK, CHIEF OF THE PORT GRAHAM VILLAGE COUNCIL

IN THE SPRING of '89 journalists rushed to the Sound from all over the world. Journalists readily grasped the fears of the local fishermen. At a hectic meeting in Cordova, Fish and Game officials presented the bad news that the herring season was canceled, that the oil was heading for the hatcheries and the pink salmon fishery was endangered. The economy and ecology of the Sound hung in peril. Then someone from the Fish and Wildlife Service stood up. "What's more," he announced gravely, "we estimate we'll be losing a thousand otters to otter heaven." What to make of the fact that fishermen cheered and clapped at this, their silver lining to the spill?

Such twists weren't reported, not because the press suppressed them, or rejected them as Exxon propaganda, but because they simply did not make sense. Like the bias that underlay the damage assessment process, many truths about the oil spill were too dissonant to be heard, too oblique to come to light.

What made sense was that sea otters were manifestly dying. What rang true were such statements as Dr. Sylvia Earle's. A nationally prominent marine scientist who toured the Sound, Earle was quoted in the *New Yorker* magazine: "Even though some will survive, their community has been destroyed forever—that's a very significant thing. I mean, if you take one of those traumatized otters and are able to nurse it back to health, then what do you do? Put it back into the water, I suppose. But where? An otter does not live as a lone being—sea otters are very tactile, very social creatures. Then, it won't be long before the whales arrive in the area, and they will begin to suffer from the contamination, too. . . ."

Reporters grasped that the crisis for the otters was not the first, nor was it the first in the history of the Natives. The victim angle was not wrong. But journalism sold them each short, the Natives and the sea otters. It underestimated their capacities to prevail. It exaggerated the hopelessness of the situation, such as was given voice by Walter Meganack. The elder's speech about the water dying was read for him in Valdez by another villager from

Port Graham. (On the tip of the Kenai Peninsula, the village was tainted after the oil drifted out of the Sound.) The speech was the most moving and oft-cited testament of the impact of the spill on the Natives. No doubt Meganack believed that the water had died. His speech was ghosted by a non-Native lawyer for the villagers, which journalists did not know.

I didn't know it then either. As is always the case, what transpired became clearer in hindsight. In hindsight I assembled a kind of baseline for the Natives and tried to see how the disaster had changed them.

In 1989 roughly five hundred Natives inhabited Prince William Sound. Several hundred lived in Cordova, out of the path of the oil. In the north, where the spill originated, there was a village of one hundred at Tatitlek. About twenty-five miles from Tatitlek, the town of Valdez also had Native residents, though not many. The most remote Native habitation was Chenega Bay in the west. Its eighty-odd residents were the one group in the Sound to experience the slick directly.

Tatitlek is just five miles from Bligh Reef. Though the oil from the first moved away from them, the villagers could smell the fumes and they were frightened. They became upset when the test burn the day after the spill blew oily smoke their way. Most upsetting of all was the advice from several authorities that their subsistence foods, such as their clams, their herring roe-on-kelp, their deer and Eastertime seal meat, should be avoided because of possible contamination.

Subsistence foods were those obtained from the environment. In 1989 the Natives of the Sound no longer relied on them exclusively. Their diet mixed subsistence resources with imported goods. The processed foods were all right—expensive to fly in or ship in, but all right. But no store could top the traditional tastes, nor the traditional feeling that came from sharing a hunt or passing around a catch. In other words, subsistence to the Natives was a symbol of identity as well as a practice of economy.

Tatitlekans did not refuse when Exxon offered to make up for the wild foods that were off limits. From Valdez the company sent milk, soda pop, pork chops, chicken—so much chicken in the month after the spill that the people started to call it Exxon duck. They weren't used to so much chicken and steak. But when it came on the national news that the Eskimos in the Sound were sick from eating Exxon's store-bought food, white Alaskans had to laugh at that, having seen the Natives buying cheese twists and burgers when they came to town. This reaction in turn caused hard feelings in the villages, or added to them, I should say.

Occasionally Exxon sent seafood. One day by mistake the shipment to Tatitlek included a case of Dungeness crab that was meant for the sea otters at the rescue center in Valdez. The box was marked "Not for Human Consumption." No one noticed the warning until several people became ill. An attorney representing the village cited this as evidence of Exxon's disregard and contempt for the Natives, to have sent spoiled food not fit for humans. I haven't found anyone else who thinks it was deliberate. But the people of Tatitlek did not miss the point that the crab, airlifted to the Sound at considerable expense, was meant to sustain sea otters.

The one creature that was separate from their subsistence, the one animal not contributing to their welfare, was getting more care and compassion than the people who stood to lose everything because the water had died. The Natives didn't make a fuss though. They rarely did. People kept their feelings to themselves. They just rolled their eyes and said, "Well, you know, what can you do, they're just so *cute*."

What attention they got the Natives did not care for. Tatitlek, being close to Valdez, was swamped with outsiders. Eric Morrison, a Native of Indian stock and the director of the Alaska Native Institute in Anchorage, was one who came. He investigated the social consequences of the disaster for an agency of the Department of the Interior:

> First seen were the reporters who came to Tatitlek not only from across the country but from around the world. It did not matter where the news people came from or their particular field of media, they were all insensitive to the community, arrogant, frightening to the children, and abusive to the elders. Reportedly they chased children and elders into homes, attempted to take pictures through residents' windows, and laughed at people who were caught off guard.
>
> The second "human" spill came from the investigators and researchers who came to Tatitlek to do social, cultural, economic, psychological, and biological research. Again, the community felt that the researchers were unconcerned about the community and were there only to procure information to fulfill their requirements and/or personal interests.
>
> The third "human" spill represented the oil spill workers or persons who camped in or near the community looking for work who drained the community of its resources and patience. This group did not draw the frustration and anger that the first two did, however.

I am glad not to have got around to Tatitlek during my early reporting. I intended to. I remember zipping over it. The little rectangular houses, the blue church and village dump, in a quaint line along the cloudy shore. The Natives were hunkered down, trying to maintain a low profile, and soon were out of sight.

The oil never hit; as in '64 Tatitlek was very close to the epicenter but was spared. The authorities believed the villagers were out of danger. Nevertheless, people found clams and mussels that crumbled to the touch. A dead starfish washed up with ulcers on it. They had heard that oil within the water can kill invisibly. When Fish and Game came and checked out the shellfish, the biologists' opinion was that the unusually cold winter had killed the mollusks. In early May a state laboratory analyzed samples of intertidal life and found no contamination. The Natives were not persuaded.

Morrison's report went on:

> Consistently, the community believed that bottom fish and shellfish were severely impacted by the spill. In that same vein, local residents were afraid to harvest local foods even after being told by experts that the subsistence food was safe to harvest. Exceptions to this pattern were a few young men who expressed the feeling that being part of the land they would harvest and suffer the consequences, saying in effect that if the ecology was destroyed they would see no reason to live.

Because researchers who were Native were so rare, I went to see Eric Morrison in Anchorage in 1990. Broad-bellied and black-haired, he was aware of the irony that a Tlingit Indian should be inquiring after Aleuts, as he referred to them. The Tlingits, who lived on the coast to the east of the Sound, were the ancient enemies of the Chugach. "Even today," he said, "Aleut elders see us and are a little afraid—Tlingits! they go, because they remember the past."

It was the warlike side of the Natives, long repressed, that was coming out when the young men in Tatitlek ate the food they feared was poisoned. Morrison explained, "Their attitude was, 'If the enemy is gonna kill me one way or another, I'm gonna eat that stuff. I will live and die by the sea.' It was a sense of martyrdom of sorts."

Or suicidal, I suggested. The suicide rate among young Alaska Natives was alarmingly high in the '80s. I heard about a young man from Chenega, a seal hunter, who was hospitalized in Cordova shortly after the oil spill. The Native was drunk and raving, alternately threatening to kill himself or to kill Exxon.

"The best warriors sometimes killed themselves after the battle," Morrison said. "We wouldn't take from others what we wouldn't take from ourselves. We believe in life recycling itself. How we come back, whether as a human or an otter, will be based on how we have lived. Is it suicide if it's not really dying?"

He shrugged. All this was beside the fact that the Tatitlek warriors lived. The food was poison only in perception, I suggested to him. The men had received bad information. Morrison shrugged again. So much was turned inward. After 1989 Eric Morrison was no longer welcome in Tatitlek. The village leaders apologized that they couldn't give him any more information because of the ongoing lawsuit over the damage to their traditional lifestyle.

In Chenega Bay, the memory of '64 was on everyone's lips, although less than a dozen of the current residents had actually experienced the earthquake. The oil came upon them more slowly than the tsunami, literally the people watched it approach on television. When it hit, many feared their village would have to be abandoned a second time. They felt a sense of apocalypse, but of isolation as well. For although helicopters, boats, state officials, biologists, fishermen, reporters, etc., swarmed over Chenega Bay, the initial focus of the emergency was not the village itself, but the AFK salmon hatchery two miles away.

Chenega is on a point between Crab Bay and the larger Sawmill Bay; the fish hatchery is located at the sheltered south end of Sawmill Bay. Patches of the slick, moving toward the southwestern exits of the Sound, arrived at the entrance to Sawmill Bay five days after the spill, which was time enough for protective action to have begun. For ten days it was touch and go, as Cordova fishing boats and other volunteers streamed in to help deploy the airlifted boom and to deflect the mousse with makeshift trolls. Oil caught the inner beaches here and there, but the hatchery and the fishery were saved.

The Chenegans were grateful for the booming, and for other help. Exxon sent fresh fruit, canned goods and extra diesel fuel for the power station. All the local skiffs were hired during the emergency, and any Native person over eighteen could have a job. A Chenega cleanup crew was put together. Twenty men and women helped wash the beaches throughout the summer. The money was good, though the daily encounter with oil did not lift their hopes about the environment.

Gail Evanoff returned to Chenega in May. Gail and Larry were out of the village that winter because their daughter was in high school in Nome. Civically, Gail was like a she-wolf defending her cubs. A lot of non-Native ears were boxed that summer. Larry Evanoff arrived later, having stayed to settle up the family's affairs.

He was always the more cautious one. He wondered why this was the second time he'd been spared. It bothered him that he hadn't been there to help, as in '64.

It was a challenge for the village to meld the efforts of younger leaders like the Evanoffs, and Chuck and Darrell Totemoff, the ones who took the phone calls and answered questions, with the taciturn authority of elders like John M. Totemoff, Don Kompkoff and Paul Kompkoff Sr. (Paul Sr., for one, chose not to have a telephone.) The elders could explain natural acts in the Sound, the ways of wildlife and of weather and even of tidal waves, for earthquakes and tsunamis had happened before and the Natives had survived. But when their oral encyclopedia had no explanation for hydrocarbon contamination, the elders were put off balance. It was one thing to know to avoid oiled game—one hunter said he had no intention, having seen a half-blind seal swimming in circles, of feeding that meat to his family. What about the oil hidden within, even when the seals looked clean and healthy? Paul Sr. was shown a runny liver from a seal shot by his son. He advised, "No, I never saw a liver like that before, this seal must be contaminated."

As the earthquake had, the spill changed everything, creating a before-and-after village. The disaster brought all manner of investigators, not only from agencies of government but also reporters, social psychologists and attorneys. A most valuable document, to all the inquiries, was a household survey of Chenega Bay by the subsistence division of Fish and Game. It had been published three years before. The report, by Lee Stratton and Evelyn Chisum, contained harvest data and other information about the first two years of the newly formed village. Here was a picture of Chenega as last seen, a statistical baseline for measuring the social disturbance of the spill. Verifiable, and a cause for deep concern, was that subsistence harvests dropped substantially in 1989, both in volume and variety of species taken.

The report cut two ways, however. Stratton and Chisum's purpose had been to compare contemporary Chenega with the '60s village. They found that the economy had changed. From a reliance on commercial fishing and cannery jobs for income, there had been a shift toward public-sector dependencies, where income was derived from government employment and transfer payments. The subsistence lifestyle and seasonal work could not pay for Chenega Bay's power plant, telephone system, satellite TV, indoor plumbing, all services that were lacking in the old village at the time of the earthquake.

Not that new Chenega was a welfare case, far from it. By the standard of bush Alaska, where the remedy for idleness is alcohol, the social health of the village was excellent. But, there being no business in Chenega other than the business of being Chenega, the people were assisted by cash allowances for their home heating oil; by employment at the village power station, the dock, the school, the tribal council, the business office, etc.; by subsidized medical care and other social services. A lifeline of support reached from over the ice-topped mountains.

The 1971 claims act had established Native corporations, which managed the awards of money and land for Native shareholders. From Chenega Bay on a wild corner of the Sound, it was but 100 miles by floatplane to Anchorage. The lawyers, accountants and investment managers were located there: the non-Native infrastructure for running Chugach Alaska Inc., which was the regional corporation, and for the local Chenega Village Corp. In Anchorage and in Juneau, Native politicians and lobbyists looked out for their groups' interests. The urban Natives were a world apart from Paul Kompkoff Sr. They were educated and they made deals, but they couldn't speak Alutiiq (the language of the Chugach and other Pacific Eskimos) or tell which ferns were good for a cold. Yet they guarded their connections to the rural villages. Elders like Paul Sr. held down the cultural fort for them.

In their comparative survey, Stratton and Chisum found that old and new Chenega were most alike in the need that people expressed for their wild fish and game. The Fish and Game investigators recorded the harvests of the '60s as best as former residents could recollect, and also the harvests between 1984 and 1986, on the heels of resettlement. Subsistence was expressed in pounds per capita, that is, by the total estimated weight of the salmon, seals, shellfish, deer, birds' eggs, cranberries, and so forth, brought into the village over the course of a year: that weight divided by the number of people in the households surveyed. The '85–'86 per capita harvest was 378 pounds, which was less than half the amount of old Chenega. The difference, one inferred, was made up by purchases from the outside.

Subsistence then dropped by half after the spill, but in aggregate amounts the drop was not nearly so great as between the time of the old and new village. As I read it, the greater decline in the use of wild foods had already occurred, and by extension, the greater damage to the Natives' traditional lifestyle. The old ways had rusted while the Chenegans were in exile. People today were able to telephone the grocery store in Cordova and receive their order of food a day or two later on the mail plane. Subsistence in the new village was a spiritual affirmative—a myth, in the highest sense—more than a material necessity. It was the myth that they needed. This distinction was not readily told in the accounting of the oil spill, where every damage required a statistic.

Chenega Bay held up better than Native villages outside of the Sound. From the edge of Tatitlek, past Chenega, past Port Graham and English Bay on the Kenai, past the Native communities on Kodiak Island, and as far as the village of Chignik on the Alaska Peninsula, the 1,000-mile reach of the oil affected the entire prehistoric territory of the Pacific Eskimos. It was as if the Alutiiqs were being singled out. The Chenega area received the heaviest contamination by far. Yet the communities beyond the Sound had more drinking and family problems, more feuds over spill jobs and wages. Chenega Bay was tighter, more religious, a happier place overall. So I learned later. In 1989 I didn't get there.

> *Hoary-faced otter*
> *Spiked hair against the slick sick*
> *Dive dive dive dive die*
> —SPILL HAIKU, *1989*

THE BOOMING of Sawmill Bay probably saved some otters from being killed, and two or three attempts to screen off smaller bays may also have been of help. But what saved several thousand animals were the natural crenulations of the southwestern Sound. Otters were able to cluster into the heads of bays and behind the arms of points, until the oil patches, hitting and missing, were either flushed from the Sound or beached.

The areas of densest population were not in the oil's path. "When I realized," said Cal Lensink, "that Orca Inlet and the Copper River Delta weren't going to get it, it was almost a feeling of exhilaration at how we'd lucked out. I could imagine half the otter population being wiped out. If you imagined the worst, and the worst didn't happen, well, it helped, when we were handling the dead animals in Valdez."

So much for the good news.

At least a thousand did not escape. Maneuvering on their backs as is their wont, sea otters ran into oil they didn't see. Their heads and necks blackened, they groomed furiously, rising half out of the water in alarm, but they succeeded only in distributing the oil over their bodies and into their gullets. Their clumped fur let icy water in. The lighter fractions of the crude burned their stomachs and pierced their lungs. In some instances acute emphysema caused air bubbles to bulge out under the skin of an otter's throat like a grisly necklace. Those animals were the quickest to go. After they were dead, ocean-action smoothed mousse over their forms like a thin chocolate frosting. Some otters tried to ward off hypothermia by hauling out on land. Winding oily trails led to their carcasses.

The first dead otter was brought to Valdez six days after the accident. Lensink, who had retired from the Fish and Wildlife Service four months earlier, volunteered to organize the wildlife morgue in Valdez. He trained other volunteers and Service personnel to inventory the seabirds and the otters. The team worked in a muddy parking lot by the temporary offices of the FWS, in front of a freezer trailer. Each creature had to be weighed and measured; identified by species and by age and sex if possible; characterized by its degree of oil coverage and general condition; and from this was noted the most likely cause of death, for a decomposed, bleached or emaciated specimen had probably died of other causes over the winter—before the oil spill. Lensink assigned each carcass a number, wrote the data down on a clipboard, and dispatched it to the freezer.

It was right that the elder of sea otter biology should take this mean and lowly job. He wasn't going to rattle. The smoke from his pipe blocked the stench. When he pulled an otter's tooth (the layers of enamel indicate the animal's age), the mouth was sometimes so rigid with death that the jawbones broke from his force and weight. He extracted fetuses the size of plump rabbits. The western Sound where the oil went was a "female" area, having been settled longer than the east. Females in the morgue outnumbered the males by two to one, and over 60 percent were pregnant.

The freezer trailer filled up with bags of birds and otters. Someone, not Lensink, dubbed it the "corpsicle." When I came to Valdez in the middle of May, I asked to be taken inside. A nonplussed FWS biologist pointed to the sealed and tagged garbage bags. She said, "Otters to your left, bald eagles to your right, seabirds straight ahead." I saw my breath pulse. In spite of the freezer it smelled. It took a quarter of an hour for the odor of death to dissipate from my jacket.

Lensink observed that the loss of so many mature breeders would disrupt the population structure in the Sound, shifting it toward a younger, less experienced and probably less productive group. He observed also that more otters remained following the spill than were here thirty years ago. A tall man with outsized hands and feet, and eyeglasses perched on top of a gray crew cut, Lensink made a large and shambling figure, seemingly aloof from the anguish over the injured animals.

"What *did* you feel?" I asked him afterward.

"I felt insulted. I could see that people were exaggerating the damages. But when you see an oiled animal—dying, screaming, under severe stress—I thought, That's not the way to go. I thought, We can do better than that."

The Prince William Sound Wildlife Rescue Fleet—fishermen who started as volunteers and then were hired by Exxon—brought in the animal carcasses. Of the 490 otters, half were picked up within the first three weeks of April. Mortalities were severe at first, then slacked off. The fact that sixty-nine, or 15 percent of the final total, were judged to have died of prespill causes is an indication of the intensity of the search. But when the assessment of the damages moved into the freezer of government secrecy, FWS scientists were noncommittal about the recovery effort. Why? The success of the recovery pointed to an actionable figure, which was the number of mortalities overall.

Obviously not every oil-killed otter was found. Some must have floated out of the Sound, others scavenged by eagles, a few sank, many were missed. FWS volunteer Lensink, with no obligation to keep quiet, wrote a paper suggesting that the recovery rate was 50 percent. At the conclusion of their studies, FWS biologists put the success of the carcass recovery at 20 percent, which led to the official estimate that five times as many sea otters died from the oil spill than were in the trailer morgues. Across the spill zone in its entirety, a disparity arose of 4,000 otters, which was the gap between Lensink's estimate 1,500 otters killed and the government's worst-case figure of 5,500.

Whatever the number, it should be pointed out that the best tests of carcass recovery were not tried. Biologists could have raced ahead of the slick, put tags on live otters and figured the proportion of the animals that later turned up dead. Almost as good: After the carcasses started washing up, they could have tagged a sample, then put them back where they were found, then waited to see the number that were eventually retrieved.

These would have been real-time experiments, seizing the terrible opportunity of the spill. Just for this reason they were rejected by the FWS. Too scientifically heartless. Not politically doable—not while people were out *rescuing* sea otters. Nor, the least objectionable of research options, was an aerial count made of the population in the western Sound in front of the scythe of the oil, though the lapse here had to do with confusion more than policy. Several months later, biologists did try to re-create the drift and recovery of carcasses, taking twenty-five from the morgue and letting them go not in the Sound but near Kodiak Island. The five turned in were the basis for the official recovery estimate of 20 percent.

"However many were killed," Lensink said, "it won't make any difference to the population, that's for certain. They are still overpopulated in Prince William Sound. Even if 1,500 died there alone [the government estimated roughly 2,500 deaths in the Sound], that's still less than the annual recruitment. The oil spill will hardly slow that down."

Annual recruitment is the number of animals that survive being pups and join the adult population. Lensink might have overstated it. Driven by the explosion in the eastern Sound, the recruitment overall—i.e., the Sound's population growth—was roughly 10 percent per year, according to a FWS study published in 1988. The spill surely halted it; and Lensink himself had noted that breeding in the west would become less productive. Still it was only a matter of when the otters would get going again, whether it took them one year or five.

Another point about Lensink is that his career bracketed the period in which biologists liked to put their hands in and manage wildlife, seeking to balance the needs of animals and of man. He considered sea otters the most interesting part of the marine ecosystem, but he thought people should be able to enjoy Dungeness crab too. Hence his "overpopulated." Younger biologists didn't care to interfere unless absolutely necessary.

Live animals came into Valdez as well as dead ones. Otters that looked oiled were netted by the crews of the rescue fleet, until the FWS forbade it and took over the job. (Technically the otter rescue was Exxon's responsibility, and the FWS was its adviser.) About 150 animals were taken into the rehab operation organized by Sea World biologists Randy Davis and Terrie Williams. Unfortunately the otters they received were more contaminated than any in their prespill experiments. Valdez was not Sea World; they had to set up in a school gymnasium. Although Exxon spared no expense in constructing the facility to their specifications and bringing on staff, by the time the operation was fully proficient the period of greatest need was past.

The otters rescued in the first two to three weeks, being the most heavily oiled, were in the worst shape. To get their fur clean required soaping and rinsing them, over and over, for two hours. Little could be done for their internal wounds from toxicity. Moreover, their haywire metabolisms were very difficult to stabilize. Body temperatures would rocket up and down even while the otters were sedated. A cleaned animal in a cage, rubbing itself hyperactively, would overheat, scream, convulse, then die, while the otter in the next cage would shiver, grow cold, grow lethargic, then die. Three-quarters of the early arrivals died in spite of treatment.

Afterward the pathologists found the principal causes of death to be shock, hypothermia, emphysema, gastric erosion and captive stress syndrome, usually in combination. How an individual tolerated stress seemed to be as important to its survival as the degree of oiling. Upon review of the records of twenty-three animals that died within ten days of capture, the government's chief clinical pathologist wrote: "Lightly oiled otters were as likely to die of shock as heavily oiled ones, suggesting that confinement was more important than direct exposure to oil. However, heavily oiled otters developed shock more rapidly and had greater numbers of laboratory abnormalities, suggesting that at the least, exposure to oil was an important predisposing factor."

Well before the results were analyzed, scientists were second-guessing the program, beginning with Cal Lensink in the muddy parking lot. "I was appalled by the inhumanity of the rescue operation," he said. "We took in animals, screaming in distress from being captured, and they later died. It would have been much better to take those heavily oiled ones and put them to sleep. We would have come out even. We didn't save any more than if nothing had been done."

Even Randy Davis had no illusions about the number of otters being saved. He told the *Anchorage Daily News* a few weeks into the effort that the lessons being gained in toxicology, animal husbandry and the like would be valuable in the *next* oil spill. Even if none of these otters were to make it, Davis said, the rehab work allowed people to release their frustration and guilt.

The images of the spill brought hundreds of volunteers to Valdez. Some on the otter center staff, which swelled to 160, were too distraught to be useful. Terri McKim, a Humane Society worker from California, helped organize the volunteers. "People who had never dealt with wildlife experienced emotions they never had before," McKim recalled. "They didn't want to leave the center at the end of their shifts. They would get attached, and if they came back in the morning and found their otter dead, they'd feel guilty. That's why we were against giving the otters names, but it was unavoidable.

"Meanwhile, all that anger was going on. Anger at Exxon each time one died. What we needed as much as anything was a grief counselor. We were all too engrossed with caring for the animals to help the volunteers get through their grief."

The operation was running smoothly by the time I got to see it in May. The less oiled animals, rescued later, received a regimen of care with the kinks worked out. Davis and Williams had learned that even though the otters shivered, they did better outside where it was cooler, airier and quieter. They were put in cages that had deep basins, circulating water and ice chunks. I watched a pair of females that were rolling about and grooming themselves. In front of their cage was a plastic cooler full of shrimp and clam meat; the sea otters were costing Exxon $50,000 a week in food alone.

I was taken to see some other females that were housed at a fish hatchery in Valdez. They were lolling on a raft in a holding tank. The sleekest and handsomest animal, at the center of the group, had been blinded by the oil. She would stay a captive; the others were being readied for release. I was not permitted to get near them. But I couldn't help but call, clucking tongue to palate and squeaking my lips, and the cute things lifted their heads in unison.

I had just got off a wildlife rescue boat, and I could report that the crisis in the Sound was ebbing. The sea otters floating off the fouled beaches, including a mother I saw with rare twins, appeared to have no need of assistance. Yet outside of the Sound at this time, new otter centers were taking in scores of animals. Exxon built a facility in Seward, just west of the Sound. By popular demand, another center was set up on the far side of the Kenai Peninsula near Homer.

The images of disaster were still fresh, and the momentum of events outpaced their rationale. The Fish and Wildlife Service, having been late and lukewarm with help in the Sound, and hectored for it by politicians and the public, was leading an aggressive capture effort. A half dozen boats and a dozen skiff crews patrolled the Kenai and Kodiak coastline. Whereas rescuers in the Sound were able to snare oiled otters with dip nets for the most part, the less tainted animals here were too lively to be netted by hand. Tangle nets had to be used. Aircraft lifted the otters, clutching ice to their chests and whistling in anxiety, to Seward and to Valdez.

The Seward center received a total of 187 animals, of which 151 survived. Over half the otters at Seward were classified as lightly oiled, and only two heavily oiled. The Homer center became a holding facility for the cleaned otters from Seward. Over the spring and summer Homer maintained 121 otters in floating pens in an isolated bay, the staff and volunteers so abstentious of noise that they used electric screwdrivers in place of hammers, and oars instead of outboard motors, and they lost but two animals.

Thus 225 of the 357 otters plucked from the spill zone were

kept alive, a goodly proportion. At the Valdez center sixty-three lived and eighty-five died—the harder fate of the animals from the Sound. Clearly the sea otters did best where the contamination was least. Still the question begged whether the rescues outside of Prince William Sound were necessary in the first place. The question is not resolved today, and it can't be, scientifically, for there is no measure of the otters that got into the oil and worked out their problems on their own.

The majority of biologists believe the rescue went on too long. Anthony DeGange of the FWS, who took part in the program and evaluated it for the agency, wrote: "Later in the spill period, probably from late May through September, capture, handling and rehabilitation were probably counterproductive. Most of the otters entering treatment centers were in relatively good condition, and many were lightly oiled or not oiled. Capture crews could no longer determine oil status on the otters they caught. There was evidence from the field that otters were surviving successfully in areas impacted by oil. It follows that the capture effort should have been curtailed long before it was."

Here was the power of public sentiment. Exxon spent some $18 million, or $81,000 for each otter that was cleaned and kept alive. The FWS biologists went along with rescue measures they didn't believe in. Really, it strikes me that the scientists had a lot in common with the Natives. They both knew what they thought, but they were diffident and didn't push it. Displays of high conviction made them uncomfortable. Both expected, from unhappy experience, to be discriminated against.

After the initial glare the Natives kept a low profile, but in August a brouhaha arose over Exxon's plan to make an exhibit of aboriginal artifacts. The cleanup crews, sometimes preceded by archaeologists, sometimes not, had come across burial sites, middens and scattered prehistoric objects. Exxon was responsible for protecting these cultural resources from the cleanup and the oil alike. Artifacts, if found, were supposed to be left in place unless archaeologists decided that the cleanup would harm them. The crews were instructed not to take anything and not to poke around above the beaches.

Unavoidably, there were incidents of thievery and vandalism. The worst that came to light was by a worker who was formerly an anthropology student. He made off with parts of a Chugach skeleton from a rock shelter on Knight Island. Other bones he hid under a log near the beach, where authorities mistook them for the remains of a drowning victim. Eventually their antiquity was identified, and the bones were reinterred in a private, Russian Orthodox ceremony. Exxon scheduled the exhibit of its collection of prehistoric tools to open in Valdez on the very day of the Native reburial.

The exhibit was a means to promote the company's cultural resources program, which besides protecting artifacts had advanced the study of archaeology within the spill zone. Exxon needed good news, and expected that the Native groups would be agreeable. But the outcry from the Chugach regional corporation and from the local corporations of Chenega, Tatitlek and Eyak was sharp and stunning. The exhibit was canceled.

I contacted John Johnson, the cultural resources manager for the regional corporation. "These quick shots don't quite make it," he said. "There are sensitive areas out there that are not to be discussed. If a prehistoric village site hits the papers, then next year it looks like a minefield. Exxon leaves, and every guy and his brother has this stuff on his mantel."

The chief archaeologist for Exxon maintained that it would have been impossible to tell from the exhibit or from its catalog where the objects were recovered. He said he had tried to be careful. Indeed, a prior research monograph, if one should dig it out of the library, gave much more explicit directions to sites. The real problem was that of corporate insensitivity vs. Native hypersensitivity, a gulf intensified by the crisis. But the double standard of race is timeless. When the grave robber of Knight Island got a $100 fine for a penalty, John Johnson wondered whether a Native would get off as lightly if he raided the cemetery in downtown Anchorage.

Having walked on the coastline of the Sound each summer for ten years, Johnson took pride in his understanding of the prehistoric treasures, the map for which he guarded in his memory. He was suspicious of others' maps, and, I think, suspicious of others' understanding. Still Johnson might be a source for me, a way in to the Natives. He was at turns helpful and elusive, a nice guy who was hard to pin down. Hearing that he was going to visit Mummy Island, an important Chugach site near Cordova, I tried very hard to get him to take me along. No way. I took some pleasure from the fact that it poured like hell all weekend while he was there with the spirits of his ancestors. I was high and dry above the lake. Truth to tell, I really didn't know what I wanted from John Johnson. His sympathy, I think.

With me for a while were my wife and youngest daughter. Our daughter was not yet five. We thought we should explain to her why we had come to Alaska. So I sketched the oil spill as lightly as I could, and she took it pretty well about the dead otters and birds. She was braving me. A few minutes later, I saw her pale shock and silent tears. My dam of determinism gave way then, after months of chipper ratiocination, and my poor wife didn't know which sobbing child to go to first.

How should a person respond to the disaster? I believed in a tough love for wildlife, in the long view of environmental disturbances, yet something had touched me in the morgue. The feelings loosed by the oil spill ought to lead somewhere, somewhere where science couldn't go.

As if sensing the yearning, psychologists came to Prince William Sound to see how people were responding. I'm not referring to the mental health specialists, who counseled people for stress and conducted diagnostic surveys. Two independent psychologists came to probe the collective subconscious. One, a Jungian analyst, had the Native model in mind. He wrote, in a notice:

DREAMS OF THE OIL SPILL

The unconscious mind has been called the inner aspect of nature. In this sense, the dream as an expression of the unconscious is nature's voice. Indigenous cultures throughout history have turned to their dreams for guidance in the face of extreme and overwhelming situations. I am interested in assembling a composite dream from dreams of individuals. Please send any dreams big or small that you wish to share, relating to the oil spill.

I sent my best dream in, and even helped collect others, but I found it strange that non-Natives in our distress over the disaster should look to the Natives' way to soothe them, our imagined Native way, and yet find no comfort in our own science. We sense that since they live closer to nature, they have a better sense of its truth. But then we exercise our own truths in their terms. I thought about this after talking with Michael Krauss of the Alaska Native Language Center in Fairbanks. I asked him why there were not many legends about the sea otter among the Native people of the Sound, at least compared to tales of other animals. The question, he said, implied that this animal was as significant to them as it was to us. Krauss suggested that we had made the sea otter our fetish.

The high point of my summer in the Sound was the release of the sea otters. Final judgment on the animal rescue program depended on the fate of the 197 otters put back into the wild. (Twenty-eight others were not fit and were placed in aquariums Outside.) The releases proved much more controversial than the captures. Rescue workers were unhappy that forty-five of the animals were going to be implanted with radio transmitters. This was a necessity if their whereabouts and survival were to be monitored, but to some the abdominal surgery was an extra dose of cruelty.

Saboteurs freed a dozen otters from the Homer and Valdez centers, presumably to spare them the implantations.

From their quarter, Alaska Fish and Game biologists warned that the otters might have picked up diseases in captivity that would threaten the wild population. In fact a flare-up of a herpes-like virus occurred at the Seward center in July. The state opposed the releases, but the FWS determined that the virus was already present in the wild population, and resolved to go ahead.

There was a debate over where the releases should take place. To put them back near the oiled shorelines whence they came made no sense, not by the presumptions of their rescue, and to put them back hundreds of miles away was also troublesome, since past translocations had shown sea otters to be capable of heroic swims back. Nonstop homing would drain energies they needed for foraging, grooming and readjusting. Nor could the FWS release sea otters into areas where they might meet the ire of fishermen.

Everybody agreed that the delay was not good for the animals in captivity. Some of the otters gnawed at their pens in stress, or swam laps back and forth, basket cases in the making. The Homer and Valdez holding facilities had problems with rogue males, the wild sea otters in whose territory the floating pens were placed. The rogues attacked the captive males through the netting and mated with the captive females.

It was decided to release otters from the Valdez center into the far bays of the northeastern Sound. In early August I got into a helicopter with a FWS biologist, six rescue staffers and six male sea otters. As soon as the engine turned over, the otters began to whistle their piercing distress calls. It reminded me of the tree frogs' trilling around the pond in Massachusetts, where one call set off the others, each pitched a fraction higher or lower than the next and all making for a vibrating cacophony. The otters' sound was louder, and cut through the rotor noise. They kept it up for the half-hour flight.

The aircraft cabin filled up with the damp heat of their metabolisms. From my seat at the rear, I could look into the cage of otter no. 024. He fidgeted and fondled his white oblong cubes of ice, pressing them to his mouth and rolling them over his face and stomach. I hadn't considered that an animal that eats seafood must defecate the same. Now and then 024 would flip over and poke his small paws and snub nose toward me through the mesh. "Hi!" I greeted him, willing closed my ears and my nose.

The day was ending when we landed at Nelson Bay. To the southwest toward Cordova, the low clustered clouds were sharply backlit, and brilliant grays flashed from the water. The spruce and hemlock on the rock bluffs wore their warmest colors. Ten years earlier Nelson Bay had been the staging ground for the crab-hungry pioneers, mostly male, moving onto Cordova. In 1989 it had a sizable mixed population. Biologists hoped that the resident otters would buffer the novelty of the place for the six being released, so they wouldn't sprint away at once.

Incongruously offshore was a Japanese freighter, come to pick up a boom of tawny logs. The Eyak Corporation, made up of Cordova Natives, was cutting its lands on the flats near town. Nelson Bay was Native land also. The timber was cached in the water until it could be exported. But I found the scene too pretty and the occasion too warm to be marred by such concerns. The freighter seemed to be part of a welcoming committee.

To win this climactic moment with their charges, the rescue staffers had held a lottery. The lucky ones took turns taking pictures and videotaping as the six cages were carried down to the shoreline. The cages were set side by side with the doors toward the bay. The FWS biologist in charge made quick work of it. At his nod, each handler sprung his or her special pal.

A ninety-pounder humped out first, barely paused, plunged, undulated in the opaque water and then dove. Twenty yards offshore he popped up like a seamount and faced us, prompting a flurry of photos, and then he rolled, lolled and disappeared for good. A white-faced specimen seemed to take his time. A clambering otter can't be said to look dignified. Flipper-kick, once, twice, thrice, good-bye. Their dark heads, like small buoys atop a long line, arced toward the freighter in the distance. The shadows lengthened across the beach, and we stood quietly with our cameras and notebooks at our sides. The sea otters were free.

It should have been the end of the story, but radiotelemetry had the cold epilogue. The sea otters with implanted transmitters, forty-five in all, were turned loose in stages in the eastern Sound. For a while they seemed healthy, if rather frenetic in their movements. A score crossed into the western Sound. Six went further, out onto the Kenai coastline, and the longest run home was by a female that swam 250 miles to English Bay on the tip of the peninsula.

Winter was the killing time. By spring twelve of the otters were known to be dead, because of the change in their radio signals. Like those used on the bald eagles, the transmitters changed their pattern of beeps if the animals stopped moving. Boat and airborne trackers picked up no radio signals at all from nine other otters, in spite of lengthy searches. One device malfunctioned, removing that animal from study.

Since the most likely cause for signals to be missing was that those nine otters were dead as well, scientists figured a loss of almost half the sample in less than a year. This rate of mortality/missing was very high. In other work on radio-tagged otters in the Sound, survival has been much better, which tended to absolve the implantation surgery (the experimenter effect) from having weakened the animals unduly.

In 1991 the researchers reported that only a third of the treated otters were still living. That is, thirty of the forty-five sampled had either died or disappeared within two years. The findings emboldened the biologists who doubted the usefulness of rehabilitation. The forty-five, they noted, were the least-oiled to start with, the healthiest otters of the lot. "Davis and Williams did a heck of a job, but. . . ." As they saw it, the heavily oiled animals died rapidly, and the others failed gradually from stress. The costly effort made no difference to the population.

Indeed: "Those guys are populationists," said Jim Styers, a rescue specialist who directed the Seward center. "We focus on individuals." He and others in the program clung to the worth of the animals that lived, down to the last beeping transmitter. Whether light or heavy, any oiling of animals was perceived as a threat. Scientists did not have all the answers about animals and oil. Else why were other scientists, the damage assessors, out trying to prove that the oil was harmful?

Randall Davis and Terrie Williams, the leaders of the effort, have kept feet in both camps. They emphasized the scientific value of what was learned, and predicted better results—in the next spill—if facilities were in place in advance. They have lobbied for rescue centers in California and Alaska. The Fish and Wildlife Service has drawn up contingency plans for a future response, so as not to be unprepared again. All sides are in accord that captivity is harmful, and that the ideal response, if it were possible, would be to net sea otters ahead of an oil slick and immediately to deposit them somewhere out of the way.

And if the oil does hit them? Repeatedly I was told, "You'll never get away with doing nothing. The public won't stand for it." The critics are bolder but they still expect to be overruled. Davis has warned that if the policy were indeed to refrain, or to do no more than put the worst cases out of their misery, the FWS must have the courage of its convictions, "because there are going to be a lot of very nasty photographs and television videos of little, furry, sick and dying animals."

Jim Styers of the Seward center made an interesting point. "If you take away the rescue," he said, "then you take away the accountability." In that view the wildlife rescue had value as a punishment to Exxon.

Exxon spent millions on the animal rescue, millions in claims payments to fishermen and Alaska businesses, several billion on the shoreline cleanup, then another billion to settle the civil and criminal charges, and still faced billions more in private-plaintiff actions. But contrition still seemed to be lacking. I submit that the correct punishment would have been for its highest executives to come at once to Prince William Sound. Not to wash animals. They should have picked the carcasses off the beaches. They should have stood in the morgue with the garbage bags and watched their breath congeal. They might have stood in for our helpless grief. Perhaps then the acute phase of the disaster could have been brought to a proper close, and the chronic phase that got under way in 1989 and still goes on might not have been so mean and chilly.

The first fish caught each year must be eaten entirely except for the gall and the gills. If anything of the fish is wasted, it will never come back again.

—KAJ BIRKET-SMITH, "THE CHUGACH ESKIMO"

THE PEAK of Mount Eyak across the lake is not often visible because of the rain clouds. The peak is slightly hooked, like the tip of a boat hook, or a bent stylus. On a rare clear dawn, streaks of buff and gray were etched from the mountain nib onto the sky. The traces of the rainstorm that went out the night before lay on the flanks of the conifers, like wispy smoke from scores of campfires. The moisture drifted low toward the throat of the lake.

The fall came on. I stood at the window at night, watching for the aurora borealis. One evening I was treated with green-hued floodlights, which lifted in horizontal bands behind the mountain, as if there were an emerald city back there and it was slowly turning up the juice. But usually the spectacle came as high thin whorls, twisting about the zenith. It was said that the northern lights were the souls of fallen Chugach warriors. The whorls, I'd hazard, were the Chugach souls. The bands from behind the mountain were fallen Eyaks.

The Eyaks were coastal Indians, an enemy of the Chugach, based in the Copper River Delta. They were a marginal people, squeezed between Eskimos and Tlingits, the smallest and most obscure Native group in Alaska. Their last village was located on the west side of the lake; the town of Cordova had swallowed it up many years ago. Just two elderly Eyaks were left. Ironically, the Natives of the present Eyak Corporation were primarily of Chugach stock. Their corporate headquarters was at the old village site.

When the Natives gathered there for a shareholders meeting, I made a pitch to come before them to ask about sea otters. Its hand strengthened by the oil spill, the Fish and Wildlife Service was about to prohibit Alaska Natives from harvesting otters for commercial purposes. I wanted to ask how people felt about that. The answer came back no.

I packed up my rooms and left for the airport, out on the flats of the Delta, where the Eyaks used to gather red salmon from the sloughs. At the gate were two well-dressed members of the corporation. They were headed back to Anchorage, presumably, after the meeting, and they were in good spirits. One Native demonstrated his golf swing to the other. That to me marked the end of the acute phase of the oil spill.

The chronic phase of the spill involved preparations for litigation, and here the Natives looked to be in better shape. Although they may not have suffered on the mortal plane of the sea otters, their injuries were ongoing and acknowledged to be greater than the purely economic losses of the salmon fishermen, say, or the aesthetic losses of conservationists.

In civil claims filed against Exxon, Native groups cited damage to their wild foods, to their coastal lands, to their style of life, to their corporate welfare and to themselves. This harm required documentation. Besides commissioning private studies by consultants, the Natives' lawyers drew upon the findings of public agencies. There was useful material, for example, in the "Social Indicators Study of Alaskan Coastal Villages," by the Department of Interior, of which the Tatitlek section was written by Eric Morrison. There was "Subsistence after the Spill," by James Fall and his colleagues at the subsistence division of Alaska Fish and Game. Fall's reports documented that the Native harvest and consumption of wild foods fell off sharply following the spill, compared to prespill levels. Of all villages, the recovery of subsistence was slowest in Chenega Bay.

A more complex undertaking was the assessment of the risks to the villagers from eating the foods in question. Fears for their health obviously cut down on the amount of their consumption. In 1989 a half-dozen federal and state agencies came together in a committee called the Oil Spill Health Task Force. Its mission was to study the foods for evidence of contamination, to weigh the risks in light of the relevant toxicology and to pass results and advice to the Native communities. The task force investigation, in various forms, went on for five years. But this research was of little use to the Natives' litigation, because the one salient finding, repeatedly conveyed to the villages, was that all subsistence foods were safe to eat as long as they were not obviously tainted with oil. The one salient response, however, was that the Natives didn't buy it.

Such was the dilemma of science in the snare of the law. The process of law allows for conflicting judgments, winners and losers, appeals and reversals—but science seeks a higher consistency. Its judgments ought to disagree only in their refinement of the truth. Serving too many masters, science failed to prove, by its own rigorous standards, that the sea otters and other wildlife resources were chronically ill from the oil, and yet also failed to prove, by the standard of popular acceptance, that these same resources were fit enough to eat. To turn the conundrum around, people believed that the wildlife was sick, though researchers did not truly establish that fact. Yet where researchers did show with confidence that wildlife was healthy, people remained skeptical. The skeptics were not only the Native people.

To me the scientific work of the Oil Spill Health Task Force was extremely helpful, priceless, because it approximated the se-cret NRDA doings. During the three years that the latter was under wraps I could infer the big picture—the direction of long-term biological effects in the Sound—from what the researchers of the task force were reporting to the villages. There was no com-munication between the two inquiries, and the NRDA project dwarfed the public effort in scope, yet the lab procedures used and the range of animals tested were the same.

The fact that the task force found deer meat to be safe, for example, helped put to rest the scenario that oil from the shoreline threatened the terrestrial food chain. The fact that aromatic hydro-carbon exposure in salmon, halibut, rockfish and cod fell off mark-edly between 1989 and 1990 indicated the transient nature of the oil in the sea. Interestingly, the two places where fish were found to be most exposed to oil in 1989 were the waters around the village of Chenega Bay and the waters around the port of Kodiak. But Kodiak City was some 250 miles away from the southwestern Sound and touched by the spill only slightly. Moreover, in 1990, when the Chenega salmon showed much less exposure to oil, the Kodiak fish were unchanged. The only explanation was that the Kodiak fish were continuously affected by background diesel pol-lution from boats and the town harbor. Subsistence users ate these fish all along, to no ill effect.

In another instance, the two investigations issued different reports based on the same collection of harbor seals. (With the seal population of the region declining, it was thought wasteful for two teams to shoot animals.) The NRDA scientists detected metabolites of oil in the seals' liver bile and traces of injury in the brain, which they suggested were worrisome for the long-term health of the seals. At the same time the health task force found that the harbor seals were clean to eat. "The levels of hydrocarbons found in the samples do not present any health risk," announced Dr. Tom Nighswander, the task force chairman. "They are so low they are virtually nondetectable." Was there not a conflict here?

Because one addressed the bile and brain, and the other the tissues of the liver, blubber and muscle, there need be no conflict. Both evaluations could be correct, as oil could hurt the animal in ways that would not show up in its edible flesh. But this was the glass half empty. Were not the brain lesions faint echoes of the acute phase that was over? Were not the liver and gall bladder and bile ridding the body of the residual hydrocarbons, a process that was highly efficient in mammals? I chose to drink of the glass half full. The two reports indicated that seals short-circuited the contamination for the benefit of host and consumer alike.

I gained a lot of good from the subsistence science, but I had to pound the telephone and the library to get it. The Sound's Native villagers had neither the time nor affinity for this new subject. It was scary stuff to them. When the report of the brain-damaged seals came out, some people in Chenega Bay thought they would suffer brain damage themselves if they ate that meat. Such were the misconceptions the Oil Spill Health Task Force had to deal with.

It was said that when the tide goes out, the table is set. What a torture of feelings, as the physical craving for clams or octopus was held at bay, but never slaked, by suspicion of contamination. I'm hungry for it, one villager said, but I don't want cancer. The hunger was not about amounts of food, since the Natives had protein available elsewhere. It was a longing for the taste of their culture, for the very taste of themselves, which was under chemical attack from yet another poisonous dose of change. I think the perception was just that fundamental—that the oil would be the straw that broke the back of their culture.

Given what was at stake, it may have been impossible for the members of the task force to reassure the Natives. But the failure of their effort, even as I drew from it my hopeful understanding, pained and preoccupied me. Not merely a miscommunication between cultures, it was a tragedy of epistemology. For in my view of history, the scientists and the Natives made a recurrent link in the Sound, as did the Natives and otters, as did the otters and scientists. They were the three base-pairs on the DNA of a long story.

Georg Steller, a scientist, was the first white man to set foot in Alaska. Bering let him go ashore on Kayak Island, southeast of Chugach Sound, in 1741. Steller wanted badly to meet the American Natives. He came across the warm remains of a meal, heard rustles (perhaps) in the trees, spied distant smoke, even discovered a Chugach storehouse—but the people never let him make contact. The scientist and the Natives missed connecting.

A century later a great smallpox epidemic broke out in Russian America. The Russians obtained the smallpox vaccine, recently developed in Europe, and attempted to inoculate the Natives ahead of the epidemic. Several doctors and hastily trained paramedics were dispatched along the coast. The majority of Natives refused to have their arms stuck. They saw the vaccinators arrive just as disease was breaking out. In a climate of oppression, they feared they were being offered the disease itself. Unknowingly they were half right, for the vaccine was the cowpox virus, which is close enough to human smallpox to spark the immune system. An Indian shaman almost had one of the medics killed. In the Sound, at least a third of the Chugach people died in the epidemic; afterward a census counted only 287 Natives.

The ultimate empiricists, they have lived by trusting their own instincts and their own eyes and ears. Now comes a medical authority called the Oil Spill Health Task Force, bearing a reassuring message. The signals they read in the environment undercut it. First and foremost, oil remained visible in the Sound and oil was a proved killer. Second, the authorities were not unified. Why would Fish and Game have closed districts to commercial salmon and herring fishing if the fish were really safe for villagers to eat? Why were the damage assessors shaking their heads if the Sound was healthy?

Then, although representatives of Native organizations sat on the task force along with government agents, and although the chairman was an Indian Health Service physician, why was the oil company serving on the committee as well? It didn't look right, especially because Exxon's toxicologist was the most positive of all that the foods were safe. (Exxon was there, like a cowbird chick in a warbler's nest, because Exxon had asssumed responsibility for the oil spill. The company paid for the collection of field samples and reimbursed the government agencies for the lab work.)

The politics were beyond the scientists' control. That part isn't my focus. But by their own methods the researchers also undercut the case they presented to the Natives.

Science took three approaches to the problem. The simplest was the organoleptic testing of the seafood, or the "sense" test, which was a standard sequence for chemical taint or spoilage. The tests were performed at the state's Department of Environmental Conservation laboratory near Anchorage, beginning a few weeks after the spill. Technicians first looked over each sample for traces of oil. Then the sample was sniffed; the fish or shellfish had been sealed in a container, so that hydrocarbon vapors might be trapped. If it passed the smell test, the sample was put under ultraviolet light, sometimes with a chemical pretreatment, because oil compounds tend to fluoresce under ultraviolet light. If still appearing clean, the penultimate step was to flash-heat the sample in a microwave oven, in order to drive off the smell of oil if oil was there. And finally, the taste test, rendered by the palates of two technicians.

Working on behalf of the fishing industry as well as the health task force, the DEC lab performed over 5,000 organoleptic exams of seafood over the course of two years. None of the finfish samples came up positive for oil. No crabs tested positive. Some of the clams and mussels did, however, look or smell of oil. The mollusks weren't brought as far as the taste stage. The lab technicians were wary of paralytic shellfish poisoning. Shellfish can absorb this toxin from a summer-blooming plankton as readily as they absorb aromatic hydrocarbons.

The advantage of organoleptic testing is its quick turnaround. In early May of '89 the DEC lab said the seafood around Tatitlek was clean of oil. At the same time state health officials issued a recommendation to all subsistence users in the spill zone that, in effect, they conduct their own organoleptic tests. They should inspect their catches by sight, smell and taste. If they came up with no evidence of oiling, the seafood was safe to eat, although "absolute assurances" of purity could not be given.

Of course, absolute assurance was just what was desired. To get it, scientists must pursue hydrocarbons at lower levels of contamination than the human senses could detect. The heavier-weight PAHs, buried within tissues, were resistant to smell or taste. Native leaders put pressure on the task force to make quantitative judgments, not simply qualitative. It is ironic and telling of their situation in the world that the Natives turned away from proofs that depended on the acute application of their senses; but this was because they and their advisers had gathered a little bit of knowledge about the sublethal effects of oil on organisms.

Therefore with chromatography and mass spectrometry, and other such complex tools as I've described earlier, the seafood was tested for specific compounds. The Department of Fish and Game initiated this second, more analytical approach. It asked the U.S. Food and Drug Administration to screen thirteen samples of fish and mollusks collected by Native harvesters. The people who collected the samples examined them for oil, smelled them, and rated eleven of the thirteen to be organoleptically clean. The FDA screening confirmed the field evaluation. PAH levels were found to be "low" in the eleven that passed the sense test, but in two others, a mussel and a clam that smelled oily (they came from Windy Bay, a particularly hard-hit bay on the Kenai Peninsula), the PAHs were found to be "high." Precise concentrations were not given.

Generalizing, the FDA noted that "these PAH levels in the subsistence shellfish samples are lower than those found in many other foods, particularly smoked foods and leafy vegetables, and do not represent a serious health hazard." If this was encouraging news, it rested on a very small number of samples. Also, it was delivered late. The drawback of constituent hydrocarbon analysis is that it's expensive and lengthy. The Fish and Game effort was meant to be a pilot study, yet not until the end of August, when the spring and summer harvest seasons were already past, did the Oil Spill Health Task Force relay the findings from the FDA to the villages.

NOAA and Exxon, meanwhile, jointly undertook a much larger study, whose results were correspondingly slower to be reported. The aim was to take PAH readings in the parts per billion and to track those levels as they altered over time. The test included more than 1,000 samples of fish and mollusks from about 150 locations. Sampling was conducted in July, August and September of 1989, and at several times in 1990 and '91. Sites were selected with input from the villagers: the fishing spots they liked offshore and the beaches that were good for butter clams, for mussels or for chitons (a rock-grazing mollusk with a segmented shell).

None of the shoreline stations selected were heavily oiled, except for Windy Bay on the Kenai and for one location in the far southwestern Sound. It was assumed that Native harvesters would avoid shellfish where contamination on the beach was heavy or conspicuous. But most sites were known to have been affected to one degree or another. The clam and mussel station for the Chenega area, for instance, designated CHE1, was located just south of the village, on Sawmill Bay. In spite of multiple booming to protect the salmon hatchery, oil did wash in with the tides onto CHE1.

The upshot of the three-year study was that the fish—primarily halibut and salmon were analyzed—were clean. That is, there was strong evidence of exposure in the liver bile of some of the fish, but the low levels of hydrocarbons taken up in their flesh were no more than could be found in fish from virgin areas of Alaska. According to the final summary, polyaromatic hydrocarbons "rarely exceeded the relatively low concentration of 30 ppb." Thus from the fall of '89 onward, with metronomic regularity, the task force issued clean bills of health for finfish to the Native villages.

The shellfish were more problematic. The majority of samples were judged either not contaminated or "minimally" so (less than 100 parts per billion). But in the meat of clams and mussels from two areas, Windy Bay and several sites around Chenega Bay, the PAH levels ranged up to one part per million (1,000 parts per billion), and in some few cases exceeded that. This was considered "heavy" contamination. This was the same level of oiling that, in the mussel beds, was thought to have caused reproductive failure in the harlequin ducks.

After the first year, however, the levels generally declined from their peaks. The advice of the task force, consistent with earlier warnings, was that shellfish from oily beaches should be avoided. The obviously polluted Windy Bay sites were out. But the Chenega tainting eased and was said not to pose a serious hazard to health.

So far everything was done according to Hoyle. The tests and the advisories were straightforward and appropriate. Advocates for the Natives objected to the limited sample size, and to the tardy reporting, but these issues were beside the point. The real trouble began when the task force tried to convert the PAH contamination of subsistence foods into the risk of people getting sick. This impulse was understandable. For the task force should do better than just crunch hydrocarbon concentrations. What did "low PAHs" or "minimally contaminated" actually mean to a villager? Having opened a Pandora's box of chemicals and numbers, the scientists sought to assure the people who asked them to open the box that the escaping PAHs were not to be feared.

This third approach to the problem was academic, in that it looked to prior toxicology. There were no case studies in the literature of oiled seafood per se. As the National Academy of Sciences declared in its 1985 tome, *Oil in the Sea:* "Thus at present there is no demonstrated relationship that chronic exposures through eating petroleum-derived PAH (polynuclear aromatic hydrocarbons) contaminated seafood are related to the incidence of cancer or other disease in humans." On the other hand: "Exceptions to these conclusions may arise in localized areas, as in the case of isolated fishing villages where seafood constitutes a major portion of the annual diet. No data are available, however, for these cases."

Chenega and other Native villages might be exceptional cases. The task force assembled a panel of government experts, including toxicologists, epidemiologists and biochemists. Besides analyzing the case at hand, the experts were asked to set guidelines, which would be groundbreaking since none existed, on safety levels for hydrocarbons in seafood.

The FDA was the leading player on the panel. Responsible for protecting the nation's food supply, the FDA had information on PAHs as a general class of contaminants. These chemicals were not high among the agency's concerns, for pollutants these days were legion, but the PAHs bore watching because they were spread wide through the environment. The compounds were present, said a 1983 agency report, "in water, air, food, and soil from such diverse sources as tobacco smoke, automobile and engine exhausts, high-boiling petroleum distillates, carbon black, coal tar, pitch and rubber tires. . . . PAH have been reported in smoked fish and meats, grilled and roasted foods, root and leaf vegetables, vegetable oils, grains, plants, fruits, seafoods, whiskies, etc." As for their major sources, the FDA put "curing smokes" at the head of the list.

In Japan and Scandinavia, where people ate a lot of smoked fish, scientists had investigated a possible link between diet and stomach cancer. Nothing was nailed down, although a particular PAH by the name of benzo(a)pyrene, a durable five-ringed benzene compound, was a prime suspect. B(a)p was identifiable in cured bacon, in smoked meats and also in mussels from polluted harbors. Usually the compound was found in smaller concentrations than other PAHs, but FDA looked upon B(a)p as a red flag. If a food tested high for benzo(a)pyrene, it would likely test even higher for the others. Then the agency would have reason for concern, for B(a)p did cause cancer in laboratory animals.

The FDA brought a broad and knowing perspective to the task force, perhaps too broad and knowing. In its earlier work for Fish and Game the agency had opined that the contamination of seafood from the oil spill was lower than could be found in smoked products. The NOAA/Exxon sampling program provided a way to demonstrate this. The Natives ate much of their salmon smoked. In the days before freezers, smoke-curing preserved a catch, and the taste was popular still. So into the 1989 analytical hopper with the others went several samples of smoked salmon, collected from Tatitlek and from a Native village outside the Sound. The idea was to put the health risks of the spill into a framework that people could understand.

It was a sucker punch: The concentration of aromatic hydrocarbons in the smoked salmon was almost 10,000 times greater than in the wild salmon. A batch of smoked fish from Tatitlek had B(a)p at twenty parts per billion, which was off the charts. By comparison, in the flesh of the most suspect wild salmon in '89—the dozen or so samples having *total* PAHs of 30 ppb—the benzo(a)pyrene component was undetectable, absent. The task force did not trumpet the comparison, it just put the results out there for the Natives to see. Cancer was out of its box.

"I hesitated to analyze those [smoked fish] samples," recalled John Robinson, the top NOAA official on the task force. "Scientifically, it did not have anything to do with our study. The danger was that we'd disturb the Natives' lifestyle and we'd regret what we had done later. But the point was, the spill was adding only a minuscule additional threat of PAHs to people who smoke cigarettes and eat smoked fish."

The scientists at the FDA were well aware that people made a distinction between voluntary risk, such as choosing to eat one's salmon smoked, and involuntary risk, such as eating foods contaminated by others that one required for subsistence. This question of choice and risk came up all the time. For example, the national flap over benzene in Perrier mineral water took place about the same time as the seafood in Alaska was being analyzed. The same FDA scientists tried to debunk the Perrier scare, noting that the environment was rife with benzene at low levels. Society tended to reject such a perspective. People may not have a choice about breathing benzene in the air, but they would drop benzene like a hot potato from a discretionary purchase.

That the villages had alternative foods, and that most people were too busy or worried in 1989 to fish or hunt for subsistence, were not the issue. The Natives viewed any consumption of tainted fish and clams, no matter how minor the parts per billion, as an involuntary risk, and therefore unacceptable. Furthermore, the Natives resented the suggestion that their own lifestyle put them at a greater hazard than the oil spill did. For it was the lifestyle itself that was under attack.

The task force pushed ahead, realizing that the perception of risk was more virulent than the hydrocarbons themselves. Starting in 1990 it sent out to the villages a monthly newsletter of its past and present activities and findings. It put together an educational video. In addition, the researchers increased the testing of fish and invertebrates around villages where the concern was greatest. Whereas Chenega had but one shellfish station in '89, eleven separate beaches were sampled in subsequent years. According to

NOAA's Jay Field, who worked with the villages on the selection of new sites, it was particularly difficult to find clam sites around Chenega, not because of the spill, but because of the sea otters and the earthquake.

I mentioned that the tainting around Chenega dropped off after '89. The one sampling place near the village whose mollusks remained "moderately" contaminated in 1990 was Port Ashton, about halfway between Chenega Bay and the AFK cannery on the shore of Sawmill Bay. Port Ashton itself had once been a cannery, now long abandoned. Decrepit piers, laced with creosote, stood in the soft sediment. The villagers were warned to stay away from the mussels, butter clams and littlenecks growing there, which was too bad, since it was about the best spot in the bay. The shellfish had hydrocarbons at less than one part per million. Later the NOAA chemists in Seattle found that the fingerprint of the PAHs in Port Ashton clams was not the usual one for the oil spill. More likely it was the creosote.

Meanwhile, in Washington, D.C., the FDA put the health hazards of the contamination into a new context. The agency produced a report from its Quantitative Risk Assessment Committee. Risk assessment, extrapolating PAH doses from lab rats to humans, brandished the long odds of contracting cancer in Prince William Sound. Later I obtained the report from the task force. Assumptions pyramiding on assumptions, the construction of the risk went up this way:

The first assumption was to convert the PAHs in the seafood into units of carcinogencity according to the potency of benzo(a)pyrene. Since scores of compounds were involved, each posing a different risk, the FDA needed to simplify matters. The committee selected nine PAHs, of known concentrations in the samples, and rated them for their suspected risk relative to B(a)p. For purposes of the argument these compounds were assumed to be human carcinogens, although none, not even B(a)p itself, were proved to cause cancer in people. Only two of the compounds besides B(a)p had been shown to cause cancer in rodents.

But converting to B(a)p equivalents was a necessity, not just a convenience, because B(a)p per se was so rare in the seafood of the spill zone. The experts threw finfish out of their assessment altogether, because not only benzo(a)pyrene but also its equivalents were so very low in the fish. The chance of cancer would have to be figured from the consumption of oiled mollusks.

However, in terms of B(a)p equivalency, the great majority of shellfish were also also uncontaminated. The committee had to take the most polluted subsample available, the clams and mussels collected from the Windy Bay site on the Kenai in 1989, to find sufficient PAHs to make B(a)p equivalents. Consolidating seven samples, they came up with a contamination factor of 30 ppb.

Let us save that number and move to the next assumption: What might be the general cancer risk to people from exposure to benzo(a)pyrene? The FDA experts were guided by an animal study published in 1981. In the study, lab rats received a fixed dosage of B(a)p for their lifetimes, which were almost three years. The model was "less than ideal," the FDA report conceded, because only one dose was administered, not a range of doses; because it produced tumors that were mostly benign, not cancerous; and because the tumors mostly appeared in the male rats, not the females. Eight of thirty-two, or one-quarter of the male rats, developed tumors before they died, whereas only two of the thirty-two control males developed such tumors. The six extra cases were said to be caused by the ingestion of B(a)p.

Now the extrapolation. The FDA applied the proportionate dose of B(a)p to a hypothetical test on a 150-pound human being, and figured the likelihood of that person contracting a cancer over his or her seventy-year lifetime. I must interject that if this leap seems rational to my reader, then both of us have been wasting our time.

A third consideration: the Native consumption of shellfish. The experts considered it their unusual good fortune to have germane data to work with instead of a generalized estimate. They had Stratton and Chisum's prespill survey of Chenega Bay households. They took the annual per capita amount of clams that Chenegans said they consumed. From that was derived the Native person's daily intake of clam meat: two grams. The two grams per day were contaminated, pursuant to the scenario, with the 30 ppb B(a)p equivalent from the oily mollusks at Windy Bay.

A Native hypothetically ingested this dose for his or her lifetime. However, the FDA committee recognized the oil wouldn't persist for seventy years. It assigned a ten-year limit to the scenario, after which time the contamination should be negligible. The foreshortening increased the odds against disease by a factor of 7.

Finally, the key calculation: The prediction was 2.5 extra cases of cancer for every 10 million people on this diet. The individual Native had two and a half chances in 10 million of developing cancer from eating the clams. And that was the upperbound risk, the worst-case odds for the worst-case tainting.

Ergo not to worry.

In order to explain the FDA's risk assessment, the Oil Spill Health Task Force held a Risk Communication Workshop in Anchorage. The date was late September 1990, following the second year of the shoreline cleanup. Representatives of the task force and the FDA met with representatives of the Native villages. Gail Evanoff, vice president of the village corporation, appeared for Chenega Bay.

Gail Evanoff was the toughest person to win over. She was the Chenegan angriest about the oil spill. A month before the workshop Evanoff led a tour of the southwestern Sound for state officials and Native leaders. Reporting on the tour in a Native newsletter, she summarized the anxiety the Chenegans felt about harvesting their traditional foods:

> An abnormal seal liver, ordinarily firm, was soft and runny. The arm of a starfish fell apart when pulled from the rocks. They have reported several dead eagles and sea gulls, a dead bear and a blind sea lion found during the past month, highly unusual occurrences prior to the spill. The animals and birds were found on land adjacent to areas sprayed with Interpel [the reference is to Inipol, the fertilizer used to stimulate the oil-degrading bacteria] and Chenega villagers' lack of trust in the Oil Spill Health Task Force subsistence food test results were communicated to Lee Stratton, the subsistence Fish and Game representative present on the tour.

When the Anchorage workshop got under way, the village representatives laid out their array of frustrations. According to notes taken by Dr. Tom Nighswander, the task force chairman:

> The perception remains that any food with hydrocarbons is not completely safe. As long as oil can be found on the beaches, there will be concern about their food despite official agency announcements. . . . The villagers need the ability to assess for themselves what risk is. They can not just listen to public bulletins assuring that there is no problem. . . . Several village representatives wanted their own scientist participating in [a long-term epidemiological study] of subsistence food.

The FDA scientist from Washington, Robert Scheuplein, then gave his talk. He stressed the gap between contamination and risk. He referred to the recent Alar scare in the Lower 48, the grossly unreasonable fear of Alar-sprayed apples. He told the group that the American diet in general, what with its fat content, chemical preservatives and other harmful impurities, posed a risk of dying of one in fifteen, as opposed to the one-in-a-million chance of cancer from eating seafood from the oiled areas. He said the most tainted of the shellfish were 100 times safer than the Natives' smoked salmon. Scheuplein's remarks, I gathered from several participants, were not appreciated. Somehow the blame seemed once more to be put back on them.

There was no meeting of the minds. Afterward NOAA's John Robinson was rueful. "All the time and effort that went into it," he said, "and we didn't get anyone to believe it. It's another aspect of the ongoing tragedy of the oil spill."

Do I make too much of this? One might argue that the failure owed simply to the divergent cultures, the scientists clumsy at communication and the Natives opaque in response. The workshop organizers admitted there should have been more village involvement in the testing program, more efforts to consult. But the problem went deeper.

The task force held a news conference in conjunction with the risk communication workshop. The headline in the *Valdez Vanguard* read: "Scientists say contamination levels high but safe." In the *Anchorage Daily News* the headline said the seafood was found "OK" for subsistence, and the lead paragraph of the article read:

> Fish and shellfish samples in Prince William Sound and the Gulf of Alaska contain trace amounts of cancer-causing residues from the *Exxon Valdez* oil spill but are safe for subsistence users to eat, according to Food and Drug Administration guidelines issued Wednesday.

The message was contradictory: threat = not threat, cancer = safety. If non-Natives were this ambivalent about foods they did not even have to eat, how could the villagers be reassured? Quantifying the odds of cancer was all right for the populationists, but most people, Native and otherwise, focused on the individual, for whom a chance of a cancer could never be too slight.

Looking back on it, NOAA's Jay Field allowed that the continual emphasis on toxicology, its very language, may have kept the threat alive in the Natives' perceptions. "But that didn't change our advice all along," Field said, "which was, 'The fish is safe. Don't eat the clams if there's oil on them, and secondarily, don't eat the clams from an oily beach even if they look clean.' "

Exactly. The circuitous chase of precision via chemistry, toxicology and risk assessment led back to the point already established by the "sense" test, and the go-round was counterproductive. The Natives were half right to flinch from the inoculation. The ancient Chugach advisory against eating the gall bladder of a fish—empirically, the gall was the repository of impurities—was just about the only wisdom they needed to know.

There was a village near Chenega. It was never daylight but always dark. People were used to it, because it was never light. Then an old baidarka [kayak] arrived. It was Raven. As he entered the smoke house he said: "What is wrong with this place since it never gets light?"

The people asked him: "Could you get the light? What do you mean by asking why none of us go for the light?" Anytime they became sleepy they went to bed, because they did not know what the light was. Raven said: "Yes, I am going away to bring the light."

Raven stayed away for a long time, but one morning he came back with his baidarka. He had a square box. It was tied up with rawhide. As he opened the box, daylight appeared. Raven said: "Now watch, as soon as the day breaks you must get up and build a fire." Since then they rose in the morning and did not sleep as long as they used to.

Next morning they called Raven in order to give him all kinds of presents, because he had brought them the daylight. He loaded his baidarka with all kinds of furs, but right behind the point he tipped over and lost them. The people did not see it. Raven swam to the beach, leaving his baidarka. He got soaking wet and could hardly swim. . . .

—CHUGACH LEGEND

TAXIING AWAY from the dock and into the lake, the plane rode downwind on twin floats. When it turned, I could see where I used to live on the far shore of Eyak. More knowledgeable than a journalist, more sensitive than a scientist, I took off at last for Chenega Bay, eighty-four miles away.

The day was June 28, still spring in the Sound, and the year 1991. We flew over Cordova and across Orca Inlet. It was fine weather. On the high bluffs of Hawkins Island, little tarns gleamed like epaulets. The still pools gave back the blue sky.

This was my fifth visit to the Sound. In Cordova, at least, the intensity was gone, the zeitgeist that bound everyone to the spill and thus to each other in spite of their differences: the free spirits, the fishermen, the Forest Service rangers, the coasties, the cleanup workers, the Texas-twanged Exxon personnel. No longer chafed by a central excitement, people had turned away and tended their own private fires.

But my people in Chenega would not let it alone. On the occasion of the second anniversary of the spill in March, villagers led reporters to beaches that were still dirty. Sleepy Bay, across the channel from the village on Latouche Island, was the notorious example. Northern Latouche was owned by the village corporation. Elders such as Paul Kompkoff Sr. gave interviews about the ongoing toll to wildlife. "Everything's dead," Gail Evanoff was quoted. Chitons had been found with mysterious white sores; Fish and Game took samples for analysis.

When the Chugach regional corporation foundered that spring, it laid its financial woes to the *Exxon Valdez*. "If Exxon had paid the Native corporation for even a fraction of the damage caused by the devastating spill," said a press release, "the bankruptcy filing could have been avoided." The spill reduced the salmon packed at the corporation's three fish plants in 1989, while the massive cleanup effort was alleged to have driven up labor and construction costs at Chugach's new sawmill in Seward.

The Natives were objecting to the settlement of the government's charges against the oil company. An Exxon source was bitter. "The spill work they got has sustained them for the past two years," he said. "At the same time they blatantly attempt to scuttle the settlement. All this is perpetuating their victim mentality."

Meanwhile, quite a different portrayal from the anthropological consultants of the Natives. In a lengthy report the consultants argued that in damaging their subsistence foods, the oil spill had damaged the culture of the Natives in manifold respects, namely, a decline, real and perceived, in the quantity and quality of natural resources; the disruption of sharing, of kinship ties and of the transmission of subsistence skills to the young; uncertainty over the future; loss of autonomy in a difficult world.

Chenega Bay was the village slowest to resume the harvest, the slowest to be free of the oil. I thought I might help them, though ostensibly I came so that they could help me. Their lead attorney in Anchorage cleared my visit. He did not promise me access to the villagers. After the plane left me at the Chenega dock, I did not hasten up the wooden stairs. I fiddled with my duffel bag and looked around.

To the left of the stairway was the wrecked foundation of the New England Fish Company, a herring saltery. Earlier in the century, herring packed in brine made an important business in the Sound. The saltery was in use as late as 1964, until being damaged by the earthquake that destroyed old Chenega.

A teenage girl came down and said hello. The arrival of the mail plane always caused a small stir. She wore leggings and tossed her long hair. "This is the boringest place," she said, rolling her eyes, too young to do anything about it.

Chuck Totemoff, the president of the village corporation, rode down the ramp on a bright red four-wheeler. Whether he expected me or not I couldn't tell from his face. Definitely there was no key to the city, but he said he'd drop my bag at the small apartment that Chenega rented to its visitors.

An older man in a pressed checked shirt was taking the sun at the top of the stairs. I stopped and had a cigarette with him. He looked like a Native Ronald Reagan, handsome, and his hair glossy black and well done. Looking closer, I saw he was cloudy from cataracts. He wore a hearing aid. He said his back was bothering him a lot today.

In short order Paul Kompkoff Sr. and I lay side by side on the wooden planks, like two new friends at a health club. I demonstrated my set of back exercises. He grasped his knees and pulled his small feet toward his chest. If he would do these every morning, everything would be OK.

The song of hermit thrushes reached us. The sweet introductory note, holding like a foot in the door, followed by a melodious trill. My favorite song from Massachusetts, and not just one but many tinkled from around the wooded shore. "Dy-yai'-yah-kirq," said Kompkoff, giving the bird's name in Alutiiq. The music was too high for his sixty-eight-year-old ears to catch anymore.

He could hear it inside, though, for he began to tell me about the summer fish camps of his boyhood. He and his relatives would paddle in kayaks to Icy Bay, the long fjord southwest of the old village. They lived in white tents on the beach for a month. He remembered awakening to the sounds of the glacier ice groaning, and the baby seals crying, and the liquid melancholy of the hermit thrush. "It was better then," he said contentedly.

Better than . . .? I broached the spill.

"On the beaches, the last two years, the smell is like a strange country. We're not enjoying, in our minds, what we eat anymore. The animals, see, they're not like us. They smell it and they're not gonna hang around. They go back to where they came from, where it's clean.

"The terns that ate the little fish that swam through the oil— the terns disappeared. They ate the little fish and died. There aren't any seals. The oystercatchers aren't here as many as before. Also the songbirds. The deer. Even the mosquitoes aren't here the way they used to be."

"That's one good thing about the oil spill," I essayed. I felt dismayed, because this wasn't PR. Kompkoff spoke with deadly assurance. Chenega's concerns had metastasized since '89, from oil's incipient poison to oil's rampant destruction of wildlife populations. Paul Jr., Kompkoff's son, was the principal seal hunter in the village, and he was convinced that the seals in the Sound were both sicker and fewer.

Paul Sr. pointed out his house to me. It was the first one past the village generator and the two-story community building. I walked along the stony thoroughfare; it had a boardwalk running beside it for the sloppy conditions of winter. The houses were prefab double-wides with metal roofs, arrayed on a sloping commons. Some people were seen here and there, paying me no mind. The village had the dusty feeling of a summer weekend when school is out. The feeling was the same every day, of people not pressed for time.

My modular apartment, very comfortable, was located beside the playground and basketball court, impeding the comfort. The floor of the basketball court was plywood on a hollow frame. Children came to the playground several times a day, as if on a schedule, with the last period going late under the midnight sun. There were giggles and punk hairdos and a pulsating boom box. I worked on my jump shot when I would rather have been sleeping, or watched reruns on Rat-net, Alaska's rural-area TV.

The next evening after supper I went to Paul Kompkoff's house. As an elder, he was used to unannounced callers, to whom he offered stories and advice. He sat at his kitchen table with coffee and cigarettes. His wife, Minnie, would refill our cups, then go back to her parakeets across the room, missing nothing that was said.

Kompkoff told me about his experience in the earthquake, about the otter and the eagle fighting over the fish, and the relatives he never found.

"Then we picked out this place to live," he said. "It was good. Good water, lots of wood."

Why didn't people reclaim the old village?

"Too many bad memories," put in Minnie, who had lost her parents also.

Their granddaughter passed through the kitchen. " 'Bye. I'm going up to play volleyball. I need my Walkman."

"The earthquake was bad," he resumed, "but things popped back. This oil. . . ."

I asked Kompkoff why Natives for so long would not talk about the spill.

"When it first happened, so many phony people showed up. Just because we're Natives, a lot of white people think we're dumb and mindless. But in our way, we're smart. Exxon said we *like* to eat Spam. Sure we do, when we don't have anything else."

People said Paul Sr. wasn't looking too well. It was true, when one adjusted one's set for Alutiiq coloring, that he appeared drained, even sallow. He tried to explain to me how the Native people were smart in the way that they knew the wildlife.

"They are our little friends," he said, brightening, "the little animals. They sing for you. Ravens will follow you on the beach. They clean up the seal parts for you."

Kompkoff said he disapproved of what Steve W———— had done earlier today. W————, a white guy who had married into the village, killed the black bear that people had been seeing the past few days. I saw the bear myself, skirting the high ground. They came down at this time for berries, because the berries ripened first near the shore. The Chenega of the early '60s harvested forty bears a year. A man would crawl into a den in early spring while the animal still slept, feel around in the dark for its head and shoot it behind the ear, but W———— engaged in no such stealth. He opened his front door in the morning, saw the bear close by and popped it. Chenega Bay harvested a half dozen black bears per year, mostly kills of nuisance animals.

Kompkoff said he would have tried to scare the bear away, or just waited until it left. W———— said to me, "If he'd've let me have my breakfast, I might've let that s.o.b. live." The bear didn't show any fear, he complained, and for that reason posed a danger to the village children.

It had been cool that spring, as the snow was still low on the mountains of Latouche. White blotches showed below the cloud cover. Between Latouche and Chenega were two islets, called Bettles and Little Bettles. The Chenega cleanup crew was currently picking up oily gravel and debris on a segment of the smaller island, and one drizzly morning I rode out to watch.

I went in a rubber Zodiac with the cleanup monitors. This year the overseer-to-worker ratio was the highest yet. For ten Natives with trowels and buckets, there was a Coast Guard on-scene coordinator, an Exxon supervisor, a DEC monitor and a FWS observer responsible for seeing that the bald eagles nesting near the work site were not disturbed. These four fellows were sharing a large apartment adjacent to mine, and were on friendly terms.

The cleanup was set to end after a third pass at the Sound's shoreline. Chenega wanted the work to continue until all the subsurface oil was removed. It wasn't to be. Even the state DEC had thrown in the towel. Only four small crews were tasked, including the crew from Chenega Bay. The DEC man told me that the segment on Little Bettles had not been recommended for treatment. The assessment was that there would be no net environmental benefit. Cost was also a criterion in 1991, because it was agreed that anything Exxon spent on cleanup could be deducted from its financial settlement. But when the village protested, work was scheduled for Little Bettles.

A sea otter floated on its back as we neared the island. The animal seemed more curious about its own protruding feet than the passing skiff. Then I saw another otter, atop an outcrop of the island, at least ten feet above the beach. I had never seen one on land before nor one that lay so still. It was dead, I was told. It had been there for a few days. Sea otters tend to haul out when they are old and ailing—that was probably the case here. But nobody in the village went to check it out. If the sea otters were ailing because of the oil spill, it was not of concern in Chenega. Since the prohibition of the commercial harvest, many thought it best to keep their distance.

Because it was near high tide, the outcrops blocked one's path around the curved shoreline. The cleanup crew was split up and people were working on separate pockets. I was put ashore next to three women. Two happened to be from Kompkoff's family. There was his daughter Sharlene and his sprightly wife, Minnie, no less, who looked bulkier in her rain gear.

The two islands, located outside the Sawmill Bay sea curtains, were smacked pretty hard in '89. "It must have been bad," commented Sharlene, "if it's still like this." Scaly patches of asphalt alternated with the black lichen on the beach's uppermost flanks. Where the water was receding the rocks were clean and covered with limpets, but their undersides shielded a film of brown oil that was quite sticky. "It's looking better," Sharlene said. "I don't know how much better, but it is."

The small stuff the workers put into heavy-ply plastic bags; the larger rocks they turned over and wiped off, or carried lower onto the shore, that the ocean might take a better shot at them. The bags full at the waterline were marked for burial in Oregon. The monitors strolled about. The work was by the hour, not by the accomplishment. Put the time in and go on to the next segment.

Clink, clink, went the ladies' trowels. They were like dental assistants, patiently poking into the cavities of the island, and the island was acting very bravely. Minnie Kompkoff made a point of scraping beneath the boulder where her daughter had just been. She wore a small smile of triumph, her glasses glinting with rain, when she came up with more gravel for Oregon.

Chenega Bay had about twenty households. In 1989 the average household earned $51,778. In 1990 it was $33,948, and in 1991, as I would learn, $24,323. The figures reflected the declining input of the cleanup employment. I feel a little uncomfortable, because this information on their finances, provided voluntarily to the subsistence division of Fish and Game, might be used to counter the Natives' claims of injury from the spill. Exxon already has it. Besides, they always maintained that the spill wages were a niggardly reward for the harm done to their way of life.

The fog licked lower on the landscape, and in the distance I heard the war cries of the ravens. I turned to face out. The Sound was flat calm. A round-faced otter was swimming in, trailed by a pearl-gray V. It swam on its front like a dog, with no apparent effort, steering with its tail. An otter swims on its front when it has a purpose, like taking on a rival. This one came right to the beach, rose up, looked us over for a minute and then swam back out.

Over the winter Exxon had touted the recovery of the sea otter population. I received a four-page brochure titled "Sea Otters Thrive in Prince William Sound, Alaska." The bulletins inside were headed: "Thousands of Otters and Pups," "A Diet of Shellfish," "Clean Water," "Clean Beaches" and "Resilient Sea Otters." The brochure contained few facts, but there were some clever generalizations. The section on diet noted that the government had declared that "ample stocks of shellfish were available and safe for humans to eat." The implication was that shellfish consumed by the animals must be safe too.

Chenega hadn't signed off on the first assumption. The Oil Spill Health Task Force was still trying to counter their perceptions. The task force had collected shellfish samples from the area two weeks prior to my visit. For information I was advised to go see John M. Totemoff, another elder of the village and uncle of the corporation president. He agreed to take me in his boat to CHE1, the original sampling station, whose clams and mussels had been analyzed since 1989.

We chugged out of Crab Bay and around the corner into Sawmill Bay. Totemoff was a short, stocky, smooth-visaged person, with ageless black hair, and like many Natives he had no angles about him, literally no handholds to me in his features or expression. He said, "I read in the paper that the oil is three hundred feet down. So I won't go for shrimp. I found a dead eagle not too long ago. I didn't see deer like I used to on the beach during spring. The seals and sea lions aren't coming in here anymore. I heard they had brain damage, maybe that's why. I hear that Fish and Game found baby salmon that had a deformed backbone." Nodding, I wrote down this flat litany of fact and fear. "They don't believe our stories," Totemoff finished. I nodded.

We landed at a fine-graveled beach. "This place has real small mussels," he said. He gestured to his right. "There were no clams found on that point a year ago." According to Fish and Game, the area of CHE1 was well picked over by clam diggers because it was so close to the village. Nor did Totemoff blame the oil. "After the earthquake," he continued, "I tried six beaches and found one clam from each beach. So I don't try too much anymore."

Just then a skiff with two men pulled up. They were non-Natives, a lawyer for the village corporation and a consultant land manager. The attorney disembarked with alacrity, wanting to know who I was. He would not put it past Exxon to send a spy posing as a writer. The reader might expect horns painted on this man, but I must say that when he relaxed Sam turned out to be a nice guy. Nice guy, bad business. He was here to brief the villagers on the status of their litigation. We talked several times during my stay. After he relaxed some more, he agreed that the lengthy tort process was making it impossible for the Natives to heal. Since Exxon wouldn't settle with the private plaintiffs, federal and state trials were in the offing, yet the court dates, to his frustration, were regularly pushed back.

Totemoff ran me down to the end of the bay and left me at the AFK salmon hatchery. I have previously described the AFK operation. This was the year that the pinks would return so heavily to Sawmill Bay that millions of pounds had to be thrown away. For a period during the '80s the aquaculture corporation and the Native village talked about Chenegans taking jobs at the hatchery, and about other cooperative ventures. With cannery work gone from the western Sound, employment with PWSAC would seem to make perfect sense, but nothing has come of it.

From the hatchery I meant to walk back to the village along the east shore of the bay. An aquaculture worker took me by skiff as far as the pilings and twisted metal of Port Ashton, about half the distance back. Port Ashton, a.k.a. CHE7, was built as a cannery in 1919. It packed salmon and herring, but was abandoned before Chenega Bay was founded. Some people in the village thought they remembered that an old fuel tank had ruptured there in the '70s. Port Ashton, in other words, was not pristine when people from new Chenega started harvesting its butter clams and littlenecks.

The stalks of wreckage reached well above my head. Down the beach on either side, jagged blocks of graywacke had loosened from the uplands and tumbled into the tidal zone. Yet the beach right around me was broad and smooth, and the site oddly peaceful, giving no impression of pollution. It must make a nice outing to come here from the village. As of 1991, the Port Ashton shellfish held the highest remaining concentrations of aromatic hydrocarbons of all the stations sampled in the western Sound.

"Nobody except Exxon argued that the oil from the spill didn't get in there," said Fish and Game's Rita Miraglia. I telephoned her because, having succeeded Lee Stratton as the subsistence representative to Chenega Bay, Miraglia passed along the findings of the health task force. The clams had been of concern since they were first tested in 1990. But if the oil spill had aggravated the light contamination of CHE7, by 1991 the chemicals were back to the preexisting creosote and whatever else.

"I'm frustrated that some people still use the site," Miraglia said. "We're telling them, These particular clams aren't good to eat. But Port Ashton's not too far away and the clams are large, compared to the CHE1 site near the village."

I felt a flash of pleasure, which I was not able to convey to Miraglia, that some people were relying on their senses at last. They were ignoring toxicology's risks and judging the clams safe to eat. Polyaromatic hydrocarbons at less than 1 part per million was a risk I would take too, though I would be happier not knowing the numbers. Of course others in the village maintained their doubts. A few traveled to the eastern Sound or as far as the Kenai to harvest their clams.

Although the task force consistently found chitons to be uncontaminated, nobody ate the chitons from around the village. I heard about the chitons with the mysterious white sores. The issue of the white sores illustrated the gap between the two paradigms, the two rival approaches to the world. Natives observed firsthand that something seemed wrong with these mollusks, and science could not, or did not, adequately explain it.

There were weaknesses in both assessments. For the Natives, the problem was that their knowledge of chitons was rusty. Caught year-round in the area of the old village, chitons used to be a highly favored item. People called them gumboots, or bidarkis. The best was the red chiton (or *Cryptochiton stelleri*, another animal with Georg Steller's name on it), which grows up to twelve inches long. Its tough but meaty foot was removed from its flattish shell and cooked up in a pan. The smaller and more common species, the black leather chiton, was popped whole into a fire for a minute or two, then the meat forked out.

The new Chenegans had less of a taste for gumboots and less of a chance to exercise it. When the Natives moved back to the southwestern Sound, the red chiton was particularly rare: because of its slow growth and long life span, most likely it had not recovered yet from the uplift of the earthquake. The sea otters may possibly have cut into the chitons too. Not as many people still knew how to look for them either. The harvests at any rate were but a fraction of what they had been. Only two or three households regularly went out for the black species, and gustation in the village depended on sharing. In the current anxiety over brain-damaged seals and cancer-causing clams, a villager surely would be concerned to see white speckles appear on the gumboots. But was it possible that the Chugach, or perhaps the inhabitants of the pre-earthquake village, would have recognized the spots?

For the scientists, knowledge was weak too, because no one had ever studied the tissue structure of chitons so as to be able to tell routine conditions from unusual injuries, let alone the injuries owing to hydrocarbon exposure.

The investigation of the sores began with Fish and Game's Rita Miraglia. After hearing the stories, she collected twenty-one black chitons from two locations in the vicinity of the village. She confirmed there were tiny white spots speckling the feet of the mollusks from one of the sites. Miraglia took the live chitons to Fish and Game's pathologist for damage assessment, Joseph Sullivan, in Anchorage. Diagnosing the white spots as "sores," Sullivan passed the specimens for analysis to Albert Sparks, an invertebrate pathologist and NRDA consultant for the state.

Sparks's report came back two months later. Miraglia summarized the outcome in a letter to me:

> In general, results were inconclusive. The samples went to a lab first for slicing and mounting on slides. Dr. Sparks only saw the slides. In retrospect, it was not clear that the lab understood what we were interested in, or whether Dr. Sparks had seen the lesions in question. After we got the report, I went back to Chenega Bay, to try to get more samples, our intent being to send these directly to Dr. Sparks. However, I was unable to find chitons with white sores. At the time, I asked people in Chenega Bay to notify me if they found any more of them.

Miraglia, the medium between the Natives and the scientists, called the results "inconclusive." That's what she was told by Fish and Game's Sullivan. But had Sparks missed the suspect lesions? His own report, cautiously prefaced, said that most tissues "appeared normal" under the microscope. The type of lesions he saw suggested that animals had been damaged during the act of collecting.

Fish and Game equivocated. Another interpreter might have gone to the village with a sanguine message: No unusual pathology, no further signs of "sores" in the wild, so no need to be concerned.

The last time I talked to Gail Evanoff about the spotted chitons, she recalled that the test showed them to be contaminated.

There is a quote from H. D. Thoreau, who was a scientist manqué, about the contribution of Indians to the understanding of nature. He said that Indians "stand between the men of science and the subjects which they study." He meant not only the priority of knowledge of the indigenous peoples, but also their closer and sharper view. In his own later work, Thoreau alternated between collecting copious data on the plant cycles, weather patterns, river heights, bird migrations, etc. of his native Concord—he hoped that by grasping nature in its variable statistical parts, a grand unifying theory might emerge from his journals—and attacking the problem indirectly, as he studied nature through the rich lore of the Algonquian Indians of Maine, Massachusetts and Canada. His research was voluminous, but he died along the paths to shaping it.

In Chenega Bay it occurred to me that Thoreau's double-barreled approach might be the only way to resolve the issues of the sick and missing wildlife. To my mind the oil retained no biological power of any significance, and I believed that the hurly-burly of the cleanup and other human activity these past seasons had scattered a portion of the wildlife. The damage assessment researchers, whose reports fanned the Natives' anxiety about the oil, really didn't know what to think about the allegations of missing animals. Science had no model to explain changes on the broad scale of the Native evidence.

Exxon for its part disputed the Native assessment. Its people did not attack head-on, but expressed a what-will-they-think-of-next? air of irritation. While in Chenega, I interviewed the Exxon representative, Michael Barker. Barker was overseeing the cleanup around the village, but his regular employment for the company was as a field biologist. He had worked on the bald eagle rescue in '89. Thick-bearded and avuncular, Barker fielded my questions well. "I'm pretty green," he maintained. "I'm an environmentalist."

I asked him about Chenega's fears of the oil. "What they knew," he said, "was that 11 million gallons killed a lot of otters and birds. They didn't see that it was the effects on fur and feathers, the hypothermia more than the poison, that did it."

What of their perception that abundance was down?

"That's a hard one. I don't know how much was here before '89. They're so emotional. The shoreline and the sea are their garden, and you can't expect people to be objective about that. We've tried to alleviate their fears about the quality of the food, but about the quantity . . . I think the fear is exaggerated."

When I suggested that Exxon should work with the villagers

on the problem, Barker flared, "Why try to convince them? I don't know that it's a worthwhile exercise when somebody's mind is made up. Anyway, their lawyer in Anchorage made us agree—I am not allowed to talk to people in Chenega Bay about subsistence or about the wildlife we see."

Wanted: Alutiiq-speaking biologist and/or scientific Chugach. Legal training not required. I wished such a person had materialized after the disaster. Certainly I was not the one. I had strong feelings but no clear ideas. Whatever clarity I had came to me later, alone before the blinking screen, and did little good to Chenega Bay.

Much later I looked into the question of the harbor seals, the species of widest concern to the village. All sides agreed that seals had declined. Adopting Thoreau's approach A, I derived several sets of statistics, from interviews and published reports.

Hunters in the village said 1991 was the worst-ever year for seals. They had to go far in the Sound to get them. Only twenty-eight were reported taken, down from fifty-five the year before. Both harvests were well below the annual average of 165 when the villagers first came together, according to the prespill report by Stratton and Chisum.

The report also indicated the take before the earthquake. Older hunters were asked about the seal harvests of the early '60s. Astoundingly, Chenega took 1,600 seals annually. Although inflated no doubt by fond memory, the figure represented the efforts of only fourteen of the twenty-three households in the old village. The overall harvest probably exceeded 2,000 seals per year.

This hunt was not subsistence. Alaska Territory for years had a predator control program. Creatures that competed with the canneries for salmon, such as seals, sea lions and bald eagles, could be destroyed at will. By dynamiting their haulout sites, game wardens killed thousands of harbor seals off the Copper River Delta in the late '50s. The Sound's Natives were enlisted in the task. From Chenega the men would run their skiffs into Icy Bay, Port Nellie Juan, Port Bainbridge, where seals liked to haul out on the icebergs. Shooting close to shore, the hunter would grab the animal before it sank, or, that failing, snag it with a grappling hook from the bottom. He turned in the snout for a $3 bounty and kept the rest for his personal use.

After statehood in '59 the control program was expanded. At its height in 1965 some 60,000 harbor seals were destroyed in Alaska. Coincidentally a market for sealskin coats developed in Europe. With the hides bringing $15 apiece on top of the bounty, the animal became an important new source of income for

Chenega, supplementing the mainstays of fishing and cannery work.

Chugach stories tell that the prehistoric Chenegans had a passion for seal. Their faces were alleged to be darker than other Chugach because of all the grease. Their 1960s descendants certainly kept up the tradition. There was so much that villagers consumed less than half of the animal, presumably just the choice parts, which would be the breast, liver and flippers, and also some of the fat, which rendered as oil was the all-purpose condiment. Such use was wasteful, but paled before the florid waste of the state program. In the minds of the authorities the cash and food benefit to the coastal villages helped to justify the control program. In any event the harbor seal population in the Gulf of Alaska was very robust at the time and did not appear to be hurt. Yet here again Natives were being induced to kill an abundant marine mammal when it was not in their interests.

The decline of harbor seals since then was not unique to the Chenega area, nor to Prince William Sound, nor was it confined to the period of the oil spill. Since the late '70s the coast of the western Gulf of Alaska has seen seals disappear for no discernible reason. At Tugidak Island, near Kodiak, once the largest harbor seal haulout in the word, a plunge of 85 percent was observed between 1976 and 1988. I have referred to the parallel crisis among the Steller sea lions. The predator control program was long since over, and biologists doubt there could have been a delayed effect. A change in the pinnipeds' food supply, caused possibly by the burgeoning fishing fleet in the Gulf or by an unknown oceanographic alteration, may be driving this unsettling phenomenon.

Fish and Game started surveying the Sound's population of seals in 1984, the year Chenega Bay was settled. Not every seal was counted. Biologists established an aerial transect, a line flown around the Sound above two dozen haulout sites. The seals there on view gave a "trend count," against which to track future changes. The trend count was believed to represent between 10 and 30 percent of the Sound's seal population. That number in turn was very tentatively said to be 13,000 seals as of 1984.

The survey was conducted next in 1988. Assuming the trend count accurately recorded the shifts in the Sound's population, biologists reported a 40 percent loss of harbor seals in the course of just four years. The direction of the change was much easier to enumerate than the precise loss. In real terms it may have been as high as five thousand animals. At any rate, two disturbances were now in play to limit the seals, the subsistence take by the Sound's Natives and the mystery take emanating from the Gulf.

Ken Pitcher, who directed the surveys for Fish and Game, did not weigh the causes in his report. The problem was too new. He was not even aware of what the Native harvest was, he told me, adding that it could not have come close to the systemic disturbance as a contributor to the seals' decline. He was somewhat surprised to learn that the harvest was as high as 550 seals per year.

The harvest figure was an approximation of my own. Fish and Game did not have a good fix on the harvests in the late '80s. Since the '70s, federal biologists have been in charge of that aspect of the resource. The Marine Mammal Protection Act permitted Natives to engage in commercial harvests, that is, sell the hides of seals and others (the sea otters lately excepted), as long as there was no waste from the activity or threat to the species. No permits, bag limits or seasonal restrictions were imposed. The NOAA biologists had no means of judging a threat to the seal population, since they did not keep tallies of the take by the villages, nor did they conduct aerial censuses.

For the Sound, the only harvest data that was available was in the household surveys directed by Lee Stratton. But she didn't cover the villages concurrently. She had harvest information from Chenega Bay for the years between '84 and '86, from Tatitlek between '87 and '89, from Cordova in '85 and '88. The Native take from Valdez, though it would have been minor, was unknown. Thus the figure of 550 seals a year was my conservative guess. It was rounded down from the sum of Stratton's averages for Tatitlek (430), Chenega (165) and Cordova (50).

Gingerly, I set this figure next to the rough estimate of mortalities in the Sound from the oil spill: 200–300. Since only eighteen seal carcasses were ever recovered, the damage assessors calculated the losses on the basis of the change in the trend count afterward. They compared the '88 count to '89, and separated the numbers from the oiled western Sound from the unoiled east. The exercise was made more difficult by the background of population decline. The deaths they came up with were about half as many as the subsistence kill on the eve of the oil spill.

In my calculation, the oil spill ranked as the third disturbance to the harbor seal population in the Sound. The NRDA study, the report that framed public understanding of the animals' plight, did not handle it that way. The oil was put first as a cause, the background decline was given as a secondary problem, and the subsistence take was not mentioned at all. The omission struck me as wrong. The Sound's overall population of seals was now perhaps as low as two thousand. It was wrong to ignore one factor, to down-play another and to play up a third when people in Chenega were so painfully preoccupied with the poisoned missing animals.

Kathryn Frost, the principal investigator of harbor seals for Fish and Game, reminded me, once again, that the science she performed was not open-ended, that the law demanded she eval-uate only the damage of the spill. When I first questioned her, she was vague about the subsistence take in the Sound. When I ques-tioned her after I got the figures, she said, "I had access to those numbers. I did not introduce them in my reports because the data is very hard to work with. We don't know where in the Sound the harvests occurred. If the harvest was greater in the unoiled part of the Sound, as we have reason to think it was, then the losses of seals we showed in the oiled areas—compared to the unoiled—would be more important. The effect of the oil might be shown to be even greater. But scientifically, I decided to leave it alone."

Then she said a startling thing: "We're lucky that the spill stopped the harvest that year." She meant that the crisis had given the seal population some breathing room.

The hunters from the village of Tatitlek, who shot the majority of seals in the Sound, were diverted in '89. After the spill, Fish and Game suggested to the men that maybe they had been going a little too far. Some hunters used to come home on weekends from jobs in Valdez and take out their far-ranging boats and high-powered rifles. A man could shoot a dozen seals, strip off the skins for sale, save a little of the meat for his friends and family and be back at work on Monday.

Tatitlek seemed to heed the warning. Frost said that their seal harvest was low in 1990. It picked up in late '91, but only to a little over 100, a quarter as many seals as before. Meanwhile the pop-ulation stabilized, according to the trend counts. Numbers hadn't got back to the '88 level, by any means, but after 1990 they no longer appeared to be falling. Frost allowed that part of the reason may be the letup in subsistence.

So there it was. Not for the first time Chenega had the oppo-site understanding. To Chenega in proud isolation in the western Sound, the spill had ruined the seals, not saved them.

"To attribute it all [the decline] to the spill is human nature," Kathryn Frost said. "We expect Native people not to respond like the rest of us. But in that way they're no different. They haven't been there that long. They may have noticed it at one level, sub-liminally, beforehand. Whether they noticed it more afterward is a real difficult psychological question. I suspect that the answer is yes.

"But I have worked a long time with Native hunters and I don't consider the Native knowledge of wildlife to be just 'anecdotal.' They know things I could never hope to know. You have to put the two approaches together. You have to be feeding harvest data back to the people all the time. You say to them, 'It's your harvest, but here are our numbers. So what do you want to do?' "

She concluded with a warning to me. "Harvest information is very sensitive. It should not be repeated lightly. Non-Natives are very free to throw around the specifics of other people's lives. It's fun to make generalizations about other people, but it's not so fun when they're made about you."

Saint Paul said, "Speak the truth with love." I always took that to mean that of the two love was paramount. Love ought to be my goal on earth higher than truth. I expect that Gail Evanoff will give me a sneak preview of my judgment.

I have saved Gail Evanoff until last, but in truth she saved me until last. She seemed to avoid me during my stay in the village. I went by the corporation office several times to talk with her. At her desk she was crisp and formal. She had the facts and figures. "We need more cleanup on the anadromous streams," she said, "and more work to mitigate the continuous sheening." Then she would turn to another matter.

Finally I presented myself at her house. I came in with the lawyer and the land manager, who were amused as I tried to wait her out. Her son lay on the couch, watching a tape of *The Godfather* on a big-screen TV. Larry Evanoff passed through silently. With their two kids nearly grown, the couple had adopted a pair of infants and started all over.

She pulled up a chair to the kitchen table, an intense woman in jeans and a windbreaker, and coiled her legs beneath the chair. I scrutinized Evanoff as hard as she scrutinized me. She was short-coiffed and wore glasses. She smoked mentholated cigarettes. The coloring of the Inupiat Eskimo—she was not from the Sound—seemed more xanthic, less ruddy, than the Chugach/Aleut/Alutiiq type. Here was the spirit-owner of the oil spill.

"Science isn't the only truth," Evanoff said. "They challenge our statements when we report them. Do they think they are the gods of the environment?

"We don't need scientists to tell us that our beaches are getting better. We have got eyes. I can understand what they are trying to dispel, the fear of hydrocarbons. What we don't appreciate, though, is those *equations*, the parts per billion. What I want to know is . . . I have collected a whole bunch of desiccated crabs. Why did they die? Did they starve?"

We went outside. A nacreous sky lowered over Latouche. Evanoff showed me several of the desiccated crabs. The carapaces were indeed bleached and empty.

She kept an oily length of boom in her front yard, where she could see it every day. "It floated in from Sawmill Bay," she said. "You betcha I keep it. I just like to aggravate my memory, as if it weren't aggravated enough."

She brought up the seals that would no longer come. When I asked her about the general decline across the Gulf, Gail conceded it was possible. She had heard of it. She would rather talk about conditions closer to home, her village in the corner of the Sound, she the surrogate mother, so to speak, and Chenega the baby that was reborn through her labor and will.

"If the fish eat the oil they may be OK to eat, if we don't know it, but the beach life. . . . It truly cuts so much out of your life when you can't rely on the subsistence foods. Taking the kids out on the beach was a day of education. You know the octopus are found under these outctrops. You say, Here are their holes. You tell them the seed pods of the brown lilies are good to eat—they're our rice. Gathering these foods fosters our kinship, who we are."

We slapped at mosquitoes. The ceiling of fog was trying to lift from over the bay.

I missed a transition. Evanoff was talking about VCRs. "Because of that activity we're not with our families anymore. We sit on our couches watching *The Godfather.*" She laughed lightly for a second. "Here I want to bring myself cross-culture, to the Aleuts, and I see young mothers not starting out the way we used to. We've lost that tangible thing. Touching it, feeling it. This last Christmas was the most depressing that I can remember. Only one house had Native foods out. Pickled seal flipper! That was the favorite house."

The hermit thrush commiserated, so sweetly. The ravens laughed farther off. The snowfields peeked from Latouche. Very early the next morning Paul Kompkoff Sr. left with Paul Jr. to go fishing. I never wished him good-bye. People said the trip on the boat would do him good. He died of a heart attack eighteen months later. His heart was broken, it was said, broken by the oil spill.

For all that, Chenega Bay turned the corner in 1991. The subsistence activities of the village picked up. Following two off-years, the consumption of shellfish and octopus came back to the level of the mid-'80s, according to Fish and Game's 1991–92 household survey. The overall harvest amount came back too, although the proportions had shifted, with the salmon, halibut and rockfish up, and the seals and sea lions sharply down. It stood to reason.

Though people remained concerned about contamination, the bottom line was that imported chicken and hamburger still cost $5 a pound.

Having been asked so often who they were and what they had lost, and having recollected and reformulated it so many times, unwittingly the villagers invigorated their old selves. The Native people absorbed another violent jolt at the plate boundary of culture, but perhaps it woke them up to what they were losing.

On another front they won a cultural victory. As I left Chenega, a district court judge in Anchorage was deciding in favor of the Natives in the matter of the harvest of sea otters. In July of '91 the court struck down the FWS's regulation against the sale of Native handicrafts. The judge ruled that as long as the Natives did not go into factory-style manufacturing, they were permitted to make items of otter fur and sell them to whomever would buy.

Conservation groups appealed the decision but were denied. The ruling forced the FWS to take seriously the Alaska Sea Otter Commission. This was a Native organization that had sought official recognition as a comanager with the government of the resource. The Service and the Native group now had no choice but to cooperate, the one to monitor the harvest scientifically, the other to monitor the subsistence by people's good sense. The otter and the Native had a lot of catching up to do.

PRINCE WILLIAM SOUND ITINERARY
July 2, 1991
Exxon Company, U.S.A.

John Wilkinson—Exxon
Karsten Rodvik—Exxon
Marguerite Holloway—*Scientific American*
Jeff Wheelwright—Book Author—Simon & Schuster

Depart Anchorage—7 A.M.
• Chenega (pick up Jeff Wheelwright)
• Bainbridge Island (BA 6 & 7)
• Latouche Island—Sleepy Bay (LA 18)
• Knight Island—Point Helen (KN 405A)
• Knight Island—Bay of Isles (KN 135B)
• Eleanor Island—Northwest Bay (EL 52B)—LUNCH
• Smith Island—"Quayle Beach" (SM 5B)
• Cordova (drop off Jeff Wheelwright)
Arrive Anchorage—between 3 and 4 P.M.

IT WAS ONE OF THOSE DAYS in the Sound when you think you'll be weathered in forever, but then it lifts enough for the aircraft to get in and get you out. Today after a dim beginning, the daylight kept building and surprisingly building over the village of Chenega Bay. The itinerary was set back only four hours. When the helicopter took off and turned north, the sky was a high vibrant blue. The helo cast its pulsating shadow onto banks of fog low along the shore, and the shadow was ringed by a traveling rainbow.

Exxon's Rodvik was the public affairs contact. Wilkinson was knowledgeable about bioremediation, the bug-boosting technique and the company's last hurrah of the cleanup. Because of our late start our guides decided to cut out the Bainbridge and Knight Island cleanup inspections. We headed directly to Eleanor.

For the fourth time in twenty months, I stepped onto the pocket beach, the segment dubbed EL 52B, in the west arm of Northwest Bay. It looked almost entirely clean, but then it had looked good the last two times. Our hosts did not press, but as we ate sandwiches on a log, Wilkinson suggested that bioremediation, if accompanied by proper tilling of the beach sediments, could degrade up to 90 percent of the oil in three years. I suggested that whether or not the stimulation helped, the bacteria would consume 100 percent of the oil in due course.

The company position was that the Sound in 1991 was "essentially cleansed" and "effectively recovered." Although I disliked the wording, I had arrived at the same conclusion. As Evanoff resented the reassurances of scientists, I did not care to be sold on recovery by Exxon. I had eyes.

Exxon's three biological consultants, who were marine pollution specialists from Great Britain, also toured the Sound in '91. They announced that they saw a lot of sea otters, among other evidence that they gave of the system's recovery. The company issued a brochure on the trio's observations. But meanwhile it guarded real data on the sea otter population. Its private researcher was David Garshelis, a wildlife biologist from Minnesota.

A decade earlier Garshelis wrote his Ph.D. thesis on the otters of Prince William Sound. He helped investigate the animals' feeding habits and also the collapse of the Dungeness crab fishery around Cordova. His credentials to do damage assessment on otters were as solid as anyone's, only he went with the Exxon side. "That I had qualms going in is an understatement," he said. "At the time I was one of the people refusing to buy Exxon gas. But they challenged me to find any long-lasting effects."

Garshelis and his team counted otters around several islands and mainland sections in 1990 and 1991. He failed to find losses in the spill zone, except at one island in the first year afterward. In general he counted gains over the last census, which had been taken by the Fish and Wildlife Service in 1984 and '85. How could this be? If his numbers were correct, the population in the west must have been on the rise since '84 (if more slowly than in the east), so that the mortalities from the spill would not register.

The government's NRDA study, by contrast, found one third *fewer* sea otters in the western Sound than in 1984. Douglas Burn, who ran a series of boat surveys for the FWS, replicated the earlier spotting methods more closely than Garshelis did, and he surveyed a greater number of shoreline segments.

Burn said Garshelis's study area was much too small to be representative of the population as a whole. Meanwhile he brooked criticism from the government peer reviewers, who caused him to retreat from his finding that otter numbers were still slipping in the western Sound. Still, as of 1991 Burn was reporting that the population had not shown any gain in two years.

Garshelis tried to understand why the two studies were far apart. He was embarrassed that his Exxon-sponsored work should be so contrary to that of the FWS, as if he were answering to the company's position on recovery. Contemptuous of the rosy impressions of the three Britons regarding the sea otters, he feared that his own report would be dismissed for the same bias. When he analyzed his rival's data, however, he felt better. Garshelis claimed that, in zones where they overlapped, Burn had counted the same number of otters as he had.

Comparing the opposing conclusions, I threw up my hands. The two researchers had defined the Sound differently. They had started with different parts, within which they created oiled zones of differing dimensions. They assumed that otters within their oiled zones could be compared with otters within unoiled zones, as if the animals were as sessile as mussels, and didn't travel about. Neither researcher had repeated the prespill survey in full—itself an incomplete snapshot of the Sound that was five years out of date by the time the spill happened.

The sea otters were reduced by the number of the carcasses that were recovered plus an unknown number more. Determining the toll by census afterward was an extremely uncertain exercise— and pointless to argue over. Garshelis said, "The engineers at Exxon shake their heads over the disparities. They've made me wonder—are we wildlife biologists really scientists?"

However many otters managed to dodge a bullet in the spring of '89, they were not necessarily spared the repercussions. I mean the potential tax on health, reproduction and survival. Garshelis made only passing attempts to get at the chronic effects of the oil; he had no permits to implant transmitters for tracking the animals. The government had transmitters and put a lot into this question. According to Bob Spies, the government's chief scientist, the combination of acute effects (the initial mortalities) and sublethal effects (most probably from exposure to hydrocarbons) had brought about a population decline of sea otters in the Sound.

Spies drew upon a compendium of FWS investigations called Marine Mammal Study Number 6. Besides estimating the initial mortalities and making population counts, Marine Mammal 6 looked at the otters' uptake of hydrocarbons, blood chemistry, choice of diet, winter-killed carcasses, pupping productivity, juvenile survival—a host of approaches. Marine Mammal 6 was huge, and like a mutating organism, it begat ever larger versions of itself over time, each stamped preliminary, none quite settled in shape. MM6 was big enough to have spawned a major battle at its core, as contract and staff biologists bit one another's backs over issues deriving mainly from their personalities. I won't detail the bitter politics.

I have said the point was to determine whether oil was taking a toll on the otters, but of course the point was not whether, but how. The best hits, besides Burn's census figures, were: 1) A greater number of juvenile otters appeared to survive in the east than in the west during the winter of '90–'91. Specifically, eight of twenty-two animals with implanted transmitters survived in the east, versus only five of thirty-nine in the west, and 2) Collections of otter carcasses in the spring of 1990 and again in '91 showed a greater proportion of prime-age animals dead over the winter in the western Sound than was considered normal.

There were puzzling counterhits in MM 6 as well, such as the fact that female adults in the oiled west evinced greater survival than those in the east, which was to say that the otters in the east took an inexplicable turn down, according to the transmitter signals. The contract biologists attributed this to a disease possibly loosed from the rescue centers.

In short, scenarios were sketched, but no hydrocarbon data, no bile or fat metabolites, no lesions, etc. indicating a link to the oil were ever measured in the sea otters in the wild. Moreover, neither trend 1) nor 2) continued beyond '91. Which brought one back to Burn and Garshelis, contesting the number of otters they tallied from the boat. Recently Spies said to me that he had not changed his opinion about the sea otters, but that "a recovery may be going on that we haven't yet detected."

What was biological recovery? It was a concept of some latitude. I had collected a sheaf of academic definitions pertaining to marine ecosystems after oil spills. All the specialists agreed on one thing: A return to the status quo ante was not possible and not required. The recovery of a marine system did not depend on the replacement of the original number of mussels, loons, sea otters, etc., in the exact same locations they were before an oil spill.

The National Academy of Sciences, in *Oil in the Sea*, held that recovery occurred when there was the same general range of life and biomass as before. This was the loosest definition. It stipulated only a return to the *type* of community, while allowing for patchiness and variations among the numbers of plants and animals.

Exxon's three British consultants issued a more argumentative definition: "Recovery is marked by the re-establishment of a healthy biological community in which the plants and animals characteristic of that community are present and functioning normally. It may not have the same composition or age structure as that which was present before the damage, and will continue to show change and further development. It is impossible to say whether an ecosystem that has recovered from an oil spill is the same as, or different from, that which would have persisted in the absence of the spill." The company maintained that by these criteria the Sound had recovered by the spring of 1991.

The Exxon Valdez Oil Spill Trustees (the Alaska and federal representatives responsible for "restoring" the Sound after the determination and settlement of damages) declared: "In a scientific sense, full ecological recovery has been achieved when the pre-spill flora and fauna are again present, healthy and productive, and there is a full complement of age classes." The government's criteria were more exacting than Exxon's. It did not constitute recovery when juvenile chitons or juvenile sea otters replaced the mature animals that had been killed. Individual populations must return to their former distributions of age and reproductive function. Recovery, in other words, was closer to the status quo ante than Exxon viewed it. And if recovery in the Sound was incomplete, as the ecosystem healed slowly, then the Trustees had reason to assist nature with their "restoration."

Recovery implied a definition of injury and a passage of time. The less rigorously one defined the injuries, and the more generally one defined recovery, the shorter would be the return to normalcy—and vice versa. Howard Feder, an experienced University of Alaska biologist, put it most simply when I talked to him nine months after the spill. "There are certain people," he said, "who will argue that the Sound will be ruined forever. And there'll be others who will say, Give it a few years and it will recover. And they will be arguing about this until one day they'll both notice that it has recovered."

There was a second forum in which to debate recovery, and that was to make the oil the focus instead of the ecosystem. Hydrocarbons persisting in the biological fabric of the Sound might possibly be doing harm. Exxon did not endorse this line of thinking. It led inevitably to the individual animal, to the one otter or the one chiton battling hydrocarbons in its system. The leader of Exxon's trio of experts, Dr. Robert Clark, believed this missed the point of recovery. "The question should be asked," said Clark in a presentation in Anchorage, "Can the organisms carry on, can they reproduce with oil on board? If so, the sublethal effects are not that significant. The organism still has its part in the ecosystem."

The most sensitive hydrocarbon test that was employed during the spill was John Stegeman's assay for MFO induction in fish. MFO, it will be recalled, is the class of enzymes that are activated in the liver to help rid the organism of aromatic hydrocarbons and toxins. When I went to see biochemist Stegeman at Woods Hole, he was no alarmist about oil pollution, but he entertained the idea that the recovery of organisms was not complete until the readings of MFO went down to zero.

"If you're sick," Stegeman said, "you're fully recovered when you have no more symptoms."

I said, "I don't know if my liver is still being affected from the bit of oil I swallowed on Block Island. I maintain that I have recovered."

Stegeman replied he could test me (I might not survive the test), and he might learn whether my liver was still exposed. "If the enzyme is being induced," he repeated, "you're still symptomatic. As long as there is exposure, there is a chance for something bad to be happening. That's not recovery." Among the remote chances, incalculable even by risk assessment, was incipient liver cancer.

In this book I have argued that the ability of science to detect and measure hydrocarbons and their metabolites far exceeded science's ability to know what to make of the measurements. The measurements actually impeded understanding. There was the acute phase of the oil spill, which was soon over in the Sound, and now the chronic phase, whose effects were unproved, most likely unprovable and diminishing fast into the background. That was the end of it as far as I was concerned. Someone else might wait for the seaweed sporelings to mature fully on the scrubbed rocks, or for the sea otters to expand again. I saw recovery faute de mieux. Such were my thoughts on my last day in the Prince William Sound.

The helicopter landed at Sleepy Bay on Latouche, where the

work crew was engaged in spraying fertilizer upon freshly tilled cobbles. LA 18 was no EL 52B. It suffered probably the heaviest penetration of the spill. The surface wasn't marked anymore, but researchers would be coming here for the rest the century to find subsurface contamination. Near the waterline, the boulders overturned by a belching backhoe were black. The members of the bioremediation team wore white suits and masks against the spray. It looked and smelled like the corpse of the disaster was being disinterred.

Sleepy Bay had a second distinction. It had the most worked-over, worried-over salmon stream in Prince William Sound. Each year the stream shifted its course, making a new mouth through the beach to the bay, and exposing its salmon eggs and fry to a new skein of oil. The caretaker of the stream was Mark Kuwada, Fish and Game's cleanup coordinator, who happened to be on-site today. After many exchanges on the telephone, it was a treat to meet him in person.

I broke off from our party. Kuwada complained about Exxon's work. He was scornful of the "net environmental benefit analysis" by which cleanup decisions were made. "It's weird science," he growled. "In meetings they jam NEBA down our throats." He remained an unreconstructed foe of the oil when other officials had given up. Kuwada wanted it out, all of it, the way Chenega wanted it out. If it were up to him, he would hunt it down to the last flicker of MFO.

"People say that the sublethal effects in salmon won't show up in the population, and therefore it wasn't a disaster," he said. "Well, we dropped a bomb on Hiroshima and that didn't have an effect on the growth of the Japanese population. Does that mean it wasn't a disaster?" For all of his passion he did not take himself too seriously, which made his passion all the more admirable. He allowed, "The people who are still out here, after this amount of time, are the ones who really care."

We went to the next stop. Approaching Smith Island in the center in the Sound, I had the sense, for the first time in my travels, that Prince William Sound was very small. The peaks that for two years bristled like a high enfilade now put me in mind of a white picket fence around a blue pool.

Quayle Beach on Smith got its name when the vice president landed here in May of '89. It was so gooey and hellish that a long wooden boardwalk was built expressly for him. The crews flushed mousse down to the waterline for Quayle's approval, and after he left they released most of the oil from the boom, just let it go offshore to come back in on the next tide. Four months later environmentalists sent dirty gravel from Smith to each member of Congress as evidence of the cleanup's failure.

Then unexpectedly, Quayle Beach became a showplace for the cleansing power of the winter storms. The strand, slightly scalloped, has a northern exposure. The fetch is seven miles to Naked Island, although Naked on this clear day seemed to lie close. After two winters of pounding, no oil was on the rocks, but there were some rubbery smudges in crevices below, and sometimes a rainbow reflection when you tilted your head to a tide pool. The shoreline was not treated in 1991.

An oystercatcher scurried and shrieked. The Sound was waveless, lambent, beneath a strong sun that was almost narcotic. We unzipped our orange Mustang suits to our T-shirts and strolled around, kicking now and again at the rounded stones.

The tour finished, we headed east to Cordova. When we were halfway there I saw something chilling on the flanks of the Sound, a sight I had never seen. A clear-cut of timber, a light-green patch of baldness glaring in the distance. The cutting was taking place on stands of spruce and hemlock owned by the Tatitlek corporation on Knowles Head.

The U.S. Congress, as a special break to the Natives, passed a measure in the late '80s allowing the regional and village corporations to gain extra income from their coastal forests. The corporations sold timber rights to loggers with whom they were in partnership. The timber was let go at a loss, because current prices were less than the value estimated for wood at the time the land was conveyed to the Natives. Then the corporations sold these paper losses to Outside companies, which used them to offset their federal tax bills. The Natives still controlled the timber. Lately they and their partners had begun to cut logs for sale abroad, or for milling at the struggling Chugach sawmill in Seward.

Not all the Natives agreed that the land should be exploited this way. The head of the Tatitlek tribal council, for instance, was disturbed by the clear-cut spreading over the ridgeline from Knowles Bay. He told me it was ugly as hell. But the corporation was charged to make earnings for shareholders.

In the far eastern Sound the Eyak corporation was cutting too. The modern Eyaks owned about 100,000 acres. The tracts being logged in 1991 were a ways out of town, but the corporation had plans to take 1,000 acres of trees from the watershed of Eyak Lake. Opponents in Cordova called the Eyak logging a slow-moving oil spill. The corporation president, who had been an outspoken critic of Exxon, replied that she liked the look of the clear-cuts. She said it opened the view so that she could take in the full beauty of the Native lands.

Because of the pressure from environmental groups, the Native corporations stood at the head of the line to receive "restoration" funds. The government was about to get a load of money from Exxon. Buying back timber rights from the Natives was as good a way to spend it as any, however flimsy the biological connections from the oil in the sea to the woods on the market. The corporations weren't shutting down their chainsaws in the interim. "Natives hold trees hostage" was a grumpy headline of the day. Whatever they did, they couldn't win.

White men have different ways of making an evaluation. You have your methods for how you're going to tell your story. I would have my own methods. Fiction or nonfiction, it doesn't matter. If it were me, I would write it from my personal feelings and I wouldn't take it from any other sources.

—HENRY MAKARKA, EYAK ELDER

THE LAKE TODAY was the same color as the sea, unusual for Eyak. When the helicopter came over the lake, we left the Sound. The flats lay ahead.

The Delta of the Eyaks is a dramatic place. It is hard by the Sound, yet the two environments could hardly be more different. They vibrate in one's eyes like complementary colors: the steep and misty Sound, all deep blues, dark greens and grays, against the tawny Delta marsh, as flat as a savanna, with distant copses of trees, pale willow scrub, streaks of fireweed, and gray-braided channels cutting through soft gray dunes.

Yet the Delta ignores the Sound. It is a vast foreground, a half million acres, that funnels toward the interior. I had flown over, driven into the Delta many times. At the point where one first senses the funnel to the north, the red-rimmed mountains with their avalanche chutes and ice lips are still far off, but they are rising in an implacable line on either side. Proceeding, one feels a mounting squeeze on the chest from the linear perspective. From high in the Copper River basin, the wind whips glacial grit head-on.

From the flats looking west, back toward Cordova, one sees a road snaking through the lower peaks bordering the Sound. The first time I rode from the airport toward the town, two years earlier, the disaster was still sharp, but I couldn't believe my good fortune to be in this place. The road planed above marsh and ponds, past the shrouded domes of beaver lodges. The shrubs by the side were just about to leaf. Through the streaked windshield I glimpsed something looming, something half veiled in the clouds. The Delta was as flat as a platter, upon which was being presented to me a mountain. The mountain bared its snowy shoulders like a bold bride to a nervous groom. Then it went by, and the view of the Sound approaching made me so high with excitement that I became a little frightened.

The helicopter set down at the airport. I had my equilibrium under control now, but I can't say that my happiness to be working on the coast of Alaska did not influence my studies and observations. What pleased me most were the ironies and auguries. I mean of man and nature, man above nature, and man, poor bird, within nature. Here is one other:

To the south the Delta meets the Gulf of Alaska. The front is screened by shallows and large sandbars, which are constituted of organic material and mountain rock ground up by the glaciers. The Copper River brings down tons of fresh supplies and reworks the area constantly, but periodically the whole game is reset by tectonics. There are tree stumps 1,500 years old among the sandbars. It is thought that the Delta gets uplifted, the forest extends toward the Gulf, the land relaxes from the shock and as it subsides the sea moves in and restores the muck and marsh. The river for all its power is fiddling on a much smaller scale.

When the Delta thaws in the spring, the area hosts the largest migration of shorebirds in the Western Hemisphere. This is why many biologists were relieved when the spill went west. Dunlins and sandpipers rest and feed here a few days before moving north. But one bird that comes and stays, making the Delta its summer home for breeding, is the dusky Canada goose. The dusky is an uncommon subspecies of the Canada goose that is common (some say too common) in the Lower 48.

The Canada goose is considered to have nine subspecies. There is no master race, only subspecies making different-sized populations. By definition, the subspecies of geese are physically capable of breeding with one another. When and if that should happen, the two strains that mated would begin to merge. Conversely, if the population of a subspecies became split geographically, with some geese migrating to one place and some to another, and if the two halves started breeding separately and stopped exchanging genes, then before long (centuries) their descendants might look a little different from each other. At that point a scientist could come and declare that two subspecies existed where there used to be one.

Something like that occurred in the case of the dusky. It got split off, and today the subspecies nests only in the Copper River Delta of Alaska, to which it migrates from wintering grounds in northwestern Oregon and southwestern Washington.

To me the differences from the goose of Massachusetts were not very noticeable. The dusky *is* darker overall, and the breast feathers—this is how carefully the specialists look—are slightly more golden than another dark subspecies of the Pacific Northwest, the Vancouver Canada goose. In the dialectic of taxonomy, lumpers do battle with splitters. The splitters, carving out fiefs, have lately carried it to the lumpers, who want to make things simpler. Although the lumpers say that the dusky and the Vancouver should be considered one subspecies, the splitters are holding firm to two.

In 1989 I attended a symposium in Cordova on the ecology of the Delta. A researcher of avian DNA gave a lecture on the unusual similarity, in terms of chromosomal patterns, among the nine subspecies of Canada goose. A couple of U.S. Forest Service biologists spoke up. They took exception to the researcher's analysis, because it implied that the Forest Service's concern for the dusky Canada goose was myopic. This really was just a goose, the geneticist seemed to suggest. It's just a Canada goose that breeds somewhere where other Canada geese are not breeding.

About the Forest Service concern for the bird. No reader should be surprised that the earthquake was involved. The dusky goose in the 1980s was perceived to be on the ropes because of what the earthquake caused to happen to its nesting habitat.

The Delta went up about six feet in 1964. Suddenly there was a new front of mud, reaching several miles further into the Gulf. Broad stumps from the past came up to air. Behind the new front, the old beach line began to dry out. The wetlands supported by tidal flooding fell under the freshwater manipulations of the river. New ponds formed. At the old boundaries between salt marsh and river slough, low sedges and shrubs started giving way to tall shrubs and thickets, the scouts sent ahead by the upland forest. It was a friendly takeover of habitat, and gradual enough for most creatures to tolerate, but the stubborn dusky appeared to get hurt.

The dusky usually nested in the open. The sweetgale shrubs and the alder and willow thickets obscured its view of predators. The coyotes and especially the bears, which like cover anyway, became more abundant as the brush thickened on the Delta. Probably they were able to sneak closer and menace the nests and nestlings more successfully than before.

Now it might be asked why the duskies did not move seaward,

and colonize the new ground, like the other creatures and vegetation that required space. (Likewise, why didn't intertidal animals, the snails, crabs and starfish on the cobble beaches of the
Sound, simply migrate down the beach to the new waterline in '64,
instead of staying high and dry to die?) In fact, the population of
the dusky goose gained at first, because new habitat opened up and
the old habitat was still being used, though slowly changing in favor
of the predators.

In 1981 the production from the nests fell sharply. Goslings
weren't seen on the Delta. Alaska Fish and Game biologists, who
had been monitoring the birds, were not caught unawares. Lead
researcher Bruce Campbell recalled, "My predecessors speculated
that the habitat would change from the quake and we'd have this
result. But when I warned that something was going wrong, nobody listened." Then the dusky population started to go down
dramatically. From a prequake high of almost 30,000 the geese
declined, according to a count taken one winter in the mid-'80s, to
under 10,000.

Wildlife biologists in Oregon and Washington, who had resisted Campbell, awoke to the problem. The trouble of the geese
might not have become an issue had not the birds been hunted in
those states during the winter. Prior to the earthquake, hunting
pressure was the principal disturbance limiting the population.
Several thousand duskies were taken per year. Game managers
thought they had done a pretty good job, balancing the needs of
fowlers with the needs of the birds, but then the habitat change in
Alaska appeared to have upset the arrangement. For several years
the hunters shot geese that were not being replaced, cutting the
population in half. Now a harvest quota was imposed, and hunters
in the Northwest groused because of the short season. There was
pressure to help the goose on the Delta.

Fish and Game's Campbell issued a report in 1988. Whereas
the primary cause of nest loss before '64 was tidal flooding, Campbell demonstrated that predation was the main problem now. The
bears and coyotes were hitting the nests hard, although he found
the losses were as great from the open nests as from the cloaked
ones.

Meanwhile, the U.S. Forest Service, the Delta's manager,
spent hundreds of thousands of dollars on artificial nests. A half
dozen designs, and some 600 structures in all, were put out in open
habitat. The most successful model was a mini-island of fiberglass.
It floated in the center of the new freshwater ponds, anchored to
the bottom. When a dusky pair adapted to it, the mammalian
predators were foiled, if not the seagulls and jaegers, the avian

predators. And the goose population stopped falling by '89. Thus, at the symposium in Cordova, the biologists who objected to the DNA findings aspersing the dusky's uniqueness were the same biologists who worked on the artificial nest program.

In 1991 the dusky population was found to be up to almost 15,000 in Oregon and Washington. About 400 artificial nests were still in place on the flats. Were the safer nests the reason for the improvement, or was it that the total bag of duskies permitted in Washington State was only forty birds per year? Was another factor at work as well?

Pat Miller, a biologist for the Washington Department of Wildlife, worked in Alaska for parts of five summers, capturing and banding the geese. He was in Cordova in '91 to put leg bands on duskies as I was leaving. Though he was impressed that the flocks had rebounded, he did not attribute it to the nesting program of the Forest Service or to better management of hunters in the Northwest. Miller observed a dramatic phenomenon upon the flats—beavers. The beavers were exploding. They turned sloughs into large ponds. They began to clear-cut the willow around the levees, opening up the habitat. The flooding behind their dams killed tall brush used for cover by bears. From the airplane Miller saw the beavers helping the geese by driving back the growth that had been spawned by the earthquake. When he got home to Washington, he gave a talk on the turnaround of the bird to a wildlife group. A local reporter wrote it up, and the story was picked up by the *Anchorage Daily News*, and so I read the news by subscription in Massachusetts: "Alaska Beavers Aid Northwest Hunters."

The headline was anthropocentric but the article delighted me. It was the moral of my story. People had measured them and declared them a special species but people could not do anything for the geese except to stop shooting them. The beavers organized their recovery. It was so neat I didn't want to poke at it.

"If you're asking do I have any data on the beaver hypothesis, no I do not," Pat Miller said frostily. "You know, a talk at a sportsmen's club is not the same thing as a peer-reviewed presentation in a journal." He took it a little hard, I thought, but probably because biologists from the Forest Service in Alaska had chided him over the story.

Dan Logan, the Forest Service district biologist, said Miller's was a great scenario—and Logan cheered the beavers on—but the effect of the animals on Delta habitat, and on the improved nesting success of the duskies, just hadn't been studied. He wished he knew if it were true. He wished he had the money for a graduate student to look into it.

Fish and Game's Campbell, to whom all the biologists deferred, was mostly on Miller's side. He was not persuaded by the evidence for the artificial nests. He had no hard evidence for the beavers' work either, but he knew that the brown bears had backed off from the Delta at about the time the goose population had turned around. Predation was way down. He could construe no reason why the bears would desist unless their habitat had been rendered less suitable. The beavers were the most likely agents of that change, and if the goose had benefited, so be it.

Uncertainties, uncertainties. At least I was out on the Delta, with a creature untainted by the oil spill.

But the geese did not escape. In 1992 Logan and the Forest Service applied for funding from the restoration budget. The biologists proposed to study the duskies in the context of the mystery geese of Prince William Sound. What was this? Geese within the Sound? Apparently some darkish Canada geese, no more than a few thousand, nested in the pools on the high boggy shoulders of some of the islands. No geneticist or taxonomist had ever checked the birds out. Were they duskies? Were they the Vancouver subspecies? Were they something else?

It would matter to policy-makers. If Prince William Sound had duskies, the duskies might have been hurt by the oil. Habitat protection might be in order. Or if they were duskies and it was decided they were *not* hurt, hunters would say that the range and population of the bird were greater than believed. They would want the bag limits loosened. Or if the goose were found to be a new Canada goose altogether, the tenth and rarest subspecies, conservationists might promote it for the endangered species list. . . . Yikes.

Funding to study the birds was denied. Bruce Campbell was wistful, although he had resolved to keep away from spill research. He was a man for basic science.

"We need to know what those geese are," Campbell said. "We just need to know."

Afterword

NATURE WENT ON turning and turning, but one part of it was stuck, literally frozen in place. For more than three years the government held the animal carcasses in the trailer morgues. When the charges against the oil company were settled, officials had no more use for the evidence. It could be disposed of. First, university scientists and museum curators from around the country were invited to come help themselves. The sea otters and birds, though ruined by oiling and thawing, had value to researchers and to the public for their skeletons.

In October 1992, the prospective new owners, wearing respirators and rubber gloves, made their selections at the facility of the Sure-Way Incineration Company in Anchorage. Thousands of seabirds, hundreds of sea otters and a score of other creatures were left over. The odds and ends of the disaster included one (1) hermit thrush, one (1) Canada goose and one (1) oil-blackened poodle. All went up the chimney to their rest.

Acknowledgments

My wife, Mia, who introduced me to Alaska in the early '80s, suggested that I do this book. It involved a career change of some risk. She has never wavered in her support.

Although most of the publishing world considered the *Exxon Valdez* a short-order disaster, best served while hot, Esther Newberg, my literary agent, and Alice Mayhew, my editor, saw merit in a broad study of Prince William Sound. Information was both voluminous and hard to come by, and I made slow progress at first. Alice Mayhew did not doubt that I would reach my goal. I am grateful for her unswerving determination and guidance, and for the able assistance at Simon & Schuster of Sarah Baker. Esther Newberg was unflappable throughout.

My book draws upon hundreds of interviews and an array of scientific literature. I thank all those who put aside their pressing business to talk to me and all those who sent me reprints of their work. The research that I used includes academic texts, articles from peer-reviewed journals and reports from the so-called gray literature of science, no less valuable. I decided against footnotes, citations and uniform attributions within the text, because I did not wish to overload the general reader. The interviewees and bibliography are given by chapter in the Sources section.

Three scientists deserve special mention. They took innumerable calls and patiently answered my questions, sometimes the same questions in successive calls, until I got it right. Subsequently they reviewed portions of my manuscript and offered corrections and suggestions. My profound thanks to Robert Spies, chief scientist for the Exxon Valdez Oil Spill Trustee Council; Douglas Wolfe, chief of the Bioeffects Assessment Branch of the National Oceanic and Atmospheric Administration; and James Payne, director of research, Sound Environmental Services, Inc. They are not responsible for any errors of fact or interpretation that remain.

A dozen other people I looked to frequently. I thank Bruce Batten, Public Affairs, U.S. Fish and Wildlife Service; James Brady, Division of Commercial Fisheries, Alaska Department of Fish and Game; Gail Evanoff, Chenega Village Corporation; James Fall, Division of Subsistence, ADF&G; David Kennedy and John Robinson, Hazardous Materials Response and Assessment Division, NOAA; Dennis Lees and Jonathan Houghton, biological consultants to NOAA/HMRAD; Jacqueline Michel, Research Planning, Inc.; Karsten Rodvik, Public Affairs, Exxon Company, USA; Usha Varanasi, Environmental Conservation Division, NOAA; and Nathaniel Wheelwright, professor of biology, Bowdoin College.

I do not cite articles or broadcasts of the news media regarding the oil spill because for the most part these were used to check my own fact-finding. I did take more than once, however, from the excellent reporting of Charles Wohlforth, Craig Medred and Hal Bernton of the *Anchorage Daily News*. Two books about the *Exxon Valdez* have been published, unread as yet by me.

The following men and women, of various affiliations, provided logistical help and general encouragement, which I much appreciated: Henry Beathard, Dave Beck, Nancy Bird, Joe Bridgman, Rick Burroughs, Kelly Carlisle, Robert Clarke, Cece Crowe, Dolores Nonella Crowley, John Crowley, Nan Elliot, L. J. Evans, Tasha Galaktionoff, David Grimes, Vivian Hamilton, Lori Harris, Kim Heron, Anne Hollister, Matthew Jamin, Dee Lane, Steven Levi, Barbara Logan, Pat Lynn, Heather McCarty, Max McCarty, Marie Motschman, Brian O'Neill, Jeff and Kim Park, Tima Priess, Steve Provant, Patricia Ryan, Kate Sexton, Linda Sievers, Helen Stockholm, Richard Stolley, Gary and Laurel Thompson, Peg Thompson, Kelley Weaverling.

Finally I wish to acknowledge two men whose gentle wisdom inspired me and who died during the course of my writing: Paul Kompkoff Sr. and Loudon Wainwright. And a third, who died years earlier, Joseph Wheelwright Sewall. He was on a long passage from New England to Alaska, not unlike mine, but made only halfway.

—J.W.

Sources

INTRODUCTION

1. INTERVIEWS
Robert Clark, National Oceanic and Atmospheric Adminstration (NOAA)
William Gronlund, NOAA
Alan Maki, Exxon

1: THE EARTHQUAKE AND THE ORANGUTAN

1. INTERVIEWS
James Brady, Alaska Department of Fish and Game (ADF&G)
Michael Castellini, University of Alaska–Fairbanks (UAF)
R. Ted Cooney, UAF
Wayne Donaldson, ADF&G
Gregg Erickson, consultant, ADF&G
James Estes, U.S. Fish and Wildlife Service (FWS)
Howard Feder, UAF
Hal Geiger, ADF&G
David Halpern, California Institute of Technology
Mohammad Hameedi, National Oceanic and Atmospheric Adminstration (NOAA)
Scott Hatch, FWS
Cecil Hoffmann, U.S. Department of Interior
Peter Holm, Prince William Sound Aquaculture Corp. (PWSAC)
Glenn Juday, UAF
Armin Koernig, PWSAC (retired)
Rikk Kvitek, Moss Landing Marine Laboratories
Dennis Lees, consultant, NOAA
Thomas Loughlin, NOAA
Lloyd Lowry, ADF&G
Carol-Ann Manen, NOAA
Kenneth Mann, Bedford Institute of Oceanography
Bruce McCain, NOAA
C. Peter McRoy, UAF
Jacqueline Michel, consultant, NOAA
Phillip Mundy, consultant, Exxon Valdez Trustee Council
Steven Nelson, U.S. Geological Survey (USGS)
Brenda Norcross, UAF
A. J. Paul, UAF
Eugene Pavia, Alaska Department of Environmental Conservation (ADEC)
Charles Peterson, University of North Carolina
George Plafker, USGS
John Robinson, NOAA
Thomas Royer, UAF
Robert Roys, ADF&G (retired)
Samuel Sharr, ADF&G
David Shaw, UAF
Robert Spies, consultant, Exxon Valdez Trustee Council
Bradley Stevens, NOAA
Robert Vadas, University of Maine
Alex Wertheimer, NOAA
Mark Willette, ADF&G
Gregory Winter, ADEC
Douglas Wolfe, NOAA

2. BOOKS, REPORTS AND ARTICLES

Adams, Kenneth. 1989. "Impacts upon Fisheries of Prince William Sound and Nearby Waters Caused by the *Exxon Valdez* Oil Spill." Testimony presented to the House Interior Subcommittee on Water, Power and Offshore Energy Resources, Valdez, Alaska, May 7, 1989.

Alaska Department of Fish and Game, Division of Commercial Fisheries. 1988, 1989, 1990, 1991, 1992. *Annual Finfish Management Report, Prince William Sound Area*.

Alaska Department of Fish and Game. 1989. *Wildlife Notebook Series*. Juneau: Alaska Department of Fish and Game.

Arctic Environmental Information and Data Center. 1991. *A Field Guide to Prince William Sound*. Anchorage: University of Alaska.

Barr, Lou, and Nancy Barr. 1983. *Under Alaskan Seas: The Shallow Water Marine Invertebrates*. Anchorage: Alaska Northwest Publishing Co.

Cairns, John, Jr. 1989. "Restoring Damaged Ecosystems: Is Predisturbance Condition a Viable Option?" *Environmental Professional* 11:152–159.

Cooney, R. T., and T. M. Willette. 1991. "Regional-Level Investigations of Pink Salmon Production Responses to Interannual Variations in Ocean Temperatures: Cooperative Fisheries and Oceanographic Studies." Presentation to the Fifteenth Northeast Pacific Pink and Chum Salmon Workshop, Parksville, B.C., February 27–March 1, 1991.

Cooney, R. T., T. Mark Willette, and Jeff Olsen. 1992. "The Effects of Climate on North Pacific Pink Salmon Production: Examining Some Details of a Natural Experiment." Presentation to the International Symposium on Climate Change and Northern Fish Populations, Victoria, B.C., October.

Duggins, D. O., C. A. Simenstad, and J. A. Estes. 1989. "Magnification of Secondary Production by Kelp Detritus in Coastal Marine Ecosystems." *Science* 245:170–173.

Dunford, Richard W., Sara P. Hudson, and William H. Desvousges. 1993. "Experimental Contingent Values for Reducing Environmental Damage from Oil Spills." *Proceedings of the 1993 International Oil Spill Conference, Tampa, Florida, March 29–April 1, 1993*, pp. 699–704.

Estes, James A., and John F. Palmisano. 1974. "Sea Otters: Their Role in Structuring Nearshore Communities." *Science* 185:1058–1060.

Elner, R. W., and R. L. Vadas, Sr., 1990. "Inference in Ecology: The Sea Urchin Phenomenon in the Northwestern Atlantic." *American Naturalist* 136:108–125.

Exxon Valdez Oil Spill Trustee Council. 1989. *State/Federal Natural Resource Damage Assessment Plan for the* Exxon Valdez *Oil Spill, August 1989: Public Review Draft*. Juneau: Exxon Valdez Oil Spill Trustee Council.

Exxon Valdez Oil Spill Trustee Council. 1990. "Restoration Following the *Exxon Valdez* Oil Spill." *Proceedings of the Public Symposium of March 1990*. Anchorage: Exxon Valdez Oil Spill Trustee Council.

Exxon Valdez Oil Spill Trustee Council. 1993. Exxon Valdez *Oil Spill Symposium, February 2–5, 1993: Program and Abstracts*. Anchorage: Exxon Valdez Oil Spill Trustee Council.

Foster, M. S., and D. R. Schiel. 1988. "Kelp Communities and Sea Otters: Keystone Species or Just Another Brick in the Wall?" In G. R. VanBlaricom and J. A. Estes, eds., *The Community Ecology of Sea Otters*. New York: Springer-Verlag.

Geiger, Harold J. 1993. "Pink Salmon Run Reconstruction and Life History Model." Fish/Shellfish Study No. 28. Draft Report to the Exxon Valdez Oil Spill Trustee Council, June.

Gould, Stephen Jay. 1990. "The Golden Rule—A Proper Scale for Our Environmental Crisis." *Natural History*, September, pp. 24–30.

Grigalunas, Thomas A., and James J. Opaluch. 1993. "Non-Use Value in Natural Resource Damage Assessments: The *Nestucca* Oil Spill." *Proceedings of the 1993 International Oil Spill Conference, Tampa, Florida, March 29–April 1, 1993*, pp. 689–693.

Hood, D. W., and S. T. Zimmerman, eds. 1986, 1987. *The Gulf of Alaska: Physical Environment and Biological Resources.* Outer Continental Shelf Environmental Assessment Program. Washington, D.C.: U.S. Department of the Interior, U.S. Department of Commerce.

Juday, Glenn P., and Nora R. Foster. 1990. "A Preliminary Look at Effects of the *Exxon Valdez* Oil Spill on Green Island Research Natural Area." *Agroborealis* 22 (1):10–16.

Lentfer, Jack W., ed. 1988. *Selected Marine Mammals of Alaska.* Washington, D.C.: Marine Mammal Commission.

Lethcoe, Nancy R. 1987. *Glaciers of Prince William Sound, Alaska.* Valdez: Prince William Sound Books.

Lethcoe, Nancy R., and Lisa Nurnberger, eds. 1989. *Prince William Sound Environmental Reader: 1989—T/V Exxon Valdez Oil Spill.* Valdez: Prince William Sound Conservation Alliance.

Lewin, Roger. 1986. "In Ecology, Change Brings Stability." *Science* 234:1071–1073.

Mann, K. H. 1982. *Ecology of Coastal Waters: A Systems Approach.* Berkeley and Los Angeles: University of California Press.

Mickelson, Pete, 1989a. "Bird, Mammal and Human Use of Perry Island in Prince William Sound, Alaska, in Summer, 1989." Prince William Sound Science Center, Cordova, Alaska.

———. 1989b. *Natural History of Alaska's Prince William Sound.* Cordova: Alaska Wild Wings.

Müter, F. J., B. L. Norcross, and T. C. Royer. 1994. "Do Cyclic Temperatures Cause Cyclic Fisheries?" *Canadian Journal of Fisheries and Aquatic Sciences*, in press.

Myren, R. T., and J. J. Pella. 1977. "Natural Variability in Distribution of an Intertidal Population of *Macoma balthica* Subject to Potential Oil Pollution at Port Valdez, Alaska." *Marine Biology* 41:371–382.

National Academy of Sciences. 1968–1973. *The Great Alaska Earthquake of 1964.* Washington, D.C.: National Academy of Sciences.

National Oceanic and Atmospheric Administration. 1980. "Environmental Assessment of the Alaskan Continental Shelf: Northeast Gulf of Alaska Interim Synthesis Report." Prepared by Science Applications, Inc., Boulder, Colorado.

Nelson, Steven W., J. A. Dumoulin, and Marti L. Miller. 1985. Geologic Map of the Chugach National Forest, Alaska. Map MF-1645-B, U.S. Geological Survey.

Nysewander, David R., and John L. Trapp. 1984. "Widespread Mortality of Adult Seabirds in Alaska, August–September, 1983." U.S. Fish and Wildlife Service Report, Anchorage, Alaska, February.

Parker, K. S., T. C. Royer, and R. B. Deriso. 1994. "High Latitude

Climate Forcing by the 18.6-Year Lunar Nodal Cycle and Historical Recruitment Trends in Pacific Halibut." *Canadian Journal of Fisheries and Aquatic Sciences,* in press.

Paul, A. J., Judy Paul, and Howard M. Feder. 1976. "Recruitment and Growth in the Bivalve *Protothaca staminea,* at Olsen Bay, Prince William Sound, Ten Years after the 1964 Earthquake." *Veliger* 18 (4):385–392.

Plafker, George, W. J. Nokleberg, and J. S. Lull. 1989. "Bedrock Geology and Tectonic Evolution of the Wrangellia, Peninsular, and Chugach Terranes along the Trans-Alaska Crustal Transect in the Chugach Mountains and Southern Copper River Basin, Alaska." *Journal of Geophysical Research* 94:4255–4295.

Prince William Sound Aquaculture Corporation. 1989–1991. *PWSAC News* (Cordova).

Rosenthal, Richard J., Dennis C. Lees, and David J. Maiero. 1982. "Description of Prince William Sound Shoreline Habitats Associated with Biological Communities." Prepared for NOAA, February.

Rosenthal, Richard J., Victoria Moran-O'Connell, and Margaret C. Murphy. 1988. "Feeding Ecology of Ten Species of Rockfishes (Scorpaeinidae) from the Gulf of Alaska." *California Fish and Game* 74 (1):16–37.

Royce, W. F., T. R. Schroeder, A. A. Olsen, and W. J. Allender. 1991. *Alaskan Fisheries Two Years After the Spill.* Prepared for Exxon by Cook Inlet Fisheries Consultants, Homer, Alaska.

Royer, Thomas C. 1989. "Upper Ocean Temperature Variability in the Northeast Pacific Ocean: Is It an Indicator of Global Warming?" *Journal of Geophysical Research* 94 (C12): 18,175–18,183.

————. 1993. "High-Latitude Oceanic Variability Associated with the 18.6-Year Nodal Tide." *Journal of Geophysical Research* 98 (C3):4639–4644.

Royer, Thomas C., John A. Vermersch, Thomas J. Weingartner, H. J. Niebauer, and Robin D. Muench. 1990. "Ocean Circulation Influencing the *Exxon Valdez* Oil Spill." *Oceanography,* November, pp. 3–10.

Sharr, Samuel. 1991. *Injury to Salmon Eggs and Preemergent Fry in Prince William Sound.* Fish/Shellfish Study No. 2. Draft Report to the Exxon Valdez Oil Spill Trustee Council, November.

Shaw, David G., and Mohammad J. Hameedi, eds. 1988. *Environmental Studies in Port Valdez, Alaska: A Basis for Management.* New York: Springer-Verlag.

U.S. Geological Survey. 1967, 1968. *The Alaska Earthquake, March 27, 1964: Regional Effects.* Washington, D.C.: U.S. Government Printing Office.

Wheelwright, Jeff. 1991. "Muzzling Science." *Newsweek,* April 22, p. 10.

Willette, Mark, and Alex Wertheimer. 1991. "Early Marine Salmon Injury Assessment in Prince William Sound." Fish/Shellfish Study No. 4. Draft Report to the Exxon Valdez Oil Spill Trustee Council, November 1991.

Wolfe, Douglas A., and Björn Kjerfve. 1986. "Estuarine Variability: An Overview." In D. A. Wolfe, ed. *Estuarine Variability.* New York: Academic Press, pp. 3–17.

2: OIL AND WATER

1. INTERVIEWS

Paul Becker, National Oceanic and Atmospheric Administration (NOAA)

Randy Buckley, Exxon

Lynn Chrystal, National Weather Service

Dean Dale, consultant, NOAA

Mervin Fingas, Environment Canada

Robert Fiocco, Exxon

Jerry Galt, NOAA

Edward Gilfillan, consultant, Exxon

Jack Gould, American Petroleum Institute

Rolly Grabbe, Alaska Department of Environmental Conservation (ADEC)

Erich Gundlach, consultant, ADEC

Charles Henry, consultant, NOAA

Raymond Highsmith, University of Alaska—Fairbanks

Jonathan Houghton, consultant, NOAA

Hans Jahns, Exxon

Dennis Kelso, Commissioner, ADEC

Marshal Kendziorek, ADEC

David Kennedy, NOAA

Mark Kuwada, Alaska Department of Fish and Game (ADF&G)

Keith Kvenvolden, U.S. Geological Survey

Dennis Lees, consultant, NOAA

William Lehr, NOAA

Alan Maki, Exxon

Alan Mearns, NOAA

Jacqueline Michel, consultant, NOAA

Scott Nauman, Exxon

Riki Ott, Cordova District Fishermen United

Edward Owens, consultant, Exxon

Walter Parker, Alaska Oil Spill Commission

James R. Payne, consultant, NOAA

Robert Pavia, NOAA

Debra Payton, NOAA

Ernie Piper, ADEC

Steve Provant, ADEC

John Robinson, NOAA

Richard Rosenthal, consultant, ADF&G

Frank Rue, ADF&G

Gary Shigenaka, NOAA

Jeffrey Short, NOAA

Bryson Twidwell, ADEC

Alex Viteri, ADEC

Art Weiner, consultant, ADEC

Douglas Wolfe, NOAA

2. BOOKS, REPORTS AND ARTICLES

Alaska Oil Spill Commission. 1990. *Spill: The Wreck of the* Exxon Valdez *Final Report*. Anchorage: Alaska Oil Spill Commission, February.

Allen, Alan A. 1991. "Controlled Burning of Crude Oil on Water Following the Grounding of the *Exxon Valdez*." *Proceedings of the 1991 International Oil Spill Conference, San Diego, Calif., March 4–7, 1991*, pp. 213–216.

Becker, Paul R., and Carol-Ann Manen. 1988. "Natural Oil Seeps in the Alaskan Marine Environment." Final Report to the Outer Continental Shelf Environmental Assessment Program, NOAA, May.

Bence, A. E., and W. A. Burns. 1993. "Fingerprinting Hydrocarbons in the Biological Resources of the *Exxon Valdez* Spill Area." Exxon presentation to the American Society for Testing and Materials, Atlanta, Georgia, April 25–28.

Bragg, James R., Shan H. Yang, and John C. Roffal. 1990. "Experimental Studies of Natural Cleansing of Oil Residue from Rocks in Prince William

Sound by Wave/Tidal Action." Exxon Production Research Company, Houston, Texas.

Ciancaglini, D. E. 1991. "The Federal On-Scene Coordinator's Role in the *Exxon Valdez* Oil Spill." *Proceedings of the 1991 International Oil Spill Conference, San Diego, Calif., March 4–7, 1991,* pp. 325–332.

Driskell, W. B., A. K. Fukuyama, J. P. Houghton, D. C. Lees, G. Shigenaka, and A. J. Mearns. 1993. "Impacts on Intertidal Infauna: *Exxon Valdez* Oil Spill and Cleanup." *Proceedings of the 1993 International Oil Spill Conference, Tampa, Florida, March 29–April 1, 1993,* pp. 355–362.

Evans, David D. 1989. "In-Situ Burning of Oil Spills." *Alaska Arctic Offshore Oil Spill Response Technology: Workshop Proceedings, Anchorage, Alaska, November 29–December 1, 1988,* pp. 47–95.

Exxon Production Research Company. 1990. *Valdez Oil Spill Technology, 1989 Operations.* Houston: Exxon Production Research Company.

Exxon Valdez Oil Spill Trustee Council. 1993. Exxon Valdez *Oil Spill Symposium, February 2–5, 1993: Program and Abstracts.* Anchorage: Exxon Valdez Oil Spill Trustee Council.

Fingas, Mervin F. 1989. "Chemical Treatment of Oil Spills." *Alaska Arctic Offshore Oil Spill Response Technology: Workshop Proceedings, Anchorage, Alaska, November 29–December 1, 1988,* pp. 27–46.

Finkelstein, Kenneth, and Erich R. Gundlach. 1981. "Method for Estimating Spilled Oil Quantity on the Shoreline." *Environmental Science & Technology* 15: (5):545–549.

Foster, Michael S., John A. Tarpley, and Susan L. Dearn. 1990. "To Clean or Not to Clean: The Rationale, Methods, and Consequences of Removing Oil from Temperate Shores." *Northwest Environmental Journal* (University of Washington) 6:105–120.

Galt, J. A., G. Y. Watabayashi, D. L. Payton, and J. C. Petersen. 1991. "Trajectory Analysis for the *Exxon Valdez* Hindcast Study." *Proceedings of the 1991 International Oil Spill Conference, San Diego, Calif., March 4–7, 1991,* pp. 629–634.

Gilfillan, Edward S., Dave S. Page, E. James Harner, and Paul D. Boehm. 1993. "Shoreline Ecology Program for Prince William Sound, Alaska, Following the *Exxon Valdez* Oil Spill: Part 3—Biology." Exxon presentation to the American Society for Testing and Materials, Atlanta, Georgia, April 25–28, 1993.

Gundlach, Erich, Eugene A. Pavia, Clay Robinson, and James C. Gibeaut. 1991. "Shoreline Surveys at the *Exxon Valdez* Oil Spill: The State of Alaska Response." *Proceedings of the 1991 International Oil Spill Conference, San Diego, Calif., March 4–7, 1991,* pp. 519–529.

Haas, Thomas J. 1991. "CAMEO-Valdez: Charting the Progress of the Spill Cleanup." *Proceedings of the 1991 International Oil Spill Conference, San Diego, Calif., March 4–7, 1991,* pp. 655–658.

Hayes, Miles O., Jacqueline Michel, and David C. Noe. 1991. "Factors Controlling Initial Deposition and Long-Term Fate of Spilled Oil on Gravel Beaches." *Proceedings of the 1991 International Oil Spill Conference, San Diego, Calif., March 4–7, 1991,* pp. 453–460.

Highsmith, Raymond, et al. 1991. "Comprehensive Assessment of Injury to Coastal Habitats." Coastal Habitat Study No. 1A. Interim Report to the Exxon Valdez Oil Spill Trustee Council.

Houghton, Jonathan P., David Erikson, William B. Driskell. 1991. "Ecological Effects of Omni Barge Treatment of an Oiled Shoreline in Herring Bay, Prince William Sound, Alaska." Final Report to Exxon, March.

Houghton, Jonathan P., Dennis C. Lees, et al. 1991. "Evaluation of the Condition of Intertidal and Shallow Subtidal Biota in Prince William Sound Following the *Exxon Valdez* Oil Spill and Subsequent Shoreline Treatment." NOAA, WASC Contract No. 50ABNC-0-00121 and 50ABNC-0-00122. Seattle, Washington.

————. 1993. "Evaluation of the Condition of Prince William Sound Shorelines Following the *Exxon Valdez* Oil Spill and Subsequent Shoreline Treatment, Volume II: 1991 Biological Monitoring Survey." NOAA Technical Memorandum NOS ORCA 67. Seattle, Washington.

Kvenvolden, Keith A., Paul R. Carlson, Charles N. Threlkeld, and Augusta Warden. 1993. "Possible Connection Between Two Alaskan Catastrophes Occurring 25 Yr Apart (1964 and 1989)." *Geology* 21:813–816.

Marshall, Michael, and Erich Gundlach. 1990. "The Physical Persistence of Spilled Oil: An Analysis of Oil Spills Previous to *Valdez*." Final Report to NOAA, Seattle, Washington, April.

Michel, Jacqueline, and Miles O. Hayes. 1991. "Geomorphological Controls on the Persistence of Shoreline Contamination from the *Exxon Valdez* Oil Spill." NOAA Report No. HMRB 91-2.

————. 1993. "Persistence and Weathering of *Exxon Valdez* Oil in the Intertidal Zone—3.5 Years Later." *Proceedings of the 1993 International Oil Spill Conference, Tampa, Florida, March 29–April 1, 1993*, pp. 279–286.

Michel, Jacqueline, Miles O. Hayes, Walter J. Sexton, James C. Gibeaut, and Charles Henry. 1991. "Trends in Natural Removal of the *Exxon Valdez* Oil Spill in Prince William Sound from September 1989 to May 1990." *Proceedings of the 1991 International Oil Spill Conference, San Diego, Calif., March 4–7, 1991*, pp. 181–188.

National Oceanic and Atmospheric Administration. 1990. *Excavation and Rock Washing Treatment Technology, Net Environmental Benefit Analysis.* Seattle: Hazardous Materials Response Branch, 1990.

National Oceanic and Atmospheric Administration. 1990. "Hazardous Materials Response." In *Report to the Congress on Ocean Pollution, Monitoring, and Research, October 1988 through September 1989.* Washington: National Oceanic and Atmospheric Administration.

National Research Council, National Academy of Sciences. 1985. *Oil in the Sea: Inputs, Fates, and Effects.* Washington, D.C.: National Academy Press.

National Research Council, National Academy of Sciences. 1989. *Using Oil Spill Dispersants on the Sea.* Washington, D.C.: National Academy Press.

National Response Team. 1989. *The* Exxon Valdez *Oil Spill: A Report to the President from Samuel K. Skinner, Secretary, Department of Transportation, and William K. Reilly, Administrator, Environmental Protection Agency.* Washington, D.C.: National Response Team, May.

Nauman, Scott A. 1991. "Shoreline Cleanup: Equipment and Operations." *Proceedings of the 1991 International Oil Spill Conference, San Diego, Calif., March 4–7, 1991*, pp. 141–148.

Neff, Jerry M. 1991. *Water Quality in Prince William Sound and the Gulf of Alaska.* Cambridge, Mass.: Arthur D. Little.

Office of Technology Assessment, U.S. Congress. 1990. *Coping with an Oiled Sea: An Analysis of Oil Spill Response Technologies.* Washington, D.C.: U.S. Government Printing Office, March.

Ott, Riki. 1987. "Oil and the Marine Environment." Presentation to Prince William Sound Community College, Valdez, Alaska, December 10.

Owens, Edward H. 1991a. *Changes in Shoreline Oiling Conditions 1-1/2 Years after the 1989 Prince William Sound Spill.* Seattle: Woodward-Clyde Consultants.

————. 1991b. *Shoreline Conditions Following the* Exxon Valdez *Spill as of Fall 1990.* Seattle: Woodward-Clyde Consultants.

Owens, Edward H., Andrew R. Teal, and Paul C. Haase. 1991. "Berm Relocation During the 1990 Shoreline Cleanup Program Following the *Exxon Valdez* Spill." *Proceedings of the Fourteenth Arctic and Marine Oil Spill Program Technical Seminar, Environment Canada,* Vancouver, B.C., June.

Page, David S., Paul D. Boehm, Gregory S. Douglas, and A. Edward Bence. 1993. "Identification of Hydrocarbon Sources in the Benthic Sediments of Prince William Sound and the Gulf of Alaska Following the *Exxon Valdez* Oil Spill." Exxon presentation to the American Society for Testing and Materials, Atlanta, Georgia, April 25–28.

Payne, James R., John R. Clayton, G. Daniel McNabb, and Bruce E. Kirstein. 1991. *"Exxon Valdez* Oil Weathering Fate and Behavior: Model Predictions and Field Observations." *Proceedings of the 1991 International Oil Spill Conference, San Diego, Calif., March 4–7, 1991,* pp. 641–654.

Payne, James R., and G. Daniel McNabb, Jr. 1984. "Weathering of Petroleum in the Marine Environment." *Journal of Marine Technology Society* 18 (3):24–42.

Payne, James R., et al. 1989. "Oil-Ice Sediment Interactions during Freezeup and Breakup." Final Report to Outer Continental Shelf Environmental Assessment Program, NOAA.

————. 1993. "Spill-of-Opportunity Testing of Dispersant Effectiveness at the *Mega Borg* Oil Spill." *Proceedings of the 1993 International Oil Spill Conference, Tampa, Florida, March 29–April 1, 1993,* pp. 791–793.

Reiter, Gary A., and Jack A. Kemerer. 1989. "Vessel Destruction: A Viable Response Option for Isolated Areas." *Proceedings of the Twelfth Arctic and Marine Oil Spill Program Technical Seminar, Environment Canada, Calgary, Alberta, June 7–9, 1989,* pp. 329–334.

Rice, Stanley D., and Charles E. O'Clair. 1991. "Petroleum Hydrocarbon-Induced Injury to Subtidal Marine Sediment Resources." Subtidal Study No. 1. Draft Report to the Exxon Valdez Oil Spill Trustee Council, November.

Spaulding, Malcolm L., and Mark Reed, eds. 1991. *Oil Spills: Management and Legislative Implications. Conference Proceedings, Newport, Rhode Island, May 15–18, 1990.*

Teal, Andrew R. 1991. "Shoreline Cleanup—Reconnaissance, Evaluation, and Planning Following the Valdez Oil Spill." *Proceedings of the 1991 International Oil Spill Conference, San Diego, Calif., March 4–7, 1991,* pp. 149–152.

Wolfe, D. A., et al. 1993. "Fate of the Oil Spilled from the T/V *Exxon Valdez* in Prince William Sound, Alaska." Subtidal Study No. 4. Draft Final Report to the Exxon Valdez Oil Spill Trustee Council, June.

3: *CHEMOPHOBIA*

1. *INTERVIEWS*

Brad Andres, U.S. Fish and Wildlife Service (FWS)

Bruce Ames, University of California–Berkeley

Rochelle Araujo, Environmental Protection Agency (EPA)

Ronald Atlas, University of Louisville

Malin Babcock, National Oceanic and Atmospheric Administration (NOAA)

Evelyn Biggs, Alaska Department of Fish and Game (ADF&G)

John Blake, University of Alaska–Fairbanks (UAF)

Timothy Bowman, FWS

Terry Bowyer, UAF

Joan Braddock, UAF

James Brady, ADF&G

Mark Brodersen, Alaska Department of Environmental Conservation (ADEC)

Edward Brown, UAF

Thomas Burk, contract physician, Exxon

Don Button, UAF

James Clark, EPA

Yoram Cohen, University of California–Los Angeles

Tracy Collier, NOAA

John Couch, EPA

Rick Cripe, EPA

Marilyn Dahlheim, NOAA

Gene Dickason, Alyeska Pipeline Service Co.

Lawrence Duffy, UAF

James Faro, ADF&G

Kathryn Frost, ADF&G

D. Michael Fry, consultant, Exxon Valdez Trustee Council

John Glaser, EPA

Ellen Hale, EPA

Kelly Hepler, ADF&G

Steve Hinton, Exxon

Andrew Hoffman, ADF&G

Jo Ellen Hose, consultant, ADF&G

James Huff, National Institute of Environmental Health Sciences

Roy Lee, contract physician, Exxon

Jon Lindstrom, UAF

Edward Long, NOAA

Thomas Loughlin, NOAA

Michael McGurk, consultant, ADF&G

Anne McElroy, State University of New York at Stony Brook

Craig Matkin, consultant, NOAA

Charles Meacham, ADF&G

Michele Medinsky, Chemical Industry Institute of Technology

Byron Morris, NOAA

Mark Okihiro, consultant, ADF&G

Samuel Patten, ADF&G

John Piatt, FWS

Roger Prince, Exxon

P. Hap Pritchard, EPA

Barnett Rattner, FWS

Patrick Redig, University of Minnesota

Everett Robinson-Wilson, FWS

Stanley Rice, NOAA

Philip Schempf, FWS

Gary Sonnevil, FWS

Robert Spies, consultant, Exxon Valdez Trustee Council

Terry Spraker, consultant, ADF&G

Janet Springer, Food and Drug Administration

John Stegeman, consultant, ADEC, ADF&G

Edward Stein, Occupational Safety and Health Administration

Joseph Sullivan, ADF&G

Alex Swiderski, Alaska Department of Law

John Teal, Woods Hole Oceanographic Institution

Usha Varanasi, NOAA

John Wilcock, ADF&G

Douglas Wolfe, NOAA

2. BOOKS, REPORTS AND ARTICLES

Abelson, Philip. 1990. "Testing for Carcinogens with Rodents." *Science* 249:1357.

Alaska Department of Fish and Game, Division of Commercial Fisheries. 1988, 1989, 1990, 1991, 1992. *Annual Finfish Management Report, Prince William Sound Area.*

Alaska Department of Fish and Game, 1993. "The *Exxon Valdez* Oil Spill: What Have We Learned?" *Alaska's Wildlife,* January–February.

Atlas, Ronald M., and Richard Bartha. 1992. "Hydrocarbon Biodegradation and Oil Spill Bioremediation." In *Advances in Microbial Ecology.* New York: Plenum Press, Vol. 12, pp. 287–338.

Babcock, Malin M., and John F. Karinen. 1991. "Pre-spill and Post-spill Concentrations of Hydrocarbons in Sediments and Mussels at Intertidal Sites within Prince William Sound and the Gulf of Alaska." Coastal Habitat Study No. 1B. Interim Report to the Exxon Valdez Oil Spill Trustee Council.

Baker, J. M., R. B. Clark, P. F. Kingston, and R. H. Jenkins. 1990. "Natural Recovery of Cold Water Marine Environments after an Oil Spill." Presentation to the Thirteenth Annual Arctic and Marine Oil Spill Program Technical Seminar, Environment Canada, Edmonton, Alberta, June 6–8.

Bailey, Edgar P., and Glenn H. Davenport. 1972. "Die-Off of Common Murres on the Alaska Peninsula and Unimak Island." *Condor* 74:215–219.

Berthou, F., and G. Balouët. 1987. "The Occurrence of Hydrocarbons and Histopathological Abnormalities in Oysters for Seven Years Following the Wreck of the *Amoco Cadiz* in Brittany (France)." *Marine Environmental Research* 23:103–133.

Biggs, E., T. Baker, M. McGurk, J. E. Hose, and R. Kocan. 1991. "Injury to Prince William Sound Herring." Fish/Shellfish Study No. 11. Draft Preliminary Status Report to the Exxon Valdez Oil Spill Trustee Council, November.

Boesch, D. F., and N. N. Rabalais, eds. 1987. *Long-term Environmental Effects of Offshore Oil and Gas Development.* London and New York: Elsevier.

Boersma, P. Dee, Julia K. Parrish, and Arthur B. Kettle. 1993. "Common Murre Abundance, Phenology, and Productivity on the Barren Islands, Alaska: The *Exxon Valdez* Oil Spill and Long-Term Environmental Change." Exxon presentation to the American Society for Testing and Materials, Atlanta, Georgia, April 25–28.

Braddock, Joan F., et al. 1993. "Microbial Activity in Sediments Following the T/V *Exxon Valdez* Oil Spill." Exxon Valdez *Oil Spill Symposium, Feb. 2–5, 1993: Program and Abstracts.* Anchorage: Exxon Valdez Oil Spill Trustee Council, pp. 52–54.

Bragg, James R., Roger C. Prince, E. James Harner, and Ronald M. Atlas. 1993. "Bioremediation Effectiveness Following the *Exxon Valdez* Spill." *Proceedings of the 1993 International Oil Spill Conference, Tampa, Florida, March 29–April 1, 1993,* pp. 435–448.

Button, D. K. 1984. "Evidence for a Terpene-Based Food Chain in the Gulf of Alaska." *Applied and Environmental Microbiology* 48 (5):1004–1011.

Carls, Mark G., and Stanley D. Rice. 1990. "Abnormal Development and Growth Reductions of Pollock *Theragra chalcogramma* Embryos Exposed to Water-Soluble Fractions of Oil." *U.S. Fishery Bulletin* 88:29–37.

Carson, Rachel. 1962. *Silent Spring.* Boston: Houghton Mifflin.

Clark, R. B. 1982. "The Impact of Oil Pollution on Marine Populations,

Communities and Ecosystems: A Summing up." *Philosophical Transactions of the Royal Society of London*, Series B 297:433–443.

Cohen, Yoram. 1992. "Multimedia Fate and Effects of Airborne Petroleum Hydrocarbons in the Port Valdez Region." Final Report to the Regional Citizens' Advisory Council, Valdez, Alaska, March.

Collier, Tracy K., and Usha Varanasi. 1991. "Hepatic Activities of Xenobiotic Metabolizing Enzymes and Biliary Levels of Xenobiotics in English Sole (*Parophrys vetulus*) Exposed to Environmental Contaminants." *Archives of Environmental Contamination and Toxicology* 20:462–473.

Dahlheim, Marilyn Elaine. 1988. "Killer Whale (*Orcinus orca*) Depredation on Longline Catches of Sablefish (*Anoplopoma fimbria*) in Alaskan Waters." NWAFC Processed Report 88-14, NOAA, Seattle, Washington.

Dahlheim, Marilyn E., and Thomas R. Loughlin. 1991. "Assessment of Injuries to Killer Whales in Prince William Sound." Marine Mammal Study No. 2. Interim Report to the Exxon Valdez Oil Spill Trustee Council, November.

Delikat, Donald S., et al. 1993. "Benzene Vapor Concentrations During a Simulated Crude Oil Spill." *Proceedings of the 1993 International Oil Spill Conference, Tampa, Florida, March 29–April 1, 1993*, pp. 805–806.

Engelhardt, F. R. 1982. "Hydrocarbon Metabolism and Cortisol Balance in Oil-Exposed Ringed Seals, *Phoca Hispida*." *Comparative Biochemistry and Physiology* 72C (1):133–136.

Environmental Protection Agency, Hazardous Site Control Division. 1989. "Final Remedial Investigation Report for Eagle Harbor Site, Kitsap County, Washington." Contract No. 68-01-7251. November.

Environmental Protection Agency, Science Advisory Board. 1991. "Alaska Oil Spill Bioremediation Project." Draft Report. Gulf Breeze, Florida, October.

Exxon Company, USA. 1988. "Material Data Safety Sheet: Crude Oil." Houston, Texas.

Exxon Valdez Oil Spill Trustee Council. 1989, 1990, 1991. *State/Federal Natural Resource Damage Assessment and Restoration Plan for the* Exxon Valdez *Oil Spill*. Juneau: Exxon Valdez Oil Spill Trustee Council.

———. 1991. *Summary of Effects of the* Exxon Valdez *Oil Spill on Natural Resources and Archaeological Resources*. March.

———. 1992. *Restoration Framework*. Anchorage: Exxon Valdez Oil Spill Trustee Council.

———. 1992, 1993, 1994. Exxon Valdez *Oil Spill Restoration: Draft Work Plan*. Anchorage: Exxon Valdez Oil Spill Trustee Council.

———. 1993a. *Draft Restoration Plan*. Anchorage: Exxon Valdez Oil Spill Trustee Council.

———. 1993b. Exxon Valdez *Oil Spill Symposium, February 2–5, 1993: Program and Abstracts*. Anchorage: Exxon Valdez Oil Spill Trustee Council.

Faro, J. P., R. T. Bowyer, J. W. Testa, and L. K. Duffy. 1993. "Assessment of Injury to River Otters in Prince William Sound, Alaska, Following the *Exxon Valdez* Oil Spill." Terrestrial Mammal Study No. 3. Draft Final Report to the Exxon Valdez Oil Spill Trustee Council, March.

Federal Water Quality Administration. 1970. "Kodiak Oil Pollution Incident, March, 1970." Summary Report. U.S. Department of the Interior, Washington, D.C., May.

Fry, D. Michael, and Leslie A. Addiego. 1987. "Hemolytic Anemia Complicates the Cleaning of Oiled Seabirds." *Wildlife Journal* 10 (3):3–8.

Fry, D. Michael, and Linda J. Lowenstine. 1985. "Pathology of Common Murres and Cassin's Auklets Exposed to Oil." *Archives of Environmental Contamination and Toxicology* 14:727–737.

Fry, D. Michael, et al. 1986. "Reduced Reproduction of Wedge-tailed Shearwaters Exposed to Weathered Santa Barbara Crude Oil." *Archives of Environmental Contamination and Toxicology* 15:453–463.

General Accounting Office, 1991. *Natural Resources Damage Assessment: Information on Study of Seabirds Killed by* Exxon Valdez *Oil Spill.* Briefing Report to U.S. Senator Frank H. Murkowski. Washington, D.C., November.

————. 1993. *Natural Resources Restoration: Use of* Exxon Valdez *Oil Spill Settlement Funds.* Briefing Report to the Chairman, Committee on Natural Resources, U.S. House of Representatives. Washington, D.C., August.

Geraci, J. R., and D. J. St. Aubin, eds. 1988. "Synthesis of Effects of Oil on Marine Mammals." Contract No. 14-12-001-30293. Report Prepared for the Department of the Interior, Minerals Management Service, September.

Gibson, Marjorie J. 1991. "Bald Eagles in Alaska Following the *Exxon Valdez* Oil Spill." *Proceedings of the 1991 International Oil Spill Conference, San Diego, Calif., March 4–7, 1991*, pp. 229–234.

Goldstein, Bernard D., et al. 1992. "Valdez Air Health Study." Summary Report. Prepared for the Alyeska Pipeline Service Co., Anchorage, Alaska, June.

Golub, Richard S. 1989. "Statement on Oil Spills and Cleanup Technology." Presented to the Subcommittee on Water, Power, and Offshore Energy Resources, Committee on Interior and Insular Affairs, U.S. House of Representatives, Washington, D.C., July 18.

Gorman, R. W., S. P. Berardinelli, and T. R. Bender. 1991. "Health Evaluation Report: *Exxon/Valdez* Oil Spill." HETA 89-200 & 89-273-2111. National Institute of Occupational Safety and Health, Cincinnati, Ohio.

Gundlach, Erich R., et al. 1983. "The Fate of *Amoco Cadiz* Oil." *Science* 221:122–129.

Hall, R. J., and N. C. Coon. 1988. "Interpreting Residues of Petroleum Hydrocarbons in Wildlife Tissues." U.S. Fish and Wildlife Service, Biological Report 88(15), Washington, D.C.

Heinz, Gary H. 1989. "How Lethal Are Sublethal Effects?" *Environmental Toxicology and Chemistry* 8:463–464.

Hepler, Kelly, Andrew Hoffman, and Pat Hansen. 1991. "Injury to Dolly Varden and Cutthroat Trout in Prince William Sound." Fish/Shellfish Study No. 5. Interim Report to the Exxon Valdez Oil Spill Trustee Council, November.

Hoffman, Andrew, Kelly Hepler, and Patricia Hansen. 1991. "Injury to Demersal Rockfish and Shallow Reef Habitats in Prince William Sound." Subtidal Study No. 6. Interim Report to the Exxon Valdez Oil Spill Trustee Council, November.

Holcomb, Jay. 1991. "Overview of Bird Search and Rescue and Response Efforts During the *Exxon Valdez* Oil Spill." *Proceedings of the 1991 International Oil Spill Conference, San Diego, Calif., March 4–7, 1991*, pp. 225–228.

Huff, J. E., W. Eastin, J. Roycroft, S. L. Eustis, J. K. Haseman. 1988. "Carcinogenesis Studies of Benzene, Methyl Benzene, and Dimethyl Benzenes." *Annals of the New York Academy of Sciences*, 534:427–440.

Krahn, Margaret M., et al. 1992. "Mass Spectrometric Analysis for Aromatic Compounds in Bile of Fish Sampled after the *Exxon Valdez* Oil Spill." *Environmental Science & Technology* 26:116–126.

Kuletz, Kathy. 1992. "Assessment of Injury to Marbled Murrelets from the *Exxon Valdez* Oil Spill." Bird Study No. 6. Draft Report to the Exxon Valdez Oil Spill Trustee Council, February.

Lee, Y.-Z., P. J. O'Brien, J. F. Payne, and A. D. Rahimtula. 1986. "Toxicity of Petroleum Crude Oils and Their Effect on Xenobiotic Metabolizing Enzyme Activities in the Chicken Embryo *in Ovo*." *Environmental Research* 39:153–163.

Lewis, Jonathan P., and Donald G. Calkins. 1991. "Assessment of the *Exxon Valdez* Oil Spill on the Sitka Black-tailed Deer in Prince William Sound and the Kodiak Archipelago." Terrestrial Mammal Study No. 1. Final Report to the Exxon Valdez Oil Spill Trustee Council, February.

Long, Edward R., and Lee G. Morgan. 1990. "The Potential for Biological Effects of Sediment-sorbed Contaminants Tested in the National Status and Trends Program." NOAA Technical Memorandum NOS OMA 52. Seattle, Washington.

McCain, B. B., et al. 1978. "Bioavailability of Crude Oil from Experimentally Oiled Sediments to English Sole (*Parophrys vetulus*), and Pathological Consequences." *Journal of the Fisheries Research Board of Canada* 35 (5):657–664.

McCormick-Ray, M. Geraldine. 1983. "Hemocyte and Tissue Changes by Crude Oil in the Blue Mussel *Mytilus Edulis*." Master's thesis, University of Alaska–Fairbanks, September.

MacFarland, Harold N. 1988. "Toxicology of Petroleum Hydrocarbons." *Occupational Medicine: State of the Art Reviews* 3 (3):445–454.

McIntyre, A. D. 1982. "Oil Pollution and Fisheries." *Philosophical Transactions of the Royal Society of London*, Series B 297:401–411.

Maki, Alan W. 1991. "The *Exxon Valdez* Oil Spill: Initial Environmental Impact Assessment." *Environmental Science & Technology* 25 (1):24–29.

Malins, Donald C., and Harold O. Hodgins. 1981. "Petroleum and Marine Fishes: A Review of Uptake, Disposition, and Effects." *Environmental Science & Technology* 15 (11):1272–1280.

Malins, Donald C., Mark S. Meyers, and William T. Roubal. 1983. "Organic Free Radicals Associated with Idiopathic Liver Lesions of English Sole (*Parophrys vetulus*) from Polluted Marine Environments." *Environmental Science & Technology* 17 (11):679–685.

Malins, Donald C., et al. 1987. "Field and Laboratory Studies of the Etiology of Liver Neoplasms in Marine Fish from Puget Sound." *Environmental Health Perspectives* 71:5–16.

Melteff, Brenda, ed. 1977. "Oil and Aquatic Ecosystems, Tanker Safety and Oil Pollution Liability." Alaska Sea Grant Program. *Proceedings of the Cordova Fisheries Institute, Cordova, Alaska, April 1–3, 1977.*

Mielke, James E. 1990. *Oil in the Ocean: The Short- and Long-Term Impacts of a Spill*. Washington, D.C.: Congressional Research Service, July.

Nakatani, R.E., et al. 1987. *Effects of Crude Oil and Chemically Dispersed Oil on Chemoreception and Homing in Pacific Salmon*. Washington, D.C.: American Petroleum Institute, June.

National Oceanic and Atmospheric Administration. 1988. "PCB and Chlorinated Pesticide Contamination in U.S. Fish and Shellfish: A Historical

Assessment Report." NOAA Technical Memorandum NOS OMA 39. Seattle, Washington.

National Research Council, National Academy of Sciences. 1985. *Oil in the Sea: Inputs, Fates, and Effects*. Washington, D.C.: National Academy Press.

Nysewander, David, and Cris Dippel. 1991. "Population Surveys of Seabird Nesting Colonies in Prince William Sound, the Outside Coast of the Kenai Peninsula, Barren Islands, and Other Nearby Colonies, with Emphasis on Changes of Numbers and Reproduction of Murres." Bird Study No. 3. Interim Report to the Exxon Valdez Oil Spill Trustee Council, November.

Office of Technology Assessment, U.S. Congress. 1991. *Bioremediation for Marine Oil Spills*. Washington, D.C.: U.S. Government Printing Office, May.

Patten, Samuel M., et al. 1993. "Assessment of Injury to Sea Ducks from Hydrocarbon Uptake in Prince William Sound and the Kodiak Archipelago, Alaska, Following the *Exxon Valdez* Oil Spill." Bird Study No. 11. Draft Final Report to the Exxon Valdez Oil Spill Trustee Council, May.

Payne, Jerry F. "Oil Pollution: A Penny Ante Problem for Fisheries." *Proceedings of the First International Conference on Fisheries and Offshore Petroleum Exploitation, Bergen, Norway, October 23–25, 1989*.

Pearson, W. H., E. Moksness, and J. R. Skalski. 1993. "A Field and Laboratory Assessment of Oil Spill Effects on Survival and Reproduction of Pacific Herring Following the *Exxon Valdez* Spill." Exxon presentation to the American Society for Testing and Materials, Atlanta, Georgia, April 25–28.

Pearson, W. H., et al. 1985. *Oil Effects on Spawning Behavior and Reproduction in Pacific Herring* (Clupea harengus pallasi)." Washington, D.C.: American Petroleum Institute, October.

Piatt, John F., Calvin J. Lensink, William Butler, Marshal Kendziorek, and David Nysewander. 1990. "Immediate Impact of the *Exxon Valdez* Oil Spill on Marine Birds." *The Auk* 107 (2):387–397.

Prince, R. C., et al. 1993. "The Effect of Bioremediation on the Microbial Populations of Oiled Beaches in Prince William Sound, Alaska." *Proceedings of the 1993 International Oil Spill Conference, Tampa, Florida, March 29–April 1, 1993*, pp. 469–476.

Pritchard, P. Hap, and Charles F. Costa. 1991. "EPA's Alaska Oil Spill Bioremediation Project." *Environmental Science & Technology* 25 (3):372–379.

Purcell, Jennifer E., Daniel Grosse, and Jill J. Grover. 1990. "Mass Abundances of Abnormal Pacific Herring Larvae at a Spawning Ground in British Columbia." *Transactions of the American Fisheries Society* 119:463–469.

Rattner, B. A., D. J. Hoffman, and C. M. Marn. 1989. "Use of Mixed-Function Oxygenases to Monitor Contaminant Exposure in Wildlife." *Environmental Toxicology and Chemistry* 8:1093–1102.

Rice, S. D. 1985. "Effects of Oil on Fish." In F. R. Engelhardt, ed. *Petroleum Effects in the Arctic Environment*. London and New York: Elsevier.

Rice, S. D., et al. 1976. "Acute Toxicity and Uptake-Depuration Studies with Cook Inlet Crude Oil, Prudhoe Bay Crude Oil, No. 2 Fuel Oil and Several Subarctic Marine Organisms." NOAA Report, May.

———. 1987. "Lethal and Sublethal Effects of the Water-Soluble Fraction of Cook Inlet Crude Oil on Pacific Herring (*Clupea harengus pallasi*) Reproduction." NOAA Technical Memorandum NMFS F/NWC-111.

Roberts, Leslie. 1989. "Long, Slow Recovery Predicted for Alaska." *Science* 244:22–24.

Rochkind, Melissa L., James W. Blackburn, and Gary S. Sayer. 1986. *Microbial Decomposition of Chlorinated Aromatic Compounds.* Cincinnati: U.S. Environmental Protection Agency.

Roubal, W. T., S. I. Stranahan, and D. C. Malins. 1978. "The Accumulation of Low Molecular Weight Aromatic Hydrocarbons of Crude Oil by Coho Salmon (*Onocorhyncus kisutch*) and Starry Flounder (*Platichthys stellatus*)." *Archives of Environmental Contamination and Toxicology* 7:237–244.

Sanders, Howard L. 1978. "*Florida* Oil Spill Impact on the Buzzards Bay Benthic Fauna: West Falmouth." *Journal of the Fisheries Research Board of Canada* 35 (5):717–730.

Schempf, Philip F., Timothy D. Bowman, and Jeffrey Bernatowicz. 1991. "Assessing the Effect of the *Exxon Valdez* Oil Spill on Bald Eagles." Bird Study No. 4. Interim Report to the Exxon Valdez Oil Spill Trustee Council, November.

Sergy, Gary A., and Peter J. Blackall. 1987. "Design and Conclusions of the Baffin Oil Spill Project." *Arctic* 40 (supp. 1):1–9.

Spies, R. B. 1987. "The Biological Effects of Petroleum Hydrocarbons in the Sea: Assessments from the Field and Microcosms." In D. F. Boesch and N. N. Rabalais, eds., *Long-term Environmental Effects of Offshore Oil and Gas Development.* London and New York: Elsevier.

Spies, R. B, J. S. Felton, and L. Dillard. 1982. "Hepatic Mixed-Function Oxidases in California Flatfishes Are Increased in Contaminated Environments and by Oil and PCB Ingestion." *Marine Biology* 17:117–127.

Spies, R. B., D. D. Hardin, and J. P. Toal. 1988. "Organic Enrichment or Toxicity? A Comparison of the Effects of Kelp and Crude Oil in Sediments on the Colonization and Growth of Benthic Infauna." *Journal of Experimental Marine Biology and Ecology* 124:261–282.

Stegeman, John J., and Bruce Woodin. 1991. "Cytochrome P4501A Induction in Fish from Prince William Sound." Draft Report to the Alaska Department of Environmental Conservation, December.

Stegeman, John J., Frances Y. Young, and Elisabeth A. Snowberger. 1987. "Induced Cytochrome P450 in Winter Flounder (*Pseudopleuronectes americanus*) from Coastal Massachusetts Evaluated by Catalytic Assay and Monoclonal Antibody Probes." *Canadian Journal of Fisheries and Aquatic Sciences* 44:1270–1277.

Straughan, Dale. 1976. *Sublethal Effects of Natural Chronic Exposure to Petroleum in the Marine Environment.* API Publication No. 4280. Washington, D.C.: American Petroleum Institute, October.

Vandermeulen, J. H. 1977. "The Chedabucto Bay Spill—*Arrow* 1970." *Oceanus* 20:31–39.

Varanasi, U., S.-L. Chan, T. K. Collier, L. L. Johnson, M. M. Krahn, C. A. Krone, H. R. Sanborn, and C. Stehr. 1991. "Assessment of Oil Spill Impacts on Fishery Resources: Measurement of Hydrocarbons and Their Metabolites, and Their Effects, in Important Species." Subtidal Study No. 7. Interim Report to the Exxon Valdez Oil Spill Trustee Council.

Varanasi, Usha, et al. 1987. "Etiology of Tumors in Bottom-Dwelling Marine Fish." NOAA Report, Environmental Conservation Division, Seattle, Washington.

————. 1988. "National Benthic Surveillance Project: Pacific Coast." NOAA Technical Memorandum NMFS F/NWS-156. Environmental Conservation Division, Seattle, Washington.

————. 1992. "Evaluation of Bioindicators of Contaminant Exposure and Effects in Coastal Ecosystems." *Proceedings of the International Symposium of Ecological Indicators, Fort Lauderdale, FL., Oct. 16–19, 1990,* pp. 461–498.

Wade, Richard. 1990. "The *Exxon Valdez* Oil Spill: The Environmental Health Response to Man-made Disasters." *Journal of Environmental Health* 52 (4):213–215.

Walters, P., S. Khan, P. J. O'Brien, J. F. Payne, and A. D. Rahimtula. 1987. "Effectiveness of a Prudhoe Bay Crude Oil and Its Aliphatic, Aromatic and Heterocyclic Fractions in Inducing Mortality and Aryl Hydrocarbon Hydroxylase in Chick Embryo in Ovo." *Archives of Toxicology* 60:454–459.

Weber, D. D., D. J. Maynard, W. D. Gronlund, and V. Konchin. 1981. "Avoidance Reactions of Migrating Adult Salmon to Petroleum Hydrocarbons." *Canadian Journal of Fisheries and Aquatic Sciences* 38:779–781.

Wertenbaker, William. 1973. "Reporter at Large: A Small Spill." *The New Yorker,* November 26, pp. 48–79.

Whipple, Frank L. et al. 1993. "A Program Approach for Site Safety at Oil Spills." *Proceedings of the 1993 International Oil Spill Conference, Tampa, Florida, March 29–April 1, 1993,* pp. 99–104.

White, Jan, ed. 1991. "The Effects of Oil on Wildlife: Research, Rehabilitation, and General Concerns." *Proceedings of the Oil Symposium, Herndon, Virginia, October 16–18, 1990.*

White, Jan, and Terrie Williams. 1991. "Saving Endangered Species in Major Oil Spill Cleanup Efforts." *Proceedings of the 1991 International Oil Spill Conference, San Diego, Calif., March 4–7, 1991,* pp. 221–224.

White, R. G., J. E. Blake, M. Sousa, and J. E. Rowell. 1992. "Influence of Oil Hydrocarbons on Reproduction of Mink (*Mustela Vison*)." Terrestrial Mammal Study No. 6. Draft Final Report to Exxon Valdez Oil Spill Trustee Council, February.

Wolfe, D. A., ed. 1977. *Fate and Effects of Petroleum Hydrocarbons in Marine Organisms and Ecosystems.* New York: Pergamon.

4: THE NATIVE AND THE OTTER

1. INTERVIEWS

Brenda Ballachey, U.S. Fish and Wildlife Service (FWS)

D. Michael Barker, Exxon

Keith Bayha, FWS

Alice Berkner, International Bird Rescue Research Center

Lydia Black, University of Alaska—Fairbanks

Edgar Blatchford, Chugach Alaska Corp.

James Bodkin, FWS

Michael Bolger, Food and Drug Administration

Douglas Burn, FWS

Bruce Campbell, Alaska Department of Fish and Game (ADF&G)

Tasha Chmielewski, Chugachmiut

Daniel Costa, Long Marine Laboratory

Nancy Yaw Davis, consultant, Chugachmiut

Anthony DeGange, FWS

James Estes, FWS

Gail Evanoff, Chenega Village Corp.

Larry Evanoff, Chenega resident

James Fall, ADF&G

L. Jay Field, National Oceanic and Atmospheric Administration (NOAA)

Kathryn Frost, ADF&G

O. W. Frost, Alaska Pacific University (retired)

David Garshelis, consultant, Exxon

Joseph Geraci, University of Guelph (Ontario)

Mara Kimmel Hoyt, Alaska Sea Otter Commission

Ron Jameson, FWS

John F. C. Johnson, Chugach Alaska Corp.

Joseph Johnson, Alaska Legal Services Corp.

Gary Kompkoff, Tatitlek Village Council

Paul Kompkoff Sr., Chenega resident

Gerald Kooyman, Scripps Institution of Oceanography

Michael Krauss, Alaska Native Language Center

Rikk Kvitek, Moss Landing Marine Laboratories

Calvin Lensink, FWS (retired)

Dan Logan, U.S. Forest Service

Henry Makarka, Eyak Village Corp.

John Mattson, U.S. Forest Service

Steven McNabb, consultant, Minerals Management Service

Pat Miller, Washington Department of Wildlife

Rita Miraglia, ADF&G

Don Mitchell, consultant, Alaska Federation of Natives

Charles Mobley, consultant, Exxon

Charles Monnett, consultant, FWS

Eric Morrison, consultant, Minerals Management Service

Tom Nighswander, Oil Spill Health Task Force

Gilbert Olsen, Alaska Sea Otter Commission

Kenneth Pitcher, ADF&G

Steve Rehnberg, Eyak Village Corp.

Monica Riedel, Alaska Sea Otter Commission

John Robinson, NOAA

Janice Ryan, Alaska Federation of Natives

Karl Schneider, ADF&G

Jody Seitz, ADF&G

Pat Selanoff, Chenega resident

Donald Siniff, University of Minnesota

Robert Spies, consultant, Exxon Valdez Trustee Council

Lee Stratton, ADF&G

James Styers, consultant, Exxon

John M. Totemoff, Chenega resident

Terrie Williams, consultant, Exxon

2. BOOKS, REPORTS AND ARTICLES

Alaska Department of Fish and Game. 1985. "Sea Otter Distribution and Abundance." In *Alaska Habitat Management Guide, Southcentral Region,* vol. 2: *Distribution, Abundance, and Human Use of Fish and Wildlife.* Juneau: Alaska Department of Fish and Game.

Alaska Department of Fish and Game, Division of Subsistence. 1992. "Community Profile Database Catalog. Volume 2. Southcentral Region, Part I." Juneau, Alaska, July.

Arnold, Robert, et al. 1978. *Alaska Native Land Claims.* Anchorage: The Alaska Native Foundation.

Baker, J. M., R. B. Clark, P. F. Kingston, and R. H. Jenkins. 1990. "Natural Recovery of Cold Water Marine Environments after an Oil Spill." Presentation to the Thirteenth Annual Arctic and Marine Oil Spill Program Technical Seminar, Environment Canada, Edmonton, Alberta, June 6–8, 1990.

Ballachey, B. E., J. L. Bodkin, and D. Burn. 1992. "Assessment of the

Magnitude, Extent, and Duration of Oil Spill Impacts on Sea Otter Populations in Alaska." Marine Mammal Study No. 6. Draft Preliminary Status Report to the Exxon Valdez Oil Spill Trustee Council, May.

Bancroft, Hubert Howe. 1886. *History of Alaska, 1730–1885*. San Francisco: A. L. Bancroft & Co.

Bayha, Keith, and Jennifer Kormendy, eds. 1990. *Sea Otter Symposium: Proceedings of a Symposium to Evaluate the Response Effort on Behalf of Sea Otters after the T/V Exxon Valdez Oil Spill into Prince William Sound, Alaska, Anchorage, Alaska, April 17–19, 1990*. Biological Report 90(12). U.S. Fish and Wildlife Service.

Bennett, M. E., S. D. Heasley, and S. Huey. 1979. "Northern Gulf of Alaska Petroleum Development Scenarios: Sociocultural Impacts." Bureau of Land Management, Technical Report 36. Alaska Outer Continental Shelf Socioeconomic Studies Program.

Birket-Smith, Kaj. 1953. *The Chugach Eskimo*. Copenhagen: National Museum Publications.

Braund, Stephen R., et al. 1993. "Effects of the *Exxon Valdez* Oil Spill on Alutiiq Culture and People." Report prepared for Cohen, Milstein, Hausfeld & Toll, Washington, D.C., and Sonosky, Chambers, Sachse, Miller, Munson & Clocksin, Anchorage, Alaska, February.

Campbell, Bruce H. 1988. "Habitat Availability, Utilization, and Nesting Success of Dusky Canada Geese on the Copper River Delta, Alaska." Alaska Department of Fish and Game, Anchorage, November.

———. 1990. "Factors Affecting the Nesting Success of Dusky Canada Geese, *Branta canadensis occidentalis*, on the Copper River Delta, Alaska." *Canadian Field-Naturalist* 104:567–574.

Chevigny, Hector. 1965. *Russian America: The Great Alaskan Venture, 1741–1867*. Portland, Oregon: Binford & Mort Publishing.

Courtright, Alan M. 1968. "Game Harvests in Alaska." Alaska Department of Fish and Game, Juneau, Alaska, June.

Costa, D. P., and G. L. Kooyman. 1980. "Effects of Oil Contamination in the Sea Otter, *Enhydra lutris*." NOAA Contract No. 03-7-022-35130. Final Report to the Outer Continental Shelf Environmental Assessment Program.

Davis, Nancy Yaw. 1984. "Contemporary Pacific Eskimo." In D. Damas, ed., *Handbook of North American Indians*, vol. 5: *Arctic*. Washington, D.C.: Smithsonian Institution.

Davis, R. W., T. M. Williams, J. A. Thomas, R. A. Kastelein, and L. H. Cornell. 1988. "The Effects of Oil Contamination and Cleaning on Sea Otters (*Enhydra lutris*). II. Metabolism, Thermoregulation, and Behavior." *Canadian Journal of Zoology* 66 (12):2782–2790.

DeGange, Anthony R. 1990. "Assessment of the Fate of Sea Otters Oiled and Rehabilitated as a Result of the *Exxon Valdez* Oil Spill." Marine Mammal Study No. 7. Report to the Exxon Valdez Oil Spill Trustee Council, January.

De Laguna, Frederica. 1956. *Chugach Prehistory: The Archaeology of Prince William Sound, Alaska*. Seattle: University of Washington Press.

Dumond, Don E. 1987. *The Eskimos and Aleuts*, rev. ed. London: Thames and Hudson.

Estes, James A. 1990. "Growth and Equilibrium in Sea Otter Populations." *Journal of Animal Ecology* 59:385–401.

———. 1991. "Catastrophes and Conservation: Lessons from Sea Otters and the *Exxon Valdez*." *Science* 254:1596.

Exxon Valdez Oil Spill Trustee Council. 1993. Exxon Valdez *Oil Spill Symposium, February 2–5, 1993: Program and Abstracts.* Anchorage: Exxon Valdez Oil Spill Trustee Council.

Fall, James A. 1990. "Subsistence after the Spill: Uses of Fish and Wildlife in Alaska Native Villages and the *Exxon Valdez* Oil Spill." Alaska Department of Fish and Game, Subsistence Division, Anchorage, November.

Fall, James A., ed. 1992. "Subsistence Harvests and Uses in Seven Gulf of Alaska Communities in the Second Year Following the *Exxon Valdez* Oil Spill." Alaska Department of Fish and Game, Subsistence Division, Anchorage, March.

Fall, James A., and Charles J. Utermohle,. eds. 1993. "An Investigation of the Sociocultural Consequences of Outer Continental Shelf Development in Alaska. A Preliminary Overview of Selected Findings from the Household Harvest Survey for the First Year of Research, 1992." Prepared by the Alaska Department of Fish and Game, Subsistence Division, for the U.S. Department of the Interior, Minerals Management Service, Anchorage, March 15.

Fazio, Thomas, and John W. Howard. 1983. "Polycyclic Aromatic Hydrocarbons in Food." In Alf Bjørseth, ed., *Handbook of Polycyclic Aromatic Hydrocarbons.* New York: Marcel Dekker, Inc., 416–505.

Food and Drug Administration, Quantitative Risk Assessment Committee. 1990. "Estimation of Risk Associated with Consumption of Oil-contaminated Fish and Shellfish by Alaskan Subsistence Fishermen Using a Benzo(a)pyrene Equivalency Approach." Washington, D.C., August.

Friends of the Sea Otter. 1989, 1990. *The Otter Raft* (newsletter, Carmel, California), no. 41 (Summer 1989); no. 42 (winter 1989–1990).

Frost, Kathryn J., et al. 1991. "Assessment of Injury to Harbor Seals in Prince William Sound, Alaska, and Adjacent Areas." Marine Mammal Study No. 5. Status Report to the Exxon Valdez Oil Spill Trustee Council, November.

Frost, O. W., ed. 1992. *Bering and Chirikov: The American Voyages and Their Impact.* Anchorage: Alaska Historical Society.

Garshelis, D. L. 1987. "Sea Otter." In M. Novak, J. A. Baker, M. E. Obbard, and B. Malloch, eds., *Wild Furbearer Management and Conservation in North America.* Ontario: Ministry of Natural Resources.

Garshelis, D. L., J. A. Garshelis, and A. T. Kimker. 1986. "Sea Otter Time Budgets and Prey Relationships in Alaska." *Journal of Wildlife Management* 50 (4):637–647.

Haggarty, J. C., C. B. Wooley, J. M. Erlandson, and A. Crowell. 1991. *The 1990 Exxon Cultural Resource Program.* Anchorage: Exxon Corporation.

Hassen, Harold. 1978. "The Effect of European and American Contact on the Chugach Eskimo of Prince William Sound, Alaska, 1741–1930." Ph.D. thesis, University of Wisconsin–Milwaukee.

Hogan, M. E., and D. B. Irons. 1988. "Waterbirds and Marine Mammals." In D. G. Shaw and M. J. Hameedi, eds., *Environmental Studies in Port Valdez, Alaska.* New York: Springer-Verlag.

Irons, D. B., D. R. Nysewander, and J. L. Trapp. 1988. "Prince William Sound Sea Otter Distribution in Relation to Population Growth and Habitat Type." U.S. Fish and Wildlife Service, Anchorage, Alaska.

Johnson, Ancel M. 1987. "Sea Otters of Prince William Sound, Alaska." U.S. Fish and Wildlife Service, Anchorage, Alaska.

Johnson, C. B., and D. L. Garshelis. 1993. "Sea Otter Abundance, Distribution, and Pup Production in Prince William Sound, Alaska, Following the *Exxon Valdez* Oil Spill." Exxon presentation to the American Society for Testing and Materials, Atlanta, Georgia, April 25–28.

Johnson, John F. C., ed. 1984. *Chugach Legends: Stories and Photographs of the Chugach Region.* Anchorage: Chugach Alaska Corporation.

Kompkoff, Don, Sr. 1970s. "Chenega History and Culture." Draft manuscript, Subsistence Division, Alaska Department of Fish and Game, Anchorage.

Krauss, Michael E., ed. 1982. *In Honor of Eyak: The Art of Anna Nelson Harry.* Fairbanks: Alaska Native Language Center, University of Alaska.

Kvitek, R. G., C. E. Bowlby, and M. Staedler. 1993. "Diet and Foraging Behavior of Sea Otters in Southeast Alaska." *Marine Mammal Science* 9 (2):168–181.

Kvitek, R. G., J. S. Oliver, A. R. DeGange, and B. S. Anderson, 1992. "Changes in Alaskan Soft-Bottom Prey Communities Along a Gradient in Sea Otter Predation." *Ecology* 73 (2):413–428.

Lensink, Calvin J. 1962. "The History and Status of Sea Otters in Alaska." Ph.D. thesis, Purdue University.

———. 1990. "Birds and Sea Otters Killed in the *Exxon Valdez* Oil Spill." *Endangered Species Update* (University of Michigan School of Natural Resources) 7 (7):1–5.

Minerals Management Service. 1993. "Social Indicators Study of Alaskan Coastal Villages. IV. Postspill Key Informant Summaries. Schedule C Communities, Part 1." U.S. Department of the Interior, Anchorage, February.

Miraglia, Rita A., and Lora L. Johnson. 1990. "Cultural Resource Protection in Prince William Sound—A Native Perspective." Presentation to the Alaska Anthropological Association, Fairbanks, Alaska.

Mobley, Charles M., et al. 1990. *The 1989* Exxon Valdez *Cultural Resource Program.* Anchorage: Exxon Corporation.

Monahan, Thomas P., and Alan W. Maki. 1991. "The *Exxon Valdez* 1989 Wildlife Rescue and Rehabilitation Program." *Proceedings of the 1991 International Oil Spill Conference, San Diego, Calif., March 4–7, 1991*, pp. 131–136.

National Academy of Sciences. 1970. *The Great Alaska Earthquake of 1964: Human Ecology.* Washington, D.C.: National Academy of Sciences.

Oil Spill Health Task Force. 1990, 1991. Monthly newsletters. Alaska Department of Fish and Game, Subsistence Division, Anchorage, Alaska.

Palinkas, L. A., J. Russell, M. A. Downs, and J. S. Petterson. 1992. "Ethnic Differences in Stress, Coping, and Depressive Symptoms after the *Exxon Valdez* Oil Spill." *Journal of Nervous and Mental Disease* 180 (5):287–295.

Parker, Jill. 1991. "U.S. Fish and Wildlife Service Response Activities Following the *Exxon Valdez* Oil Spill." *Proceedings of the 1991 International Oil Spill Conference, San Diego, Calif., March 4–7, 1991*, pp. 243–246.

Pitcher, Kenneth W. 1975. "Distribution and Abundance of Sea Otters, Steller Sea Lions, and Harbor Seals in Prince William Sound, Alaska." Alaska Department of Fish and Game, September.

———. 1990. "Major Decline in Number of Harbor Seals, *Phoca Vitulina Richardsi,* on Tugidak Island, Gulf of Alaska." *Marine Mammal Science* 6 (2):121–134.

Rebar, A. H. 1993. "Clinicopathologic Alterations in Oiled Sea Otters Dying Acutely in Rehabilitation Centers." Exxon Valdez *Oil Spill Sympo-*

sium, February 2–5, 1993: Program and Abstracts. Anchorage: Exxon Valdez Oil Spill Trustee Council, pp. 274–275.

Reger, D. R., J. D. McMahan, and C. E. Holmes. 1991. "Archaeological Damage Assessment on State Land, 1991." Interim Report to the Exxon Valdez Oil Spill Trustee Council, November.

Rotterman, Lisa Mignon, and Terri Simon-Jackson. 1988. "Sea Otter, *Enhydra lutris.*" In J. W. Lentfer, ed., *Selected Marine Mammals of Alaska.* Washington, D.C.: Marine Mammal Commission.

Schneider, Karl B. 1978. "Sex and Age Segregation of Sea Otters." Alaska Department of Fish and Game, Juneau.

Simon-Jackson, Terri. 1986. "Sea Otter Survey, Cordova, Alaska—1986 (Orca Inlet to Cape Suckling)." U.S. Fish and Wildlife Service, Anchorage, Alaska.

————. 1988. "Take of Sea Otters by Alaska Natives (through 1986)." U.S. Fish and Wildlife Service, Anchorage, Alaska.

Siniff, D. B., T. D. Williams, A. M. Johnson, and D. L. Garshelis. 1982. "Experiments on the Response of Sea Otters *Enhydra lutris* to Oil Contamination." *Biological Conservation* 23:261–272.

Starr, S. Frederick, ed. 1987. *Russia's American Colony.* Durham: Duke University Press.

Stern, Richard O., and Douglas E. Gibson. 1982. "Cultural Resources Survey of the New Chenega Village Site, Evans Island, Alaska." Alaska Department of Natural Resources. Anchorage, Alaska.

Stratton, Lee. 1990. "Resource Harvest and Use in Tatitlek, Alaska." Technical Paper No. 181. Alaska Department of Fish and Game, Division of Subsistence, Anchorage.

Stratton, Lee, and Evelyn B. Chisum. 1986. "Resource Use Patterns in Chenega, Western Prince William Sound: Chenega in the 1960s and Chenega Bay 1984–1986." Technical Paper No. 139. Alaska Department of Fish and Game, Division of Subsistence, Anchorage.

Townsend, Richard, and Burr Heneman. 1989. *The* Exxon Valdez *Oil Spill: A Management Analysis.* Prepared for the Center for Marine Conservation, Washington, D.C., September.

Varanasi, Usha, et al. 1990. "Survey of Subsistence Fish and Shellfish for Exposure to Oil Spilled from the *Exxon Valdez,* First Year: 1989." NOAA Technical Memorandum NMFS F/NWC-191. Seattle, Washington, December.

Walker, Ann Hayward, and L. Jay Field. 1991. "Subsistence Fisheries and the *Exxon Valdez:* Human Health Concerns." *Proceedings of the 1991 International Oil Spill Conference, San Diego, Calif., March 4–7, 1991,* pp. 441–446.

Williams, Terrie M. 1990. "Evaluating the Long Term Effects of Crude Oil Exposure in Sea Otters: Laboratory and Field Observations." In Jan White, ed., *The Effects of Oil on Wildlife: Proceedings of the Oil Symposium, Herndon, Virginia, October 16–18, 1990.*

————, and Randall W. Davis, eds. 1990. *Sea Otter Rehabilitation Program: Exxon Valdez Oil Spill.* Published jointly by Exxon Company, USA, and International Wildlife Research.

Wynne, Kate. 1990. *Marine Mammal Interactions with the Salmon Drift Gillnet Fishery on the Copper River Delta, Alaska, 1988–1989.* Alaska Sea Grant College Program Technical Report No. 90-05. Fairbanks: University of Alaska.

Index

About the Author

A graduate of Yale and the Columbia School of Journalism, Jeff Wheelwright was the science editor of *Life* magazine for eleven years. He now lives on the central coast of California.